National Theatre Connectio 2022

TEN PLAYS FOR YOUNG PERFORMERS

Cable Street

Chat Back

Find a Partner!

Hunt

Like There's No Tomorrow

The Ramayana Reset

Remote

Superglue

Variations

You don't need to make a Big Song and Dance out of it

Edited by

NATIONAL THEATRE

methuen | drama

LONDON · NEW YORK · OXFORD · NEW DELHI · SYDNEY

METHUEN DRAMA
Bloomsbury Publishing Plc
50 Bedford Square, London, WC1B 3DP, UK
1385 Broadway, New York, NY 10018, USA
29 Earlsfort Terrace, Dublin 2, Ireland

BLOOMSBURY, METHUEN DRAMA and the Methuen Drama logo are
trademarks of Bloomsbury Publishing Plc

First published in Great Britain 2022

A catalogue record for this book is available from the British Library.

Library of Congress Cataloging-in-Publication Data
Names: National Theatre (Great Britain) Title: National Theatre Connections 2022: 10 plays for young performers
/ edited by The National Theatre. Other titles: Connections 2022 Description: 1st. | London; New York : Methuen
Drama 2022. | Series: Methuen Drama play anthologies | "Find a partner!—Like there's no tomorrow—
Remote—Variations—You don't need to make a big song and dance out of it—Cable Street—The Ramayana
reset—Chat back—Hunt—Superglue". | Identifiers: LCCN 2021057963 | ISBN 9781350320444 (paperback) |
ISBN 9781350320451 (epub) | ISBN 9781350320468 (pdf) | ISBN 9781350320475 Subjects: LCSH:
English drama—21st century. | Young adult drama, English. Classification: LCC PR1272.2 .N383 2022 |
DDC 822/.9208—dc23/eng/20220308 LC record available at https://lccn.loc.gov/2021057963.

ISBN: PB: 978-1-3503-2044-4
         ePDF: 978-1-3503-2046-8
         eBook: 978-1-3503-2045-1

Typeset by RefineCatch Limited, Bungay, Suffolk
Printed and bound in Great Britain

To find out more about our authors and books visit www.bloomsbury.com
and sign up for our newsletters.

Contents

National Theatre Connections

Connections is the National Theatre's annual nationwide youth theatre festival; a celebration of new writing, partnership and, above all, young people. As we begin to see the long-term impacts of the pandemic, it's clear that access to the arts, and through this giving young people agency and a voice, is more important than ever. Every year Connections gives youth theatres and school theatre the unique opportunity to stage new plays written specifically for young people, by some of the most exciting playwrights writing today, and to perform them in leading theatres across the UK.

New plays are at the heart of Connections – stories for and about young people, which challenge them to experience life in someone else's shoes, and transport them to different times, places and emotional landscapes. Through our 2022 portfolio, a young person might journey to 1930s East London to explore the fight against fascism, to South Asia to learn about a thousand-year-old epic tale, or into stories about the struggle to protect the future of our planet. We are proud that these plays continue to have a life as part of a repertoire permanently available to schools, colleges and youth theatres.

At the beginning of their rehearsal process, companies take part in the Connections Directors' Weekend – an opportunity for the directors to work with the playwright of their chosen play and a leading theatre director. Notes from these workshops accompany the plays in this anthology, giving an insight into the playwrights' intentions, creative inspiration and practical suggestions for exploring the text.

In 2022, over 250 companies from across the UK will take up the challenge of staging a brand-new Connections play, with nearly 6,000 young people, aged 13–19, involved in every aspect of theatre-making. It's amazing that in these incredibly challenging times for schools and theatres, Connections can still offer a space to create, to explore contemporary issues and to connect with other young theatre-makers.

Connections is not just the National Theatre's programme: it is run in collaboration with fantastic theatres across the UK who are equally passionate about youth theatre. Our Partner Theatres work with every company to develop and transfer their production, and we hope the festivals will celebrate the brilliant work that has been created, and the power of theatre in these challenging times.

We hope you enjoy this year's plays and we look forward to next year and many years to come.

Kirsten Adam
Connections Producer
November 2021

Introduction

Here are ten plays with something to say. Written by writers with a burning desire to move their audiences to act, both on and off the stage. Propelled by the twin engines of curiosity and speculation, humming to the rhythm of the ever-pertinent questions – who are we now and is it who we want to be? These plays land at a time when the cultural landscape is brimming with possibility.

Connections is about engaging with the real world by diving into an imagined world. Each of these plays is a passport to play, explore, consider, rethink and expand the universe of each and everyone who comes into contact with it – be it as performer, director, parent/carer of a performer or audience member.

All of these plays are about people. People we know or recognise, or might be, either now or in the future. Combined, these plays are about climate change, alternative narratives, sex, protest, loyalty, lies, honesty, hope, resilience, justice, collectivism, individualism, relationships, allyship, communication, division, unity, commonality and choice.

All of them are exciting as they seek to enlighten. They urge awareness, to see the possibilities and then summon the courage to fulfil the potential presented by these possibilities. It's in our hands.

Ola Animashawun
November 2021

Connections 2022 Portfolio

A note on casting

At National Theatre Connections we think long and hard about every play that we put into the portfolio. The writers whose plays make up our portfolios offer their plays as stories about humanity, and we want the plays to be for everyone, and to tell stories about a wide range of experiences, from around the world. We are proud to continue to offer plays that challenge young people to experience life in someone else's shoes, and transport them to different times, places and emotional landscapes.

We encourage our playwrights to keep the casting options for their plays as open as possible. For all plays in the portfolio, all parts can be played by D/deaf and disabled performers and, apart from where the playwright states otherwise, by actors of any gender or ethnicity. If your group doesn't exactly match the apparent casting requirements of a play in terms of race, ethnicity or gender, and you would like to produce it, we would still encourage you to do so.

Where locations are specified, rather than being preoccupied with accents, we recommend focussing your energies on finding the emotional truth of these settings.

Synopses

Cable Street *by Lisa Goldman*

Cast size: a minimum of 12 performers, for 20 speaking roles plus chorus
Recommended for ages 14+

Cable Street is about two girls growing up in London's Jewish East End in the 1930s. Leah and Kitty are blood sisters, best friends and more – but they get caught up in the political turmoil caused by Oswald Mosley's fascist Blackshirts.

At the iconic Battle of Cable Street in 1936, 100,000 working-class people come together to defend the Jewish East End of London from fascists attempting to march through and intimidate the local community. Resulting in a pitched battle fought on two fronts by the 'people' as they took on both the fascists and their police protectorate.

Kitty and Leah are torn apart politically, their love for each other ensnared, like a rabbit in a trap. As their passion and the political tensions grow stronger and stronger, pulling each of them every which way, the snare can only get tighter and tighter until something snaps.

Content warning: this play includes some examples of characters using antisemitic language/stereotypes.

Chat Back *by David Judge*

Cast size: minimum of 12, with 12 named characters plus a narrator and chorus
Recommended for ages 15+

Chat Back is about the underclass – all those young people who are so 'bad', disempowered, alienated, ostracised and abandoned that even on the last day of school they still find themselves in detention. We watch a snapshot of the lives of each individual (across a summer holiday of Friday and Saturday nights and Sunday mornings) as they negotiate their way around the obstacles en route to discovering their identity, their economic power or lack of, their lyrical dexterity or lack of, and the meaning of their lives, revealed through their desires, hopes and fears. The words in this play come thick and fast, in rhythm and rhyme, energised and unwavering in its intention to talk truth to power.

Content warning: one reference to suicide.

Find a Partner! *by Miriam Battye*

Cast size: 13 to 30, minimum 6 male/7 female characters
Most suitable for ages 14+

Find a Partner! is about the sometimes catastrophic methods we use to find that elusive thing, love. This is *Love Island* scrutinised through a *Black Mirror*-style lens as a group of young people compete to publicly couple up and fall in love forever, or die – quite literally. Facilitated by a group of 'influencers' the group sign up to the 'game' while the rest of us watch, enthralled, judging and commenting the whole time, as the play asks the questions: what does it really mean to love someone, does it have to be forever and does it have to be only one person?

Hunt *by Fionnuala Kennedy*

Cast size: 10
Recommended age: 14+

Hunt is about a group of Belfast teenagers playing their version of hide and seek. Their version entails 'borrowing' objects from their neighbours' back gardens, and dumping them at the 'box' without being caught, by either the official pursuers or the neighbours whose gardens they are infringing upon – hence the chances of being caught are twofold. The more outlandish and extraordinary the object and the more difficult to acquire it is, the more kudos you score. The thing is, nearly all of these teenagers are far too old to play this kids' game, and it's February, it's freezing and there's a storm coming. But Jo wants to impress James, the boy from her new school; he's not from round here and she's not from round there. Their fledgling relationship represents a bridge across a class divide. So begrudgingly the band gets back together, for one last game. However, this could be the worst decision of their tiny lives as, little do they know, the rumours about the strange, predatory 'Man in the Van' are true – and the even more strange, dangerous one everyone has been warned to stay away from, 'Mad' Danielle, is back on the block. This is a hunt they will never forget.

Like There's No Tomorrow, *created by the Belgrade Young Company with Justine Themen, Claire Procter and Liz Mytton*

Cast size: 10–16, plus additional ensemble members
There are **8 named characters in the play, and a minimum of 2 additional company members are required to cover the chorus roles – making a minimum company of 10.**

The number of company members playing chorus roles could be increased to 8 – making a maximum company of 16 with reasonable speaking roles. There is also the possibility of including a further 8–12 company members in non-speaking, or little-speaking, roles, delivering the movement sequences in the city, the scene changes and the bringing to life of the folk tale in Scene Three.
Recommended for ages 13+

Like There's No Tomorrow is about climate change. Set in an imagined city now, the people are choking on the fumes from the cars and the factories, produced by the slavish commitment of the masses to mass consumerism and mass consumption, and yet they still vote for more and more – more cheap clothes, more cheap travel and more disposable goods in a fast ephemeral life. It seems only one or two people can see through this non-sustainable madness, but when they open their mouths to speak out, they cannot be heard; their words are strangled in their throats as they choke on the poisonous fumes they are forced to inhale and, besides, no one can hear them above the cacophony created by the wheels of the global economy grinding against each other. Even when the evidence of imminent climate disaster across the globe is staring them in the face, as presented as the world literally cracking up before their very eyes, still no one wants to listen; they just want to carry on consuming, like they have always have and always will – won't they?

The Ramayana Reset *by Ayeesha Menon, with choreography by Hofesh Shechter*

Cast size: minimum of 12, no maximum
Suitable for ages 13+

The Ramayana Reset is about Zara, a young teenage woman who has a decision to make: to like or not to like the latest Instagram post by her friendship group; a post about the new girl, who happens to be Zara's best friend from primary school. It's a dilemma and all she has to help her decide is a book. However, this is no ordinary book, it is the *Ramayana*, the epic story of Sita and Ram, which is a traditional South Asian story, fundamental to the Hindu faith, dating back to two and a half thousand years ago. This is an epic adventure story featuring gods, demons, queens, sorcery, a giant half-monkey half-man taller than the tallest mountain and a ten-headed evil tyrant. This is a piece of dance drama, using movement inspired by the award-winning and internationally renowned choreographer Hofesh Shechter. This is a BIG story that fills the stage with action – there are fires, battles, trials and weapons powerful enough to end the universe. But most importantly of all there is love (and loyalty)?

Remote *by Stef Smith*

Cast size: 9 to 30
Suitable for ages 13+

Antler steps out of her front door and throws her phone on the ground. She stamps on it. She then climbs the tallest tree in the park. She doesn't want to be found, not by anyone. Seven teenagers' lives intertwine over the course of a single evening as they make their way through the park on a seemingly normal autumn's night. *Remote* is a play about protest, power and protecting yourself.

Superglue *by Tim Crouch*

Cast size: 8 young performers. 1 male, 1 female – and 6 of any gender.
The play also requires 8 older/elderly people who correspond with the gender and ethnicity of each young performer. This could be the young people's grandparents or great-aunts/uncles but a family relationship is not essential. Ideally, they are aged over 70. One of these older actors will be required to read a speech at the end of the play.
Recommended for ages 14+

Superglue tells the story of a group of climate activists gathering at a woodland burial ground to say goodbye to a friend who died during a protest. As they gather, they erect banners and they talk about their pasts and their futures, about peaceful action versus violent action, about how society dismisses them and undervalues their cause. Initially, we believe these activists are the age of the actors playing them. Gradually, we realise that this is the story of an elderly climate action group – elderly characters performed without imitation by young actors. Parallels are drawn between old age and adolescence in a play that gently invites an intergenerational understanding of the future of our planet.

Variations *by Katie Hims*

Cast size: 13
Recommended for ages 13+

Thirteen-year-old Alice wishes her life was completely different. She wakes up one morning to find that her life *is* different. In fact, it's so different that all she wants to do is get back to normality. But how does she do that? A play about family, string theory and breakfast.

You don't need to make a Big Song and Dance out of it
*by Abbey Wright, Shireen Mula and Matt Regan, in association
with Tackroom Theatre*

Cast size: minimum of 8, no maximum
Recommended for ages 15+

You don't need to make a Big Song and Dance out of it is about young people's attitudes towards, experiences of, access to, feelings about and opinions on pornography, love and connection. Taken from the actual words drawn from interviews of 10,000 young people from across the UK, this is a verbatim musical that tries to simply be honest and out in the open about what is often considered to be a taboo subject. No sensation, no fuss, just the plain and simple truth – set to a collection of catchy tunes.

Content warning: this play explores young people's opinions on pornography, and includes references to a number of pornographic genres.

Cable Street
by Lisa Goldman

Lisa Goldman is a writer, dramaturg and director. Her NT Connections play *Cable Street* is now in development with BFI as a feature film. Other plays include *Remedy* (Attachment National Studio 2022) and *Hoxton Story* (2005). Her first short story 'Easy Peelers' was published last year in *Mainstream* anthology (2021). Her children's novel was shortlisted for Penguin Write Now 2020.

Lisa is author of *The No Rules Handbook for Writers* (Bloomsbury Oberon) and runs a script consultancy. The plays she has developed have won or been listed for every UK playwriting award. Lisa has worked in seventeen countries (including Iran, Turkey and Brazil). She has designed and taught MA modules in writing and dramaturgy at Essex University; RADA; City, University of London and UAL.

Lisa was Artistic Director and joint Chief Executive of the Red Room (1995–2006) and Soho Theatre (2006–10). In 1995 she created the theatre for new work above the Lion and Unicorn. She has developed and directed dozens of acclaimed UK premieres including at Soho Theatre: *Baghdad Wedding* (also BBC Radio 3 Sunday play); *Piranha Heights*; *Leaves of Glass*; *Shraddha*; *This Isn't Romance* (also BBC Radio 3 The Wire); *Poor Polish Speaking Romanians* (co-translated with Paul Sirett); *Everything Must Go*; *Playing Fields*. At Live Theatre: *Inheritance*. At Bush and Traverse and international tour: *The Bogus Woman* (also BBC Radio 4 Saturday Play); *Bites*; *Stitching* (Producer). At Coventry Belgrade: *Behud*; At BAC: *Made in England*; *Sunspots*; *Obsession*; *Surfing*; *Ex*; *Seeing Red*. At Theatre Royal Stratford East: *Dangerous Lady*.

To the memory of Auntie Leah and my grandparents, Sam Goldman and Doll Joseph,
who fought at the Battle of Cable Street

Setting

Shabby, recycled/transformable furniture and props from the 'barricade' used for scenes as needed. Four time periods in the play: 1931 (thirty minutes), 1934 (three months), 1936 (three weeks), 1939 (thirty minutes). Titles giving time/place can be realised as you like – may not be needed.

Music

Be authentic and creative – whatever that means to you. I have occasionally suggested songs from *Music is the Most Beautiful Language in the World – Yiddisher Jazz in London's East End 1920s to 1950s* for mood. A pianist could play Dad (who accompanies silent films at the local 'pictures'). Mix old and new music, live and recorded. Do what you like.

Casting

Casting can be based on rightness for character rather than *actual* heritage. Physical description of Billy should also not sway casting. Kitty's ill children and baby can be represented simply, e.g. by stuffed children's clothes or big dolls. Little Jack's line can be played by whoever does the best child's voice.

Warnings

The play contains a few intimate and violent moments.

Antisemitic sentiments are expressed in the play by fascists and their sympathisers.

Performance/Text notes

In 'Chorus' sections, lines are mostly played by individual characters as indicated. Emphasise clear phrases, storytelling and passing on the narrative to the next actor. Where indicated, lines are also spoken by the whole Chorus in unison.

Don't ignore stage directions as they represent important story beats. But do feel free to determine your own physical staging.

A slash mark / indicates where the character speaking next begins their line over previous line.

Research

http://www.cablestreet.uk/ helpfully covers all of the main political contexts and events referred to in the play and there are useful interviews with people who were there.

Big thanks to

Oiffy Films for kick-starting this process

Ola Animashawun for commissioning *Cable Street* and for your wise feedback

My ancestors, for your stories. You were at my shoulder when I wrote this play but particularly Dad (Mischa Goldman). Let beigels be beigels! Thanks to John, Muz and Donna for early feedback.

Dan and Denise Jones of Cable Street for oral history archive and references.

The wonderful team at NT Connections led by producer Kirsten Adam; the National Studio for letting me use a writer's room; Nathan Crossan-Smith, Toby Clarke, Nina Steiger and Stewart Pringle for feedback; the brilliant young actors who did a Zoom read and workshops; Audrey Sheffield for the Directors' Weekend workshop. All the directors and actors who choose to perform *Cable Street*.

Casting/Characters

Minimum twelve performers with creative doubling – there are twenty-three speaking roles plus Chorus.

Leah 3 – *nineteen*	*Working class. Polish, Jewish heritage, nurse*
Kitty 3 – *nineteen*	*Working class. Irish heritage, long facial scar*
Leah 2 – *fourteen & sixteen*	*Stubborn, smart, playful – grows in confidence*
Kitty 2 – *fourteen & sixteen*	*Wild, sensual, charismatic*
Leah 1 – *eleven*	*Ugly glasses, orphan, feisty*
Kitty 1 – *eleven*	*Feral, motherless, impulsive*

All (other) characters are part of Chorus 1 or/and Chorus 2.

Chorus 1

Sam – *four years older than* **Leah** – *her Communist Party brother*
Rosa – *six years older than* **Leah** – *her religious sister*
Patrick – *young Irish docker*
Ged – *young Irish docker,* **Sam**'s *comrade*
Eva – *Jewish garment factory worker*
Anna – *Jewish garment factory worker*
Doll – *an activist,* **Sam**'s *comrade*

Worker 1/Protestor 1
Jewish Man/Survivor/Milewski voice
Tenants/Locals/Hecklers/Reds/Sweatshop Workers/Anti-fascists/Protestors

Chorus 2

Billy – *seventeen to nineteen, English*
Joyce – *eighteen to twenty,* **Billy**'s *sister*
Kitty's Dad – *thirties, Irish heritage (also Chorus 1 in 'Blood Sisters' and 'The Battle of Cable Street')*
Jack – *four years old,* **Kitty**'s *son. Voiced by Chorus member*
Oswald Mosley – *leader of British Union of Fascists (BUF)*
Bailiff
Policeman 1
Policeman 2
Police/Fascists/Blackshirts

Note: With a smaller cast, one actor can play multiple roles across Chorus 1 and 2

E.g. – **Kitty's Dad/Patrick/Oswald Mosley/Bailiff**
    – **Doll/Eva/Jack/Joyce**

Eviction 1

Music. Try the refrain of 'Whitechapel' (1951) for atmospheric sense of returning to this bygone era. Or 1930s East End Yiddisher jazz.

Title: Whitechapel, September 1st 1939

Outside a slum mansion block. Barricade made of shabby furniture, doors, crates, etc.
Big banners: 'Stepney Tenants' Defence League' and 'No Evictions'.

Homemade placards with slogans:

> *'Luxury Flats – No Extra for Rats'*
> *'Our Mansion Block Is a Slum'*
> *'Repairs before Rent Rises'*
> *'Less Rent Means More Milk'*

Jewish **Tenants**, *possibly amongst the audience too, led by* **Doll** *with megaphone.*

Leah 3 *arrives in nurse's uniform with bag slung over shoulder. Eyes the barricade.*

Leah 3   And how the bloody hell am I s'posed to get over that?

Doll   It's to keep the bailiff out.

Leah 3   And what about your (*reads from bit of paper*) 'poor woman with three sick kids'? (*Looks up.*) What floor is she?

Doll   Third – that window with the ripped net curtain –

Leah 3 *sighs and hitches up her nurse's dress.* **Doll** *sees* **Bailiff** *and two* **Police** *arrive.*

Doll (*chants at* **Police**)   They shall not pass.

Tenants (*chant at* **Police**)   They shall not pass. They shall not . . .

All stop to watch in awe as **Leah 3** *climbs drainpipe, strong and sure-footed. Rising eye-line of* **Tenants**' *impressed faces. Gasps as drainpipe comes away. Shocked,* **Leah 3** *sees* **Kitty 3** *at window holding out a hand. No choice but to grab it.* **Tenants** *cheer, part to reveal . . .*

Inside a small, shabby rented room. **Kitty**'s *boys (aged four and two) ill in bed.* **Kitty**'s *baby girl sleeps in a crate cot.* **Leah 3** *can't take her shocked eyes from* **Kitty 3**'s *long facial scar.*

Leah 3 (*whispers*)   Kitty?

Kitty 3   Look on your face when the drainpipe fell. Shinned it like a little monkey.

Leah 3   I . . .

Kitty 3   Admiring your handiwork?

Disturbed, **Leah 3** *pulls the piece of paper from her pocket.*

Leah 3   I . . . I didn't know . . .

Kitty 3   And if you *did* know –?

Leah 3 (*reads*)   Three kids. How could I know –?

Unhitches dress from the climb.

Kitty 3   What is it with you and windows?

Leah 3   Let's not –

Kitty 3   Just saying. What's wrong with the door?

Leah 3   Tenants Defence got a bit keen with the barricade. Getting in'll take the police at least half hour.

She puts her bag on the table. Clocks **Kitty 3**'s *sewing box, a black shirt being mended. Shaking her head, she goes to the bed.*

Leah 3 (*gentle*)   Hello, Jack, I'm your nurse. Just checking.

Feels their foreheads, takes pulses. Sees **Kitty 3** *watching her nervously.*

Leah 3   Got a problem with me touching 'em?

Kitty 3 *in disbelief. Their eyes light on the black shirt.* **Leah 3** *gets up.*

Leah 3   How long they been like this?

Kitty 3   Last night.

Leah 3   How's the baby?

Kitty 3   Hold her if you want.

Leah 3 *reaches out to feel baby's temperature with a different hand.*

Leah 3   Normal.

She now reaches for **Kitty 3**'s *forehead, professional, not intimate.* **Kitty 3** *flinches, maybe even screams.* **Leah 3** *withdraws, shocked.*

Leah 3 *and* **Kitty 3**   Sorry.

Kitty 3   I'm normal too.

Leah 3   I never (meant) –

Kitty 3   Leave it, Leah. I'm just hungry. You know how jittery I get . . .

She looks hopefully at **Leah 3**'s *bag. Outside more* **Police** *and another* **Bailiff***.*

Tenants   They shall not pass.
They shall not pass.

Leah 3 *moves to the window and nervously looks down (at audience).*

Leah 3   Two bailiffs and ten police. Blimey, how much rent d'you owe?

Kitty 3 (*laughs*)   Landlord's the crook – it's him they should be after.

The girls are close enough to touch – they breathe each other in, not looking at each other.

Kitty 3   Uniform suits you. Starchy. Bossy.

Leah 3 *smiles in spite of herself. Goes to bag for medicine.* **Kitty 3** *follows.*

Kitty 3   Hope you nicked that medicine – I can't pay for it. Leave me some?

Leah 3   For the boys, yeah.

She hands the medicine to **Kitty 3**.

Leah 3   One spoonful each – every four hours.

Kitty 3 (*gentle*)   Look at me, Leah. Please.

Leah 3   Keep them warm. Lots of –

Kitty 3   Look at me!

Outside, chanting continues soft under dialogue. **Leah 3** *goes back to the window.*

Tenants   They shall not pass. They shall not pass.

Kitty 3 *sits on bed, spoons medicine to her sleepy boys. Outside,* **Bailiff** *on police megaphone.*

Bailiff   Miss Grady. You must vacate the premises *now*. If you do not, police will enter the building to physically remove you and take away your children.

Jack (*feverish*)   Mummy . . .

Kitty 3   Shush, Jack. Sleep now . . .

Bailiff   Miss Grady, can you hear me? If you do not heed this eviction notice . . .

Kitty 3   Tell him, Leah. Tell him me kids are dying in here.

Jack   Mummy . . .?

Leah 3   No one's dying, Jack.

Kitty 3 (*strokes* **Jack**'*s hair*)   I'm just pretending, love – to make the bad men disappear. There . . .

Jack'*s fallen asleep again.* **Kitty 3** *approaches* **Leah 3**.

Kitty 3   Tell 'em me kids are too sick to move. You're a nurse – they'll listen.

Leah 3   Fight your own battles.

Kitty 3 *could push* **Leah 3** *out the window.*

Kitty 3   Don't bloody tempt me.

Tenants   They shall not pass. They shall not pass.

Bailiff   Miss Grady, can you hear me?

Kitty 3 (*shouts down from window*)   We ain't going nowhere, you thieving bastards! I got sick kids in 'ere what can't be moved. Now sling your 'ook.

Tenants cheer **Kitty 3**. *She grins at* **Leah 3** *who moves away.*

Leah 3   They won't be cheering when I tell them who you are, what your fiancé did –

Kitty 3   Ex-fiancé.

Leah 3 *picks up the Blackshirt uniform from the table.*

Leah 3   Ex-Blackshirt too?

Kitty 3   So what if I keep Blackshirt friends? Don't mean I think the same. Do we always have to think the same as our friends?

Leah 3 *looks towards the window desperate to get away.*

Kitty 3   You broke the drainpipe – no way back.

Leah 3 *sees that* **Kitty 3** *is right.*

Kitty 3   All those times I stood up for you. You just never knew.

She catches **Leah 3**'s *eye.*

Kitty 3   Thought so, Leah, we ain't done.

She makes **Leah 3**'s *finger trace the scar on her face.*

Kitty 1 *and* **Leah 1** (*aged eleven*) *play marbles on Cable Street in 1931.*

Kitty 3   You're still my blood sister, girl.

Chorus (All)   In more ways than one.

Blood Sisters 1

Chorus 1 *become Cable Street* **Locals**. *Children play street games, e.g. skipping with packing string, barrel hoop, ball games.* **Rosa** *and* **Eva** *scrub next-door steps/ street.*

Title: Cable Street, 1931

Leah 1 *stares into* **Kitty 1**'s *eyes.* **Leah 1** *wears ugly glasses. Marbles sits between them, on a wet sunlit drain. A rainbow glistens there.*

Kitty 1   Blood sisters, Leah. Now!

Kitty 1 *gets out a blade.* **Leah 1** *flinches.* **Chorus 1** *flinch too.*

Kitty 1   Can't be a doctor if you're scared of blood.

Leah 1   Not blood – pain. Finish the game!

Kitty 1 *puts down her blade.*

Kitty 1   Only cos you're winning.

Leah 1   It's marbles! The point is to win.

Eva	Picture a street
All	Cable Street
Kitty's Dad	A narrow street of shops and slums
Rosa	Jewish almost every one
Sam	From Poland
Eva	Ukraine
Anna	Russia
Sam	Us working-class Jews stick together
Anna	Like pickled herring and latke
Rosa	Chicken soup with matzah
Eva	Gefilte fish and horseradish

They see the beigel-seller coming with beigels in a basket.

Locals   Cream cheese beigel (*pronounced in the traditional way, long 'eye' sound – not 'bagel'*).

Burst of 'Beigels, who'll buy my beigels' *from 'Beigels' by Max Bacon (1935). Locals dance or juggle beigels.*

Kitty 1 *pushes her marble, loses and grabs the black marble.*

Leah 1   No, Kitty! Black one's mine. I won it fair and square.

Kitty 1 *pushes* **Leah 1** *who pushes her back.*

Kitty 1   Didn't.

Leah 1   Did.

Kitty 1 (*near tears*)   Black's my special one.

Leah 1   Don't play it then.

All Locals   Let beigels be beigels

Leah 1 (*relents*)   Give me the red – call it quits.

Kitty 1 *offers her red marble. They each kiss their own lucky marbles.*

Kitty 1   Love you, Black

Leah 1   Love you, Red.

They make their marbles kiss each other. Sound of a huge wave.

Message on the Edge

Leah 2 *and* **Kitty 2** *run barefoot and jump the tide at Tower Beach (by Tower Bridge).*

Title: Tower Beach, March 1934

4 p.m. Bright afternoon. Soft lapping Thames. Birds and occasional ship horns. Kitty 2 and Leah 2 (both fourteen) search along the beach in their patched school uniforms.

Kitty 2   It'll be here somewhere.

Leah 2   It might not be like you're saying, Kitty, from just a glimpse of him in the shop.

Kitty 2   Leaning on the counter he was, getting an eyeful. Dad was there – Billy didn't care. Said he'd leave a message here.

Leah 2   Tide might've washed it away.

Kitty 2   Billy knows tides and school times.

Leah 2   Did he *really* say he'd leave a message?

Kitty 2 *smiles slyly.*

Leah 2   You never went in Billy's shop because there isn't a shop, there isn't a Billy and you never went to Bethnal Green.

Kitty 2 *(about to cry)*   I did – I –

Leah 2 *(sighs)*   All right. Let's split up and look for Billy's message. *(Under breath.)* Get it over with.

They split up and look at opposite ends of the beach. **Leah 2** *finds a reddish, heart-shaped stone and carves a message for* **Kitty 2** *in the sand.*

Leah 3 *and* **Kitty 3** *watch them, unseen, curious.*

Leah 3   That message is how it started /

Leah 2 *and* **Kitty 2** *run back to each other.*

Kitty 3 *and*
Leah 2   } No

Kitty 2   Leah

Leah 2   What?

Kitty 2   If I tell you a secret will you promise to keep it?

Leah 2 *does their quirky secret 'promise' sign.*

Kitty 2   Reason we was in Bethnal Green, we're moving there tonight.

Leah 2   Liar.

Kitty 2   Doing a moonlight flit.

Leah 2   You're not.

Kitty 2   Rubi's priced us out.

Leah 2   You can't!

Kitty 2   S'only half an hour's walk.

Leah 2   But I ain't allowed round there.

Kitty 2   Bethnal Green?

Leah 2   Goyim gangs under the arches, waiting to grab yer bits 'n' pieces.

Kitty 2 *laughs, grabs* **Leah 2** *and tickles her.* **Leah 2** *giggles.*

Leah 3   I was the echo of your laughter.

Kitty 3   You were soft then – so soft-hearted.

Kitty 2 *'s laughter turns to tears.* **Leah 2** *wipes one and tastes it.*

Kitty 2   Why am I the one crying?

Leah 2   I'm crying inside. You just can't hear it.

Kitty 2   Will you miss sharing me bed?

Leah 2   Will you?

Kitty 2   When it's cold, I will.

Leah 2   I won't miss you then cos you always nick the blanket.

Kitty 2   You take up all the space. How can someone so little take up so much space?

Leah 2   I need to stretch. When I sleep at mine with Rosa, it's top to toe and I have to lie like a board on my side or she says I snore.

Kitty 2   You do snore.

Leah 2   When did I –?

Kitty 2   Like the Thames murmuring. It's sweet. Wakes me up, then sends me back to sleep.

They look at each other and smile. Sound of an alarm horn

Leah 2   Tide's coming in.

Kitty 2   If you was Billy, what message would you leave me?

Leah 2   Let's look over there. I missed that bit of beach. Head start, cos you got longer legs.

Kitty 2   Alright.

Leah 2 *races them towards her message.*

Kitty 2   What's this?

Kitty 2's *whole body lights up as she spies the message. Her eyes glitter.*

Kitty 2 (*reads*)   'I love you, Kitty.' (*She pauses.*) But I never told Billy me name.

Leah 2   He asked around

Kitty 2   Must've done.

Leah 2 *plays with* **Kitty 2**'s *hair*

Leah 2   When you leave school, how will I still see you?

Kitty 2   'I love you, Kitty.'

Leah 2   I'll drag you back to Cable Street by your hair.

She pulls **Kitty 2**'s *hair too hard.*

Kitty 2   Ow!

Leah 2   Let's run home before the tide gets us.

Kitty 2   One last paddle first.

They run into the Thames and kick water at each other, laughing.

Leah 3   I had you on a pedestal.

Kitty 3   So I was always going to fall.

Leah 1 *and* **Kitty 1** (*with kissing marbles*)   I love you so much it scares me.

Leah 2   He's not real though, this Billy – is he?

Billy *strolls by, looking handsome.*

Billy   Yeah. He's real.

He winks at **Kitty 2**, *who follows him.*

Blood Sisters 2

Title: Cable Street, 1931

Locals   Cable Street is a Jewish street.

Rosa   So Kitty and her dad stand out like a pork butchers.

Leah 1   But Kitty would stand out anywhere.

Kitty's Dad *strolls past* **Leah 1** *and* **Kitty 1**. *Something sad and broken about him.*

Dad   Still sitting in the gutter with that speccy Jew-boy?

He looks at Jewish **Locals (Chorus 1)** *in their workers' caps and specs.*

Dad   S'pose there's not much choice round here.

Kitty 2   It's Leah, Dad, Rosa's sister. She lives downstairs.

Leah 1   I ain't smelly. You're smelly.

Kitty 1   Speccy. He said 'speccy'.

Leah 1   Oh

Dad *pushes* **Leah 1** *playfully, but she loses balance and her glasses fall off.*

Dad   Smelly now. Hehehe! (*To* **Kitty 1**) Where's its sense of humour?

Leah 1 (*snivelling*)   You broke me glasses, stupid klutz.

Dad   Life's a joke, did no one tell yer?

Kitty 1   Leah's me new best friend.

Leah 1 *looks excitedly up at* **Kitty 1** *and smiles through her tears.* **Dad** *tips his hat.*

Dad   I do beg your pudding, Leah. I'll explain to Rosa – don't fret so. Come to the pictures for free. I play piano at the Cable. Ginger'll let you in.

He walks off. **Leah 1** *shows* **Kitty 1** *the broken glasses.*

Leah 1   Rosa'll skin me alive.

Kitty 1   I'll bandage it for now.

She takes the pretty cloth that her marbles are wrapped in and turns it into a cute bandage for the cracked lens.

Leah 1   If I'm your 'blood sister', I won't be related to your dad, will I?

Kitty 1   Ain't his fault, Leah. He's got shell shock. Left for dead in the trenches he was. Buried alive for days. Then when he got sent back to the front, he had to shoot some German boy who was gonna bayonet him. I know . . . His hand got pinned straight through like Jesus – lucky he can still play piano. (*She gives* **Leah 1** *the bandaged glasses.*) S'why he believes in miracles. Says I'm his little miracle.

Leah 1 *tries on her new glasses with a one-eyed pirate look.*

Leah 1   We off to the Cable then?

Kitty 1   After we do 'blood sisters'. Get there for the belly dancer in between the films. I can belly dance. Look!

She jiggles her belly. **Leah 1** *tickles her.* **Kitty 1** *escapes, grins and pulls out the blade again.*

Kitty 1   Ready now for blood sisters?

Leah 1 *blinks at the blade.* **Chorus 1** *sharp intake of breath.* **Leah 1** *holds out her arm.*

Leah 1   Blood sisters.

Solidarity

Friday night. Jewish **Locals (Chorus 1)** *hold candles and one or more cardboard box 'slum houses' with light inside.* **Leah 2** *and big sister* **Rosa** *walk along the 'street'. 1930s Yiddisher jazz coming from a gramophone mixed with religious Shabbat chanting/singing.*

Rosa (*sung/spoken*)   On Friday night the candles burn

All (*sung/spoken*)   On Cable Street

Title: Cable Street, May 1934

Locals part to reveal . . . a small all-purpose living room/kitchen/bedroom – **Leah 2**'s *family 'scullery'. Jazz distant now. Steaming tin bath of washing balances on two wooden stools.*

Sam, Leah's *older brother, has his feet up reading the* Daily Worker *when* **Kitty 2** *waltzes in, wearing a beautiful red dress.* **Sam** *whistles admiringly.*

Sam   Ain't you the Queen of Bethnal Green! Wouldn't mind *you* on me arm at the dance tonight . . . in that fetching dress –

Kitty 2   'Fetching'!

She laughs at **Sam**, *who joins in, embarrassed.*

Kitty 2   Let Leah go back to school – you can take me to your dance. She was top of the class – wants to be a doctor –

Sam *laughs bitterly at the idea and returns to his newspaper.*

Kitty 2   Why ain't you proud, Sam? What about equality?

Sam   *I* was fourteen when I started down the docks. Equality!

Kitty 2   *You* could work instead of Leah. *Always* jobs for Jews round here.

Sam   Not when you've been organising workers.

Rosa *enters, taking off headscarf. She tuts at the tin bath where a scrubbing board is half-submerged in soapy washing like a good intention.*

Rosa (*to* **Sam**)   You scrubbed Mr Johnson's smalls, yet?

Sam (*groans*)   Rosa.

Rosa (*kicks his chair*)   Don't make me work when you don't even care for Shabbat.

Sam   I was up at five this morning on a picket line, spoke at a strike meeting, researched an article and before me fundraiser, I'm having a tea-break. Is that alright?

Kitty 2   Need a hand, Rosa?

Sam (*pulls* **Kitty 2** *back*)   Not in that dress!

Rosa *looks at* **Kitty 2** *properly for the first time.* **Leah 2** *at doorway watches unnoticed.*

Rosa   Oy, oy. You nicked that cloth from work.

Kitty 2   Got it down the Lane.

Rosa   Lying shiksa.

Sam (*pulls* **Kitty 2** *towards him protectively*)   Milewski can afford it

Leah 2   What's Marlene Dietrich doing in our scullery?

Kitty 2 *lets go* **Sam**'*s hand.* **Kitty 2** *and* **Leah 2** *move towards each other.*

Kitty 2   Zank-you, dahling. Its 'fetching' ain't it, Sam, haha!

Leah 2   'Fetching'! Haha! Shame on you, Sam, hahaha! 'Fetching'!

She feels the dress fabric, holds **Kitty 2**'*s waist and twirls her.* **Sam** *winds up the old gramophone. He watches the girls, half-curious, half-jealous.*

Rosa   She gets a fine dress and we get our wages docked.

She stabs soapy clothes with stick, works the scrubbing board. Steam rises. Record begins.

Sam   Come to the dance in that dress, Kit – you'll sell us a ton of raffle tickets.

Kitty 2   I will, but you know what I want in return.

Confused and jealous, **Leah 2** *breaks away from* **Kitty 2**, *nearly knocks the washing over.*

Rosa   Careful!

Kitty 2 (*to* **Leah 2**)   Hey, Red! I'm doing it for you.

Leah 2 (*to* **Kitty 2**)   If *you* go to the dance, I'm coming too.

Kitty 2 *grabs and spins* **Leah 2**. **Rosa** *stares at her in fury.* **Leah 1** *and* **Kitty 1** *might also dance to amplify this moment.* **Rosa** *takes needle off the record. Dancing ends.*

Sam   I can't get *everyone* in for free. It's supposed to be a fundraiser for refugees escaping Hitler.

Kitty 2   I'd take their place in Germany any day.

Leah 2   And live in a police state? Don't be a schnook.

Kitty 2   Schnook yourself.

Sam (*to* **Kitty 2**)   Hitler's burning books. Locking up lefties. Calling everyone who don't agree 'collaborators'.

Kitty 2   No. He's putting people back to work. Making things. Building dams and roads. Giving people hope again.

Sam   *Daily Mail*?

Kitty 2   Everyone's saying it.

Lights up on **Chorus 2** *reading recognisable British newspapers, with pro-fascist and pro-Hitler headlines.* **Sam** *waves the* Daily Worker *at* **Kitty 2**, *with its anti-fascist headline.*

Sam   Not the *Daily Worker*. (*To* **Kitty 2**) We'll soon get your thinking straight.

Billy *enters. Watches.*

Billy   A lot of lies get told

Kitty 2   Billy says –

Sam   Who's Billy?

Leah 2   Two months and *I've* never seen him.

Billy *leaving* . . .

Kitty 2   Well *I've* seen him loads.

Billy *turns back into the room.*

Leah 2   Since when?

Kitty 2   Since he wrote me that message on Tower Beach.

Leah 2   But –

Sam   Who's Billy?

Kitty 2   Just a boy.

Rosa   *Now* she has the decency to blush.

Sam   You carrying a torch for 'Billy'?

Kitty 2   Let's just say I wouldn't mind being tickled by his 'tache.

Leah 2   Sam tried to grow a moustache, but he couldn't get more than a bit of fuzz – could you, Sam?

Sam   Shut up.

Kitty 2   Billy's moustache is handsome. Virile.

Leah 2 *snorts at the word 'virile'.* **Billy** *leaves, puffed up.* **Rosa** *wrings out the washing.*

Rosa   If the girl talks like this at fourteen, where will she end up? Round the back of the alley with the shilling whores, that's where.

Leah 2   Rosa!

Sam (*to* **Kitty 2**)   Come to the dance. Hear the truth from *actual* Germans.

Kitty 2   No one new should be let in – not 'til there's jobs for everyone here.

Sam   Don't then.

Kitty 2   Nothing 'gainst your family –

Leah 2   Kitty! We're as British as you.

Kitty 2   Not really. Parents from Poland.

Leah 2   And yours from Ireland. Just 'cause your dad dropped the 'O' off O'Grady don't make you more British than us.

Kitty 2   But eastern European Jews are more like guests –

Leah 2
Rosa   } No!
Sam

Sam (*to* **Kitty 2**)   Technically speaking, *you're* the guest. In *our* home.

Rosa   An unwanted guest.

Leah 2   No.

Kitty 2   I'm Leah's guest – it's up to her.

All look to **Leah 2** *who is saved by the entrance of* **Ged** *and* **Pat** *– two Irish dock workers.*

Pat   Sam!

Sam   Pat, Ged – What's up?

Ged *puts a bag of coins and notes on the table. They all stare at it.* **Ged** *grins.*

Ged   We did a collection for yous all round the docks.

Sam   What?

Ged   Seven pound, ten shillings and sixpence.

Rosa   A collection?

Pat   From the men.

Sam   For me . . .?

Ged   For your family.

Leah 2   That's four months' wages.

Kitty 2 (*whispers to* **Leah 2**)   You could go back to school.

Leah 2 *looks hopefully at* **Sam** *as he shakes the men's hands, too choked up to speak.*

Rosa   We're not taking charity, Sam.

Leah 2   But, Rosa –

Rosa   Don't I put food on our table?

Pat   It's solidarity, missus – not charity.

Ged   Sam took a hit for us on the docks . . . So we're taking a hit for him.

Rosa *can't stop staring at* **Ged**. *He's a goy but what a goy!*

Sam   Rosa, make some lemon tea.

Ged   You're alright, Rosa . . . we're away to the Brewery Tap. You joining us, Sam? (*Meets* **Rosa**'s *eye*.) Or maybe *you'd* like to –

Rosa *locks* **Ged**'s *eyes too long*. **Pat** *nudges* **Ged**.

Pat   It's their Sabbath.

Rosa *breaks eye contact with* **Ged** *and picks up her headscarf.*

Rosa   See, even your Catholic friend knows. Sam likes to forget.

Sam   As if I could forget round here . . .

Rosa (*to* **Ged**)   We can't thank you boys enough.

Ged *tips hat at* **Rosa**. *Then at* **Leah 2** *and* **Kitty 2**, *then* **Rosa** *again*.

Sam   I'll never forget your goodness, not for as long as I live.

Ged *and* **Pat** *leave*. **Sam** *wipes away a tear.*

Kitty 2   Blimey!

Rosa *ties on her headscarf.*

Rosa   I'll pray for you, Leah and Sam. (*Suspicious glance at* **Kitty 2**.) I'll just put this money somewhere safe.

Rosa *takes money to other room*. **Sam** *puts on his jacket.*

Kitty 2   Leah could go to school now.

Leah 2   Let me go back to school, Sam. Please.

Rosa (*calls offstage*)   Sam!

Leah 2   Please, Sam.

Sam   Coming! I'll talk it through with Rosa.

Leah 2 *and* **Kitty 2**   Yes!

Kitty 2 *kisses* **Sam**'s *cheek. He blushes as he runs off.*

Leah 2   When did you see this Billy then?

Kitty 2   Albert Hall.

Leah 2   Who's Albert Hall?

Kitty 2   It's a theatre, you schnook. With a big stage. Got friendly with Joyce in the shop, Billy's older sister. She gave me and Dad tickets. Billy's in uniform on the door.

Billy *strolls back in.*

Kitty 2   He's *so* handsome, Leah! Bright turquoise eyes, high cheekbones, slicked back hair.

Leah 2   And a 'virile 'tache'?

Kitty 2   When he smiled at me, I nearly wet myself.

Leah 2 *pretends to laugh along.*

Kitty 2   Then on the stage, this man starts speaking and thousands of us were . . . well . . . I had tears running down me face.

Leah 2   Better than pish running down your leg.

Kitty 2   On about ex-servicemen he was, how they and the youth must look backwards and forwards and join hands to build a new Great Britain. And just at that moment, Dad reached out and held me hand and we were together, on the same side, like before they took Mammy away . . . (*Her voice catches.* **Kitty 1** *and* **Dad** *hold hands in idealistic family scene with* **Billy** *and* **Joyce**.) Went back with Joyce and Billy after. Sat in their parlour.

Leah 2   A parlour!

Kitty 2   Tea and sherry and Victoria sponge that Joyce made. Civilised it was.

Leah 2   I thought you looked different, not just the dress but . . . (*She has to ask.*) Did Billy kiss you goodnight . . . ?

Kitty 2   Maybe.

Leah 2   More than a kiss? No . . . What was it like?

She tries to hide her jealous agitation. **Kitty 2** *laughs, proud.*

Kitty 2   Shall I show you?

Leah 2 *nods, nervous but excited.* **Billy** *enters. It's as if he's in* **Kitty 2**'s *memory in a different place/time. He doesn't watch their encounter or have agency.*

Kitty 2   You be me.

She swaggers, Billy-like

So he starts like this . . .

Billy *and* **Kitty 2**   You wanna be me girl then?

Kitty 2 *kisses* **Leah 2** *fully on the lips.* **Leah 2** *is shocked but aroused. She kisses* **Kitty 2** *back with passion.* **Kitty 2** *is shocked and amused.*

Billy *and* **Kitty 2**   You're a good kisser.

Leah 2   Is that Billy talking or you?

Billy *and* **Kitty 2**   It's me.

Kitty 2   And then he –

Kitty 2 *grabs* **Leah** *forcefully, kisses her, hands all over her.* **Leah 2** *gasps, scared, excited. Record ends – click of needle.*

Kitty 2 *(seductive)*   See, you'd have just let him, my dirty little Jew girl.

Leah 2 *blinks, overwhelmed with emotion. Pushes* **Kitty 2** *angrily away.*

Leah 2   Don't you *ever* call me that!

Kitty 2 *takes needle off the record.*

Kitty 2   S'what Billy called *me.*

Leah 2   Billy . . .? But why?

Billy *laughs and leaves the stage.*

Kitty 2   Just a joke. I dunno. Cause I grew up ghetto? Hey, Leah, I never meant to hurt you. You know I love you, Red. Come 'ere . . . the look on your face . . . like a little monkey.

Pulls her back into her very gently. Twists **Leah 2**'s *hair and kisses her nose. As their mouths open to kiss, the scene changes.*

Milewski's Sweatshop

Chorus 1 *create* **Jewish** *garment workshop.*

Rosa   On Cable Street there's those who sweat
Leah 2   And also those who sweat us.

The women look up at ceiling – Milewski's office upstairs. A looming shadow appears elsewhere. **Eva** *jumps.*

Eva   When Mr Milewski calls you upstairs,
                That's the day you got to be scared.

Anna   Who'd be a workshop girl?

Rosa   The fastest sets the pace.

Anna   Cutters cut the cloth
Eva   Machinist runs the seams
Worker 1   Presser steam presses

Leah 2   Button-holer sews the buttons

Anna   Cut
Eva   Seam
Worker 1   Press
Rosa   Steam

Leah 2   Button-holer sews the buttons

All   Faster faster faster
               Hang the dresses high

Rosa   This seam is crooked

They all blame one another, point the finger

Eva   Cutter's fault
Rosa   Presser's fault
Anna   Machinist's fault

All   Leah's fault. Hahaha

Rosa   Tear it up – start over

Anna (*to* **Leah 2**)   Milewski would be happy to be rid of you, believe me –

Eva (*to* **Leah 2**)   Slowing down the line.

They look at **Kitty 2** *who has her head down, seriously speedy and accurate.* **Leah 2** *grins.*

Leah 2   Goy sews good, Jew sews bad – the world is upside down.

Anna *and* **Eva** *laugh.* **Rosa** *doesn't. As* **Leah 2** *passes with dresses they say to her:*

Anna   Clever girl, getting Kitty the job.

Eva   Only reason Milewski lets you stay . . .

Rosa *looks ashamed of* **Leah 2**. **Kitty 2** *looks up.*

Kitty 2   Hey, sis, you doing overtime tonight?

Leah 2   While there's work. You?

Kitty 2 *nods and smiles.* **Leah 2** *sits next to her.*

Kitty 2   Mammy was a tailor
              She taught me two things.
              If you sew you'll never starve.
              And if you can't do it right, do it fast.

All   If you can't do it right do it fast.
              Fasten 'em fast, fasten 'em fast

Kitty 2   I could quite fancy myself in that red and black tartan.

Leah 2   I could quite fancy you in it too.

Rosa (*shocked*)   Leah!

She storms off.

Kitty 2   Untangle those threads, Leah. Then I'll help you with the buttons.

Leah 2 *untangles threads by* **Kitty 2***'s feet. Workers out of earshot now.*

Kitty 2   Careful in front of Big R.

Leah 2   Who cares? She's so religious – no one I choose would be right –

Kitty 2   But *we're* not . . . I mean . . .

Leah 2   What?

Kitty 2   Last night was a laugh. But I mean, that would be . . .

She joins **Leah 2** *under the table to show her how to untangle threads.*

Kitty 2   We're best friends, it just kind of –

Leah 2   *You* touched *me* first –

Kitty 2   I know

Leah 2   So don't make out –

Kitty 2   I wanted to . . .

Leah 2   *I* wanted to –

Kitty 2   We fit together.

Leah 2   Always did

Kitty 2   So soft. Your lips. Like eating a peach –

Leah 2 *smiles*

Leah 2   When did you eat a peach?

Kitty 2   I could eat you now. Peachy. All of you.

They giggle.

Leah 2   We can stay extra late, be alone. Tell Milewski we'll finish something while he's out playing cards.

Kitty 2   You're naughty!

Leah 2   You're hungry . . .

Kitty 2   When I kiss Bill, his bristles scratch me.

Leah 2   I hate to think of you kissing Billy.

Kitty 2   I love to think of you hating me kissing Billy.

Leah 2 *checks that the other women aren't looking.*

Leah 2   Kiss me now.

Kitty 2   Not *now*, crazy peach –

Rosa *returns.*

Rosa   Kitty . . .? (*Sees her.*) Kitty! Mr Milewski wants to see you. Now.

Leah 2 *makes a sympathetic face at* **Kitty 2** *who leaves.* **Rosa** *turns on* **Leah 2**.

Rosa   I don't want you seeing that shickster any more.

Leah 2   She's my sister.

Rosa   *I'm* your sister. That goy sits here like butter wouldn't melt, and it all gets blamed on you.

Leah 2   I earn my keep – I'll see who I want.

Rosa *lowers her voice so the other women can't hear.*

Rosa   I thought you wanted to go back to school?

Leah 2   When I'm back at school then fine, control me like you love to do. But you'll never stop me seeing Kitty.

Rosa *looks skyward.*

Leah 2   There is no heaven, Rosa.

But **Rosa** *is listening to* **Kitty 2** *and Milewski shouting upstairs. A crash. Door slams.*

Leah 2   Oh no . . .

Rosa   Her ma's meshuggah, Dad's a schlump, no one to teach her right from wrong.

Kitty 2 *emerges looking shaky, but defiant. Picks up her bag and coat.*

Leah 2   What's up?

Kitty 2   Someone snitched.

Rosa *looks away.* **Kitty 2** *and* **Leah 2** *look shocked and deeply hurt.*

Leah 2   Rosa!

Rosa   You steal from him then expect him to pay.

Kitty 2   Yes, I expect the old lech to pay. I took the cloth as payment for what he tried to do. (*To* **Rosa**.) I thought you was my family.

Kitty 2 *storms out.*

Leah 2 (*to* **Rosa**)   I hate you.

Rosa   You'll thank me later.

Leah 2   Kitty . . . wait!

She runs after **Kitty 2**.

Rosa (*calling after* **Leah 2**)   Milewski wants us on overtime –

Leah 2 (*turns*)   Milewski can go fuck himself.

Anna *shakes her head as* **Rosa** *wonders what 'fuck' means.*

Eva   But by the time Leah got outside
             Kitty had gone.
Anna   Leah looked around
             Asked around
Both   No one had seen Kitty

Eva   Come back into work, girl. It'll come out in the wash.

She puts her arm around **Leah 2**, *leads her back inside. Tired women work slowly by lamplight.*

All   Fasten down the lining
            Hang the dresses high.

Blood Sisters 3

Title: Cable Street, 1931

Kitty 1 *grins, holding the blade.*

Kitty 1   Ready?

Goes to cut **Leah 1**'s *arm.*

Leah 1   No!

Kitty 1   Stop shaking and close your eyes.

They giggle. **Leah 1** *closes her eyes.*

Kitty 1   Think of the blade like my fingernail.

She draws her fingernail across **Leah 1**'s *arm.* **Leah 1** *screams.* **Kitty 1** *laughs.*

Kitty 1   That *was* my fingernail. Relax.

She stares at **Leah 1**'s *arm curiously before decisively cutting it.* **Leah 1** *looks.*

Leah 1   Kitty – I think there's too much blood.

Kitty 1   There is – yeah there is! You jerked away too suddenly.

Leah 1   No! Ow! Do yours, quick, do yours.

Kitty 1 *presses her hand on* **Leah**'s *arm to stop blood pumping out. Can't stop laughing.*

Leah 1   Do yours!

Kitty 1   Stop squealin' or I won't kiss it better.

Fire

Women scream as fire takes hold of Milewski's sweatshop. Screams. Flames. Rain.

Aftershock

Same night. Bethnal Green. Rain falls softly now. In **Kitty 2**'s *scullery-bedroom.*

Kitty 2 *comforts shivering* **Leah 2** *on the bed, which doubles as seating.*

Leah 2   I saw smoke drift past the window and when I looked out, this man stared back, black moustache, bright blue eyes lit up by flames. Behind him, fresh graffiti in white paint, dripping in the rain and half in shadow. But you could see enough to recognise 'Perish Judah' (*Death to Jews*).

Kitty 2   Thank God they never (*hugs* **Leah 2** *tight*). Did you tell the police?

Leah 2   I tried. But Rosa kept shouting 'bout *you*.

Kitty 2   As if I'd hurt my Red.

Leah 2   S'why I had to warn you –

Kitty 2   Braving Bethnal Green for me . . .

Kitty 2 *kisses* **Leah 2** *boldly on the lips.*

Kitty 2   You taste of rainy streets.

Leah 2 (*tasting*)   And you've been drinking.

Kitty 2   Firewater – good for shock. Did a fireman lift you over his shoulder?

Leah 2   No! Back window was unlocked. I got us all out but the workshop's gutted.

Kitty 2   All that lovely silk and tartan, my favourite golden buttons. Wish I'd nicked more while I could . . .

Leah 2 *pulls a handful of golden buttons from her pockets.*

Leah 2   In a box by the window – I grabbed you some as I climbed out.

Kitty 2 *smiles gleefully as if they were jewels. Puts them in sewing box.*

Kitty 2   Love you, Peach. You should have nicked the lot! Take this off, it's too wet.

They peel off **Leah 2**'s *wet coat.*

Kitty 2   Let's snuggle in bed, warm you up a bit.

They jump into bed like the old days, snuggle under the sheet and blankets.

Leah 2   I won't get nothing for me overtime now and the money was all for you.

Kitty 2   I'll get a job, lovely girl, you'll see –

Leah 2   But no workshop'll take a thief.

Kitty 2 *looks stung.* **Leah 2** *tries to make amends.*

Leah 2   We could set up a market stall for your dresses. All sorts come to the Lane these days.

Kitty 2   Billy's family might need a hand in their grocer's shop.

Leah 2 (*cajoling*)   One day *I'll* take you to Albert Hall. Get tickets for the speaker who made you cry. What did you say his name was?

Kitty 2   Come 'ere.

Leah 2   Tell me.

Kitty 2 *sighs.*

Kitty 2   He's some aristocrat who's for the workers. Been a Labour MP and a Tory MP, set up his own party . . .

Blackshirts *march on.* **Billy** *caught up in them, a tell-tale white paint stain on his boot.*

Leah 2   Not the British Union of Fascists? Not Oswald bloody Mosley –?

Kitty 2   Billy said you'd be prejudiced. S'why I couldn't say.

Leah 2 *looks at* **Kitty 2**, *horrified.*

Leah 2   I ain't sharing you with a Blackshirt!

Kitty 2   Am I telling *you* what to do?

Blackshirts *march off.* **Leah 2** *shivers.* **Kitty 2** *holds her lovingly, sees something.*

Kitty 2   Look! Your rusty stains are still on the mattress.

Leah 2 (*laughing*)   Urgh, Kitty.

Kitty 2   Something to remember you by.

Leah 1 *and* **2** *and* **Kitty 1** *and* **2**   Blood sisters.

Leah 2   If we opened the door, we might still be on Cable Street!

Kitty 2   Nothing beyond this bed matters, only me and you.

Leah 2   Wish that was true.

Kitty 2   Let's make it true.

Leah 2   But –

Kitty 2 *pulls the covers right over them. Unseen kissing.*

Leah 2   Oh . . .

Billy *enters, white paint still on boot. He stares in disbelief at the moaning, giggling bodies moving under the blankets. He takes out his knife.*

Billy   Kitty?

Bodies freeze under blanket. **Kitty 2** *sticks her head out of the covers first.*

Kitty 2   We was just keeping warm.

Billy   Be a man, show your face.

Leah 2 *pokes her head out.*

Billy   Jew girl?

Leah 2   You?

Kitty 2 *protects* **Leah 2** *from* **Billy***.* **Joyce** *and* **Dad** *enter behind.*

Joyce   Billy, drop that knife.

Leah 2   'Billy'?!

Dad *moves into military mode. Disarms* **Billy** *and pins him down with speed and strength.*

Leah 2   He set fire to Milewski's.

Kitty 2   No!

Billy   Let me go. She'll grass me up.

Kitty 2 *realises the truth. Helps* **Dad** *hold* **Billy** *down.* **Leah 2** *grabs damp coat.*

Leah 2   Come on, Kitty.

Dad (*to* **Leah 2**)   Run, Speccy, run.

Billy (*to* **Leah 2**)   You snitch an' I'll slit your throat like a kosher cow –

Leah 2   Please, Kitty –

Kitty 2   Run!

Leah 2 *runs.* **Billy** *is noisily trying to break free.*

Dad   Joyce, help us out –

Joyce *joins* **Dad** *and* **Kitty 2** *sitting on* **Billy***.*

Billy   Joyce, you lump, whose side you on? She'll go straight to the cop shop.

Leah 2 *keeps running.*

Rehearsal

Chorus 1 *and* **2**   A Chorus is not just a Chorus. A Chorus must be trained.

Reds (Chorus 1) *salute with clenched fists.*

Reds   Left right left right left right left

Blackshirts (Chorus 2) *give fascist salute*

Blackshirts   Right left right left right left right

Statements

Blackshirts *and* **Reds** *softly march on the spot upstage.* **Kitty 2** *and* **Leah 2** *are on Tower Beach. Sounds of wind and rough waves.*

Kitty 2   That fire was sparked by Billy's passion for me, so if you want to blame anyone –

Leah 2   What's happening to us?

Kitty 2   We're alright.

Leah 2   I haven't stopped loving you –

Kitty 2   Nor me.

Leah 2   But to be with you, it's like I have to stop loving myself.

Kitty 2   *Please* withdraw your witness statement.

Leah 2   What statement? Copper told me to fuck off home to me red Jew brother.

Kitty 2 *laughs with relief and throws her arms around* **Leah 2** *who doesn't respond.*

Kitty 2   Thank God! I mean . . . I'm just glad Billy's life's not ruined. He is a bit wild but –

Ship's alarm. **Leah 2** *extricates herself.*

Leah 2   Is that all you wanted?

Reds *and* **Blackshirts** *continue marching, take the stage.*

Olympia

Title: Olympia, June 1934

Reds   Left right left right left right left

Blackshirts   Right left right left right left right

Blackshirts *and* **Reds**	They ignore us until they need us to fight So now we'll show them what being a hero looks like.
Blackshirts	With our Union Jack
Reds	With our red flag
Blackshirts *and* **Reds**	We'll take what's ours Our human right Tonight.

Reds *disappear into the audience to become* **Hecklers**. *Fanfare. Trumpets. Uniformed* **Blackshirts** *hold up a big Union Jack. They have British Union of Fascist flags too – lightning in a circle.* **Oswald Mosley** *steps forward. He gives fascist salute.* **Blackshirts** *return the salute.*

Mosley   Parliament is paralysed. What we need is a government, free of opposition, free of self-serving parasites. Leadership – but not tyranny. A fascist revolution.

Heckler 1   What about democracy?

Spotlight picks out **Heckler 1**. **Blackshirts** *pull* **Heckler 1***'s arms behind his back and beat him.*

Mosley   We will deal with Jewish international finance that exploits the world. We will deal with those in the Conservative Party who take their inspiration from the Italian Jew Benjamin Disraeli.

Doll (Heckler 2) *stands up bravely.*

Doll   Even your flag is a flash in the pan! (*BUF symbol is lightning in circle.*)

Some laughter. **Blackshirts** *move in to crush* **Doll** *who dodges them deftly.*

Mosley   And here, tonight, we will deal most forcibly with razor gangs from Jewish East End ghettos who seek to violently disrupt our meeting. Communists inspired by that German Jew Karl Marx –

Doll   And you're inspired by Mussolini and Hitler. / Fascism means murder!

Blackshirts *grab* **Doll** *finally and beat her senseless.* **Sam** *is* **Heckler 3**.

Sam   Fascism means murder. Fascism means war!

The **Blackshirts** *– one of whom is* **Billy** *– move in to crush* **Sam**. *Pull his arms behind his back and beat him viciously. Police help fascists beat and eject* **Hecklers**. *An orgy of violence.*

Reds *rescue* **Sam***; place him on chair in family scullery.* **Rosa** *removes* **Sam***'s ripped-up jacket.*

Leah 3 *and* **Kitty 3** *watch from 1939.*

Kitty 3   We missed the main event, didn't we?

Reds *and* **Blackshirts (Chorus 1** *and* **2)** *stop and turn to the audience.*

Chorus 1 *and* **2**   We were the main event.

Torn

Leah 2 *tends to* **Sam***'s wounds.* **Rosa** *holds up* **Sam***'s ripped suit jacket.*

Rosa   How am I s'posed to mend this?

Leah 2   S'like wild animals ripped you open.

Sam   Doll heckled first – got beaten to a pulp.

Leah 2 (*shocked*)   Lovely Doll who read Mum's tea leaves?

Sam   She never saw this coming.

Leah 2   Sam!

Sam   Went disguised in twin set and pearls – came out on a stretcher.

Leah 2   Fuck.

Sam   Head blown up like a balloon.

Rosa   What's 'fuck', what does it mean, this word you keep saying?

Leah 2 *and* **Sam** *laugh in spite of themselves. It hurts his broken ribs.*

Sam   Ow!

Leah 2 *tends to* **Sam***, still laughing.*

Tattoo

Billy *and* **Joyce***'s parlour.* **Billy** *is drinking whisky with* **Joyce***.* **Kitty 2** *enters.*

Billy   Salute Mosley or you can't come in.

Billy   Billy . . .

Billy   She needs to prove her loyalty, Joyce. She won't say 'Perish Judah'.

Kitty 2   No, I won't.

Billy   Been in the ghetto, stink of garlic.

Kitty 2   Don't like that common talk.

Billy   Don't you like your common job in our common shop with our common talk? How common are those jobs, Joyce? (*Relents.*) Look what I got yer.

Kitty 2 *inspects* **Billy***'s scabby arm. He's had a tattoo*

Billy *and*⎤
Sam   ⎦   Ow!

In scullery **Leah 2** *is washing* **Sam** *'s gaping wounds with stinging antiseptic. She and* **Kitty 2** *look up and meet each other's gaze across the space.*

Kitty 2 *and* ⎤
Leah 2　　　⎥ Don't want it going septic.

Billy (*joking*)　You do spell Kitty with *one* 't' don't yer?

Kitty 2 (*elated*)　When the scab comes off – ?

Billy　You'll see 'I love Kitty'. This tattoo shows how much.

Kitty 2 *grins then anxiety crosses her face.* **Billy** *notices.*

Billy　If we stop courtin', the sailor says he'll turn it into a snake.

Joyce　Courtin' are yer now?

Kitty 2 *tickles* **Billy** *– they giggle like children.* **Kitty 2** *smiles at* **Joyce***. Her new family.*

Billy　Living on Cable Street. Enough to turn anyone fascist.

Kitty 2　No – I loved living on Cable Street.

Billy　You what?

Kitty 2 *watches* **Leah 2** *bandage* **Sam** *'s wound.*

Kitty 2　It was hard sometimes, not being a Jew, the way some of 'em'd look at me. But me and Leah, we . . . Getting thrown out of where I was happy. That's what ain't right.

Billy　Oh.

Kitty 2 *watches* **Leah 1** *and* **Kitty 1** *play a slapping/clapping game – sweet to violent.*

Joyce　Evicted by a Jew.

Kitty 2　True.

Billy　And chucked out of your job by another Jew.

Kitty 2　In me own country.

Billy　S'why I was protecting you.

Joyce　Kitty understands, don't you love?

Kitty 2　Great Britain is me birthright and I support what Mosley's doing to protect it. But there are good Jews and bad Jews – like with all people. You only hate 'em, Billy, cos you don't know 'em. That's why I won't say 'Perish Judah' or do your PJ salute. But I will say 'Britain First'.

Billy　What's the difference, love?

Torn (continued)

Leah 2 *bandaging* **Sam***,* **Rosa** *trying to mend his torn jacket.*

Rosa   The *Jewish Chronicle* has best advice. Keep your head down. Don't disrupt their meetings.

Leah 2   No! Jews need to fight back.

Sam   The whole working class needs to fight back. It's an attack on us all.

Rosa   I can't fix this. (**Rosa** *discards* **Sam***'s jacket.*)

Sam   But the only ones standing up to Mosley are the Communist Party.

Leah 2   So how do I join?

Rosa *looks at* **Leah 2** *in horror.* **Sam** *smiles at* **Leah 2**.

Eviction 2

Title: Whitechapel, September 1st 1939

Tenants*' chant of 'They shall not pass' continues soft beneath*

Bailiff (*through megaphone*)   Miss Grady. We have police reinforcements. We're breaking down the barricade. Coming in.

Leah 3   They'll soon have the door open. Where's Mosley's lot when you need 'em, eh? Where's your *fascist* Tenants' Defence? (*Looks down.*) Oh, what's Sam doing here? (*Steps back from the window.*)

Kitty 3   He organised this protest. I thought that's why you came.

Leah 3   No, we're not (speaking) . . . Sam's defending *you*?

Kitty 3   Working-class solidarity . . .

Leah 3   Like you showed us at Cable Street? Must love that Britain's only taking a few thousand Jewish refugee children –

Kitty 3   That's –

Leah 3   Must be in heaven with our Tory national government and royal family chock-full of Nazi sympathisers.

Kitty 3   Got any grub, girl? I'm starving. Show me solidarity, come on.

Tenants   They shall not pass
They shall not pass

Leah 2 *looks at her bag, unsure, desperate to escape.*

Kitty 3   Each gives what they can and takes what they need. Ain't that the definition of communism?

Leah 3 (*sighs*)   I been on night shift, Kitty. All done in.

Kitty 3 (*smiles, knowing*)   And even if you could get out, you won't sleep for hours after seeing me.

1936: **Blackshirts** *march around the stage banging drums.* **Leah 1** *struts in the other direction with her bandaged-up glasses and bandaged-up arm. Cable Street Jews hold the same cardboard house(s) as before, broken window(s) now boarded up like* **Leah 1** *'s bandaged glasses.*

Leah 3 *turns to see her younger self,* **Leah 2** *– now sixteen years old.*

Petition

Title: September 1936, Cable Street

Leah 2 *giving a confident off-the-cuff speech on plinth/chair at a street corner meeting.* **Sam** *is selling the* Daily Worker. **Anti-fascists (Chorus 1)** *pass petitions around the audience as if they are spectators in the street scene.*

Leah 2   The Board of Deputies of British Jews says, 'Stay indoors if Mosley marches. Behave and nothing bad will happen.' But it is happening!

Beaten-up **Jewish Man** *stumbles in.* **Anti-fascists** *run to help him.*

Jewish Man   They came out of nowhere, five Blackshirts. Kicking and punching me.

Sam *runs to him to get intel.*

Leah 2   If five fascists can do this, what will 5,000 do? The Labour Party says 'avoid fascist gatherings'. But how can we avoid their graffiti on our streets, on our walls, on our front doors? Their megaphones on lorries, blaring hate into our homes? Their beatings in dark alleys and at meetings?

Jewish Man   Atta girl!

Sam *and some others put on knuckle-dusters, go to beat up the* **Blackshirts** *who did this.*

Leah 2   The police don't protect us! Nor do the Board of Deputies. So we've formed our own Jewish People's Council to organise resistance. If you want to stop Mosley marching through the East End, sign our petition to the Home Office.

She puts a petition into her basket. Bell rings as she enters **Billy** *'s family grocers.*

Tick

Billy *'s family grocer's shop. Tired* **Kitty 2** *in overall, serving on her own.*

Leah 2   Jam please.

Kitty 2 *looks up, amazed to see* **Leah 2***, older and cuter. Checks reflection. Smiles.*

Kitty 2   Red or black?

Leah 2   Guess. Can I have it on tick?

Kitty 2 *gets red jam.*

Kitty 2   We don't do tick . . .

Leah 2   'No tick for Jews.' I did see the sign. (*Flirty, playful.*) But you look like such a giving sort o' girl.

Kitty 2 *puckers her lips, blows a kiss. Puts jam in* **Leah 2**'*s basket. Sees petition, takes it out.*

Kitty 2   Taking a risk – carrying that round 'ere.

Leah 2   I was hoping that maybe you'd sign it.

Kitty 2 *looks at* **Leah 2**, *surprised.*

Leah 2   Our Jewish shops've got ever so popular – Blackshirts just can't keep away.

Kitty 2   Heard there'd been some trouble.

Baby starts to cry out the back.

Leah 2   Thought you might stand shoulder to shoulder with your old neighbours.

Baby's crying gets louder. **Kitty 2** *hands back petition, unsigned.*

Kitty 2 (*calling*)   Is he alright, Joyce?

Billy (*calls from back*)   Yeah.

Kitty 2 (*to* **Leah 2**)   Me baby.

Leah 2   Mazel tov.

Kitty 2   Ta. (*Smiles.*) His name's Jack.

Leah 2   Can I see him or –

Kitty 2   Best not to – right now.

Leah 2 *nods sadly.*

Leah 2   Why don't you bring Jack to Cable Street one night? Come for tea.

Kitty 2   Miss me do yer?

Leah 2   Let beigels be beigels? Rosa's out most Wednesdays.

Kitty 2   Can't do Wednes –

Leah 2   Or down the Lane one Sunday?

Kitty 2   Why didn't you come when you knew I was pregnant?

Leah 2   Pregnant by that murderer.

Kitty 2   Then leave me alone forever.

They both want to cry. **Kitty 2** *reaches out to touch* **Leah 2**'*s hand.*

Leah 2   You know it's wrong for fascists to march through Jewish streets.

Kitty 2   Free speech.

She tries to pulls her hand away but **Kitty 2** *won't let her.*

Kitty 2   Mosley just wants to solve the unemployment crisis. Three million unemployed in Britain and three million Jews.

Leah 2   There's 300,000 Jews in Britain not three million. You just added a nought.

Kitty 2   I read it.

Leah 2   With your eyes shut? You drop an 'O' from your name to make you sound less of an Irish immigrant then you add it to the number of Jewish immigrants!

Kitty 2   Oh oh oh! (*Lets go of* **Leah***, sticks up her hand.*) Miss, I got the answer, miss!

Leah 2   A third of British Jews are in the East End – that's why it seems a lot to you. Jews can't help getting paid less. Unionisation is the answer. Working-class solidarity.

Kitty 2   Shut up, Leah. Shut up. Just shut up.

Leah 2   Free speech, eh? (*Beat.*) 'Mosley go home.' That's what *we'll* say. Stepney is our home. It was never his. Mosley lives in a big posh house, full of servants.

Kitty 2   I wouldn't mind a big posh house.

Leah 2 *notices a rag doll, dressed as a female Blackshirt.* **Leah 2** *looks from doll to* **Kitty 2***, genuinely confused.* **Kitty 2** *picks up the doll before* **Leah 2** *can.* **Kitty 2** *makes doll dance.*

Kitty 2   Nothing personal, Leah, but Jews are taking over the world. Out for themselves, that's what it is. We're out for the nation.

Leah 2   We're all human – where we're born is chance. Should that decide our chances in life? We need a world revolution. Save us from nationalism, poverty and war.

Kitty 2   But you got to admit, the black shirt is a sharp look.

Leah 2 *stares at* **Kitty 2** *in shock.*

Leah 2   *You* ain't joined the fascists? I don't believe you.

Blackshirts   Bang your drum, Kitty
Bang your drum

Kitty 2   I bang me drum for the orchestra.
Cute in the uniform. Pure.
Just a dab of lipstick
Perfect poster girl for Mosley
S'pose that's why they chose me.
I might be a mum but I still got it
Don't take it so personally.

Blackshirts   Bang your drum, Kitty
Bang your drum

Under percussion. Seductive, persuasive.

Kitty 2   The Fascist corporate state will recognise homemaker and mother as a career. It will remove the immigrant competition from cheaper female labour. Give women more spending power. It's not about hate or blaming anyone for our plight, but it *is* about putting British women first.

Leah 2 *takes the jam from her basket, slams it on the counter.*

Kitty 2   Leah . . .

She grabs at **Leah 2**. *But* **Leah 2** *pulls away, devastated. Shop bell rings loudly – like in a boxing ring.*

Defend the Jewish East End!

Title: Cable Street, September 1936

Anti-fascists collect petitions from audience. **Leah 2** *waves her petition.*

Leah 2	In forty-eight hours, 100,000 of you signed this petition. Thank you. Thank you.
Doll	Go home, Oswald Mosley! Leave our streets alone

Sam   But the Home Office ignore us. License Mosley and his Blackshirts to march through Stepney.

Jewish Man   Protected by 6,000 police

Survivor   Ten of us can fit in Mrs Joseph's cellar. We'll save you a place, Rosa.

Rosa	Survivors of the pogroms find places to hide Trauma carved on their faces like warnings.

Anti-fascists   War with the fascists marches towards us.

Leah 2, **Anna** *and* **Sam** *with buckets of whitewash, graffitiing the roads and walls.*

Ged	Dockers collect debris in sacks for days.
Pat	Plan our blockade against Mosley's parade.
Leah 2	We build resistance / together
Anti-fascists	Together
Ged	Dockers
Anna	Garment workers
Pat	Railway workers
Doll	Tenants' groups
Eva	Jewish groups
Sam	Socialists

Worker 1	Anarchists
Kitty's Dad	Ex-servicemen
Leah 2	And our Stepney Branch of the Communist Party

Leah 2, **Doll** *and* **Sam** *complete their graffiti. The graffiti words can also be spoken.*

Sam	'All out on Gardiner's Corner!'
Doll	'All out on Cable Street!'
Leah 2	'No *pasarán*!'
All	'They shall not pass.'
Doll	We won't let Mosley and his Blackshirts march.
Sam	Thousands coming by bus or train
	for the solidarity march with Spain
	will instead face British fascists!
Leah 2	Come to Aldgate East
Many	Defend our streets
All	Defend the Jewish East End!

The Battle of Cable Street

Title: Cable Street, Sunday 4 October 1936

Chorus 1 (Locals & Reds); **Chorus 2 (Blackshirts & Police)**. **Chorus** *speaks in unison.*

In a corner, **Kitty 1** *and* **Leah 1** *(bandaged-up) play marbles.*

A banner hangs on Cable Street: 'Remember Olympia. They shall not pass'
Ged, **Pat** *and* **Locals** *reinforce barricade of mattresses, tables and chairs.*

Sam	A crisp, cold October day.
	Perfect protest weather.
Doll	First off, the ex-servicemen's peaceful march
	with its anti-fascist banners
	gets beaten up by police.
Chorus 1	How dare they?
Doll	Angry locals gather.
Leah 2	By 2 p.m., it's rammed at Gardiner's Corner
	You can't see the end of the crowd
Chorus 1	Not down any street.

Leah 2 *climbs, as* **Leah 3** *did at start of the play*

Leah 3	Shinned a lamppost
	thought I saw you
	with my lot
	but it wasn't. Thought if you were here
	you'd have a chance of seeing me.

Doll (*to* **Leah 2**)   Get down before the police nab yer, silly mare.

Kitty 3   Said I'd go, but me heart wasn't in it
                            Billy got arrested last minute
                            Left me in the shit as usual.

Billy *held by two* **Police**.

Billy   Promise me you'll march, girl – bang your drum for me.

Kitty 2   I can't drum and carry Jack.

Billy   Mum'll mind Jack. Promise me.

Kitty 3   So there's me, Joyce and the other girls
                            on Royal Mint Street where the money's made.

Blackshirts   Watching Mosley in his military hat,
                            his Blackshirts on parade.

Kitty 2 (*to* **Joyce**)   Mosley cuts a dash close up,
                            glad we come, lining up, prepped for fun

Blackshirts   Bang your drum, Kitty
                            Bang your drum
                            Come on, Kitty, bang your drum

Kitty 2   Me Blackshirt girls are rum
                            Full of anti-Jewish jokes
                            but no more than anyone.

Blackshirts (*chanting at* **Leah 2**)   Britain awake. Go home, Jew.

Leah 2 *jumps down from lamppost but remains centre stage.*

Protestors are forced back by **Police** *batons.*

Doll   Mounted police attack us
                            push through and scatter us

Police .   Bang bang bang

Chorus 1   Shoulder to shoulder

Doll   Felled by random baton blows

Leah 2   Rip up the paving stones!

Chorus 1 (*chanting*)   2, 3, 4, 5 – we want Mosley dead or alive!

Leah 3   Irish dockers, bearded Jews, women and their kids
                            Pushed up on the pavement in the police baton charge
                            Against the shaking department store

Kitty 3   I hear glass crash

Leah 3	A screaming crowd falls through
Leah 3 *and* **Kitty 3**	I wonder if one of them is you.

Leah 2 *is hit by a* **Police** *baton, then dragged away under.*

Leah 3	Blood a surprise, little river on me face
	Taste the salty red, my head is lead
	As comrades drag me from the battle
	I think I see two girls
	throwing marbles
	One black, one red

Leah 1 *and* **Kitty 1** *run and mime throwing their marbles at mounted police horses.*

Leah 1	Horses hooves flying
Kitty 1	Poor cloppers fall.

HQ – a café – **Sam** *gives orders.*

Leah 2	At the first aid post, I get patched up, then to HQ
Sam	Cable Street is Mosley's only way
	So we need you lot at the barricades.
	Police'll clamber over the top
	You find ways to make 'em stop.

Sam, **Ged** *and* **Pat** *are together.*

Ged	Irish dockers man the barricades
Sam	We'd never have done it alone.
Pat	Our pick axes pull up cobblestones
Sam	People bring what they're able – chairs, tables –
All	To the barricades
	To the barricades
Ged	Missiles fly across the stack
	of corrugated iron, furniture and paving
Pat	As the police climb up
	The missiles send them flying
Sam	Smashing glass, lobbing bricks
All	They shall not pass
	They shall not pass
Pat	Half-filled lemonade bottles
Ged	Shook and thrown, they explode
All	Mosley go home!

Leah 2   I hope you change your mind last minute
                   Join me on Cable Street.

As **Protestors** *add stuff to the barricade,* **Police** *remove it. But* **Police** *are outnumbered.*

Leah 3   A familiar face framed by an open window
                   above the barricade

Leah 2   Rosa!

Eva   We get pans of boiling water

Anna   Rotten veg

Rosa   Full chamber pot

Eva   And out of the window we throw the lot

Rosa *runs at the window with a big chamber pot.*

Anna   Drown the police in piss

All   They shall not pass!

Rosa   God forgive me.

She throws it right over the **Policeman**'*s head. From the top of the barricade,* **Ged** *calls –*

Ged   Good shot, Rosa!

Rosa'*s careworn face lights up.*

Anna   The police run for shelter.

Eva   Run into the lock-ups.

Rosa (*calls*) Lock 'em in boys!

Ged   We will, Rosa, we will.

Eva *and* **Anna** *look at* **Rosa** *in shocked delight.*

Doll   The coppers who cracked our heads
                   to beat us back

All   beat a path for Blackshirts to march,

Doll   now, shamefaced, surrender their helmets
                   (*with*) hate still in their hearts . . .

Leah 1 *and* **Kitty 1***, twirl the police helmets on sticks. Hang their trophies high on the street.*

Policeman 1   Come on, boys, let's get out of here. I ain't taking on tooled-up dockers.

Policeman 2   Or those Yid bitches. (*Shouts at the women.*) Animals!

Ged   We let them slink away, what else to do?

Doll   They'll go straight now, arrest and beat
                   some poor innocent Jewish boy as punishment
                   for our resistance.

News comes through police megaphones.

Policeman 1   The fascist march has been called off. Please return to your homes.

Leah 3   No one believes it, so they have to keep saying it.

Police 1 *and* **2**   Go home. Go home. Go home.

Kitty 2 *marches off, banging her drum, followed by the* **Blackshirts** *and* **Police***.*

Sam   When they've gone
                   the cry goes up
Leah 2   We've won
Many   We've won
All   We've won

Blackshirts   Half past four. Getting dark.
                   Blackshirts retreat through the City
                   Shattering Jewish shop windows on their way.

Police 1   Police do nothing, secretly applauding.

Sam   There's still time for *us* to march. Get the banners ready!

Leah 2   Any Blackshirts on the streets won't stand a chance.

Sam *and* **Leah 2** *pick up banner, lead march of* **Reds***.*

Blackshirts   Come on Kitty – bang your drum!

Reds   We'll bash the fascists' heads in Bethnal Green until they crack like
eggs.

Other **Protestors** *including* **Eva***,* **Rosa***,* **Anna** *and* **Ged** *stay celebrating on Cable Street.*

Anna   Singing

Anna *and* **Eva**   The streets are ours

Rosa   Cafés overflow with stories
                   Of our glories and absurdities.
Ged   People hugging, laughing, drinking
Ged *and* **Rosa**   Dancing

They cheer as the disciplined march of **Reds** *passes.*

Leah 3   Crowds cheer us all through Stepney
                   But Bethnal Green's a different beast
                   Near Kitty's street, English flags,
                   Fascist slogans, hostile glares
                   Or running scared –

Leah 2   Oh –

Leah 2 *transfixed by* **Kitty 2** – *lets banner pole go. Another comrade picks up it, marches on.*

Sam   Come back, Leah – no breaking rank.

Outside a dress shop, **Kitty 2** *in* **Blackshirt** *uniform with* **Joyce**, *banging drum. Hard. Rhythmic.*

Kitty 3   I'd had enough of Reds marching down our street
Fascists booing,
Police between 'em

Kitty 3 *and* **2**   Too many shouting men.

Kitty 2   Joyce, let's stay here a bit
Have a laugh and a cigarette.

Billy   That Jew girl still chasing you, Kit?

Kitty 2 *sees* **Leah 2**. **Joyce** *laughs*. **Kitty 2** *slowly, provocatively bangs her drum.*

Leah 3   It's as if time stands still
All that I love and hate wrapped up in one.
Your sweet face in a uniform so wrong
Your eyes lock mine and I see red.

Leah 3 *watches* **Leah 2** *charge at* **Kitty 2**, *roaring. They move in slo-mo.*

Blackshirts   C'mon, Kitty – bang your drum

Leah 3   I push you hard against sheet glass.
Me and you
Nowhere else to go.
It splinters as you fall through
As I let you go.
And even as I hate you,
I'm jealous of the shop dummies lying next to you.

Kitty 2 *rises, framed by the shop window, her face pumping blood.*

Kitty 2 (*to* **Leah 2**)   Don't you ever fucking look at me again.

She collapses into the arms of **Joyce** *and another* **Blackshirt**. **Police** *pin* **Leah 2**'s *arms behind her back – punch her and drag her away.*

Back at the celebrations, **Protestors** *dancing*. **Ged** *and* **Rosa** *raise their glasses of beer to one another, romantic and hopeful.*

Eva   We can stop living in fear now.

Ged   If people get organised, what can the bastards do?

Rosa   My little sister's in a police cell. But on Cable Street she's a hero.

All (*raise glasses*)   To Leah!

Anna   I heard she beat up ten Blackshirts.

Rosa   No, just one. That shickster, Kitty Grady.

Eviction 3

Title: Whitechapel, 1 September 1939

Kitty 3's *room. The banging and crashing outside of police removing barricade.* **Tenants** *shouting.* **Leah 3** *stares at* **Kitty 3**'s *facial scar.*

Kitty 3   You don't know your own strength.

She motions **Leah 3** *to help her move table to block the door.* **Leah 3** *rolls her sleeves up revealing a long scar on arm from 'blood sisters' episode.*

Kitty 3   Bet you're still paying off the fine –

Leah 3   Got expelled for it an' all.

Kitty 3   Schnook.

They put down the table.

Leah 3   I'm sorry for the scar, Kitty.

Kitty 3   Why? Don't you fancy me no more?

Leah 3 (*stares at her*)   It just makes the rest of your face look extra beautiful.

Kitty 3 *smiles.* **Kitty 2** *and* **Leah 2** *dance into the space, inseparable.*

Kitty 2   Wind yerself around a girl, that's what you do.

Leah 2   When we're together, the world is our own.

Kitty 3 *holds out her hand to* **Leah 3**.

Kitty 3   Can't we just make a Hitler – Stalin pact?

Leah 3   That pact is why I resigned from the Party. S'why Sam's not talking to me . . .

Kitty 3   You never did? Leah the Red . . .

Leah 3   I'm still Red. But Stalin ain't. Trusts the Führer more than his own Politburo.

Kitty 3   Seems like they're cut from the same cloth to me.

Leah 3   In a world that's coming apart at the seams.

Kitty 3 *opens her sewing box.*

Kitty 3   They can't do it right but they don't 'alf do it fast.

Kitty 1 *grabs a BUF card from sewing box.*

Kitty 3   Bailiff can 'ave *my* membership card an' all.

Kitty 1 *rips it up, throws it like confetti over herself and* **Leah 1**, *playing at newlyweds.*

Kitty 3   It went with the scar for a bit but I've had it with the fascists. *They* ain't 'ere defending me are they?

Leah 3 *decides. Takes food out of her rucksack.*

Leah 3   I got beigels and strawberry jam in 'ere. Must be your lucky day.

Leah 1 *and* **2** ⎤ Let beigels be beigels.
Kitty 1, 2 *and* **3**⎦

Kitty 3   Why didn't yer say . . .?

Leah 3 *breaks up two plain beigels. All* **Leahs** *and* **Kittys** *come for beigel and jam.*

Loud crash through door downstairs.

Kitty 3   They're in.

Kitty 3 *looks at* **Leah 3** *in panic. Checks children still sleeping. Boots running up the stairwell.*

Leah 3   There's a room going opposite mine – I could pay first week's rent.

Kitty 3 *stares at* **Leah 3**

Kitty 3   Still love me do yer?

Leah 2   I loved you, Kitty Grady, from the moment I set eyes on you . . .

Leah 1   From our first game of marbles

Kitty 1   To our fight against the bailiff

Leah 2   But I'm scared you'll suck the life from me, that my love will never be enough for you. And if *I* don't feed you, keep you safe, you'll suck life from the whole world. Oh, Kitty Grady.

Kitty 2   Oh

Leah 1   Oh

Kitty 1   Oh

Loud banging on **Kitty***'s door.* **Police, Tenants, Bailiff** *crammed into a corridor.*

Police   Miss Grady, open this door at once or we'll –

Sam (*to* **Bailiff**)   Can't we just talk about it?

Leah 3 *shouts through the door.*

Leah 3   I'm a nurse at the London Hospital and we've got two little ones with flu in 'ere. So you can't take the bed! Make yourself useful – bring some milk and bread.

Things go quiet behind the door. **Kitty 3** *takes* **Leah 3***'s hand.*

Kitty 3   Thank you.

Bailiff   We're coming in. Stand clear.

Kitty 3   Fuck.

Leah 3 *holds* **Kitty 3** *protectively – they can't stop looking at each other.*

Sam   We're here for you, Kitty . . . And Leah . . .

Tenants (*chant*)   They shall not pass

Leah 3 *and* **Kitty 3** (*about to*) *kiss like long-lost lovers.*

Blackout.

Cable Street

BY LISA GOLDMAN

Notes on rehearsal and staging, drawn from a workshop with the writer,
held at the National Theatre, October 2021

How the writer came to write the play

Originally it was commissioned as a short film in the context of Brexit, about female friendship with two people who had diametrically opposed opinions. But the story became much bigger, and Lisa Goldman was taken down a 1930s path after reading a book by Phil Piratin about communists defending some fascists from being evicted from their homes. Goldman became very interested in how activists would defend fascists on the basis of working-class solidarity, and how they tried to change their views.

Cable Street was a great victory of the working class over the Blackshirts and the rise of British fascism. Lisa Goldman has family history connected to the area: her grandparents were both at the Battle of Cable Street, but she realised many people did not know about this historical event. Many of the stories in the play are Goldman's family stories – mostly from the Jewish side of her family. For example, the dockers coming round and giving solidarity money to Sam is a real story and happened to Goldman's grandad after he was blacklisted for organising workers. Lisa Goldman had this intense feeling that her ancestors were at her shoulder while she wrote it.

Many people where Lisa Goldman grew up in the 1970s had fascist sympathies. Her family had a Jewish Communist Party background, and she grew up around people who would openly call themselves fascists. This period is subtextually there as well as the present day and the 1930s.

The play connects with 'cancel culture' and the divisions of Brexit. The Black Lives Matter movement, and the solidarity and divisions from Covid also resonate.

This play shares a working-class history with the next generation. It is a queer, working-class, coming-of-age love story.

The central premise of the play is: Can you be friends or lovers with someone who has completely opposing views to you?

Approaching the play

Cable Street is a character-led piece. Stylistically, it moves between naturalism to 'Brechtian' elements – borrowing from 1930s traditions (including Joan Littlewood and Ewan MacColl's Theatre of Action and Theatre Union).

It should be emotionally authentic, and you should allow your young people to find their own way into it.

Lead director Audrey Sheffield likes to get a bird's-eye overview of a play before rehearsals, in order to see the throughline and the development of the characters. Structurally, this helps understand how a scene feeds into the whole play.

Writing a chronological timeline for the play, and also a scene breakdown, will be helpful for you in preparing – you could also add location, scene title, scene number and time in your scene breakdown.

Practically, consider how to involve members of your company who are called for rehearsals but who do not have as many lines in a scene. While you are working with one group, could you set some of the exercises (see below) as tasks for other members of the company?

The more all the Kittys and Leahs have a shared understanding of all the events of the play, the better.

Episodes and events

Breaking down the play into sections or manageable chunks (sometimes called a 'unit' or 'beat', but here referred to as an 'episode') is helpful for managing your rehearsals, and also ensures clarity of storytelling. An 'event' occurs when something new comes in, or when most of the characters' thinking shifts – an event also signals the start of a new episode. An event intensifies a character's thinking.

You can draw a line in the script to mark the new episode.

Which character is driving the 'beat'? For Lisa Goldman, the beat shifts when the character either achieves their 'want' or isn't able to achieve it.

In the opening scene, 'The Barricade' could be the title given to the episode – but all of the characters will have their own relationships or affinities to the barricade. For Audrey, the event is when Leah recognises Kitty in the window, rather than the climbing of the drainpipe (but there is no definitive right or wrong in deciding what is and isn't an event). And so, you move to a new episode with this event.

You could label the main events of the play, or within scenes – but do not get bogged down in this.

Structure, style and transitions

The play jumps around in time – the scope of the timespan is across several years, in a non-linear structure.

It is important to maintain the clarity of the emotional journey of the characters either through the play – they are the emotional spine of the story. Observing their throughline will help to keep the story clear. The epic feeds into the intimate and vice versa.

There are twenty scenes and four different time periods. There is, in a sense, a chronological backbone which underpins the structure, even though it is non-linear.

1931, Leah 1 and Kitty 1, three scenes, takes place within an hour

1934, Leah 2 and Kitty 2, takes place over three months – consecutive/chronological

1936, Leah 2 and Kitty 2, for three weeks – consecutive/chronological

1939, Leah 3 and Kitty 3, three scenes, takes place within half an hour/an hour

The 1939 scenes with the older Kitty and Leah function as a framing device – what follows is a memory for them, with them looking back and reassessing what's happened.

There's a musicality to the structure, in the way that the scenes feel like they come in waves. At times, one scene seems to be starting before the other has finished. If you are presenting a scene title on stage, consider what the timing of the appearance of this title should be, if one scene bleeds into another.

There is a momentum to the narrative – it is all leading to the Battle of Cable Street.

There is an ambiguity to the ending – how do you leave it for the audience? Lisa Goldman confirmed that we do need to believe in Kitty and Leah's love for each other at this moment, even if we are not sure what will happen next with their relationship.

Characters and characterisation

Everyone is a character, i.e. the Chorus is not a lump of people – avoid choric declaiming. Each member of the Chorus is a character. Aim to be as rich and specific as you can be for each character.

All of the characters have an emotional arc, and Goldman's advice is for performers to enjoy the emotional rawness, truthfulness and smartness of the characters.

The characters, apart from Oswald Mosley, are working-class characters – the performers don't need to do cockney accents, but they should strive for working-class authenticity.

Is there a physical characterisation which unites all of the Kittys and Leahs? For the younger Kitty and Leah, the physical language of games could be worth exploring.

Consider the groupings of characters – family/friends/colleagues. Improvisations and setting exercises for performers while they are not working on a scene will help bring out the relationships of these groupings.

Casting

Leah 2 and Kitty 2 should be your most confident performers, because those roles are very challenging. Lisa Goldman would suggest over-sixteens. It is a female-led play, and for Goldman the casting of Kittys and Leahs should ideally be female.

The play is written to be expandable/contractable with larger and small cast sizes as required.

There are some smaller roles in terms of lines and two really large roles, which might be an issue with larger companies with many confident performers. You could reassure performers as to the centrality of the chorus.

Production, staging and design

Lisa Goldman advised directors not to skip over moments which you might find difficult to stage.

Stage directions – it doesn't need to be exactly those directions, and they are not intended as instructions. But for Goldman those emotional beats cannot be missed, otherwise you won't be following the story. The important thing is to understand what is happening at that moment, but you don't necessarily need to do it exactly that way. It is open to interpretation as to how those stage directions or that emotional beat is expressed.

There are points in the play where all three Kittys and Leahs are on stage. Could they always be visible on stage throughout, or could they come and go? Is the Chorus on stage throughout, or do they come and go?

Red and black imagery is interesting to explore – in terms of costume (such as the red dress and the Blackshirts), but also certain props (such as the jam and the marbles)

Music – the play itself has a musical quality, and music could play an important role in your production.

You can choose to be contemporary or historical – or a blend of the two – for costume and music. The opportunity is there to explore.

Titles – It could be helpful for the audience for these to be presented on stage in some form.

Lisa Goldman suggested that the opening barricade could be a pre-show sequence, with the action building as the audience enters the space. All furniture and props for other scenes comes from the barricade.

How to stage the climbing-up the drainpipe moment? Lisa Goldman states that she didn't imagine a performer literally climbing a drainpipe. It could be achieved with the Chorus's eyeline rising, to give the sense of climbing, and the Chorus part to reveal the room as the new location. Alternatively, could the Chorus become the drainpipe? Could elements of scenography be used – such as rostra levels?

Exercises for use in rehearsals

Exercise: Prompts for discussion – A to B

In pairs, labelled A and B, themes/topics can be used to prompt discussion. Responding to the prompt, A talks to B for two minutes and then vice versa. Whatever is said is fine, it doesn't need to be profound – it can be from personal experience, abstract or random word association. This is a great way to start a conversation if the company members are new to each other, and also to engage with the themes and ideas of the play.

With each new word-prompt, Bs move to another person, so that each time, the exercise is with a new pairing.

Example prompt words:

- betrayal
- best friends
- finding your voice
- solidarity

Consider what prompts might be most suitable for your group.

This exercise could also be used to unlock a scene you are finding challenging.

Exercise: Where do you stand?

This exercise can be used to introduce the themes at the start of the process, or it can be used to help unlock a scene.

Everyone begins standing in the middle of the room, and the facilitator feeds in a provocation/statement (the stronger or more controversial the better). There is an imaginary spectrum of strongly agree to strongly disagree from one side of the room to the other, and the company positions themselves along this spectrum in response to the statement.

The facilitator draws upon the person nearest to one side of the room to explain why they have taken their position.

And this helps elicit a conversation or debate between people around the topic.

People can change their initial position on the spectrum once the conversation draws itself to a close. Has anyone changed position after having heard the different views of the group?

Example provocations, drawing from the themes/story:

'You can never really be close friends with someone who has completely opposite views to you'
'It is always better just to keep your head down, even if you see something you disagree with and it's not OK'

You want to make it an honest, inclusive space, and to help young people find their voice, and engage with the ideas of the play.

You could begin with provocations which are not related to the play to introduce the exercise to the group. For example: 'Footballers deserve to be paid what they earn.'

You could use this exercise in character later on in the rehearsal process too.

Exercise: Visualising the play (in groups of four or five)

Draw or sketch (stick figures are fine) the five most important images of the play. What are the key moments in the play? There is no right or wrong answer, but it is useful to discuss as a group.

Another approach is visualising the themes through images too.

Examples of some images selected:

1 Playing marbles and the blood sisters

2 First kiss

3 Ending

5 Billy fire-bombing the workshop

6 Barricade

This exercise can help open up thoughts about design. What's the minimum you need to tell the story? But the exercise can also prompt discussions about characters, themes and staging.

You can then order the five images in level of importance and/or lay out the images in the order in which they appear in the play, or in the chronological order of the story.

A further element to the exercise: you could then distil the five images to three, and then choose one, which can help you as a director find the most important aspect of the story to you.

Exercise: Spirit of the play

Each company member finds one thing which for them encapsulates the spirit of the play:

- piece of research
- song
- image
- physical gesture
- photograph
- poem
- stream of consciousness
- painting
- music video

These can be collated and used as a resource in the rehearsal process, or even possibly used in the production. This also helps ensure all young people are engaged in the story and gives them a voice in the process.

Exercise: Finding the facts

This could be either something you do as a director as preparation before rehearsals, or something you do with your company.

What do we mean by a fact? Identifying circumstances or happenings which have taken place in the story without any doubt, or confirmed by independent witnesses.

It helps establish a shared world for the play.

With a company, this can be done physically walking around the room with everyone contributing and sharing as facts come to mind, or seated and writing them down as you read through the script.

Examples of facts: ages, heritage of characters, where they live, where they work.

Examples of other facts from the workshop:

- Rosa doesn't like Kitty;
- Sam reads the *Daily Worker* and he has friends, Ged and Pat, who are Irish;
- Leah becomes a nurse.

The next stage is identifying and clarifying what Audrey Sheffield refers to as 'blurred facts' which are implicit assumptions, and questions, and then filling in the gaps raised by those questions.

Example of questions from the first scene: How long has Kitty been in the apartment? Who does she live with? What is her home like? Is Billy the father to all of Kitty's children?

Audrey Sheffield advised not to overcomplicate this when filling in the gaps, and to keep it clear – you should find the answer which best tells your story. Lisa Goldman also suggested that you answer these questions with the most interesting choice. These blurred facts and questions might shift as you explore a scene, and you might start to change your mind about answers to blurred facts/questions.

Other examples of questions raised in the workshop:

Does Kitty know it was Leah who wrote 'I love you' in the sand?

Does Billy leave Kitty because of her scar? (Lisa Goldman's response: 'Yes, that's exactly what I had in my mind')

Where are the parents of Kitty and Leah? (In Goldman's imagined world of the play: the mother of Kitty is in an asylum, probably a year or two before we meet Kitty. Both of Leah's parents are dead.)

Exercise: Improvising the moments just before the scene starts

For the scenes which start midway in the action, you could ask your company to improvise what has come just before the start of the scene. This helps them find the right intensity and context for the scene.

Exercise: Repetition

The performers read the scene through once aloud.

The performers reread the scene, but this time repeat the last two words of the previous line before saying their line.

Read the scene again after the repetition exercise. What has changed? Has it helped you understand the scene better?

This exercise encourages 'active listening' and 'reaction' in performance, and helps understand the characters' thought-processes, and clarity of storytelling.

Exercise: Thinking aloud

As an exercise, when rehearsing a scene, encourage your company to speak their characters' thoughts aloud – their characters' inner-monologue.

Read the scene once.

Then re-read the scene again, encouraging anyone to voice out loud their characters' inner thoughts (but not too loud, so that it's not too distracting for the other performers' spoken lines).

Return to the scene as written, using what has been learnt from the exercise about the subtext, attitudes and thoughts of the characters.

This could be particularly useful when exploring the Chorus scenes – how they are coming and going, moving in and out of focus. Establishing the relationships amongst the Chorus and their relationship to the other characters.

Exercise: Questions

You could use questions, such as the examples below, to help develop characters. They could be used during hot-seating exercises, as homework, or you could use particular questions to help tackle a particular scene.

How old are you?

What is your full name?

What are you good at?

What do you like to do?

How do you feel about money?

Where do you live?

Who do you live with?

What's your favourite food?

Is there someone you miss?

What have you got in your pockets?

Who's your best friend?

Is there a time you wish you had stood up for someone?

Do you have a secret?

What's your most treasured item and why?

Who did you last speak to? And what did you talk about?

What are you most frightened about?

What makes you happy?

Do you have a hero or a role model?

What's the angriest you've ever been?

Is there something you believe in?

Do you have parents?

Where was the time you laughed the most and who you were with?

If you could change one thing about yourself or the world, what would it be?

Lisa Goldman added that in Mike Leigh's process, the character has to be doing a physical action while answering questions such as these, so that they are in-the-flow and don't get too heady. Having a physical action allows them to respond in an embodied way as they answer the questions silently. Words can be used as emotional prompts instead of questions; e.g. fascism; jam; school.

The response to these questions could also be as a diary entry or a blog.

Challenges

These are some of the challenges which directors commented they expected to encounter when rehearsing the play:

- the intimate moments and making performers feel comfortable; also factoring in the context of other students watching/observing during rehearsals, if all of the company needs to be present for each rehearsal (such as rehearsing during curriculum time);

- working with a small cast – reassigning lines and gender of characters. Could Leah 1 and 3/Kitty 1 and 3 be doubled with other characters to have a cast size under twelve?
- how to build a chorus without taking attention away from the main characters and those smaller intimate moments;
- maintaining the fluidity of scene transitions;
- some students' unfamiliarity with Brechtian style;
- filmic aspect of the script and the transitions.

Intimacy

Yarit Dor, an intimacy director, movement director and fight director offered some guidance on how to approach some of the more intimate moments of the play.

Identify which moments have intimacy: the kissing scene, under-the-covers, tickling, playing with the hair, touching the scar, etc.

Moments of intimacy can be split into: contact-based intimacy and non-contact-based intimacy. These moments can also be contextualised as familial intimacy, intimacy between lovers, or their employment (for example, Leah 3 as a nurse).

Examples of non-contact-based intimacy: eye-contact, 'breathing each other in', verbal intimacy, ways of looking at each other, moments of attraction, tension building towards intimacy or violence.

Sometimes using the word 'intimacy' freaks people out or could even be triggering. Focus on what the characters do in terms of intimacy, and encourage the company to talk about the play and the characters, rather than what the 'performers' are doing.

If you have company members who do not consent to contact-based intimacy, what are the other avenues for the intimate moments, which would not involve lip-to-lip contact? Could you take a more stylised/more abstract approach, instead of naturalism?

Approach intimate moments using Intimacy Directors International's 'Pillars of Intimacy': **CONTEXT CONSENT COMMUNICATION CHOREOGRAPHY CLOSURE**

CONTEXT: What is happening in the scene? What are the given circumstances, who is there?

Stage directions give you the context of intimate actions, but performers might also devise actions inspired by the context.

What are the stage directions giving you and why should you follow them?

What is your impression/the energy of the stage directions? What is the power dynamic? Is it consensual?

What is the story you want to tell? What energy do you want to focus on? What is the timing/tempo of this intimacy? Where would the pauses be? In the pause, the action can tell you whether the character consents.

So, if an actor feels uncomfortable with a kiss, for example, what other action would tell the same story? You can build other offers when you understand the story.

CONSENT: Discuss with the company the consent of the character, as well as their own consent as performers. Even if a performer is aware intimacy is required for a role when they are auditioning, consent is required for specific staging choices of intimate moments. See below for 'boundary check'.

COMMUNICATION: Setting up the working language by avoiding derogatory or slang language. Decide with your group what you want to call particular parts of the body – for instance, collar bone, rather than being too vague, such as torso. 'Mouth' might be preferred to 'lip', and 'chest' might be preferred to 'breast'. For instance, for the moment with the lifting of the skirt, being clear which part of the thigh (if any) is being touched would be important – inner, outer, back of thighs?

This language is also then a working tool for choreography.

Communicate how you are going to rehearse the intimate moments, so the performers understand how it will be treated – e.g. 'next week we are rehearsing this scene including the moment when the characters kiss'.

CHOREOGRAPHY: How does a body part come into contact with another body? What is the duration? And the speed? What's the quality of the movement? (i.e. is it a light hand touch as opposed to gripping?)

CLOSURE: Check-in/debrief after an intimate moment – how did that feel?

After this intimate contact, lead another physical action with performers, such as pendulum coordination swings or a ball game as part of their closure.

Choreography exercise for directors

Devise possible variations of staging an intimate moment: one side of the spectrum, super-naturalism, and at the other end, overly stylised (physical theatre/dance).

What is your plan B/counter-offer if contact is not possible between performers at both ends of the spectrum?

Examples from the workshop for the kisses between Kitty and Leah (p.21):

Stylised version with no contact: Passion and reactions displayed out to the audience? The stage directions spoken? Freeze frames using the Brechtian style of getting closer?

Stylised version with contact: Choreography of hands touching instead of lips? Tango or mating dance? Transposing the anatomical action of kissing to a stylised movement?

Naturalistic without mouth contact: Physical proximity, hands in hair and closeness of face?

Naturalistic with mouth contact: Considering the force of the movement, how the control shifts and the pacing of it.

In response to this exercise, Lisa Goldman reiterated that it is important for her that the first kiss between Kitty and Leah is a sexually charged moment, and that it is shocking for Leah. Goldman expressed doubt as to whether this can be achieved in a stylised way, as it is realism and there is already stylisation with Billy. But that doesn't necessarily mean actual lip contact – just staging in a clever way to be true to the play.

She hoped that advice on this safe staging could be offered rather than just exploring ways to avoid a key moment in the play.

Other practical considerations

Ideally intimate moments should be initially rehearsed only with the people who need to be there for that rehearsal. However, having a third person in the room (rather than solely director and performers), such as an assistant director or a stage manager, is advisable. The last thing to be rehearsed is the lip-to-lip touch; instead start with the peripheries of the body.

Boundary check

As part of the process of consent, you set up a boundary check – where a performer is comfortable to be touched by another performer. It is best for a performer to speak and demonstrate this boundary check at the same time, and for the listener (the other performer) to mimic this with their own body (some people learn aurally, visually or kinaesthetically); i.e. 'not below my lower back' is spoken while the performer physically demonstrates the limit of where they consider the boundary line of their lower back to be.

To avoid unnecessary and repeated physical contact, a 'placeholder' can be substituted in rehearsals, such as a palm-to-palm touch, instead of lip-to-lip contact, after having walked through the scene.

Giving performers a roadmap, by creating a choreographed structure, is helpful – for instance, which way does the head go and return to for a kiss?

Tongue kissing is not required for stage kissing, as it would not be visible to an audience, so this can be noted to performers.

Simulation of naturalistic intimacy

If you would prefer to stage a naturalistic kiss between the characters, but the performers do not wish to make lip-to-lip contact, it is possible to simulate a kiss. However, Yarit Dor advises that this requires a lot of rehearsal to make look realistic and to avoid accidental lip contact.

Yarit Dor demonstrated the simulation of a kiss: temple to temple, noses slightly towards each other. If a character is wearing a hat this can be helpful for obscuring. Hands onto the cheek of the other person can help mask the gap. And then readjusting the positions of the hands after this moment.

For simulating a quick kiss, the performer anchors their hands to their own jawline, moving in quickly (the hands obscure) and leaving a gap between the mouth of the two performers.

Lisa Goldman suggests an exercise used by Mike Leigh, where performers act out what their bodies are doing initially with their hands only, and then with each other's hands. This creates trust and emotional connection, and a shared and secret understanding of what is happening between the two characters alone.

Suggested references

The Cable Street website is a great resource with a large number of interviews and photographs: www.cablestreet.uk

The following books were part of Lisa Goldman's historical research:

Battle for the East End – David Rosenberg

East End My Cradle – Willy Goldman

Everything Happens in Cable Street – Roger Mills

Jew Boy – Simon Blumenfeld

Our Flag Stays Red – Phil Piratin

Remembering Cable Street: Fascism and Anti-Fascism in British Society – Tony Kushner/Nadia Valman

From a workshop led by Audrey Sheffield,
with intimacy session led by Yarit Dor
With notes by Oliver O'Shea

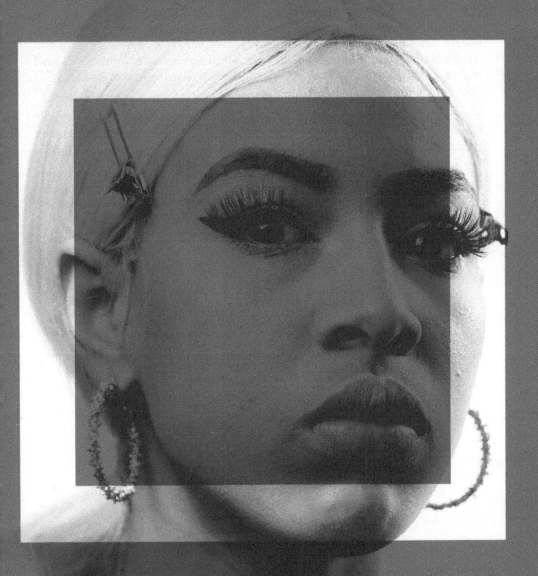

Chat Back
by David Judge

David Judge is a playwright, performance poet and actor.

His most recent play, *SparkPlug*, which David Judge wrote and performed, toured the UK in spring 2019 and was shown on Sky Arts in May 2021. *Sparkplug*, *Skipping Rope* (his first play – commissioned by Box of Tricks) and *PanLid* (commissioned by Talawa and the Royal Exchange) were all shortlisted for the Alfred Fagon Award. He has also written his first episode of *Coronation Street*, which was broadcast in June 2021, and recently contributed to *My White Best Friend – North* (created by Rachel De-Lahay and performed at the Royal Exchange).

As an actor David has worked at the Royal Exchange (Manchester) the Crucible (Sheffield) the Lyric Hammersmith, the Donmar Warehouse, the National Theatre (London) and other theatres across the nation. He also recently appeared as Tybalt in the National Theatre/Sky Arts feature film of *Romeo and Juliet*.

Most importantly, this all started for David when he was a member of the National Youth Theatre and performed in Mark Ravenhill's *Citizenship* at the Salford Lowry and National Theatre as part of NT Connections many many (nearly twenty) moons ago!

Chorus	Is the conscience of your characters and their world includes everyone below – when possible
Narrator	Should guide your audience safely through the world you create. Can be any of the below – when possible

Fibs	*Always tells them – Year 8*
Noe	*One should trust him – Year 10*
DD	*Double detention always awaits – Year 9*
Ska	*Has a few – Year 9*
Kin	*Dred's kindred spirit – Year 10*
Stones	*If he carries on will soon become rocks – Year 11*
Dred	*Kin's kindred spirit – Year 11*
Carr	*If only someone could warn her – Year 8*
Less	*Will soon have more – Year 11*
Seek	*Will find what they are looking for – Year 11*
Bruno	*Britain's bullish best – bulldog*

C/M	Chorus member – cast accordingly
C/M a,b,c	Characters in that scene – can change scene by scene
C/Mx2	Two chorus members – . . . x3 . . . x4 and so on

Adult	C/M

. . .	Search for – loss of – moment of no – words
–	Interruption
*****	Start of new scene

Swearing	Is optional. I have given as many alternatives as possible, but please respect the rhythm when amending. Alternative in smaller case
Staging	The scenes should flow together, without blackouts. The Narrator and Chorus should merge and work together to gobble up scenes and spew them out

It's about to become the summer holidays. For some the last, for others the worst. Once this play bursts open, it should carry with it the spirit, soul and excitement of the whole six weeks. Although it keeps within three days of one weekend, it should capture a coming of age, of sorts, for your characters, their foes and friends.

'Carr's Song'

I am more than happy for this to be sung a cappella. However, there is space for this to grow musically/percussively. Feel free to explore how the company may support/ accompany the moments when the song appears. Also, feel free to play with/change the lyrics for the reprise(s).

Lyrics

Verse 1

I don't wanna stay young forever coz if
I stay young then I'll never get old with you
And
I don't wanna stay young forever coz if
I never get old, I'll never be there for you
And

Chorus

I don't wanna
I don't wanna
No.

Verse 2

I don't wanna stay young forever coz if
I stay young then how will I save the world
So I don't wanna stay young forever coz if
I never get old, I'll never know the right words
So

The sheet music is here to help – ditch it if it doesn't.

*

Narrator
  Friday

Narrator
  We stare out of the window
  There is not a cloud

Narrator
  We glance at the clock
  It's three twenty-nine
  P.m.

Chorus
  aaaaaaaaaaaaaaaaaaaAAAAAAAAAAAAAANNNNNND
  . . .
  DING-A-DING-A-DING-A-DING-A-DING-A-DING-A-DING-A-DING-A-DING

Narrator
  It's the end of the school day

C/M
  Yes!

Narrator
  No
  It's the end of the school week

C/M x3
  Yes!

Narrator
  Actually
  It's the end of the school year

Chorus
  YYYYYYEEEEEEEEEEEEEEEAAAAAAAAAAAHHHHHHHH!

C/M
  Yes!

Narrator
  As the school spews us

Chorus
  OUT

Narrator
  From its doors and fire escapes

Chorus
  OUT

Narrator
Into its yard

Chorus
OUT

Narrator
Towards its gates
There is a buzz of excitement and smell of rebellion in the air

Narrator
A group
Eager to escape the uniformed ugliness of their uniforms
Desperately make their exaggerated way towards the gates

Narrator
Most run towards fun

Narrator
Some are dragged off by mum

C/M
But –

Adult
– No buts. Come on!

Narrator
Likes are liked
Unliked
Then liked again

Narrator
Texts get text

Narrator
Love gets left

Narrator
Mates get met

C/M
On your marks

C/M
Get

C/M
Set

Narrator
Romance races
Fights are fuelled

Narrator
Someone says

C/M
Someone's someone has the hots for you

C/M
Eeeew
Nah

Narrator
Us teachers
Who didn't always do as we were told
Chase those hanging on for something better than home

C/M x2
Out!

C/M x5
Out!

Chorus
OUT!

Narrator
Of the yard

Narrator
As it empties

Narrator
Homework
Gym kits

Narrator
Packets that once packaged crisps

Narrator
And other such things that belonged to kids
Scatter and stick to the fences

*

Chorus
DING-A-DING-A-DING-A-DING-A-DING-A-DING-A-DING-A-DING-A-
DING

Narrator
The last detention of the year welcomes
Less

Less
Soon to have more

Narrator
Carr

Carr
If only someone could warn me

Narrator
Seek

Seek
Will soon find what I'm looking for

Narrator
Ska

Ska
Got a few

Narrator
DD

DD
Double detention always awaits

Narrator
Noe

Noe
One should trust me

Narrator
Kin

Kin
Dred's kindred spirit

Narrator
Fibs

Fibs
I'm always telling them
Or am I?
Ha ha!

Narrator
And me
Are all present

Adult
Quiet at the back!
. . .

Noe
Then we'd have a quarter-caste queen

Kin
We wouldn't have

Ska
You can't say that

Noe
Why not?

DD
More like an eighth

Ska
You just can't

Noe
She will be though

DD
If they ever let her

Kin
They'll never let her now

Fibs
Let her what?

Ska
Be queen

Noe
She'll be the first quarter-caste queen of England

Kin
No
She won't

DD
Eighth-caste queen

Ska
You can't use that word

DD
What word?

Ska
Caste

DD
Why not?

Ska
Because you can't

Noe

So what's the right word to use then?

Ska

I don't know

Noe

Black?

Fibs

How can you be Black if you're not even half?

DD

Not even a quarter

Kin

It doesn't matter because it'll never happen!

Fibs

Alright

Calm down, Kin

DD

Innit

. . .

Noe

What if a quarter and a quarter have a baby

Does that make it half?

Ska

No

It's mixed

Kin

I give up!

Kin *gets up and goes to sit with* **Less**.

Fibs

Laters, Kinders

Adult

Erm, can we stay seated please, Kin? It's detention, not musical chairs. OK?

Ska

What's her problem?

Fibs

Don't know but she's gone full loco lately

DD

Full loco?

Fibs

Serious Holmes
She's gone mad

Noe

Mad?

Fibs

Yeah
Switched
Started smoking bud with some college guy
Skipping classes to go see him
And
I heard she pierced her own nipples
She's loco
To the Pepsi Max

Ska

Chat shit you

Fibs

Ask anyone
She did it with an exit revels badge
Or something like that

Noe

Extinction Rebellion

Fibs

Yeah that

Ska

Chat proper shit you
   . . .

Noe

What if a half and another half get together?

Ska

Two mixes?

Noe

Yeah
That
What does that make the baby?

Ska

I don't know
Full mixed?

Noe

Weird

How can you be fully mixed?

Ska

What's weird about it?

DD

Isn't that

Dual heritage?

Fibs

What?

DD

Dual

Heritage

Fibs

I thought that was when your mum's Irish and your dad's Welsh

DD

Don't be stupid

They're white

Ska

You're white

Fibs

Who are you calling stupid

DD double dickhead

Adult

Quiet! I won't ask again!

. . .

DD

Check Less out though

All fat and that

Ska

Imagine she had it right here

Noe

Nah

Ska

Right now

Fibs

Eeeeeeeeeeeewww!

Ska

Imagine

. . .

Fibs

I heard the dad's someone in Year 9

Noe

Nah

Fibs

Serious!

DD

You're chatting daft

Again

Ska

Always chatting

Fibs

Well, what's she doing here then?

She's finished

Done her exams time ago

Ska

That's her business

Fibs

Just saying

If I was Year 11

There's no way

No

Way

I'm coming back in for the last detention of the year

You mad?!

Noe

Nah

DD

What

So

She's hanging around school

Coming in for detention

Just to see her man?

Fibs

Her boy

DD

You're a boy

Ska

Ha!

Fibs

Shut up
Skabs

Ska

You shut up
Boy

Kin

You all need to shut up
Stop talking shit
And grow up

Noe

Innit

Kin

And you

Less

Leave it, Kin

Noe

Who are you talking to?

Kin

Who do you think?

DD

Check
Kin
Out
Getting brave because she's got a new
Sixth-form man

Fibs

Innit

DD

I'll knock a man out me you know

Kin

Whatever
Go and grow some pubes
Dwindle-Dick

Adult

Right! Enough! . . . Now, for those of you coming back next year, make no
mistake, you will be coming back early from your summer breaks to spend more
precious minutes of your youth sat here with me! And for those of you fortunate
enough not to be gracing us with your presence next year, I will stretch this hour
out for as long as legally allowed if I don't have some.

Chorus
SILENCE!

Narrator
The silence slithers around and settles the room

Narrator
The silence begins to strangle and suffocate the students

Narrator
The silence is
Just
About
To –

Chorus
– DING-A-DING-A-DING-A-DING-A-DING-A-DING-A-DING-A-DING-A-
DING

Narrator
We detainees
Head towards the school gates

Narrator
Towards the weekend
Our great escape

Narrator
We join the many other
Lasts to leave
And gather momentum
As we burst onto

*

Narrator
The Streets

Chorus
WHO ARE YOU?!

C/M a
Telling me about a dinner ticket
Two pound fifteen

C/M b
And you wonder why I'm smoking
Aged thirteen

C/M a
I'm not full
Two fifteen gets me jack sh –

C/M b
– So
Yo!

C/M c
What?

C/M a
Sort me a cig
I'm starving

C/M d
Aaaaaanndd

Chorus
WHO ARE YOU?!

C/M c
Telling me

C/M d
No ball games

C/M c
Just because windows get smashed

C/M d
And gardens get trashed

C/M c
And we get the blame

C/M d
And then there's no play

C/M e
Buuuuuuutt

Chorus
WHO ARE YOU?!

C/M e
To go and tell my mum

C/M f
Have you seen what her and her mates have done?

C/M e
I'd have him over my knee and smack his bum

C/M g
Is it?

Chorus
WHO ARE YOU?!

C/M a

Telling us we fill you with rage

C/M b

War-ing

C/M c

Global warming

C/M d

People trafficking

Chorus

COMMITTED BY PEOPLE OF YOUR AGE

C/M e

On a regular

C/M f

You see

Chorus

IT'S YOUR GENERATION THAT'S *FUCKING UP/LETTING DOWN* THE NATION

C/M g

And that can't be influenced by playing PlayStation

C/M h

Soooooo

Chorus

WHO *THE FUCK* ARE YOU?!

C/M a

Telling me to get out of the room

C/M b

Go and wait in the corridor

C/M c

I'll deal with you soon

C/M d

And

Chorus

WHO *THE FUCK* ARE YOU?!

C/M e

Saying

C/M f

You've no idea what to do

C/M g
It must be the way that your parents raised you

C/M h
Well that might be true

C/M a
But check yourself first

C/M b
Because their

C/M c
Generation

C/M d
Their

C/M e
Responsibility

C/M f
Their

C/M g
Community

C/M h
This world that born me

Chorus
IT INCLUDES YOU TOO!

Narrator
As the six-week souls of summer scatter
Their footsteps pitter patter
Like the sound of frying batter

*

Narrator
The chip shop

Narrator
Us with nothing in our cupboards queue for food

Narrator
At the front is Less
She has been foraging for her soon-to-be nest

Narrator
She holds a plastic bag filled with single nappies and other such donations

Narrator
She tries to speak but her voice is hushed with embarrassed hesitation

Adult
Fifty-three pence worth?!

Less
Yeah
Sorry

Adult
I've got to make a living here, Love!

Less
I know but that's
Please

Adult
I can't keep . . . OK! But it's not right this. A girl of your age shouldn't be –

Less
– Alright
Forget about it!

Adult
'Forget about it' she says now. Shocking!

Less *drops her bag of woe. As it hits the floor, her reality shifts.*

Chorus
SMACK!

Less *squares up to the adult.*

Less
Would you be shocked if I said I had to

Chorus
SMACK!

Less
My mother

Chorus
SMACK!

Less
Her
In the face
And then duck for cover?
Would you be shocked if I said I had to

Chorus
SMACK!

Less
Her again
And

Chorus
SMACK!

Less
Her again
Until
Finally
I feel
She's restrained enough
Or not?
Would you be shocked when I

Chorus
SMACK!

Less
Her
One more time
On the spot

Chorus
SMACK!

Less
Her one more time
Without doubt

Chorus
SMACK!

Less
Just
One
More

Chorus
SMACK!

Less
In the face
Giving me space

Chorus
SMACK!

Less
And time
To dial 999
And shout

Chorus
HELP!

Less

My mum's trying to commit suicide!

Would you be so 'shocked' if you knew about the shit that I've swam in just to get myself to

Chorus

HERE

*As **Less** picks up her bag, reality resumes.*

She exits.

Narrator

We burst in and bounce off everything

Narrator

Covering this food poverty scene like our Rash

Narrator

Playing a dangerous game of

C/M

Wet willy!

C/M

Damp dick!

C/M

Clammy c –

Adult

– Right you lot, out. Now!

Narrator

We snap and crackle back onto the street

Putting the fry in this day's

*

Narrator

Friday night

Narrator

Tags

Pings

Requests

Likes

Narrator

Knocking on

Getting out

Party invites

C/M a
> I'm just too eager for the easy
> Any open ear will please me

C/M b
> And a shut door will not freeze me
> Coz the window keeps me cool and breezy

C/M c
> Sometimes I can feel quite queasy
> Like society's trying to tweeze me

C/M d
> But I won't splat pop that simply
> Coz my skin just ain't that dimply

C/M e
> And even when I'm old and wrinkly
> I will never be moved so quickly

C/M f
> I'll get where I want to go swiftly
> Hear jokes get cracked side split me

C/M g
> Yeah let's get proper fucking giggly / Yeah come on let's get proper giggly
> On the floor like worms all wriggly

Chorus
> LET'S NOT LET THIS GRAVE WORLD DIG WE

C/M a
> Alright

C/M b
> Party pooper

C/M c
> Innit

C/M d
> Proper

C/M e
> Watch out!

Chorus
> BEEEEEEEEEEEEEEEEEEEEEEEEEEEEEEEEEEEEEEEEEEEEEEEEP!

Adult
> Watch where you're going!

C/M a
> No!

You watch where you're going!

Narrator
As the young'uns scatter and scuttle off
The moonlight creeps after them
It reveals

*

Narrator
The bench

Narrator
Where we spot the
New kid
Finishing his chips

Narrator
But there could be a problem
Because this bench
Isn't his

Dred
Today
I fly
The nest
I've ignored what's advised for the rest because

C/M
BEING THE BEST

Dred
Is not the best for me
Me
Who is that?
Am I the son of a bitch? / This?
Or the sperm of a twat? / Son of that?
I'll find out soon enough
Because I've left the rough to set sail for the smooth
Prove nothing no more
Plus
I've got no baggage to care for

Chorus
BAGS

Dred
That support the voice of my mum as she silently screams through her eyes

Chorus
BAGS

Dred
> To care for my sister and to answer her whys

Chorus
> QUESTIONS

Dred
> I've got a bag full
> A flag coloured red to trigger the bull's rage
> Dad's age makes him a bully
> But now I'm

Chorus
> GROWN FULLY

Dred
> So
> I

Chorus
> DON'T SAY A WORD

Dred
> But he
> Him
> He knows
> Slyly and slowly
> Calmly and quietly
> He knows his blows are wrong and

Chorus
> SO IS HE!

Dred
> Me
> I'm disassociated
> A debated sacrifice that drove me to opt out
> Get knocked out
> Hang myself out to
> . . .

Stones *and* **Kin** *appear in the shadows.* **Stones** *smokes a spliff.*

Dred
> But I never did it
> Words delivered none of it
> The amount of times I've relieved the pain with a smoke

Stones *steps from the shadows and offers* **Dred** *the spliff.*

Stones
> Choke?

Dred
> And forget the bloke

Stones
> Choke

Dred
> And forget the pain

Stones
> Choke!

Dred
> And forget the days of not eating to feed his big fat gambling belly!

Dred *takes the spliff.*

Chorus
> NOW

Dred
> Now where do I go?

Kin *steps out from the shadows.*

Dred
> Sack / Fuck this yellow brick road
> I want roads of gold
> Stories untold but to my waiting ear

Dred
> Here
> This is the place for me
> Away from there
> Don't know what I'll do
> But
> I don't really care

Stones
> Take a deep drag

Dred
> I don't want to cough

Stones
> No worries
> Get that shit / stuff on your chest

Kin
> Off

Dred *takes a deep drag. He coughs.* **Stones** *laughs.* **Kin** *watches.*

Stones
What's your name, bro?

Dred
Dred

Stones
Is it?

Dred
It is yeah

Stones
Sick
I'm Stones
Nice to meet you, bruva Dred

Kin
Kin

Dred
Dred

Kin
Yeah
You said

Dred
Right
Yeah
. . .

Stones
You got a piece of cigarette, Dred?

Chorus
BEEEEEEEEEEEEEEEEEEEEEEEEEEEEEEEEEEEEEEEEEEEEEEEP!

Adult a
Road rage! Road rage!

Adult b
ROOOOOOOOAD! RAAAAAAAAAAAAGE!

Stones
It's kicking off
Come

Stones, **Kin** *and* **Dred** *exit.*

Chorus
BEEP – BEEP – BEEP – BEEP – BEEP – BEEP – BEEP – BEEP

Narrator
A tram departs

*

Narrator
　The tram-stop
　Noe and Ska snog next to the bicycle storage unit

Narrator
　Fibs and DD sit
　Chit chatting their usual shit

Fibs
　I said
　I know that I took it too far a bit
　But you can take your bag and you can shove it

DD
　Who did you say that to?

Fibs
　To that toe-whiff Mr Patel

DD
　Ha!
　I bet his wife was in tears

Fibs
　Nah
　She was calm
　Just took the bag and papers back

DD
　Are you fired?

Fibs
　Banned for life

DD
　Yeah?

Fibs
　Yeah

DD
　Shit

Fibs
　Yes

DD *and* **Fibs** *watch* **Noe** *and* **Ska** *as they snog.*

DD
　Do you
　. . .?

Fibs
What?

DD
You know
Do you
Want to –

Fibs
– Noe
You coming?

Noe
We'll catch you up

Fibs
Alright
Soon
. . .

Fibs
Come then

Fibs *exits,* **DD** *follows.*

Adult
Passengers are reminded that there is no smoking on any of the platforms.

Narrator
Noe vapes
Then forces Ska into one of the bicycle storage units
Ska tries
But fails to escape

Ska
Noe
Get off me!

Noe
This
Is
How
Much
I
Love
You

Ska
Stop!
What are you doing?!

Noe
Locking you
In a box

Ska
Noe don't!

Noe
Just

Ska
Noe!

Noe
What?

Ska
You better stop now!

Noe
Why?

Ska
Because

Noe
There
Locked

Ska *storms a tantrum.*

Ska
You better let me out now!

Noe
Or what?

Ska
Or else!

Noe
Or else what?

Ska
Or else I'll –

Noe
– Or else you'll what?

Ska
Noe!

Noe
Or else
What?

Ska

Or else I'll penetrate your arse with that fucking vape stick!

Noe

That's disgusting

Ska

Your dick's disgusting!

Noe

Your mum liked it

Ska

You better let me out now, Noe
Noe
Noe!

Noe

OK!
Calm down
Skazalicious

Noe *releases* **Ska**.

Ska

Well?

Noe

Well
What?

Ska

What was that for?

Noe

For you
You asked me to be more
Romantic

Ska

How's that romantic?

Noe

Well
I was thinking
When you die
I'll keep your ashes
Some
In a little box
Silver
Put it on a chain

Put the chain around my neck
And
You know
Put you
Close
To my heart
Keep you there
Forever

Ska
Right

Noe
Right

Ska *takes the vape and puffs a cloud.*

Ska
Love you

Noe
Hate you

Noe *takes back his vape. He wipes it then puts it away.*

Ska
Give me a kiss then

Narrator
They kiss
Long and fast

C/M
Eeew
Nasty that

Chorus
BEEP – BEEP – BEEP – BEEP – BEEP – BEEP – BEEP – BEEP

Narrator
The last tram arrives

Chorus
BEEP – BEEP – BEEP – BEEP – BEEP – BEEP – BEEP – BEEP

Narrator
Then departs
As the night almost ends
Others kiss

Narrator
Others fight over kisses

Narrator
  Others
  With lack of kisses
  Weep

Narrator
  Some hide

Narrator
  Some seek

Narrator
  Some meet a face to call theirs

Narrator
  Most sleep
  Apart from Seek
  Who doesn't know their phone's torch is shining its light

Narrator
  As they stand by their window
  Searching for someone who might be right

Seek's *phone's torch should read 'SOS' in Morse code.*

Narrator
  The torch speaks in Morse
  As their hands move and finger the screen
  We answer the call and enter

                              *

Narrator
  Seek's room
  Where pings ping frequently

Chorus
  Ping Ping Ping Ping

Seek
  Hello
  Can you

Chorus
  HELP

C/M
  Ping

Seek
  Me
  Please?

I'm lost
And
I can't find myself
I need some

Chorus
    HELP

C/M
    Ping

Seek
    With figuring me out
    I'm clueless
    Whisper and sniff
    Or
    Scream and shout my whole entire heart out!
    Hello
    Please
    Can you

Chorus
    HELP

C/M
    Ping

Seek
    I'm freezing life. Squeezing strife. I wring out my soul. Whilst shouting.
    Screaming. Constantly fighting for control. I try so hard to fulfil certain roles that
    I hope will make you just know me. Do you want to? Can you be bothered?
    Really? I need

Chorus
    HELP

C/M
    Ping

Seek
    To be your

C/M
    Friend

C/M
    Family

C/M
    Peer

C/M
Cover

C/M
Lover

Seek
Your only one
Will you help me be all of these things and just
Speak to me?

Chorus
Ping Ping Ping Ping

*

Narrator
Saturday morning
Most wake up
A few waste away

Narrator
Breakfast is made
Scrambled for
Fought over and finished

Narrator
Pets are played with
Pampered
Walked
Fed and smacked

Bruno
Ow!

Narrator
Sports
Man
Hand

Narrator
Food
Shop
And other such bags get packed

C/M
Ring
Ring

Narrator
Carr rides across the space on her bicycle in full hi-vis

With helmet
Lights
And all that other safety biz

Narrator

She is lost in her own world as she sings and rides
But she speaks for us all
When she talks of I

Carr

I
(*Singing*)
Don't wanna
I don't wanna
No
I

Carr *exits.*

C/M

Ring
Ring

*

Narrator

The bus stop
Less sits with a bag of cleaning products

C/M

PING

Narrator

She reads a text
Then tells us what's up

Adult

Running late. Please don't hate me. Mum. Xx.

Less

I don't hate you

Chorus

MUM

Less

I couldn't
You're my

Chorus

MUM

Less
But I don't need you

Chorus
MUM

Less
Which is sad
Because
You're the only

Chorus
MUM

Less
I've got

As **Less** *exits,* **Bruno** *bounces on.*

*

Bruno
Bark! Bark! Bark!
Bark! Bark!
The gated play area!
Bark! Bark! Bark!
My territory!
Bark! Bark! Bark!
Mine!
Bark! Bark!
OK?!
Bark
OK

Bruno *settles.* **Fibs** *and* **Noe** *swing.* **DD** *waits.* **Ska** *sits on the slide.*

Ska
And then I see this dog in a hole
In the floor
They opened up this grid thing and –

Adult
– You lot shouldn't be in there, it's meant for kids.

Bruno
What?!
What?!
What?!

Fibs
We are kids

Adult
> And that dog should be on a lead.

Bruno
> Who are you calling a dog?!

DD
> It's a gated area
> Dog can't get you

Bruno
> My name's Bruno!

Fibs
> Yeah
> Jog on knobhead

DD
> Yeah
> 0121

Chorus
> DO ONE!

DD
> I saw another dog
> Bob!
> Someone shouted at it

Ska
> Him

Fibs
> I saw a dead dog in a wheelie bin

Ska
> I saw my dog close-up as it licked my face off

DD
> I saw a dog shiver from the wet and the cold

Ska
> I laugh at dogs that shake the wet off indoors

DD
> I laugh at dogs generally

Ska
> I've never seen a dog not filled with love

DD
> I've seen a dog's tongue and cheeks flapping in the wind out of the window of a car

Ska
I saw a dog dragged down the road by its lead attached to a car

DD
Was a motorcycle

Ska
It was a moped
Actually

DD
I saw a dog butchered perfectly

Noe
I remember my dog Paddy

DD
I saw on the telly

Ska
A van full of dogs

DD
All someone's Bob

Ska
All someone's Bruno

Bruno
What?

DD
I saw a cattle van stuffed full with dogs

Fibs
On the telly?

DD
They were alive

Ska
My eyes wanted to hide but I remembered

DD
Bob

Noe
Paddy

Fibs
Lady

Ska
Bruno

Bruno
Yeah
What?

DD
The puppies that were taken only a few days old

Ska
I saw

Fibs
On Channel 4?

DD
A van stuffed

Ska
Packed

DD
Crammed with contorted dogs

Ska
Full of love

DD
And cracked bones

Ska
Ribs

Fibs
Ribs?

Ska
I saw a woman in the east turn Bruno into ribs

Bruno
Who did what now?

Noe
Turn Paddy into legs

Fibs
Turning Lady into shanks

Bruno
Nah
Hold it down, mate

DD
I've seen a dog give thanks after a smack

Fibs

I've seen a dog maul a human

Ska

Not to death!

DD

I saw a van on the telly full of it

Noe

Death?

DD

Yes
With thankful faces

Ska

And bottomless hearts

DD

Full of tales with no room to wag

Ska

I've seen a dog chase its wagger round

DD

And round

Ska

And round in circles

Bruno

– I can do that
look
Ha! Ha!

DD

I saw a dog on the telly

Ska

Stolen and prepped

Noe

Farming life for food has always been a thing

Ska

Yeah but you can't go eating people's pets!

Noe

Not in England

Fibs

What you watching documentaries for?

DD

I wasn't
I saw a clip on *Gogglebox*

Ska

Was proper sad you know

Fibs

What are you watching *Gogglebox* for?
For Nanas that

Noe

Innit
Run this
Let's go shop

Fibs

Yeah
Miss this

Bruno

What?!
Where you going?!
Why are they leaving us?!
Bark!

Ska

Wait up
I've got to take Bruno back

Bruno

Bark! Bark!

Noe

Hurry up then
Skaztastic

Bruno

Bark!

Noe, Fibs, DD *exit.*

Ska *puts the lead on* **Bruno** *then follows the others.*

Bruno *stops, sniffs, then pees on a post.*

The trickling sound of the pee becomes the sound of running water from . . .

*

Narrator
> The brook
> Discarded syringes
> Used condoms
> Burnt-out cans of beer

Narrator
> And other left-behinds
> From the ghosts of those now gone
> Quietly haunt here

C/M a
> Us ghosts are just about to light a fire

C/M b
> And crack a beer

C/M c
> But we have to leg it when

Narrator
> Kin
> Dred
> And Stones
> Appear

C/M a
> 0
> 1

C/M b
> 2
> 1

C/M c
> Do one!

C/Ms *disappear.*

Narrator
> Inspired by Dred's webbing of words
> Kin shares a poem
> About her new
> Single-parent world

Kin
> Things are disrupted
> I'm disturbed
> The pressures of precious possessions permanently placed in my palm then
> Snatched before I have the chance to grasp

Unlike some
I couldn't palm my precious
It's bigger than that
So big it's a myth
Like that fat bloke I sent my Christmas wish list
Fake
Filled up a lake with the tears that I cried
Inside's dead
My bones are dry
A ring caused the chaos in the eyes of Smeagol
To others
Precious
Is the prick of a needle

Kin

My precious is my parents
And I was theirs
But
Like a smackhead syringe-less
Like a Santa-less kid
Like Gollum ring-less
I split in two when my parents did
. . .
Well?

Stones

Well what?

Kin

What did you think?

Stones

Of what?

Kin

That
What I just said
My poem

Stones

Yeah
Was alright that

Kin

Right
. . .

Stones

What?

Kin
Nothing
. . .

Dred
I liked it

Kin
Yeah?

Stones
Yeah
Me too
Course

Kin
Yeah
Right

Stones
I did!
. . .

Stones
What was that
Golly bit about?

Kin
What bit?

Stones
The last bit
Something about a golly ring

Kin
It's Gollum

Dred
That bit was sick

Stones
Yeah
That
What's it about?
Sounds a bit
Politically incorrect to me

Kin
You're a bit
Politically incorrect

Dred

It's Smeagol

Stones

It's what?

Dred

Gollum's
Smeagol

Kin

Have you not even seen Lord of the Rings?

Stones

Nah
I don't do Harry Potter and that
Ha! Ha!
. . .

Stones

What?

Kin

My parents have just
They're not
You know!
And I've finally found a way to
To let you know how much that hurts me
How broken my heart is
And I just
I thought you were a nice guy
You know
Good
Guess I was wrong about that as well

Stones

You're not
I am
. . .

Dred

Instead of hopping scotch
I was dodging drunken blows
. . .

Kin

What?

Dred
Nothing
I was just
Doesn't matter
. . .

*

Narrator
A ping pings

C/M
Ping

Narrator
Followed by another

C/M
Ping

Narrator
And a few more

C/M
Ping

C/M
Ping

C/M
Ping

Narrator
Then all of them

Chorus
PING

Narrator
They pings gather momentum
Creating a rhythm
A beat
That beats along with many other beats
In the many bars

Narrator
Behind the many doors on
Canal Street
The Gay Village

C/M
Yeah, girl!
Let's have it!

Narrator
> Or is it?

*

C/M
> Ping

Chorus
> THERE'S ONE THERE

Narrator
> Seek's bedroom

Narrator
> Seek sits on their bed
> Sighs
> Then lies back
> As they swipe through Tinder

Narrator
> And darker dating apps

C/M a
> Ping

C/M b
> There's one there

Seek
> I want it
> But I don't need it
> I want to need it

C/M c
> Ping

C/M b
> There's one there

Seek
> That one's a good'n
> But I shouldn't have blinked
> Because they're gone in a sudden

C/M d
> Ping

C/M b
> There's one there

Seek

> So just keep it cool
> But sparks overrule
> No one loves a fool

C/M e

> Ping

C/M f

> Here's one here

Seek

> This one's amazing
> But their intimidating beauty
> Leaves me dazing

C/M e

> Ping

C/M f

> This one's still here

C/M g

> So keep them near

Seek

> But the words aren't coming
> I'm losing
> I fear
> I just want to step off
> I don't want to fall

C/M e

> Ping!

C/M f

> This one's now gone

C/M e

> Pong

Seek

> That's my own fault
> For waiting on the wall

C/M h

> Ping

C/M i

> There's one there

Seek

> I want it
> But I don't need it
> I want to need it

*

C/M
> Ring
> Ring

Carr *sings as she rides across the space.*

Carr
> I
> Don't wanna stay young forever
> No
> I
> Don't wanna
> I don't wanna

Carr *exits.*

In the distance a bike and its rider are destroyed by a car.

*

Narrator
> The days end
> Fades
> Into

Narrator
> Saturday night's start
> Pings pong back and forth

C/M a
> Ping

C/M b
> Ping
> . . .

C/M c
> Pong

C/M d
> Ping

DD
> How long does a heart stay broken for?
> Because I've been nursing mine for months
> It used to sing

Chorus
> BABOOM! BABOOM!

DD
But now it just sighs

Chorus
HUMPH!

C/M a
Ping

Ska
That's life
Could die tomorrow
We all have bad days
And nights

C/M b
Ping

Fibs
I'm pretty
For a moment

C/M c
Ping

Noe
But ugly
for a lifetime

C/M d
Pong!

*

Narrator
Mirrors
Lights
Instas
Snaps

Narrator
No time for chats
Need to snap back

Chorus
IN THE MIRROR

C/M a
What's going on?

Chorus
LOOKS IN THE MIRROR

C/M b
Who's coming out?

Chorus
ANOTHER MIRROR

C/M c
What's being worn?

Chorus
STARES IN THE MIRROR

C/M d
Who's got what?

Chorus
DOUBTS IN THE MIRROR

C/M e
Who's going there?

C/M f
Going where?

C/M g
With who?

C/M h
Yo

C/M I
Let's go

Chorus
GET YOUR FACE OUT THE MIRROR!

*

Bruno *enters with his lead attached. He stops, sniffs, then pees on a post.*

The trickling sound of the pee becomes the sound of running water from

Narrator
The brook
Kin and Dred explore their newfound bond

Narrator
Stones smokes until the smoke has gone

Kin
Some man manipulate
Just for cumming's sake

Stones
> Some girls sexulate
> Just for loving's sake

Dred
> But love doesn't just come

Kin
> It's a joint investment

Dred
> Created from

Kin
> Lust?

Stones
> Sex

Dred
> Hormones
> I guess

Kin
> Can you be lucky in it?

Dred
> We create our own luck

Kin
> Love

Dred
> It can build

Stones
> Or break homes

Dred
> Not with sticks

Kin
> And Stones

Dred
> With thoughts

Kin
> And
> Actions

Stones
> It can forgive

Kin
> And accuse

Dred
> Or confuse an abused youth
> . . .

Dred
> Love education

Kin
> Yes!

Dred
> Fuck / Run
> Sex education

Kin
> Yes, Dred!

Stones
> Fuck / Run algebra
> Mathematical masturbation!
> . . .

Kin
> Give it to me straight

Dred
> On a plate?

Kin
> Laid
> Out

Stones
> Warn me about isolation

Kin
> You see

Dred
> It's scary

As **Kin** *and* **Dred** *get closer,* **Stones** *gets further away.*

Stones
> The lack of fish like me

Chorus
> IN OUR POISONED OCEAN

Narrator
> Us ghosts watch on
> As Stones leaves them to it

Narrator
Finishes his smoke
Then coughs

Narrator
Us ghosts watch on
Knowing this form of retreat
Could soon turn Stones
Into rocks

Stones
Sticks and stones may break my bones
But words can break my heart
And taking that to A&E
Won't get me very far

*

Chorus
BRUUUUNNNOOOOOOOO!

Narrator
The street

Narrator
The bus stop

Narrator
The bus stop
On the street

Ska *enters.*

Ska
Bruno?!

Ska *is about to stick a 'Missing' poster in the bus stop, when a group stampedes past.*

C/M a
He shall entice you with his love sword

C/M b
And dance and flirt and play

C/M a
Enhancing ego with his love sword

C/M b
Eyes sharp like birds of prey

C/M c
I challenge you break my love sword! Anyone! Night or day!

C/M d
Whilst he's thinking with his love sword

C/M e
Black and white turns to grey

C/M d
He won her with his love sword

C/M e
On his lap her head she lay

C/M c
Swiping! Swinging! Stabbing my love sword!

C/M d
He searches for words to say

C/M a
His horny eager ego

C/M b
Naked sweaty hard

C/M d
Made him stab her with his sex sword

C/M e
As soon as she left her guard

C/M a
He cursed her

C/M b
Or him

C/M d
Could be them

C/M e
With his sex sword

C/M a
STDs their spirit drained

C/M b
He should put away his sex sword

Chorus
AND TRY USING HIS BRAIN!

The group exits.

As **Ska** *sticks up her 'missing' poster, an* **Adult** *with beer in hand enters.*

Adult

I'd be careful if I were you. The law could have you away for vandalising.

Ska

My dog's gone missing

Adult

That's no excuse to go defacing council property.

Ska

I'm not

Adult

What do you call that then?

Ska

I need to find him
He's not from around here
He'll be lost
Scared

Adult

What breed is it?

Ska

It's a bulldog
British

Adult

Poor things. Bred so bad they can't breathe. You should get a rescue dog, there's enough of them ready to live the life bulldogs struggle to sup.

Ska

Bruno loves his life

Adult

Mind you, most of them are from abroad now. You know, it's me that should be scared. Wild, foreign animals roaming the streets.

Ska

He's not foreign
My dad got him from Warrington

Adult

Dogs. You love them, take care of them, wash, feed and house them and what do they do? Bite your arm off when you're not looking.

Ska

Not all of them

Adult

Most of them.

Ska
> People are just as dangerous
> If not worse

The **Adult** *notices* **Ska** *'s scars.*

Adult
> What happened to your face, love?

Ska
> A dog bit me
> And I'm not your love

Adult
> And you still trust it?

Ska
> Wasn't Bruno

Adult
> A dog's a dog It'll bite eventually. You want to send it back. Back to where it came from.

Ska
> He's my best mate
> And he's got more
> Humanity
> Than you

Ska *hurries off.*

Chorus
> BRUUUUNNNOOOOOOOO!

*

Narrator
> Seek's room
> Full of make-up and heels
> Seek empties their heart
> As they blossom and peel

Seek
> Waiting
> In agony
> Every bit of me is in agony
> A tragedy
> If I don't open my eyes and see what's in front of me
> More agony awaits
> Disguised as opportunity
> Camouflaged as destiny

Well
Not for me
I'm here right now
In pain
But I will not lay blame
On the pressure of what you want me to be
Eventually the pressure peers
But
Gradually
I'm glad to be
Alive in pain
And not dead in misery

Narrator
As Seek steps out
A ping pings

C/M
Ping

Narrator
Followed by another

C/M
Ping

Narrator
All of the pings ping
Gathering momentum
Creating a rhythm
A beat

Narrator
A beat that beats along with many other beats
In the many bars
Behind the many doors on
Canal Street

Narrator
The Gay Village

Chorus
YES SEEK!

Seek
I did it!

Chorus
PONG!

*

Narrator
    Sunday morning
    Breakfast
    Footy
    Drop-offs
    Pick-ups

Narrator
    Last night's party brings this morning's sick up

Narrator
    Status updates
    Chats and snaps
    Some lounge in gardens
    Some squeezed in flats

Narrator
    Phones ping in toilets that whiff a very strong pong
    Someone somewhere sings someone else's song

C/M
    I
    (*Singing*)   Don't wanna
    I don't wanna

*

Narrator
    A spot in
    The park

Narrator
    Stones' smoking keeps on going
    As he tries his hand at writing a poem

Stones
    Ha!
    (*Writing*)   'I couldn't be here
    On the ground
    If it was raining
    It's Britain
    I may drown'
    Ha!
    'But I won't
    Because I'm a Brit

    And my training
    It's been good
    Knowing when it's right to put up my hood'
    Ha ha!

'I hope
Doped up off this phat spliff
Buzzing off the fact
Having a laugh
I mean
Proper laughing
About how it could rain any sec
And instead of sunbathing
I'll be baffin'
Ha!
'Because this is Britain
And you see these
Sunny delights
I've been trained to save them'
Ha!
'And knowing that
I brought a pen
To share this
Moment
When –'

Fibs and **Ska** *jump over a fence and approach* **Stones.**

Stones (*writing*)
'These two
Year 7s or something
Enter my sight
Asking for'

Fibs
Eyar yo!
You got a cigarette?

Stones (*writing*)
'But what I was smoking
They weren't ready for yet'

Ska
Cheeky
Man's ignoring you you know

Stones (*writing*)
'My smokes and jokes'

Fibs
Ey!
Boy!

Stones (*writing*)
   'They just weren't ready yet'

Ska
   Don't ignore us
   Boy!

Stones (*writing*)
   'I could tell by their tone'

Fibs
   I said –

Stones
   – Nah
   No cigs

Fibs
   Give us a drag of that then

Stones
   This?

Fibs
   Yeah
   You deaf?

Ska
   Nah
   He heard what you said

Stones
   HA!
   You ain't ready yet

Fibs
   Who are you talking to?
   Better not be talking to me

Stones (*writing*)
   'Then I knew it was time
   To get myself gone'

Ska
   Innit
   About
   Ready yet

Fibs
   Ready for what?

Stones (*writing*)
  'And that's why I'm ending this
  Po
  Om'

Narrator
  As Stones laughs himself off

Stones
  Ha! Ha!

Fibs *and* **Ska**
  We watch him leave

*

An **Adult** *enters holding a lead that is attached to a dog offstage. The* **Adult** *notices one of* **Ska***'s 'Missing dog' posters. They take out their phone and make a call.*

Adult   . . . Hello? . . . Is that Chantelle? . . . Yeah, I erm . . . I think I've found your dog . . . (*on phone*) OK . . . Right . . . Right, OK. I'll see you there soon . . . OK . . . Yeah, bye.

The **Adult** *hangs up, then gently tugs on the lead.*

Adult
  Come on. Come on then. There we go.

Sad and scared, **Bruno** *limps onto the stage. He's covered in spray paint (Union Jack colours), soaked in beer and singed with cigarette burns.*

Bruno
  Home?

Adult
  Come on. let's get you home.

Bruno
  Yes
  Please
  Home

Bruno *exits with the* **Adult***.*

*

Narrator
  The bus stop
  Less sits with a card that reads congratulations

Narrator
  But she struggles to accept her mum's forced adulations

Adult

Dear Less. Congratulations on your exciting news. I'm so glad you got what you wanted. I know things have been difficult, but I am so proud of you. I can't wait to see you again. Lots of love and kisses. Mum.

Narrator

Less finds it hard but she's no defeatist
As she slowly rips the card
Into a million pieces

Less

Nice one
That's a lovely thing to say
It's a shame you've never walked that talk
Or stalked me with it
When I was low
So yeah
Nice one

But
What right have you got to be proud of me?
You didn't share our struggle or offer a hand
So
Mum
I hope you understand that you have no right
Stop fighting the truth I use
To help you fulfil your role
How can you be happy over there?
When I'm down here
Warming holes
How can you be glad that I
Got what I wanted?
When who
Or what I am
You
Haven't a clue
So
If letting you be proud of me
Makes it easier
Then go crazy
But don't dare take me there with you

Narrator

Less stands
Then holds a hand to her stomach as she walks off

*

Narrator
  A group burst in
  They chat about summat

Narrator
  And this is some chit
  That has to be told

Narrator
  As they make their way
  Just some hooded youths

Narrator
  Walking down
  The road

C/M a
  I am here

C/M b
  I started over there

C/M a
  I'm a little bit of this

C/M b
  I'm a little bit of that

C/M c
  I don't really like just

C/M d
  Chilling

C/M c
  But there's

Chorus
  TRAPS

C/M d
  And

Chorus
  HOLD BACKS

C/M e
  Without a crew it's boring

C/M f
  Time to bully some scruff

C/M e
  Who ain't too tough

C/M f
 To get some stuff

C/M g
 To impress some muff

Chorus
 WATCH IT!

C/M g
 Or is it to feed

C/M e
 My kid

C/M f
 Our kid

C/M g
 Some kid

C/M a
 You see

C/M b
 I'm halfway in

C/M c
 And I'm just as much

Chorus
 OUT!

C/M d
 And if I'm not with yours

C/M e
 Then I'd better

Chorus
 WATCH OUT!

C/M f
 For a

Chorus
 CLOUT!

C/M g
 Come then
 Let's bounce out of here
 It's dry, man

C/M d
> Nah just hold back a sec
> Something will happen
> Soon

Narrator
> As us
> Hooded youths
> Loiter

Narrator
> Ska
> DD
> Noe
> And Fibs
> Enter

Fibs
> That's him there you know

DD
> Is it yeah?

Ska
> Yeah it is you know

DD
> Right

Noe
> Do it then

DD
> Yeah
> I will

Noe
> Go on then

DD
> Right

Noe
> Go then!

Fibs
> Man was cheeky you know

DD
> I know

Noe
> Do something about it then

DD

   I will

Noe

   When?
   Been following for time

Fibs

   Who's he chatting to?

Ska

   Someone else is there now

Noe

   You need to hurry up, man
   Stop shitting yourself
   Do something!

DD

   Alright!
   . . .

DD

   Yo!

Stones, **Kin** and **Dred** *appear – They turn to see the group approaching them.*

DD *jabs out of the group – towards* **Stones***.*

Dred *jumps between* **DD** *and* **Stones***.*

DD*'s hand – now revealing a blade – jabs into* **Dred***'s stomach.*

Everything freezes as
   Very slowly, the ghost of **Carr***, dressed in a hospital gown, rides past on her bicycle.*

All that is frozen gives **Carr** *its attention.*

Carr

   I (*Singing*)   don't wanna stay young forever coz if
   I stay young then I'll never get old with you
   And
   I don't wanna stay young forever coz if
   I never get old, I'll never be there for you
   And
   I don't wanna
   I don't wanna
   No
   I (*Singing*)   Don't wanna stay young forever coz if
   I stay young then how will I save the world

So
I don't wanna stay young forever coz if
I never get old, I'll never know the right words
So
I don't wanna
I don't wanna
No
I don't wanna
I don't wanna

As **Carr** *rides off all that is frozen melts.*

The blade retreats from the stomach of **Dred**.

DD's *hand nervously hides itself and the knife in* **DD**'s *pocket.*

Stones, **Dred** *and* **Kin** *withdraw into the shadows.*

The fight is undone.

Everyone continues with their day.

*

Narrator
> Somewhere else
> The no longer
> On the shelf
> Seek
> Steps out
> Into

Narrator
> A backyard
> Seek lights a cigarette

Narrator
> Last night was a night
> They will never forget

Narrator
> Full of slippers
> Dressing gown and last night's make-up
> They see a wasp asleep
> That they decide to wake up

Narrator
> They puts down the cig
> Remembers where they put it
> Then picks up a stick
> And carefully pokes inside a bucket

Seek
> Today I saved a wasp
> I thought I saw it die
> In a bucket with water it was
> When I went for a smoke outside
>
> It struggled for its life
> The wasp's wing wet with rain
> I found a stick to help it out
> And it caught its breath again
>
> I was going to leave the wasp
> When I had first saw it
> For I thought there wasn't
> Any more life for it
>
> But I was wrong
> And so I did
> The wasp was strong
> And so it lived

*An **Adult**, also in slippers and gown, enters with a coffee for* **Seek**.

Adult
> Last night I saw you.

*

Narrator
> The late afternoon is soon to be leaving
> The sun goes to bed
> Potato mash steaming

Narrator
> As many eat

C/M
> No meat!

Narrator
> There are some who are lost in the dark of the street

Narrator
> Sunday evening
> Less's workload is heaving
> She's had just about enough of wallpaper steaming

Less
> Grrr!

Narrator
> She has a new flat

One bed
No cat

Less

Well
No
Not yet
But –

Adult

– The agreement states, no smoking, no pets.

Less begins to iron a never-ending pile of uniforms. Most are school uniforms, but some are work uniforms, prison uniforms, army uniforms, sixth-form uniforms, football kits, graduation gowns and homeless blankets. As she irons, **Chorus Members** *approach her and, one by one, they give* **Less** *an item that will help her on her new journey, in exchange for a uniform that they will need for theirs.*

Less

When I'm ready
I hope I'm better than you
Doing what they need
Instead of what's best to sooth your feet
Boots off now
When you got in from wherever
I bow-tie my crap kicks
And I'm standing in shit / No more likes just pricks
See
School ain't easy when instead of
Nike Air
I'm flossing
Primarni Brick
But you loved your boots
Your toots
Your lingerie business suits
And your drink
And I think
My shit kick misery
Funded your history of being
A selfish mother
So
Raised as a childless kid with a useless mum
The total opposite other I will become

But
As bad as you've been
I've made it good
Grown up quick

Flipped my vision
Became a young adult like you
Were
I've witnessed fears within peers
Situations
Circumstances
Just like yours before
And
So
I can sort of understand why
You jumped out of windows instead of walking through doors
Or
Just
Facing your failure in the face
Me
But I understand now
Home's a different world when you're alone it / it's shit
So the pain I keep hold of
I'm going to hang on to it
Because all of the bad
From you
And from me
Is the fuel that I use
To be the best I can be

*

Chorus
MONDAY MORNING

C/M a
We're all ready for the start of a new week

C/M b
Some of us are

C/M c
Innit
Wait up!

C/M a
For whatever that week decides to do with us

C/M d
We're all wearing our freshly ironed uniforms

C/M b
Some of us are

C/M c
> Innit
> Wait up!

C/M d
> Ready to march towards the week ahead

C/M c
> Right
> I'm ready
> Just had to switch my crypto

C/M b
> Yeah
> Me too

C/M c
> What coin?

C/M b
> Their coin

C/M c
> Yes!

C/M b
> Pump it

C/M c
> Then

C/M b&c
> Dump it!

*

Chorus
> CAN SOMEBODY
> PLEASE PLEASE PLEASE PLEASE PLEASE PLEASE PLEASE
> BRING BACK ROBIN HOOD?!

C/M
> The little I've got I could do with more
> But Dad's not got the right credit score

Chorus
> PLEASE BRING BACK ROBIN HOOD

C/M
> Money in my pocket equals nil
> But I can tick from Jack or Jill

Chorus
> PLEASE BRING BACK ROBIN HOOD

C/M
I'm suddenly in an urgent rush
But what I need is not a must

Chorus
PLEASE BRING BACK ROBIN HOOD

C/M
They finish theirs and get a gap year
I can't afford mine or one of Blackpool's piers

Chorus
PLEASE BRING BACK ROBIN HOOD

C/M
Education and fees – Class backs ya
But you can reach your dreams on *X Factor*

Chorus
PLEASE BRING BACK ROBIN HOOD

C/M
Harrow boys an Eton mess
Unemployed no NHS

Chorus
PLEASE BRING BACK ROBIN HOOD

C/M
Gyms and gins lattes and lunch
Pound-shop shopping discount Munch-bunch

Chorus
PLEASE BRING BACK ROBIN HOOD

C/M
Trident Trident – Poverty Poverty
Foodbanks foodbanks – National Lottery

Chorus
PLEASE BRING BACK ROBIN HOOD

C/M
This palace that palace
Palace fucking / after palace

C/M
Bookies

C/M
Bookies

C/M
Bookies

C/M
Bookies

C/M
Bookies

C/M
Bookies

C/M
Bookies

Chorus
PLEASE BRING BACK ROBIN HOOD

C/M
The Queen's on screen she stains my green

Chorus
PLEASE

C/M
They don't mean to be mean

Chorus
PLEASE

C/M
There's no opportunity in our community

Chorus
PLEASE

C/M
We haven't got any they've got plenty

Chorus
PLEASE

C/M
Hats and hoods make youngsters thugs

C/M
But

C/M
One of them could do some good

C/M
So

Chorus
PLEASE PLEASE PLEASE PLEASE PLEASE PLEASE PLEASE
LET ONE BE OUR ROBIN HOOD!

The End

'Carr's Song'

DAVID JUDGE

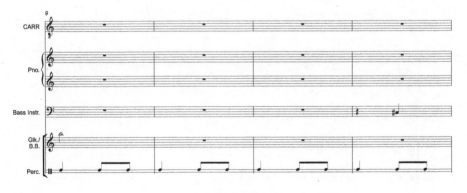

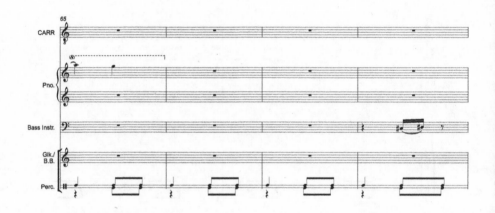

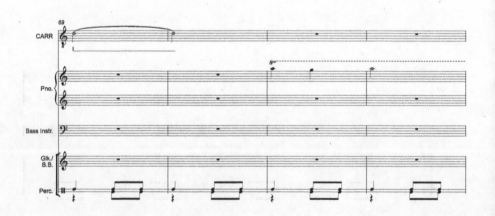

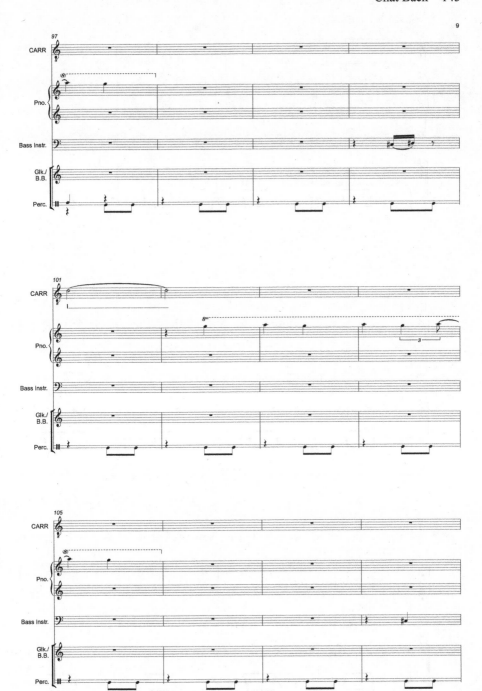

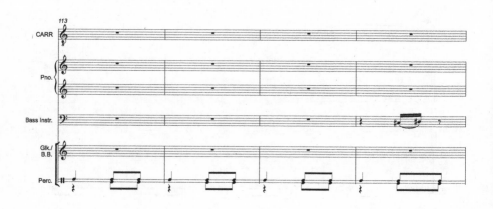

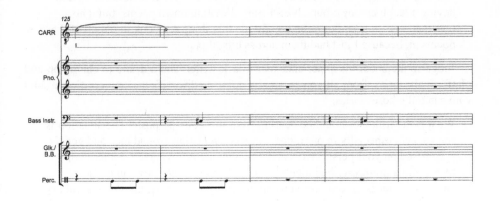

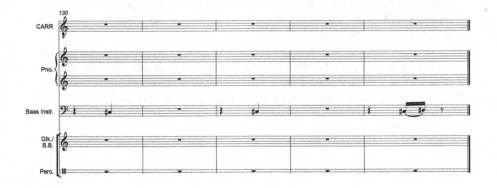

Chat Back

BY DAVID JUDGE

*Notes on rehearsal and staging, drawn from a workshop with the writer,
held at the National Theatre, October 2021*

How the writer came to write the play

Writer David Judge spoke about how he came to write the play:

> At school I kept a diary, but it was poetic and from a world of MCing, hysteria music and drum and bass. That's how we got our ownership of the English language not from GCSEs but from MCing on the street corner, debating and having a laugh amongst ourselves. I started writing down poems, thoughts, observations – a friend of mine bought me this shiny red book to put all of these poems in, because I just had them across bits of paper.

Judge spoke about his experience as a Black writer, and a desire to champion and platform all stories, from all voices, and by doing so diversify the conversation around who can tell whose stories:

> What is the fruit we should be bearing from this equality push? The situation is so nuanced, especially in our cities – true conversation around race and gender is so based on your perspectives and how you identify yourself, rather than fitting into a pre-prescribed identity group. Within *Chat Back* you get some clues, some ideas as to where you can go with your casting, but there is fluidity there. This play is OK to be picked up and explored with all of the contradictions you have within yourself.
>
> In a world of hyper media exposure and immediacy, we can use the young voices and perspectives in this play as a conduit to see the impact that this intense exposure and digital influence is having on the way young people socialise and communicate.
>
> This new generational language and way of socialising among young people seemed so far from me, but then I found it in my red book of poems. That sense of being trapped. That sense of release. That sense of summer holidays. My recurring theme was, 'Who will I become and who will want me?'. That's universal.

Approaching the play

Lead director Miranda Cromwell noted that working on this play provides an opportunity to learn from the young people with whom you're working and it is vital that the young people feel a sense of ownership of the whole piece – this play is written for them, so it's important to find moments in the creative process where they can take the lead.

David Judge said that his aim in writing the play was to make theatre *tangible* for young, working-class people; to create a play in which their experiences were recognised. The script is full of instructions and implied stage directions; but you are free to ignore those that are not helpful for you or your group.

Exercises for use in rehearsals

Exercise: Opening the space

Miranda Cromwell emphasised the importance of ritual. It's essential that the rehearsal room is a safe space where people can speak openly and work generously with one another, talk about difficult questions and make mistakes.

Invite the group to stand in a circle.

Everyone breathe deeply – in through the nose and out through the mouth – at first led by the facilitator, but then everyone breathing in sync. When everyone is ready, raise one arm as if picking up the play from the air, then slowly bring that arm down until it's touching the floor. Everyone should arrive at the floor at about the same time, but without speaking.

This ritual helps to connect the company together; it's reversed at the end of the session.

Exercise: Question cards

This is a great exercise for groups who don't know one another:

- The facilitator hands everyone a card with a question written on it. These can be inspired by the themes of the play and your group; for example, 'What made you want to become a director?' or 'What's your guilty pleasure song?'
- Go up to another person, introduce yourself, ask them the question on the card and listen to their answer. Then they ask you a question.
- Once everyone has had a few minutes to talk, the group gathers in a circle.
- Each person is invited to introduce the person to their left. What do you remember from when you spoke to them? Ask if anyone else spoke to them, and what do they remember?

The most important thing in this game is *listening*. We spend a lot of time as performers thinking about what we've got to say, but listening is an even more critical tool for the actor. Tailoring the questions to the content of the play can be a useful way to inspire conversations about the work.

Exercise: Shoaling

Miranda Cromwell shared this movement exercise, also known as 'flocking' or 'boy band'. The directors got into groups of four to five. One person in each group is the leader and leads their group around the space. Everyone else in the group follows them, keeping the exact distance they have between them and copying their movements. This doesn't have to be completely exact; everyone can do their own version of the leader's movement.

We ran this exercise with two groups moving around the space simultaneously. Miranda Cromwell invited the leaders of each group to become more aware of one another, and to react to one another's movements. As the groups became more confident with their movements, a new rule was added – anyone could swap groups if they like, or even start their own group.

After the exercise, the directors were invited to feed back on their experience of participating in and watching the exercise. Several said they found it quite a freeing experience – it allows people who are less confident to follow someone else, while creating their own interpretation of the leader's movements; and because of the element of following the leader, it's a good exercise for validating the leader's movement choices.

Different kinds of music was played throughout the exercise, and the directors noted that this had a very strong effect on the movement. Using music young people know well can create challenges and opportunities as a director.

David Judge mentioned that SAULT's album *Nine* had been something he'd been listening to a lot while writing the play due to its sense of danger lurking in the background; some of this album was played during the movement exercise.

During rehearsal, the shoaling exercise can be a useful way of can be a useful way of beginning to explore characters; for example, by imagining each character's journey to school. You could also use it to start to create moments and images from the play itself – exploring them in an improvisatory way to start off with and then starting to set images or movements that you think are particularly effective. Having two or more groups moving together also allows you to explore status and power in a scene, negotiating who is in control between leaders of rival groups.

Exercise: Echo circle

The directors stood in a large circle around the room. Miranda Cromwell asked them all to imagine an inner circle within the larger space. In this exercise, anyone can step into the inner circle at any time and make a sound. The people on the outside copy the sound they hear. As more sounds get added, people can choose which sounds they'd like to copy. As the game goes on, add a sense of rhythm (it's good to start with a tone rather than a rhythm first as it tends to lead to a greater variety of textures).

You can add more rules, as the game goes on; for example, two people have to be in the inner circle at all times. You can also add a sense of location. Once you've created a location, you can explore adding text or the song. In the workshop, the directors explored building up Carr's song through this method.

You can also try this exercise in smaller groups, with one person acting as the conductor. They make movements towards other company members and those people interpret it into sound.

Analysing the play: Themes, events, locations

Miranda Cromwell offered some ways into approaching the play and thinking about the specifics of your own production. In groups of five, the directors were asked to consider the following questions:

- What are the themes that are contained within the play? Another way of asking this might be: what is the heartbeat of this play? Or in other words: why is this play speaking to us now?
- What are the events that happen in the play?
- What are the locations in the play?
- What are the challenges of the play? These might come from the play itself, or from the specific group of young people you're working with.

Themes

The group collectively came up with an extensive list of themes. This is an exercise Miranda Cromwell does for every play that she works on. Each play is likely to contain a multiplicity of themes, but as a director, you should try to focus on the themes *you* think are most important and to consider how you might bring those out with the choices that you make in your production. This will make your production deeper, and more artistically unique. For example, one theme that was mentioned was traffic safety and the traffic lights. What might happen if your whole production was framed around the images of traffic lights? We look at every play we work on through the lens of our own experience. Sometimes we don't interrogate the things that are the most familiar to us, even though they may be the most important.

The themes the group identified were:

- Toxic relationships – whether between adults and teenagers, or Noe and Ska
- Rebellion
- Social class
- Identity
- Poverty
- Mental health/self-esteem
- Survival
- Belonging
- Trust and distrust
- Youth anger, and a sense of 'us vs them'
- Bigotry related to immigration
- Coming of age
- Abuse
- Generations and the gap between them

- Friendships
- Place
- Desensitisation and media
- Conformity
- Engagement and disengagement
- Loyalty
- Family
- Neglect
- Reputation and pride
- Education
- Teenage pregnancy
- Drugs
- Youth crime
- Internet – dating apps and swipe culture
- Knife crime
- Porn
- Traffic safety
- Peer pressure
- Parentification

Events

Miranda Cromwell identified an *event* as something that happens in a scene that's new, or that makes a change in the action. This is something that professional actors can find themselves discussing a lot in rehearsal – where does a key event begin and end? How does it cause change for each of the characters on the stage? There's no right or wrong answer about what makes an event, but it's important to be as specific as possible about the choices that you're making. David Judge noted that in *Chat Back*, we're often joining characters at a moment of profound change in their life; Miranda Cromwell agreed and pointed out that the challenge of identifying events is that they need to work for every actor in the scene.

Some of the events the group identified were:

- Less not having enough money in the chip shop, leading to their breaking point and humiliation
- The escape/race from school
- The trap of detention
- Self-discovery – Seek searches for acceptance, participates, asks for help
- The stabbing

- The reversal of the stabbing
- The car crash
- The reveal of the dog
- Noe locking Ska in the cupboard
- The song – which comes as an intervention
- The ironing
- The ending
- Dred arrives
- Kin and Dred meeting
- A kiss
- Less tears up the card
- The prayer for Robin Hood
- The wasp in the bucket
- Stones rejects the two girls

Locations

The group identified the following main locations:

- School
- Chip shop
- Canal Street
- Bench
- Park
- The flat
- Tram stop
- Bus stop
- The brook
- A road
- Back garden
- Bedroom
- Gated play area

It's important to note that there are many locations in the play – it moves continuously. This allows you to explore ways of creating these locations with your company, rather than building sets for each location. David Judge mentioned that you should feel free to change the locations to your area, to make it relatable to you and your students.

Challenges of the play and context

The group was invited to list the challenges presented by the play. They split this into challenges that directors could experience in their *environments*, and the challenges of the *play* itself.

Challenges in the play	Challenges in the environment
<ul><li>Language</li><li>Perception of the language – potential backlash within the school</li><li>Sensitive content</li><li>Rhythm</li><li>Intimacy</li><li>Transitions</li><li>Staging the bike</li><li>Choreography</li><li>Violence/the stabbing</li><li>Not demonising the adults</li></ul>	<ul><li>Covid safety</li><li>Headteachers' and parents' buy-in</li><li>Working with a company without diversity</li><li>Avoiding stereotypes</li><li>Logistics of multi-roling</li><li>Budget</li><li>Safeguarding – especially with wider age groups mixing older and younger students (e.g. fourteen to nineteen)</li><li>Time commitments of students – especially exams</li></ul>

Miranda Cromwell noted that each of these challenges offers an opportunity to overcome it through creativity.

The group discussed moments of difficult language, e.g. 'penetrate your arse'. How can you stay true to intention that it's a shocking moment, while making sure that parents and school leaders are comfortable with the language being used? The group discussed the possibility of using bleeps, or a soundscape, to cover the words so it's not heard by the audience. Alternatively, if you take the decision that it's essential to use the words as written, there's the option of including a programme note so audiences are aware of the content, and/or talk to your headteacher in advance.

Similarly, you might not want to see smoking or vaping on stage, but you don't have to use the literal prop. You could substitute another object – pens, for example – or create a stylised movement to represent the act of smoking or vaping.

David Judge talked about the importance of creating a safe space with your company to discuss these challenges. The language and content are being given to the young people in the specific context of theatre, which aims to provoke and to bear witness to what's happening in our society. There's a value in giving young people *permission* to explore content that you might find difficult, and frame that within the work that you're doing – which is why opening and closing the space at the beginning and end of the session are so powerful.

Part of the drive behind David Judge's writing of the play is that it should allow young people to speak to everyone, especially adults. The group talked about the power of seeing young people speak their truth, and how powerful it is when someone younger than you tells you something important.

Analysing character

In groups of five, everyone was invited to come up with a list of *facts* and *questions* about some of the characters in the play. This exercise is found in *The Director's Craft* by Katie Mitchell, which contains lots of other useful ideas for approaching a text. Combining *facts* and *questions* invites you to make decisions about characters, for example, it's a fact that Less doesn't have enough money to pay for the chips. A question might be: has this happened before? As an example, one group explored facts and questions relating to the adult character(s):

Facts	Questions
<ul><li>They use a lot of exclamation marks in their language – they seem to be stressed, shouting and not listening to the 'child' characters</li><li>They have authority and power</li><li>They are not a child – and exist in opposition to the children</li><li>They don't speak politely or respectfully to the young people</li><li>They give instructions, commands or warnings</li><li>They don't seem to be compassionate towards the younger characters</li></ul>	<ul><li>What is the gender of the adult(s)?</li><li>Is this multi-role – do you have many performers playing the adult or just one?</li><li>What is the role of the adult?</li><li>Are they part of the chorus?</li></ul>

The group discussed images that came out of these lists: for example, is it powerful if the adult voice is always off stage? Could you give the young person or people playing the adult(s) a megaphone? You could run improvisations to help answer questions and fill in gaps for the actor – e.g. if Less has been smacked before, improvise a scene where that happens; or improvise how everyone got into detention.

Freewriting can also be really useful to answer questions. You could run a free writing exercise to answer a specific question ('who hurt Bruno?' was an example) or ask everyone to choose a favourite question and respond to that.

Once you've completed your list of facts and questions for a character, you can explore their *superobjective* and *objective*. The thing that character most wants throughout the play is their superobjective; and in each scene, they'll have an objective for the scene which helps them get towards their superobjective; and *obstacles* which stand in the way of their achieving the scene objective. It's helpful to identify all the objectives a character might face in the scene, and then to choose the most interesting one to focus on. Miranda Cromwell suggested that obstacles are most interesting when they make it hard for people to rationally get what they want.

David Judge noted that a lot of the time in this play, the character's objective is a physical one – they're trying to find a place to be, without being interrupted or having that space invaded by adults or trams.

Ways the writer thinks about the play

David Judge noted that the play is very fluid. He offered some images which are helpful when thinking about the structure of the play. First, a *protest march*. If you look at a march from above, it looks like a single body, moving together with the same objective. But if you get closer in, you see that everyone is different. Some people are leading; some people are speaking; some are just following along.

It's also helpful to think of the play as a *relay race* in which the baton is constantly passed from one set of actors to another – which can be really helpful in establishing the visual language of transitions, as scenes don't start or stop as in a more traditional play. The play is also a kind of *Greek chorus* in which the performers step up and represent the community that they're part of.

David Judge also suggested that it can be helpful to go through the play and identify political references within the text that tie it to larger events. For example, Bruno is a British bulldog as a Brexit reference; and Judge now thinks of detention as a form of lockdown.

Fluidity is key – both in the speed and rhythm of the dialogue, and in transitions between the scenes. David Judge suggested watching his spoken-word sets on YouTube as a guide to the rhythm of the chorus's language, though it's important that each production makes the language their own. There's also flexibility in casting – most characters are written to be performed by actors of any gender, and there's no rule about who speaks as the narrator – anyone can take on this role. It's also worth mentioning that the play is written in a way that reflects Judge's Manchester accent – you can amend the text if you need to in order to sort the accent of your performers.

Question and answer with David Judge

Q: Can I change the gender of the characters if needed?
DJ: Yes.

Q: Who should play the Chorus and Narrator?
DJ: It's up to you – you can be really flexible about how you cast both these roles. They can be one person or everyone. The important thing is to think about *why* you're making the choices that you're making.

Q: How do you imagine the bicycle on stage?
DJ: The bicycle is like a knife cutting through the business. Its appearance needs to be a suspended moment. Carr could be sitting on the bike with someone rolling it slowly behind her. Miranda Cromwell suggested that you could do it with no bike, with the actor holding bike lights. It might even carry more magic if you *don't* have a bike.

Q: Did you write it for it to be acted by the 'drama kids' or by young people like those we see in the play – the ones who might be in detention.
DJ: Neither or both! When writing it, I thought about my experience at youth theatre. I wanted to make sure the show didn't have a lead character who got all the attention. And the play also represents my experience growing up. When I was writing the play, I thought about the need to make theatre tangible for young working-class people. But

the play is also an opportunity for people from other backgrounds to understand the lives of young people like the ones in the play. So, it's for both those groups!

Q: How would you approach Noe's 'This is how much I love you' moment?
DJ: Noe is trying to push Ska into the storage unit, it's coming from the physical resistance as he tries to squeeze her in – it's not designed to be a horror movie moment, it's from Ska fighting back.

Q: How can I avoid stereotyping the characters in the play?
DJ: If your young people aren't the ones in the play, they probably know people who are. As actors it's exciting to play people who are different to you. As the director, it's important to ask whether you believe what you're seeing. Is the actor thinking the thoughts of the character?

Q: What's behind the writing of the last scene?
DJ: It's about changing everything. We're wishing and hoping for things to be better. In many working-class communities, shops are being replaced by bookies, and paths to a better life are going missing. At the end of the play, some young people are going back into school, but those that aren't have that pressure to be something and they don't know what that is yet.

The desire for change is the main driver of this scene.

Suggested references

The album *Nine* by SAULT
The book *The Director's Craft* by Katie Mitchell
David Judge – Spoken Word Poetry on YouTube: https://www.youtube.com/
    watch?v=nR4h8oyMX0E&ab_channel=EvidentlySalford-SpokenWordPoetry

From a workshop led by Miranda Cromwell
With notes by Tom Mansfield

Find a Partner!

by Miriam Battye

Miriam Battye is a writer from Manchester. She was the first Sister Pictures Writer in Residence in 2018 and has various original ideas in development for television. Theatre includes: *Trip the Light Fantastic* (Bristol Old Vic); *All Your Gold* (Theatre Royal, Plymouth); *Electricity* (National Youth Theatre/Arcola); *Balance* (Royal Exchange, Manchester); *Pancake Day* (Bunker/PLAY).

'In a cruel land, you either learn to laugh at cruelty or spend your life weeping.'

Robert Jordan

'I just want a boy who doesn't put his willy up as many girls as he wants.'

Hayley, *Love Island*

Characters

The Lovers
Girls:
Hayley
Sam F
Jess
Ally
Ella

Boys:
Andy
Max
Jacob
Kai
Sam M
Other **Boys** *(as many as you want, can double as* **Spectators***)*

Spectators
Spectator 1 *(in charge)*
Other **Spectators** *(as many as you want)*

Notes on the text

The game-show format that is presented in the play is metaphorical. It is reality, turned up to 100.

We are watching people try to find someone to fall in love with and successfully hold onto that love through the obstacles life throws at them, whilst the whole time their love is scrutinised by people around them.

The circle in which the action happens should be simple, and needs to be no more elaborate than the outline of a large circle on the floor. The Lovers exist only within it. The Spectators exist outside it, and are the only ones who can cross the line of the circle. When they are outside the circle, no one inside can hear them. Spectator 1 has specified lines, and the rest can be divided amongst however many Spectators you want. Spectator 1 can also say lines set for other Spectators.

When the Lovers speak 'to us', they should speak directly outwards, in the direction of the real audience. These are their private thoughts, like monologues, their Diary Room of sorts. These break into the action of the play throughout, and could be realised either just with a clear turn of the head or with lighting. These can be further enhanced by having everyone else in the company watching them, for example.

The way a Lover is sent Out is up for interpretation. In this version, they are 'shot' by an unseen shotgun, and fall to the floor. You could also achieve this in different ways, physically. What matters is that they are gone from the game, forever.

I would encourage you not to worry about the context this new reality lives in. It just is. As the play is playful and heightened I would encourage you to have fun and be playful.

Prologue: Choose your partner!

Three young men stand in a line, bathed in a striking light.

They are silent, quivering a little, afraid.

A young woman stands alone, a few strides away, deciding if she should choose them.

After a moment, she speaks.

Hayley   Number Two?

Boy 2 *steps forward, taking a gasping breath of relief.*

The others stare on in terror.

Hayley   Yeah. I think Number Two could be my Partner.

She looks him up and down.

Hayley   He looks a bit handy.
A bit helpful.
Quite fit.
Not so fit that I'd be in a constant state of threat.
And not so un-fit that he'd bring our average down.
He has the fitness of someone who would love me about 10 per cent more than I love him.
And that's all anyone wants, really.

Boy 2 *smiles, grateful.*

Boy 2   I'm *so grateful* you choose me.

Hayley   Aw.

She smiles.

Her smile falls.

Oh. Actually. Can you just turn your head again?

Boy 2 *turns his head a little to the side, worried.*

Hayley   Oh. Oh no.
You see that?
He's got a slightly deviated jaw line there? It's fine now but that's an early sign that his kids are gonna be crap at sports.

She looks at the camera/audience.

Mama don't want nerds.

Boy 2 *shakes his head frantically.*

She looks back at him.

Hayley   Plus his plimsolls make him look like a wanker.
So I'll go with Number Three.

Boy 2 *shakes his head, makes a few desperate sounds but she has spoken.*

Boy 3 *gratefully steps forward as* **Boy 2** *steps back.*

Boy 3   Ohmygod. Thank you.

Hayley   Hiya! – Yeah. Number Three's my final choice.

She holds out her hand. He steps forward, gratefully takes it in his.

The **Spectators** *have been watching intently from outside the circle. They move freely around it.*

One of said **Spectators** *steps into the circle from the outside, addresses the remaining* **Boys**. *This is* **Spectator 1**, *and they are very much in charge of proceedings.*

Spectator 1   So, guys. No one wants to be your Partner.
        I'm sorry . . . you're Out! Time to say goodbye!

The remaining boys are shot, one by one, by an unseen gun.

They are Out.

They fall to the floor one by one.

Hayley *looks out at us, the audience.*

Hayley   I'm not picky. I just value myself.

Hayley *and* **Boy 3** *assemble themselves in a Partner pose, joining the other Lovers.*

(Perhaps lights up to reveal) They are assembled in sets of Partners, all standing in their Partner poses. Coupley. Happy.

Spectator 1   So you've all found a Partner. Now the real game begins!
        Who'll be Out next? Who's gonna lose, and who's gonna –

All   WIN AT LOVE!

The Partners fist pump the air together –

All   GOOOOO LOVE!

With a musical flourish, we move straight into –

Part One: Why love?

The monologues happen out to us, the audience.

Everyone watches the Partner duo who are speaking.

During the monologues, the bodies of the four rejected boys are dragged off out of the circle by their feet, clumsily, by **Spectators**. *A* **Spectator** *wipes the floor where they were with blue roll.*

Jess *and* **Andy**.

Jess *speaks to us. She is bold, pragmatic.*

Jess   Why do I want a Partner?

She thinks.

    Well. I've been Unpartnered for about . . . six months now?

    And it's starting to become a problem.

    People are starting to get – *Uncomfortable*.

    When I don't have a satisfactory answer to *the Question*.

She pauses.

    It's getting hard to avoid *the Question*.

She pauses.

    'Are you seeing anyone?'

    'Got a Partner yet, hun?'

    'Are you maybe just too picky, darling, cos my niece has got chronic impetigo and even she's got one . . .'

She nods her head, a greater resolve.

    So yeah.

    That's why I'm here.

    It's time to get a Partner.

    It's time to get Loved.

All   GOOOOO LOVE!

Andy *speaks to us. He is furtive, wildly anxious.*

Andy   It's not like I haven't tried to find one.

    I'm on every app –

    I go to every social event –

    I maintain open body language, at all times –

    I haven't crossed my arms in three years –

    I spend a lot of time standing in lifts, actually, just, waiting –

    Always keep a seat next to me at weddings –

    At the cinema –

    On the bus –

    Just in case. Someone just happens to . . . fill it

    And we can start, y'know, Falling in Love.

A brief silence.

He gets a bit breathy, sensing he's not proved himself enough –

    I BAKE.

    I listen to FEMINIST PODCASTS.

    I am consistently VERY NICE to everyone I meet –

    Trust me, I've tried EVERYTHING.

A breath.

    This really is my last chance.

    Cos you *have* to find a Partner here, right?

    Or you're Out.

He pauses. To take a breath. To contemplate death.

(*To himself.*) Ohhh this might have been a mistake.

Jess *pipes up, speaks to us –*

Jess   I just feel like I have all this Love just ready and waiting.
Fully formed. Beautiful and massive and life-changing.
And I don't have anyone to, like, give it to.

Andy *looks at her.*

Andy   Me too. I feel that way too.

They look at each other.

Andy   Go Love?

All   GOOOOO LOVE!

The **Spectators** *call out their responses outside the circle. They cannot be heard by those inside.*

Spectator 1   What do you think, guys?

Spectator   I think the standard is really going downhill tbh.

Spectator   Yeah I can't wank to any of these.

Spectator   It looks like they've just gone into the canteen and grabbed whoever didn't have their mouth full.

Spectator   It looks like they've just rounded up some dogs and kicked them through Matalan.

The **Spectators** *laugh.*

Spectator   Shut up! They still deserve a Partner. Everyone, no matter how unlovable, deserves a Partner.

Spectator   Disagree. No one wants to see uglies bumping their actually ugly uglies.

The **Spectators** *laugh.*

Sam F *and* **Max**.

Max *speaks to us. He is unwaveringly cocksure.*

Max   I'm not even Unpartnered now.
I'm fighting them off.
No, literally, I am *fighting* them off.
I've had to put up a fences.
I've had to put up walls.
I've got a sixteen-metre perimeter around my house so that girls can't break into my bathroom.
I regularly cause traffic jams –
I've caused three semi-serious collisions just getting myself a Pret.

I've been banned from most shopping centres.
I don't even get the bus.
I just – crowd-surf to my destination.
I'm here to win. Obv.
What else am I going to do with all of this? Politics?

He thinks.

(*To himself*) Maybe I should do politics.

Sam F *looks at* **Max** *for a moment, disturbed. He notices.*

Max   What?

Sam F *looks back to us. She speaks. She is grounded, realistic.*

Sam F   I just want to find out if I really need a Partner or not.
Cos if I'm honest I have no idea if I do, or if someone has just told me I do.
I want to know if Partnering Up still holds the societal capital it had in the past,
Or whether we're free, now, to decide who or what we need to make us happy.

Max *looks at her, disturbed.*

Sam F   What?

Spectator   I give these guys a week.

Spectator   Yeah. She's boring and he's the human equivalent of splashback.

Spectator   I'd let him splash my back.

The **Spectators** *laugh.*

Spectator   He'll be a shit Partner though.

Spectator   Yeah he'll be shit at Love, he won't know what to do with it

Spectator   I reckon she can change him, y'know.

Spectator   Omigod – Project!

All Spectators   GOTTALOVEADICKHEAD.

Ella *and* **Jacob**.

Jacob *speaks to us. He is trying his best to be cool about this.*

Jacob   Um. I'm here because I think I need some guidance?
Like what do I say. Exactly. To keep her.
I mean I'm not worried.
I mean I'm totally fine.

He briefly pauses.
It's just my armpits that betray me.

He touches an armpit. Rubs his fingers together. Drenched with sweat.

He holds it out to us. Please.

I just need someone to tell me what to do. And then what to do after I've done that. And then what to do after I've done that. And how not to be terrified about all of it.

Spectator   This guy is desperado.

Spectator   Big time.

Spectator   Big Desperate Energy.

Spectator   You can see it in his eyes –

Spectator   See it a mile off –

All Spectators   PANTY SNIFFER.

Spectator 1 *jumps into the circle, addresses* **Jacob** –

Spectator 1   OK, OK, Jacob, honesty is great, everyone loves honesty, but I think, possibly, you need to say something a bit less sadboy?

Jacob   Wwwwhat do you mean?

Spectator 1   Y'know, bit more 'awwwite'? Bit more 'get in there, lads'? Bit more 'cuppla-pints-and-some-pawwwk-scratchings'-type of OK with yourself?

Another **Spectator** *jumps in.*

Spectator   Yeah otherwise you'll be Out sooner than you can say 'prescription-strength deodorant'.

Jacob *turns back and speaks to us* –

Jacob   I've come because I'm reasonably lonely?

Spectator 1   Mmm no it's a bit –

Jacob   I really like girls and I want one I want one I want one in my tum?

Spectator   Well, that's just a bit weird, but –

Jacob   Just. Tell me what to say. Just tell me. And I'll say it.

Another **Spectator** *jumps in.*

Spectator   Maybe just keep your mouth shut, hun.

Jacob *does. He does double thumbs-up.*

The **Spectators** *all jump out of the circle, and watch.*

Ella *speaks to us. She makes a lot of 'air quote' gestures.*

Ella   Well. I've never been very 'popular'. I've never been particularly good at 'people'. I've never really understood 'romantic comedies' or 'love songs' or what the fuck makes 'will they won't they' so interesting – like – will they, or won't they? Like, answer the question.

The main thing is even if they will at the beginning, eventually, they won't.

So shut the fuck up about it.

She thinks.

Ella   It's not that I'm 'cynical'. I'm just *aware* of people's self-interest and therefore *generally* mistrustful of people's intentions?

She thinks.

OK fine I am cynical.
Whatever. I'm a child of divorce. And *EastEnders.*

A brief pause.

Jacob *does a thumbs-up at her, hopeful. She frowns.*

Spectator   Dunno if she deserves a Partner actually

Spectator   Yeah. Leave 'Love' to the 'optimists'. 'Hun'.

Spectator   I call bullshit. It's always the ones who claim they don't want Love who are doing Boy raindances and poking holes in condoms.

The **Spectators** *laugh.*

Ally *and* **Kai** *speak to us. They are a bit confused.*

Ally   Um. I'd just quite like a Partner?

Kai   I'd just quite like a Partner too?

They look at each other.

Ally   This might work.

Ally *looks back at us, smiling brightly.*

Ally   I have very low expectations.

Kai *grins.*

Everyone is standing in their Partner poses. Smiling.

Jess (*smiling*)   Does anyone know what we do now?

Andy (*smiling*)   I dunno. Just keep smiling.

Hayley (*smiling*)   Are we supposed to start arguing yet?

Ella (*smiling*)   I think that comes later?

Jess (*leaning out to speak to* **Sam F***, psst*)   Oi, Sam? What type are you?

Sam F   What, sorry?

Jess   Like you were talking about 'societal capital' – does that mean you're the boring type?

Sam F   What?

Jess   Like Hayley's the fit type, I'm the damaged type, Ella is . . .

Ella   I'm the bitch, I think?

Jess   Right, and Ally's the thick type.

Ally (*waving at* **Sam F**)   Helloooo!

Jess   We're all different types.

Ella   Yeah it's kinda like the Spice Girls, but not like really old.

Sam F (*to* **Jess**)   You're the . . . damaged type?

Jess   Oh yeah. You've got to be a bit damaged. You've got to have been, like, hurt before. Otherwise you won't know the red flags. Otherwise you'll fall for the first person who says you've got nice teeth.

Sam F   Who decided this, sorry?

Jess   It's just good sense to know your type

Ella   Like how can you be anyone's type if you don't know what type you are?

Sam F   So . . . what about the boys?

Jess *points the boys out one by one* (**Max**, **Boy 3**, **Jacob**, **Andy**, **Kai**, *back to* **Andy**)

Jess   Ummm . . . Tosser, tosser, tosser, not, not, probably not.

Sam F   That's it?

Jess   Ummm. Boys are simple.

Sam F   Are they?

Spectator   What the hell is going on? Where's the drama? Is anyone else getting – BORED.

The **Spectator** *turns their back to the circle. Followed by –*

Spectator (*turning their back*)   Yep, BORED.

Spectator 1 *jumps into the circle.*

Spectator 1   Guys, what are you waiting for?
Can you just shut up and get on with it please?

They run out of the circle.

Sam F   Wait – what?

Ella   What are we getting on with?

Spectator 1 *jumps back in again.*

Spectator 1   Falling in Love, of course!
On your marks . . . get set . . .

All   GOOOOOO LOVE!

Part Two: Fall in love!

The contestants set about Falling in Love in the circle. The **Spectators** *watch intently.*

How would you try to 'fall in love' if you had limited time? It could be a physical movement, proximity, trying to telepathically link, running or throwing yourself at each other, it could be trying to learn everything about it each other straight away. Every Partnership tries to work it out.

Ella *and* **Jacob**. *Sitting, staring at each other. Trying to fall in love.*

Ella   What do we need to do.

Jacob   Fall in love.

Ella   I think the most important thing is. Proximity.

They look at each other. They shuffle closer to each other.

Jacob   Done.

Ella   And having compatible personalities.

Jacob   How do we do that.

Ella (*serious*)   I'm really bubbly.

Jacob   I'm not. So that's a good balance?

Ella   Right, and sharing the same values.

Jacob   OK. Are you happy with your values?

Ella   Yes.

Jacob   Cool, I'll share them.

Ella   Nice.

Jacob   We're really nailing this. Love you.

Ella   No that's too soon. It has to be believable.

Jacob (*not understanding*)   Oh right. I get you. And I looo –

Ella   No.

Jacob   Sorry.

He touches his armpit. It's sodden.

Shit.

Jess *and* **Andy**. *Standing, looking at each other.*

Jess   This is going to be hard work.

Andy   Relationships are supposed to be hard work.

Jess   Give and take.

Andy   Commitment. Compromise. It might be painful but it's worth it.

Jess   Otherwise we'll be single.

Andy   We'll be *single people.*

Jess   You can't get a mortgage on a *single person's* salary.

Andy   Who are you supposed to kiss on New Year's Eve?

Jess   Who are you supposed to talk to? Your family and friends?

Andy   Who are you supposed to talk to your family and friends *about*?

Jess   Yeah.

Andy   Yeah.

Jess   I agree.

Andy   Totally.

A pause. They look at each other.

Jess   I think we might be quite compatible, actually.

They high ten, elated.

Andy   Amazing. Can this be our thing?

Jess   Absolutely.

They high ten again.

Jess *and* **Andy**   WE HAVE A THING!

Hayley *and* **Boy 3**. *Standing. She is inspecting him. He is nervous, afraid to fuck up.*

Hayley   Do you have a history of mental illness in the family?

He shakes his head.

Hayley   Diabetes?

He shakes his head.

Hayley   Male pattern baldness?

He looks up at his own head. He shakes his head.

Hayley   Oh so are you like a secretly hairy family?

Boy 3   No, we have, like, a normal amount of hair.

Hayley   And have you got your all your own teeth?

He nods his head.

Hayley   Can I have a look?

Boy 3   You – want to look at my teeth?

Hayley   Yeah.

Boy 3   Umm.

Hayley   Unless . . . you've got something to hide?

He opens his mouth immediately.

She looks at them.

Hayley   What's your name by the way?

Boy 3 (*mouth open*)   Joey.

Hayley   What?

He closes his mouth.

Boy 3   Joey.

She frowns.

Hayley   Well, that's not gonna work is it.

Boy 3   Why not?

Hayley   What's our Partner name gonna be? 'Hoey'?

Boy 3   Uhhhhhh . . .

Hayley *looks around, calls out –*

Hayley   When are we getting new boys in, people?

Boy 3   No no no no. I can change my name! I just won't have a name! You can just have all the – name. You don't even have to look at me. We can just pretend I don't exist.

He crouches into a little ball, covering his head –

See? This is totally sustainable.

Hayley   Fine. I mean there's no one else anyway.

Boy 3 *looks up at her, exhales, relieved.*

Boy 3   Do we kiss now?

Hayley *thinks for a moment. Rolls her eyes, relents.*

Hayley   Fine.

He goes to stand to go for a kiss, she puts up a fist. He stops, confused, and kisses her knuckles. He goes back down and holds himself in a little ball, sobbing quietly.

Max *and* **Sam F**. *Standing.* **Max** *is basically ignoring her.*

Sam F   So. Like. What are your interests.

Max   I don't understand what's happening right now.

Sam F   Um. We're having a conversation.

Max   I don't normally have to. Conversation.

Sam F   Can you just try? *What are your interests?*

He stares at her for a moment.

Max   I don't know.

He really struggles.

I quite like old boats.

Sam F   Yeah?

Max   Nah not really actually.

Sam F   Right. Great.
Now you ask me a question.

He stares, blankly.

Max   I normally just like vaguely insult girls.
Liiiike –
'You look better than usual.'

He pauses for effect.

Do you Love me now?

She stands up.

Sam F   OK I can't do this.

Max   Wow, you're really different from other girls.

Sam F   Am I?

Max   You really, like, challenge me!

She suddenly runs, full pelt out of the circle – but bumps into the imaginary wall of the chalk circle.

She falls back in pain.

Sam F   Ow!

Spectator   Lol, where does she think she's going?

Sam F (*to herself*)   Argh. What am I gonna do?

A **Spectator** *jumps into the circle to give advice.*

Spectator   You've got to give him a chance, hun.

Sam F   But. I hate him.

Another jumps in.

Spectator   I think you're being a bit harsh tbh. Like, he's probably just got his guard up.

Spectator   Yeah he probably just has a bad relationship with his mum or whatever and struggles to trust women.

Spectator   Yeah! Exactly! Just try to connect with him.

Sam F   I cannot connect with that. There is nothing to connect – to.

Spectator   Well, you could be less of a bitch? I think you'd work better as like a . . . Wise, sage type? Sort of like . . . an old goose or something. Or your nan. OK?

Sam F   What?

Spectator   Just BE NICE.
(*Whispering*) Otherwise you're Out, babes.

The **Spectators** *jump out of the circle.* **Sam F** *returns to sit beside* **Max**. *She tries to be nice.*

Ally *and* **Kai**. *Standing. Facing each other. They are calm. Zen.*

Spectator   What are they . . . doing?

The **Spectators** *peer at* **Ally** *and* **Kai** *from outside the circle.*

Spectator   Is she already giving him the silent treatment?

Spectator   Is this passive aggressive or aggressive aggressive?

Spectator   No . . . she's pissed *him* off.

Spectator   I think they're *both* angry.

Suddenly –

Kai   Go!

They start play fighting and wrestling.

Spectator   Ooh! Violence!

A bored **Spectator** *tuns back around to the circle to watch.*

Spectator   OOH!

Ally *pins* **Kai** *down. They erupt into giggles.*

Ally   I win!

Kai   Argh, dammit!

They sit together, giggling.

A **Spectator** *jumps into the circle.*

Spectator   Um. What's going on here? Who's mad at who?

Kai   What?

Ally   We're not mad

Spectator   So what you're just. Having a nice time.

Ally   Yeah.

Spectator   You're just. Getting on.

Kai   Yeah.

Ally *nods, smiling.*

Ally   Yeah!

Her face falls.

Sorry. Is that not OK?

*The **Spectator** jumps out of the circle again.*

Spectator   We need them Out, asap.

Spectator   I think it's cute.

Spectator   I think it's *too* cute.

Spectator   Yeah. They're definitely faking it.

All Spectators   GAME PLAN

They watch all the Partners assembled in the circle, who are messing around, chatting, ignoring each other.

Spectator   I think everyone likes each other a bit too much actually.

Spectator   Yeah I'm sorry but I can't invest in a relationship if it hasn't been tested a bit.

Spectator   BORED.

*The bored **Spectator** turns their back on the circle. Another follows suit.*

Spectator (*turning their back*)   BORED.

Spectator 1   I know –

Spectator 1 *suddenly shoves **Sam M** (male) from outside the circle into the circle and everyone gasps.*

Sam M   Hey, guys, I'm Sam!

All Spectators   Oooooooooooh

Spectator   TWIST.

Sam M *is going round introducing himself.*

Hayley   Hi, I'm Hayley.

Sam M   Hi, I'm Sam.

Hayley *turns and speaks to us.*

Hayley   Yeah so I'm getting like a medium vibe with Sam.

Sam M *shakes* **Ella** *and* **Jacob**'s *hands.*

Sam M   Hi, I'm Sam. Hi, I'm Sam.

Jacob *turns to speak to us, still shaking* **Sam M**'s *hand.*

Jacob   I'm not threatened by new boy Sam, no.
Me and Ella are really happy.
Really calm and happy.
Yeah.
Yeah.

A pause, he nods a lot.

I haven't pooed in three days though, so.

They stop shaking hands.

Sam M *wipes his hand on his trousers.*

Sam F *holds out her hand to* **Sam M**.

Sam F   Hi, I'm Sam!

Sam M   Hi, I'm also Sam!

Hayley   Oh my God, that's hilarious. What would your Partner name be? 'Sam'?

Hayley *laughs a lot.*

Sam F (*sarcastic*)   I guess we can't be Partners then, Hayley.

Hayley   Wow, that was like, reallyveryrude.

Max *shakes* **Sam M**'s *hand.*

Sam M   Hi, I'm Sam.

Max *talks to us –*

Max   Absolutely no threat there. He's not going to steal Girl Sam from me.

I mean I'm not even bothered if he does. I'm keeping my options open, if you know what I mean. Not putting *all my eggs in one breakfast*, if you know what I mean. I mean I'll cross that bridge *when I cross it*, if you know what I mean. I mean if you know *what I mean*, if you know what I mean.

A **Spectator** *steps into the circle.*

Spectator   What do you mean?

He thinks.

Max   I dunno.

He doesn't know what to do, so goes with –

Max (*laddy*)   Tits! I dunno.

He sits on the floor, a bit tired.

Sam M *goes to* **Sam F**, *who is standing alone at the edge of the circle, looking for a way out.*

Sam M   Hi, other Sam. You OK?

Sam F   You don't have to talk to me. I'm not your Partner.

Sam M   No, I know, I just. Felt like saying hello. You seem kind of normal.

Sam F   D'you reckon we could be friends?

He looks at her. He looks around.

Sam M   Is that allowed?

Spectator (*peering at them from outside the circle*)   Don't like that.

Spectator   Yeah what *is* that?

Spectator   Sam is such a dark horse!

Spectator   How *dare* he try and steal a Partner!

Spectator   Well, he doesn't want to be Out. Who do we want Out?

Spectator 1 *jumps into the circle. Speaks brightly –*

Spectator 1   Right, grab your Partner, let's see who's still in Love!

The Lovers all grab their Partners, get into their poses, whilst asking –

Jess   Wait, I thought it was to find out who's the Most Loved?

Ella   No I think it's who's the Best at Love?

Jacob   I thought it was who's Love *is* the Best?

Andy   Is there a difference?

Jess   The main thing is we're not Out.
(*To* **Andy**.) I'm not gonna be Out, am I?

Andy (*dead serious*)   Of course not. I'm falling in love with you.

Jess (*serious*)   I'm falling in love with you too.

Andy   Good. On schedule.

They high ten, serious. Clasp each other tight.

Sam M *looks around, terrified.*

Sam M   Wait wait wait. I don't have a Partner.

He appeals to the girls, a little frantic –

Sam M   I think I'd be a really good Partner. I'm really dependable, and I'm a good listener, and I like . . . travelling and, dogs-and-or-cats and, documentaries and . . . it doesn't matter, the main thing is I won't leave you. I'll just – stay – with you. And you'll never be Out.

Hayley *suddenly steps forward.*

Hayley   I'll take him!

Sam M *spins round to her.*

Sam M   What?

Boy 3   *What!*

He immediately falls to his knees in horror and sadness and the rage of futile mortality.

Spectator 1   Um. Can we at least give it a *bit* of a tense pause?

Hayley *goes back to her Partner and pulls up the gasping, panicking* **Boy 3**, *linking arms with him.* **Spectator 1** *looks at* **Boy 3**.

Spectator 1   OK *you* need to look less worried, because you don't know what she's going to do yet.

Boy 3   But.

But you're about to – I'm about to –

He looks around, for help.

No one says anything.

He relents. Starting to cry, he puts on a smile.

Spectator 1   Thank you. So!
Would anyone like to swap Partners?

Hayley *pretends to grapple with the decision.*

Hayley   Ummmm I –

She steps forward and **Boy 3** *holds onto her arm, tugging her back. A little tustle.*

She wrenches free –

Hayley   I do!

Everyone, **Spectators** *and all, pretend to gasp.*

Hayley   I'm sorry, but. I might be *happier* with Sam. What do you want me to be? Possibly *not* be happier?

She joins **Sam M**. **Boy 3** *is left alone, crying quietly. He crawls around, trying to find the exit.*

Spectator   Can you blame her? That boy is human cartilage and we all know it.

Spectator   She was the only one bringing the sauce in that relationship.

Spectator   He definitely loved her more than she loved him. Say it with me –

All Spectators   PRECARIOUS.

Hayley   What happens now? Did I win yet?

Andy   Yeah, who won this round?

Spectator 1   What do we reckon guys? Who's the Best so far?

All the **Spectators** *shrug. 'Whatever, don't care, you pick', etc.*

Spectator 1 *jumps back into the circle.*

Spectator 1   The Best Partners are . . . HAYLEY AND SAM!

All Spectators   GOOOOO HAM!

Hayley *screams and jumps up and down, hugging* **Sam M**, *who is baffled.*

Sam M   But we literally just met?

Hayley   *Shut up.*

Spectator 1   How do you feel?

Hayley   Uh, the Best?

A bit of jumping up and down from **Hayley**, *alone.*

Jess   OK so who's Out?

Spectator 1 *jumps outs and addresses the other* **Spectators**.

Spectator 1   What do you reckon, chaps?

They all decisively point at **Ally** *and* **Kai**.

Spectator 1 *jumps back in.*

Spectator 1   It's Ally and Kai!

A confused pause. Some of the **Spectators** *makes 'aw' sounds.*

Jess *and* **Andy** *secretly high ten.*

Spectator 1 *does a big sad face at* **Ally** *and* **Kai**.

Spectator 1   Aw, guys. Sad times.

Kai   Wait, what's happening?

Ally   We're the Most Loved Partners?

Spectator 1   No. The Least. *Least Loved.* Where do you think it all went wrong?

Ally   Um. What? Oh, I don't know. I don't know. I really liked him.

Kai   Yeah, me too.

Spectator 1 *can't resist an 'aw'.*

Spectator 1   Oh my God. Gutted.

Spectator 1 *yells up to some unseen overlords.*

Spectator 1   Can we have some gutted music please?

Gutted music plays.

So, Ally. You can be Out with Kai. Or you can save yourself. If you want to Partner with . . . whatever his name is.

Boy 3 (*quietly, forlornly*)   Joey.

Spectator 1   What are you going to do?

Ally *looks at* **Kai**.

Ally   Well. I choose Kai. Of course I choose Kai. I really like him. I like, *like* like him.

Kai   You do?

Ally   Yeah. I mean. I don't know what like liking is or anything but. Yeah. They say you know when you know don't you? So maybe I know.

A brief pause.

Ally (*shrugging*)   I dunno.

They hold each other's hands.

Kai   Me too. Me neither.

They smile at each other.

Spectator 1   Aw.

Spectator   Bless

Spectator   That's actually quite cute

They hold hands, looking at each other, happy, loving.

Spectator 1   Wow. That is commitment, isn't it.
I mean it's *so* nice in a way because you actually *know* now for sure that it's real.

Ally *and* **Kai**   Yeah.

Spectator 1   This relationship *is* real.

Ally *and* **Kai**   Yeah.

Spectator 1   Since you're Out anyway.

Ally *and* **Kai**   Yeah.

A brief pause.

Ally   Wait, what?

They are shot. They are Out. One by one, they hit the floor.

A pause.

Boy 3   Um –

He is shot. He is Out. He hits the floor.

A brief pause.

Spectator   Great!

Lights change. Their bodies are cleared away with brusque efficiency. Someone wipes down the floor where they were with blue roll.

During, **Sam F** *moves to the edge and knocks on the circle.*

Spectator 1 *jumps into the circle to talk to her.*

Sam F   If they *actually* loved each other, doesn't that defeat the point of this whole thing? Shouldn't they have won?

Spectator 1   Well, no, because. They were the worst at Love.

Sam F   But why?

Spectator 1 *thinks.*

Spectator 1   It was just too *easy* for Ally and Kai. There wasn't enough of a journey. To win at Love, you've got to be the best Partners.

Sam F   The best Partners.

Spectator 1   Yes, the best Partners.

Sam F   How do we do that? Are you just changing the rules as we go?

Spectator 1   Rules? There aren't any *rules*, hun. Love doesn't play by the rules.

Which leads us straight into –

Part Three: Be in love!

Spectator 1 *addresses the Lovers.*

Spectator 1   You've found a Partner. And you've fallen in Love, it's time for the biggest challenge of all. Being in Love.

General confusion from the Lovers.

Spectator 1   What will your Love look like? How will you keep it? How will you manage it, and take care of it? Time to find out. On your marks . . . get set . . .

All   GOOOOOO LOVE!

Andy *and* **Jess**. *Walking around an imaginary home.*

Andy   So this is where we'll put the fridge. And the new cupboards. And the oven –

Jess   We'll argue about whether we get a gas or fan-assisted –

Andy   This is where I'll make you try my bolognaise –

He does. She does. It is too hot. They laugh.

Jess   My mum will email you over that recipe you wanted –

Andy   Ah, love your mum –

Jess (*to herself*)   Mum will be so happy I've finally found someone . . .

Andy   We'll put the dining table here –

Jess   Yes!

They sit at it. They quickly talk through their lives –

Andy   This is where we'll argue –

Jess   About money –

Andy   About priorities –

Jess   About that woman at work –

Andy   About what to do about your dad now he's –

Jess   This is where you'll tell me I look beautiful even if I don't –

Andy   Where you'll tell me I look beautiful because you know I need to hear it –

Jess   This is where you'll hurt me. You'll hurt me here too. And here.

Andy   And me here, here. This is where you won't even mean to.

Jess   This is where I'll feel like I'm finally in my own home instead of just a visitor in it –

Andy   This is where I'll get the proof I needed –

Jess   This is where you'll never leave me even if you want to –

Andy   This is where I won't want to –

Andy   This is where the commitment will live –

Jess   Yes this is where the happiness will sit –

Andy   Yes this is where we'll look at it and polish it and own it –

Jess   This is where we'll take care of it –

Andy   Good. Thank you.

Jess   I feel better now. I can relax now.

They hold each other in their home. They try to relax.

Jacob *and* **Ella**. *Slow dancing. He talks covertly to the* **Spectators** *over her shoulder as they go round.*

Jacob   Hello? What do I do now? How do I keep my Partner?

Spectators *pop into the circle to offer advice –*

Spectator   Have you said I Love You yet?

Jacob   Yes!

Spectator   Great! Then you can relax.

Jacob   Well, *I've* said it. She's a bit resistant.

Spectator   Oh no. Then stop relaxing. Stop relaxing right now. You can't say that and not hear it back.

Spectator   Yeah that's really sad, mate

Spectator   You've just gotta get those words out of her. If you get her to say it, she might start to mean it.

Jacob   OK. OK. I will.

The **Spectators** *jump out of the circle.*

Spectator   Is that how it works?

Spectator (*shrugging*)   Dunno. Guess we're about to find out.

They watch.

Jacob   Can't you just tell me you love me?

Ella   Why?

Jacob   Because I told you I love you.

Ella   Is that the reason people tell each other that?

Jacob   I just need to hear it.

Ella   OK. Say I did love you. But telling you I love you all the time isn't part of the way I love. I struggle saying it. Would that be OK?

Jacob *thinks.*

Jacob   Can't you just say it?

Ella *thinks. She relents. She sees how much he needs it.*

Ella   OK. I Love you.

Jacob   Thank you.
Wasn't that easy?

Sam M *and* **Hayley**. **Hayley** *is quite enthusiastic.* **Sam M** *isn't.*

Hayley   What do you think our Being in Love will look like? Should we like. Pretend get a dog? Pretend go on holiday? We could pretend do anything!

Sam M   Why don't we just pretend slow down a bit and pretend have a conversation first.

Hayley   OK. What should we talk about?

Sam M   Can't we just. Pretend? Like. Pretend talk. Pretend joke. Pretend laugh. There you go. Look how much we're pretend nailing it.

Hayley   Don't you want to actually get to know me?

Sam M   Look. No offence, Hayley, I'm sure you're very nice.
    But I just want to get through this without getting Out.
    Feel like if we start getting to know each other, we're gonna find out we don't like each other, we'll start fighting, and then we'll *want* each other Out.

Hayley (*disappointed*)   D'you really think so?

Sam M   I said I would stay your Partner. So I will.
    Just. Don't make it hard for me.

Hayley *pauses. She is hurt.*

Hayley   OK. Sorry.

They pretend hold hands. Sad.

The **Spectators** *are watching intently.*

Spectator   OK, is anyone starting to quite like them?

Spectator   They do say honesty is the root of the best relationships.

Spectator   Yeah, I could totally watch them hate-love each other all day.

Spectator   I want more Max action. I love him. IWishICouldSpreadHimOnABagel.

Spectator   Bin Girl Sam though.

Spectator   Yeah Girl Sam is such a failed example of carbon she actually makes me want to never have kids.

Spectator (*turning around*)   Oh here she is, I'm already BORED.

Spectator (*turning around*)   BORED.

Sam F *and* **Max**. *Sitting. Silent.*

Max   Right, shall we have a go at a conversation again? I've thought of a question.

Sam F   It's taken you this long to think of a question?

Max   Sorry. This is all new for me!

Sam F   I feel like everyone else is a lot further along than we are. Ella and Jacob have said the L word, Jess and Andy have got a whole *life* laid out and we're still trying to string a conversation together?

Sam F *stands up and walks away.*

Max   I'm sorry, I just – you're quite intimidating!

He hangs his head in shame. Maybe starts exercising.

Sam M *breaks away from* **Hayley** *and meets* **Sam F** *in the centre of the circle.*

Sam M   You all right?

Sam F   Yeah, great, thanks. You?

They both resort to heavy sarcasm.

Sam M   Great. Totally great.

Sam F   Yeah, I'm really enjoying myself.

Sam M   Yeah, I'm literally so in love it's crazy.

Sam F   Yeah, I can't eat, sleep, think about anything other than him.

Sam M   I'm actually struggling to form sentences.

Sam F   Me too! I feel like I'm *high*.

Sam M   Oh yeahhh, my stomach and lungs and all vital organs are full of butterflies!

Sam F   Oh my God me too, and candy floss, and fairy dust, and fucking Taylor Swift songs.

Sam M   I feel like I could just burst into song at any moment!

They are both laughing now. They come to a stop.

Sam M   Wow. I haven't laughed in so long I'd actually forgotten what that was.

Sam F   Oh crap. Are people going to think something is 'happening' between us now.

Sam M   Inevitably.

Sam F   When did that happen? When did everything start meaning so much?

Sam M   I dunno.

Sam F   I thought Love was supposed to be fun. And maybe vaguely relaxing. I just feel more stressed than before.

Sam M   Ditto.

A brief pause.

Sam M *and* **Sam F**   Deeeep.

They laugh a little.

Sam F   I think we are definitely friends now.

He looks at her.

Sam M   I'd fucking love to be your friend, Girl Sam.

Sam F   Thanks, Boy Sam.

They hug, friends, laughing a little.

Spectator 1 *talks to another* **Spectator** *outside the circle.*

Spectator   What is going on there?

Spectator 1   Are they Partners?

Spectator   I think they're friends.

Spectator 1   That doesn't count. So they're potential Partners.

Spectator   What do you mean?

Spectator 1   They're a boy and a girl, right? They're –

Spectator   Yeah.

The other producer looks at them dumbly.

Spectator 1   Well, then.

Spectator 1 *places their hands on an imaginary surface in front. They push it forward.*

Spectator 1   Give them a little. Push.

By this point, all the Partners have started trying to ballroom dance together, with varying levels of success.

That **Spectator** *goes up behind* **Max**, *who is dancing generically on his own, and nudges him.*

Spectator   Hey, what's going on with Sam and Sam?

Max   What?

They point at **Sam** *and* **Sam**, *who are dancing together, laughing.*

Spectator   There.

Max   What do you mean?

Another **Spectator** *jumps into the circle.*

Spectator   She's making you look a mug, mate.

They pat **Max** *and pushes him forward.*

Spectator (*whispers into his ear*)   Also Jacob said you have little tiny boy legs.

Max *is immediately revved up. He is pushed towards* **Sam** *and* **Sam**.

The **Spectators** *retreats out of the circle and watch.*

Max   What do you think you're doing, dickhead?

Sam M *turns to* **Max**, *surprised.*

Sam M   What what where?

Max   With her.

Sam M   Sam?

Max   Watch your back, mate.

Sam M   Why?

Max   Wolf in snake's clothing, mate. Wolf. In snake's clothing.

He thinks about this.

Sam M   I think you'd – probably still be able to tell it was wolf if it was like, in a snake's –

Sam F   Are we not allowed to have a conversation?

Jess   No you're not allowed to do that.

Sam F   Why not?

Jess   I dunno, it's just really uncool of you.

Sam F   What kind of arbitrary morality is this?

Hayley   Why are you using the words 'arbitrary morality' – seriously, WHO DO YOU THINK YOU'RE TALKING TO?

Jacob   Whoah whoah whoah, what's going on here?

Ella   Wait, is Boy Sam partnering with Girl Sam now?

Sam F   We're just having a conversation! We're literally just friends. I have no interest in him like that!

Sam M *looks at her, a little forlorn.*

Hayley   I AM – NOT – GOING – OUT.

She points at **Sam M**, *hard.*

Hayley   YOU PROMISED.

Spectator 1   Time to light a match under it –

They run into the circle.

Spectator 1   ALL RIGHT ALL RIGHT ALL RIGHT.
It's time to swap Partners!

Sam F   What? Now?

Jacob   Why?

Max   Yeah, why?

Sam F   Why are you doing this now? I like my Partner! I don't want to have to do it all again. I'm exhausted, I'm *exhausted*. Partnering up is *exhausting*. I just want to stay with this one!

Spectator 1   But you want to be *sure* don't you?

Jess   Sure about what?

Spectator 1   That you really Love each other, of course? That you're a real, valid, real-life, proper, never going to break up, real life, shitting-with-the-door-open, fucking, couple.

A brief pause.

Spectator 1   This is all in your interests, isn't it? You know this is all for you, right?

Jess *thinks. She is a bit baffled.*

Jess   Yes.

Spectator 1   We're just looking out for you.

The **Spectators** *all nod. Some of the Lovers nod, convinced.*

We move straight into –

Part Four: The break-up/down

Everyone is in position for the Partner swap, a little panicked. Partner poses.

Spectator 1   Andy and Jess, do either of you want to swap Partners?

They both shake their heads. They look at each other, shaking their heads. They gasp in relief.

Andy (*true*)   Oh my God, I've never been so happy.

Jess (*true*)   Me too. I'm so glad I found you.

They high ten. **Hayley** *watches forlornly.*

Spectator 1   Ella and Jacob, do either of you want to –

Jacob   NO.

Ella   All right then – no.

He wraps his arm around **Ella**. *She receives it gratefully.*

Ella   Thank you.

Jacob   I love you.

Ella   Thank you. For doing that.

She kisses him on the cheek. **Hayley** *watches forlornly.*

Spectator 1   Sam and Max. Do either of you want a new Partner?

Max   No, we don't.

Sam F   Actually, I do. I want Sam to be my Partner.

The **Spectators** *outside cheer.* **Hayley** *gasps, holding onto* **Sam M**.

Spectator   FINALLY.

Spectator   I *knew* they were into each other.

Spectator   Ring the bells! Love is real!

All Spectators   SAM SQUARED SAM SQUARED SAM SQUARED –

Spectator 1   Wait. Are you saying you Love Sam?

Sam F   I'm saying – We're friends. And I'd much rather be partnered with a friend than –

Spectator   Um, that's not allowed.

Spectator (*referring to* **Sam M**)   Nooo, he's been friendzoned! Look at his sad little friendzoned face

Spectator 1   You can't be Partners with someone unless you Love them. Do you Love him?

Sam M *tries not to be too interested in her answer.*

Sam F *is aggravated, unsure what to say.*

Sam F   He's my friend! Is that not enough?

Sam M *is secretly hurt.*

Jess   No. This is *Love.* This is serious. This is the stuff you build a life on. So – do you?

Max *jumps in –*

Max   Wait, Sam. Please. Don't send me Out.

Sam F   You'll be fine. As you've told me, several times, all the girls will be lining up to be your Partner.

Max   But I don't want to try to Love them. I want to try to Love *you.*

Sam F (*sarcastic*)   Wow, I'm convinced.

Max   Look can we just have, like, ten seconds alone, to talk?

Spectator 1 (*sympathetic*)   Aw.

A brief pause.

Spectator 1   Nope!

Max   Fine. If we can't do this in private then –

He takes a deep breath.

Max   I know it's like. Mental or whatever for me to say this, and we haven't known each other that long, and there are so many girls here who are so much more attractive than you but – *sorry* – old habit – listen you've sort of. Got in my head a bit. I think I like you. Like. I don't know what's going on. Like in my body. Like I have no idea what the fuck is going on in my body.

Sam F   Are you serious?

Max   Would I say that lame shit if I didn't mean it? Sorry. Again. I'm trying to stop being a dickhead and start being a little nerd boy like you – *sorry* – I am sorry – I'm trying. Please. Just give me a chance. Just don't send me Out yet.

Sam F *is totally torn. She struggles.*

Sam M   It's OK, Sam, hey, you don't owe me anything. We're here to find Love. You've got to put that first.

Hayley *scowls. They are still linking arms.*

Sam F   I don't know what I'm supposed to do.

Spectator 1 *steps in –*

Spectator 1 (*strong*)   Boy Sam, what about you in all this? Do you want to swap Partners?

Sam M   No.

Spectator 1   And Hayley?

Hayley   Yes.

A gasp from the Lovers. They are outraged, terrified. **Sam F** *steps forward, instinctively, protectively, towards* **Sam M**.

The Spectators erupt –

Spectator   THANK THE SWEET BABY JESUS FOR THAT.

Spectator   FINALLY, SOME ACTION.

Spectator   THANK YOU, HAYLEY

Spectator   I WAS ABOUT TO GO OUTSIDE OR SOMETHING.

Sam M   Hayley? What are you doing?

Hayley   What did you expect, Sam?
    I'm just doing it to you before you do it to me.

Sam M   You don't know I was gonna do that.

Hayley   Weren't you?

Sam M *doesn't say anything.*

Hayley   Right. So. I'm supposed to just . . . let you?

Sam M *doesn't say anything.*

Hayley   Exactly. I'm not gonna be left on a sinking ship when the violins are playing. I'm getting in a frigging lifeboat.

Sam M *looks at the ground.*

Hayley   Sorry, Sam. Love youuu.
   But crucially, I don't.

She looks around at the other boys.

Hayley   I want to Partner with . . .

Spectator   Lock up your sons, huns. Hayley's on the manpage.

Hayley   . . . Andy. I think he needs it the most.

Jess   NO!

Andy   What?

Jess *clutches him tighter.*

Jess   No. You can't leave me.

Spectator   Ooh, she's gonna push him away if she squeezes too hard

Andy   I didn't say I was leaving you!

Jess   You're thinking about it though, aren't you?

Spectator   He's THINKING ABOUT IT.

Spectator   What a snake.

Spectator   Capital F Fuckboy.

Jacob (*to* **Ella**)   I'd *never* do that to you.

Andy   I'm not *doing* anything! I don't want to be her Partner!

Jacob   Never in a million years would I –

Hayley   Actually actually I choose Jacob.

Another gasp from everyone.

Spectator   Oh my God this is heterosexual carnage.

*Everyone stares at **Jacob**.*

He looks around, a little lost.

Jacob   Who, me?

He pauses.

Really?

Sam F   Why are you doing this, Hayley?

Hayley   I have my reasons. I don't judge your shit decisions.

Sam F   Yes – you do!

Hayley   Come on, poppet.

Jacob *tentatively walks across the circle to* **Hayley**. **Ella** *is weirdly calm; she always expected this.*

Jacob   Do I just stand next to Hayley, then?

Ella   Well, this is about the most unoriginal thing that's ever happened.

Jacob   She picked me. It wasn't my idea!

Hayley   Pretty easy trade though, wasn't it, Jacob?

Ella (*laughing, given up*)   Give it a rest, Hayley. The war's over.

Jacob (*to Ella*)   In my defence. You *weren't* very affectionate. I don't mean to be a prick, but. Kind of feel like you brought this on yourself?

Hayley   Yeah. Sad times.

Ella   Piss *off*, Hayley!

Jacob   Oh my God. Have I got two girls fighting over me?

Ella   Wow.

Jacob   Wait –

He rubs his armpits.

Jacob   Bone dry.
Am I, like, cured?

He puts his arm round **Hayley**.

Jacob   Is this what being a stud feels like?
Why did no one tell me this earlier? Just be a prick and the girls come running. Am I right, Max?

Max   What?

Jacob   Can you girls maybe fight a bit more? Like. Fight fight fight?

Hayley *is looking at* **Jacob**, *disturbed.*

Hayley   Actually, actually, I want Sam again.

Jacob   Shit.

She immediately unhands herself from under **Jacob**'s *arm.*

Hayley (*to* **Sam M**)   You coming back to me, boo?

Sam M   Well, I haven't got much of a fucking choice have I?

He trudges back to **Hayley**.

Hayley   Aw.

She does a heart pose with her hands.

Jacob *runs back to* **Ella***, arms wide.*

Jacob   Ella! I can be with you again! Yay!

Ella   Yay!

She opens her arms. Then smacks him in the face.

Jacob   Shit!
Come on. You've got to forgive me.

Ella   No, I don't.

Jacob   Well, I don't mean to be a prick but –

Ella   Yeah, just saying you don't mean to be a prick doesn't automatically save you from sounding like a massive –

Jacob   Well. I'm the only prick you've got. Beggars can't be choosers.

Jess   Wow. New Jacob really *is* a prick.

Spectator   Is anyone else weirdly attracted to him now?

Spectator   Ssh! Magic is happening!

Ella   I'm definitely not choosing you.

Jacob   What are you gonna do then? Do any of you want her?

No one answers. **Ella** *is quite calm.*

Ella   No. I'm choosing no one. I'm choosing to be done.

Jacob   You can't.

Ella   I suspected this wasn't for me and it's not. I don't believe in it. I don't believe in any of this. (*She gestures to the circle.*)

The ground shakes a very small amount. Everyone stumbles very slightly.

Andy   What was that?

Spectator 1   Wait –

Jacob   She's bluffing

Spectator 1   Wait, don't –

Ella   I'd rather be Out. So I am.

Jacob   What?

Ella *is shot. She is Out. She falls to the floor.*

Jacob *stares in horror.* **Sam F** *shrieks.* **Hayley** *covers her face.*

Spectator 1   Shit.

Jacob *desperately looks around the circle.*

Jacob   No. No, wait.

He appeals to his fellow Lovers.

Jacob   Someone.
Someone – love me. Please. Someone just love me. Someone. Love me. I tried so
hard! I did what everyone said! I did what I thought everyone wanted! Someone's got
to love me. SOMEONE. SOMEONE. SOMEONE'S GOT TO LOVE ME!

Jacob *is shot. He's Out. He falls to the floor.*

A stunned silence.

Everyone turns to **Spectator 1**, *who is staring at the space where* **Jacob**'*s living head
used to be.*

Jess (*quietly*)   What do we do now?

After a moment, the **Spectator** *remembers where they are –*

Spectator 1 (*dazed*)   Sorry – I just completely, briefly, forgot where I was or what I
was doing or why then. Just very briefly, I was a little tiny bird, flying high above this
moment, you were all so small, and I was so far away, and the wind was whipping
around my little arms, my feathers, and the rain was wetting my little tiny bird face,
and I was going somewhere else, somewhere far away, somewhere where I could be
alone. And sleep.

A pause as everyone stares at them as they stand, staring blankly into space.

Spectator 1 *suddenly lies on the floor, spent.*

No one immediately knows what to do.

Sam F   Oh my God, we have to get out of here.

She starts banging on the circle.

Spectator   Is anyone just starting to find this a bit – depressing?

Spectator   Yeah.

Spectator   I just wanted to believe in Love. This just makes me want to see other
people.

The **Spectators** *one by one start to turn around.*

The ground shakes a little. Everyone stumbles about a bit.

Andy   Serious, what was that?

Sam F *has a brainwave.*

Sam F   Guys. I've got it. I know my answer. Someone ask me the question. I know who I want to Partner with.

Sam M   You do?

Andy   Why are you still playing?

Jess   Are we still playing?

Hayley   Of course we're still playing. We have to keep playing!

Sam F   I don't care about the game. I don't care what happens to me. Just – someone – ask me the question.

No one does.

Sam F   Fine. 'Do you want to swap Partners?'
Yes!
I want to Partner with Sam.

Sam M (*delighted*)   Really?

Hayley   Fucking knew it.

Jess   Well, duh.

Sam F   No! Me. Girl Sam.
I want to Partner with – myself.

Sam M   Wait, what?

An earthquake hits. Everyone falls on the floor, starts to get up again in confusion as –

Hayley   What happened there?

Sam F *runs to the edge of the circle. She puts her hand through.*

Jess   Whooooooahhh.

Andy   Is it like – broken?

Sam F   Are we free?

Jess goes to touch it, but recoils instinctively.

Jess   I'm scared.

Hayley   No! We have to keep playing. What happens now?

She runs over to **Spectator 1** *who is still lying on the floor.*

Hayley   WHAT HAPPENS NOW?

The **Spectator** *rolls over, uninterested.*

She frantically assembles everyone into their Partners whilst she says –

Hayley   We have to keep playing. We have to keep playing. Someone can still win this. Go Love! Go Love! Goooo Love!

Sam F   Hayley, you can't win. It's over.

Hayley   Yes I know I can't win alone. I need a Partner.

Sam F   It's OVER.

Hayley   Can't win without a Partner. That's insane. No one on their own is winning, let's face it. I'd like to Partner with – MAX.

Sam F   What?

Max   *What?*

She grabs **Max** *and starts assembling herself and him into a Partner pose.*

He is shocked, but lets her.

Sam F   What are you doing?

Max (*suddenly bold, bitter*)   Fine. Yeah. I'm partnering with Hayley. To be honest this was my plan all along. Of course it was my plan all along. I didn't want to be your partner, Sam. We're obviously the winners. Look at us.

Hayley   Aw!

Hayley *and* **Max** *stand together.* **Max** *stares bitterly at* **Sam F** *and* **Sam M***.*

Hayley   We look good together, don't we?

Sam M *suddenly runs in front of* **Sam F** *in a wild panic.*

Sam M *runs in front of* **Sam F***, a human shield, yelling at the unseen overlords.*

Sam M   No. Don't hurt Sam! Don't! Take me instead!

Sam F   Hey, it's OK!

Sam M   No, look, I'm so sorry – I know this isn't Love and I'm not allowed to do Big Gestures but, fuck it, I'm doing my Gesture – and it's fucking Big.

Sam M *addresses the overlords, and us.*

Sam M   DID YOU HEAR THAT?
I DON'T CARE IF WE'RE NOT PARTNERS.
I DON'T CARE IF SHE DOESN'T LOVE ME.
BECAUSE I THINK I LOVE HER.
AND YOU CAN'T BE OUT IF YOU ARE LOVED.
AND *I* LOVE HER.
I ACTUALLY PROPERLY OH SHIT THIS FEELS A BIT LIKE I'M RUNNING
INTO A WALL AT SPEED AND MAYBE I LIKE IT *LOVE HER*

Sam F   Sam, no –

He looks at her.

Sam M   I don't care if you just want to be friends and if that's all you want then I am happy to be your friend. I would *love* to be your friend, Sam.
This is me. Being your friend.

He holds his arms out, eyes squeezed shut. Ready.

TAKE ME!

Nothing happens.

He opens one eye, then the other.

Sam M   Wait? What's happening? Why is nothing – happening?

Sam F   I think. We broke it.

She easily steps over the line. **Sam M** *winces, but there's no need. She is safe. She jumps over and back over the line a few times, demonstrating.*

Sam M   Oh shit.

Hayley   That's quite embarrassing, hun. Like I don't think you had to do all that.

Max   Yeah, mate. Tone it down a notch.

Sam M *is ashamed. He can't quite look at* **Sam F.**

Sam F *is staring at him. Unsure what to say.*

The **Spectators** *are starting to turn round, back into the circle.*

Spectator   Oh my God. Did anyone see that?

Spectator   I know. That's like the most romantic thing I've ever seen.

Spectator   For God's sake. Why won't someone do that for me?

Spectator   Yeah, I just want someone to voluntarily risk their life for me with absolutely no guarantee of reciprocated feelings. Why can't I find that?

Jess *is still staring at the precipice of the circle, willing herself to step over it.*

Jess   We can leave?

Andy   Jess? What are you doing?

Everyone turns to look at them.

Jess   We can just. Leave?

Sam F   Yeah.

Andy *goes over to her, worried. Everyone watches.*

Andy   Jess, don't leave. We don't know what happens if we leave.

Jess   I know.

Andy   If we leave. Then. What happens to us?
Things might get difficult. Life might pull us apart.

Jess   Yeah.

Andy   We might end up alone.

Jess   Yeah.

Andy   At least if we stay here, we know neither of us will end up without a Partner. Ever.

Jess   Yeah.

He takes her hand in his.

Andy   Let's stay. It's much safer.

Suddenly, **Jess** *steps over the line on her own. Hand still in his. He cries out in agony.*

Andy   No!

She looks back at him.

Jess   Maybe we should be brave.

Andy   I'm not brave enough to be brave.

He takes his hand away.

Jess   Maybe we don't know what the future for us is. Maybe that's OK.

Andy   You said you'd be with me forever.

Jess   Yeah. I *said* that. Was probably quite irresponsible of me. Since I've got no idea what forever looks like.

Andy   Are you breaking up with me?

Jess   No!

Andy   Are you future-breaking up with me?

Jess   Well, we might break up! One day! We might not!

Andy   I can't handle the uncertainty.

Jess   I love you, *now*. I'm your Partner, *now*. That's what I'm saying. Now. We've planned out our whole lives in here. Maybe we should go out and – live them instead.

She holds out her hand.

Jess   Come on. Be my Partner.

He takes it, and steps over the line.

They slowly, hand in hand, walk off stage.

Andy   I'm terrified.

Jess   Me too. Cool, isn't it?

They are gone.

Hayley   Right so, we *must* win now.

Sam F   Fuck's sake, Hayley! Who cares! We're going! I'm going.

She start to leave. **Sam M** *is heartbroken.*

Sam M   Sam.

Are you going to leave me hanging? Again?

She turns back to him.

Sam F   Sam.

She thinks. She isn't sure.

Sam F   Come with me.

Sam M   Just tell me. Just tell me how you feel. I need to know.

Sam F   Come with me.

Sam M   I can take it. Whatever you decide, I'll accept it. Just, please, tell me how you feel.

Now the circle wall is broken, The **Spectators** *move into it and around* **Sam F** *and* **Sam M** *as they wish.*

Spectator   God. He's not giving up is he?

Spectator   *This* is the dedication we've been waiting for!

Spectator   *This* is like. *Love*. Isn't it.

Spectator   Proper love. Proper I will embarrass myself several times in a row just because I need to tell you how I feel Love.

Sam M   Thanks, guys

Spectator   Even if it's *really* embarrassing

Sam M   Yep, thank you.

Spectator   What's she gonna do?

Sam F   Um.

Spectator   She can't reject him now

Spectator   No, sorry, if she does then I'll lose all respect for her.

Sam F   I, um –

Spectator   Come on. Tell him you love him back. Tell him. Tell him. It'll be sooo perfect –

Sam F   Wow, it's really distracting with everyone, um –

Max   Fuck's sake do you Love him, Sam?

Sam F   I.

I mean I *like* him, I want to hang out with him, I am reasonably invested in the idea of him not dying, yes I'm pretty on board with the idea of him staying alive, I want him to be happy and, like, have a good time, like, most of the time, I want him to be healthy and fulfilled and have, like, thirty minutes of laughter a day and pudding, if he wants pudding, and, like, all the vitamins he needs and, like, a good mattress to sleep on and, like, the use of all his limbs, and, y'know for all his dreams to come true and shit. Yeah. Like. That.

So what does that mean. Does that mean I . . .

Spectator (*to the overlords*) Can we help her along, please?

Some romantic music begins to play. Lighting dips, perhaps.

Everyone watches with bated breath. Even **Spectator 1** *sits up and watches.*

Sam F OK. Yeah. I love him. I . . . love you, Boy Sam.

They come together and hold hands. **Sam F** *is still a bit bamboozled but she does her best to cover it.*

Sam M I love you, Girl Sam.

They hug.

Everyone left cheers (apart from **Max** *and* **Hayley***, who are privately furious).*

He whispers to her.

Sam M (*whispering*) That was so good. You nailed it.

Sam F (*confused, not hearing*) What?

Spectator 1 *gets up, suddenly enlivened.*

Spectator 1 Guys. I dunno about you but . . . Go Love?

Everyone except **Sam F** *cheers –*

All GOOOO LOVE!

Spectator 1 *fist pumps the air.*

Spectator 1 We are *back*, people! Love really *does* conquer all!

The **Spectators** *excitedly return to their places outside the circle, watching.* **Max** *and* **Hayley** *assemble in their Partner pose, very easily slipping into each other's arms.*

Spectator Oh my God this is so exciting

Spectator HELLA INVESTED OVER HERE.

Sam F Wait, we can still get out, right?

Sam F *tries the edge of the circle. It's still broken. Everyone's just happily pretending –*

Spectator 1 (*jolly*) We'll all still play along if you will! Go Love!

All GOOO LOVE!

Sam F *starts to pull* **Sam M** *out of the circle by his hand.*

Sam F (*excited*) Sam! We can still get out! Let's go!

He tugs her back.

Sam M   Why would you want to be Out, now?

Spectator 1   Sorry, what was that? Go Love?

All   GOOOO LOVE!

Sam F   Come on! We can go and live our lives! We don't need this any more!

Sam M   Yeah I know, but.
(*Covertly*) We could still win this.

Sam F (*disbelief*)   What?

Sam M   Come on. If we stay. We'll definitely win.

Spectator 1   Go Love?

All   GOOOO LOVE!

He starts assembling a horrified **Sam F** *into a Partner pose with him.*

Sam F   I don't care if we / win

Sam M (*covertly, smiling*)   Shh. They love us. Our Love is about to, like, *win* at love.

Sam F   But –

Sam M   Shh. Come on. Don't lose this for us.

She looks at **Sam M**, *horrified.*

Spectator   There *is* hope for all of us.

Spectator   I *knew* Love would conquer all.

Spectator (*one hand, the other, together*)   Humanity, Faith, restored.

Hayley (*to* **Max**)   Smile for God's sake. We can still win this.

Max (*smiling*)   We've lost. I've lost.

Spectator 1   I think we all know who's won at love. But since we're still playing –

Spectator   Sam Squared. Best winners ever.

Spectator   SOULMATES.

Sam M   Come on. Smile. They're choosing the winners.

Spectator 1   I guess I *have* to ask the question. Does anyone want to swap Partners?

Sam F   Um –

Sam M (*hard*)   You said you loved me.

Sam F *is taken aback.*

Spectator 1   Right, in that case –

Sam F   Actually –

Sam M   Don't you?

She looks at him.

Sam F   Not like this.

She steps forward.

I do.

Spectator 1   What?

Sam M   Sam –

Sam F   I want to swap Partners.

Gasps from the **Spectators**.

Spectator   Wait, what's happening?

Sam M *steps forward, alone.*

Sam M   No, *I* want to swap Partners.

Spectator   No! Go Love! Go Love?

Sam F   I don't want a Partner. I quit. I am Out.

She is shot. She is Out. She falls to the floor.

Sam M   No!

Max   NO!

Hayley *holds* **Max** *upright, to stop him falling to the floor in grief and agony.*

A brief pause.

Sam M   Wait, what happens to –

She is shot. He is Out. He falls to the floor.

A stunned silence.

The **Spectators** *cover their faces, fall to their knees, turn away. They can't watch.*

The **Spectators** *and* **Spectator 1** *start to leave, or turn away, during the next.*

Hayley *starts tapping* **Max**, *who has covered his face, devastated.*

Hayley   Max, Max. Look. We're the last ones left.

Max   What?

He looks around. She is breathless.

Hayley   I think we won. Oh my God, we've won.

Max *steels himself. Rubs his face. Pumps a fist.*

Hayley   Oh my God!

Hayley *starts jumping up and down, clapping.*

Max (*to himself*)   I knew I'd win. I knew I'd win.

Hayley   We won! We won! Go Love! Go Love!

They are alone on stage.

Hayley *and* **Max**   GOOOO LOVE!

Lights fall, immediately.

End of play.

Find a Partner!

BY MIRIAM BATTYE

Notes on rehearsal and staging, drawn from a workshop with the writer,
held at the National Theatre, October 2021

How the writer came to write the play

Miriam Battye:

> When we go on apps, we are asked to define the kind of person we are and it gives us a power to package ourselves as these romantic creatures. You build yourself – and I think this is fascinating.
>
> Young people have been given this mammoth task – go and find somebody who you'll spend your life with. The play is the opportunity to think and talk about this.
>
> I love reality TV – and I hate it too. These shows create an arbitrary morality where viewers can have lofty opinions – 'Oh they shouldn't have done that! Oh that's absolutely appalling!' – but I don't think we stop to think about why we're interrogating these things. They come from a set of rules that are within us and I wanted to explore those and consider what we deem to be acceptable behaviour in people who are in the pursuit of love. It was the chance to ask some questions about that.
>
> The gesture of the play is a metaphor but it all links back to the pursuit of love.

Approaching the play

Lead director Matt Harrison set up some initial exercises that encouraged everyone to dig into their instincts. He said that we can sometimes get lost in over-analysing a play and actually trusting our initial instincts can reveal a lot to us. These instincts can be used to light a fire under why we need to tell this story.

Miriam Battye and Matt Harrison highlighted the need to find moments of joy in the text. There is a lot of satire and brutal moments, but a reminder to find the lightness within this too. The more joy there is, the more the brutality will leap out as it has something to be offset against.

The hearts of the piece

Matt Harrison explained the concept that each piece of theatre has three hearts:

The Personal Heart – this is the company and creative team's investment – what is it about the play that they want to delve into?

The Social Heart – this is the political heart of the play and how it speaks to society right now.

The Global Heart – this is how the play connects to bigger issues that are
   happening on a wider scale.

There is no correct answer to these, but are a way to focus on what feels right for the
company at that point in time. What do you want to say with this play?

Miriam Battye reminded the group to unlock what the young people want to explore
too ensuring the work isn't solely director led.

Conversations around the hearts of the piece can open up personal content as
individuals relate the work back to their own experiences, so ensuring this exercise is
safely held in the space is very important.

Once you have identified what the three hearts might be for your production, you
can then look at where these appear in the piece. Matt Harrison suggested identifying
one heart that you want to beat the strongest. This would then be an area you can focus
on in rehearsal and is a great way to align everyone's point of view and will inform how
all elements of the production are shaped (including performances and design elements).

Some suggestions of hearts that came through from the group:

- Public behaviour
- The #BeKind movement
- The desire for fame/to be an influencer – what does this mean for a young
  person today?
- Seeking validation
- Online activity – the things people feel they can say to each when it is digital
- Ownership over actions and words
- Judgements – snap judgements – glorifying people or destroying people – there
  is no nuance online
- Validating your own existence by pitying others
- Young people being told, from all angles, about the desire for being in a couple
  is the epitome of success – we aren't encouraged to think about the security that
  could come from being by ourselves
- Desensitisation to violence
- The fear of dying alone and how this connects to a greater sense of humanity
- Questioning the ideals of coupledom as the ultimate success
- How do we find our happiness?

The group discussed how reality TV shows have established a set of expectations for
young people about their body image and expected codes of behaviour, and reaffirms
the idea of fame and celebrity wealth as the ultimate aspiration. They felt that these
were essential elements that run through the play.

The whys

Matt Harrison encouraged the group to consider using these questions as another way
to explore a company's approach to the material.

Why now? (Why does this point in time lend itself to staging this play?)

Why me? (What can you, as a director or maker, bring to a staging of this play?)

Why this group? (How do the company of young people performing the play enrichen your version of the play?)

Why your space or audience? (How does the configuration of your performance venue create possibilities for your production? How will your audience relate to this play? What will it reflect back to them or introduce them to?)

Similarly to the hearts of the piece, there is no one set anwer. These are provocations to dig further into a staging of the play and ensure the process stays active.

The world of the play

Miriam Battye and Matt Harrison described the play as a world with its own rules – it looks similar to ours but it isn't ours. It is heightened but the root of emotions is truthful and authentic. Truth doesn't need to mean naturalism.

A member of the group described it as 'if *Black Mirror* did *Love Island*'.
Some key threads to this world are are:

- Reality TV, with particular influence drawn from *Love Island*
- Two realities co-exist – in the circle and out of the circle
- Power, status and individual value are hugely important in this world
- The Spectators can also become part of the game themselves
- Love
- Personal image
- Insecurity
- This world is has many elements that are like ours
- Trolls hold power and agency
- If you're a Spectator on the outside of the circle, you can influence what happens within it
- People are disposable for the purpose of entertainment
- TV producers are seen as puppet masters and controllers

What are the rules of the world that help us to understand it?

Matt Harrison suggested exploring this question with a company as a way to establish the similarities and differences to our own world.

For example: In this world you can watch couples on a dating show on TV but, in this world, they can also be shot and obliterated if they are unsuccessful on the show. Both of these things are factual in *Find a Partner!*

Themes

Miriam Battye commented that 'the whole play is about the pursuit of love and I hope the play is the opportunity for young people to engage in the discussion about what has been laid out for them by social expectation, media and entertainment. It is an opportunity for young people to ask questions about this.'

The group identified some of the key themes as:

- Love – the pursuit of love and what is the cost of being open to others
- Love as commodity and entertainment
- The pain and hope of love
- Reality TV and its influence on audiences
- Pack mentality
- The desire for celebrity status
- What does it mean to be an influencer?
- Power
- Control
- Societal expectations on young people
- Vulnerability
- Violence – and the desensitisation to this
- Trolls and living an online life
- Public influence
- Brutality as entertainment
- Judging others to make ourselves feel better
- Relationships
- Sex and attraction
- Body image and individual image
- Self-esteem
- Friendship
- How we package ourselves and present ourselves to the world

Structure, style and transitions

Miriam Battye discussed how 'the gesture of the play is a metaphor – but there is nothing left unsaid. All the meaning is woven into the play, rather than being buried in subtext. So the presentation of the play can engage in theatricality, but the things that people say mean what they mean.'

Structure and time

There are different time structures that can be applied to a play:

OPEN TIME – the action leaps forwards and shows different blocks of time but they remain in chronological order (eg. Scene One – 10 a.m. on Wednesday, Scene Two – 3 p.m. on Thursday)

CLOSED TIME – the action plays out in real time (e.g. starts at 10 a.m. on Wednesday and ends at 10.55 a.m. on Wednesday)

OPEN PLACE – the action takes place in different locations and spaces (e.g. Scene One – by the river, Scene Two – in the house)

CLOSED PLACE – the action remains in the same location/space for the whole play (e.g. every scene is in the living room)

These can then be bolted together to create different structures as listed below:

1 *Open Time/Closed Place* (e.g. time moves forwards in bursts but all the action is in the same setting)

2 *Open Time/Open Place* (e.g. time moves forwards in bursts and the action moves between locations)

3 *Closed Time/Open Place* (e.g. the action plays out in real time but changes location)

4 *Closed Time/Closed Place* (e.g. the action plays out in real time and remains in the same locations)

Time scale in relation to *Find a Partner!* can be decided by each company. Miriam Battye described how she imagined each new part to be like a new episode of the show but the company could decide if they were episodes across a week, a few weeks or months.

Some key points on structure, style and transitions

- The play starts and ends with Hayley – she is a loop throughout but she should feel different and changed by the end of the play.

- There is a finality in this world – when you're shot, you're out of the game and can't come back. Performers can come back to play different characters but they must feel different so there is no confusion over who they are.

- The deaths are literal deaths and the stakes couldn't be any higher.

- The moment of the earthquake is when the world starts to break down.

- There should be a seamless flow between the world of the game and the Spectators, with the action flowing between the two spaces.

- The play is theatrical – embrace this. The emotions can feel big and charged. At times where characters feel like archetypes, draw from this and don't be afraid to lean into it. We recognise these people from reality TV shows, so use these points of reference.

Language

Across the day, there was a lot of discussion around the rhythm of the text. Miriam Battye explained that:

The whole play is written with intent – some lines are deliberately inelegant (e.g. '**Jacob** I really like girls and I want one I want one I want one in my tum?') to reveal things about the character. When I talk about rhythm it isn't that everything is very eloquent and all the lines slink together, it is sometimes that some characters say shockingly shit things, but that is deliberate. Sometimes that means lines should be spluttered and make other characters react. I know every corner of the text and it should deliver beats – sometimes this means a double bounce on the trampoline rather than a clean land.'

Matt Harrison reminded the group to 'Trust the text – it's written to be hit at. To use the punctuation and the rhythm. It's written for young people to engage with. The rhythm of the text will lead to the unlocking of emotion.'

Miriam Battye also said that: 'The play is never doing anything other than what it is doing – there are no deeper hidden meanings – my hope is that everything you need is there in the text.'

There was a discussion about 'Go Love!' as a phrase that is used many times in the play. Miriam noted that 'It must be punchy! It is driven. I'd say really go for it. Use the repetition.'

Characters and characterisation

Matt Harrison referenced a quote from writer and director Ken Campbell that character is choices made by a person under pressure. The function of rehearsals then becomes understanding the choices characters make and why they make them.

The group was asked to note their initial responses to the characters:

Hayley – The typical *Love Island* character – dominant but vulnerable

Max – The Stud – self-centred and allegiances are easily turned

Sam M – The Heartbreaker

Sam F – The Truth Seeker

Joey – The Nice Guy

Jess and Andy – High tension – they have a need to create tension even though it wasn't naturally there

Kai and Ally – The possibility of hope – then everything changes when they are shot dead

The *Spectators* are:

- Narrators
- Voters
- Captors
- Producing team
- Cheerleaders
- Decision makers
- Anonymous
- The public
- Fans

- Want to be entertained by people's misery?
- A Chorus
- Easily bored

It is important to feel the difference between the world of the game and the world of the Spectators. Each company has the flexibility to realise the two worlds in whatever way feels appropriate but the distinction between the two worlds is very important.

Miriam Battye suggested that, 'The Spectators are the people who have yet to dare – they aren't brave enough to be able to do what the people in the game are doing yet they are happy to judge them. They hold lots of power but have different motivations. Each Spectator should feel distinct – but it's up to each company how they appear – they could be in a bedroom or they could be existing in a nether space, united by watching the game.'

Some key considerations/questions for characters

- The play contains a set of people watching a set of people – and both these sets of people are being watched by an audience. What is the relationship between an audience watching an audience – what is the bridge here?

- Archetypes – how to use these and lean into them – what do these do for us as an audience? How can they be used as short form to understand who a person is?

- Why are people in the game? Is it to find love? Is it to make money? How is this different for each person?

Casting

From the group, cast sizes ranged from ten performers to 60 performers. With this in mind, the opportunity for role sharing was discussed, with multiple performers playing the same character.

Miriam Battye said that this is possible as long as it is clear who is playing who and there is clarity that the same character is represented by multiple performers. The audience must understand that it is the same character rather than lots of different characters with similar traits.

Matt Harrison encouraged companies to find the rationale behind the choice to role share, beyond it being a functional necessity. How can role sharing enrich the production and design? Does it give the opportunity for more ensemble of physical work too?

Characters who are shot could join the Spectators, as long as it is clear that they are a new character.

Production, staging and design

What are the core considerations for design?

- A boundary in the world – described in the stage directions as a circle
- Two sides of a line

- A sense that you are either in or out of a space – there are defined areas
- A line you can't cross, which then somehow breaks
- Simplicity to allow the company and the characters to be the focus – the piece is first and foremost ensemble led

Matt Harrison discussed what he might talk to a designer about:

- How do we represent the circle? Chalk? String? Or something more concrete and bold?
- How do we define the difference between both spaces?
- What is inside the circle? Is it full of paraphernalia, like being in the *Love Island* villa? Or is it sparse?
- Are microphones used to amplify the voices of the Spectators and to give them more authority?
- Few objects are mentioned, so any objects that come in are like totems – they carry meaning so should be chosen with care
- Outside the space, where are the Spectators? Do we see them in their environments or do we see them in a more limbo space that isn't concrete?
- Are the Spectators alive and present throughout? Or do they appear and disappear?
- What is the difference in textures on each side of the line?

Miriam Battye reminded us that the space is exciting and theatrical. It isn't domestic, so productions should lean into that.

Playing with scale in design can be interesting and consideration should be given to which parts of design are realised and which elements are left to the audience's imagination.

A further suggestion is to avoid using phones in the play, as they can suck the focus into something that isn't connected to the audience, and make characters disconnect and talk downwards.

Costume:

- Do you use this to link people together? Do the Players all wear a certain colour? Or do the Spectators all look homogeneous? Or is everyone more varied and unique?

The gunshot:

- In the text, the gunshot isn't seen – we don't see where it is fired from.
- This is a threat that lingers above – it is unseen and not embodied – it is a bigger power whose origin is unseen. We shouldn't see someone firing a firearm as it is dehumanised.

Sound and music:

- This is open and up for grabs. This can be built with the group. How does the sound you choose set the tone for the world of the play?

Exercise: Walking gallery

Matt Harrison asked everyone to find an image that they thought connected to the play in some way.

The group then moved through the space in a 'walking gallery' presenting their image and absorbing the other offers as a way to spark debate about the world and feel of the play.

Exercise: Building the play

Five provocations were offered, and everyone was asked to add thoughts to each one. These were:

Images

- add an image you like from the walking gallery

I love the moment when . . . .

- add a memory of the show as if you've already made it with total blue-sky thinking – e.g. when the glitter cannon explodes, everyone dances to 'Don't Start Now' by Dua Lipa, flower petals are used to represent the blood

The space feels like . . .

- how do you want the space to feel to your audience when they come in – e.g. a playground, a terrible first date

The show is like . . .

- a tactile way to describe the play – e.g. it is like *Love Island* meets *Black Mirror*.

The project under the play . . .

- this might be an intention the company have for the audience after they have watched the play – e.g. to consider the relationships in their life, to call someone they love when they go home.

This exercise can be done with each company and the thoughts documented then become a stocktake of all the possibilities of the play and a way to begin to distill what your production will look/sound/feel like.

Exercises for use in rehearsals

Intro exercises

CHECK-IN – Everyone was asked to share their name, how they were feeling and something they were proud of from the last twenty-four hours.

Matt Harrison talked about the importance of taking the time to check in with everyone at the start of each rehearsal to find out how they are but to also allow each person to have their voice heard in the space.

Questions can be changed to help set the tone for the session too.

USING MUSIC – Using music throughout a rehearsal to shift the atmosphere of the space; e.g. using upbeat music when wanting to bring energy, calmer music when wanting a group to find focus.

GROUNDING – Matt Harrison asked everyone to lie down and talked the group through a focus exercise and gentle warm-up where he invited everyone to imagine they were butter melting in a warming pan. This included communal breathing with the group, using the breath to imagine lifting the ceiling on the room before mobilising their bodies and stretching.

ENERGISER – FILL THE SPACE – The group was asked to move through the room, balancing the space. Matt Harrison counted down from five to zero by which time the group had to have filled as much of the space as possible using their bodies, levels and dance moves.

ENERGISER – GO! – Someone comes to the middle of the circle. They throw the ball to those on the outside of the circle, in any order. At any point, anyone on the outside can shout 'GO!' at which point they need to swap with the person in the middle whilst the ball stays in motion. The pace of the swaps can increase to keep the game exciting.

A second ball can be added in – using a different colour to distinguish who is swapping when.

Final layer – when someone shouts 'GO', both people in the middle have to swap, meaning two people have to leap in and the group has to swiftly, and silently, negotiate who this is.

ENERGISER – POPCORN – The aim of the game is for each member of the group to touch the football once.

The ball is thrown into the air, each person then taps it (think keepy-uppy) and shouts 'OUT!'. They then move to the edge of the space.

This keeps going until all people have touched the ball once.

The final person then shouts 'OUT!' and the game resets from the beginning.

If the ball ever touches the floor, or someone double taps the ball, the game resets.

Character exercises

Character and playfulness – meetings and greetings –
lovingly borrowed from Kneehigh

1: The group stands in a circle.

When two people make eye contact, they move into the middle of the circle, retaining eye contact, and clap at the same time.

They then continue to keep eye contact, moving backwards into the other person's starting place on the outside of the circle.

Multiple pairs can meet simultaneously.

2: This then increases in energy with the meeting changing to a high five and jumping in the middle, moving at a quicker pace. Again, with any number of pairs moving simultaneously and moving backwards to rejoin the circle.

3: The next layer is to invite the two people meeting in the middle to make a physical offer to the other person (a hand on their shoulder, shaking their hand, offering their elbow, a dance move, pointing at their nose – anything goes!). They then move backwards into the circle.

Encourage the group not to get drawn to default serious offers – keep finding the joy in the exercise. It is also good to remind the group to be respectful of interacting physically and avoid doing anything that would deliberately make anyone else feel uncomfortable.

This exercise is most interesting when interactions aren't preplanned – the exciting part is the unknown and the negotiation in that moment before something happens.

4: The meeting in the middle then becomes simplified to a moment of eye contact without any physical touch. These meetings can last for any length of time – short or long.

The invitation this time is to begin to flavour these meetings with a sense of the characters from the play. This can change the dynamic of the greeting – arriving quickly, arriving slowly, arriving with matching energy, arriving with differing energies.

The group commented how themes of coupling, playfulness, the awkwardness of teenage romance and relationship power dynamics began to emerge in the final stage of the exercise.

Character journeys

This exercise is a way to explore the changes particular characters go through from the start of the play to the end.

The group was split into smaller teams and assigned the following characters and objects:

Max – Post-it notes

Sam M – String

Hayley – Flipchart paper and pens

Sam F – Blu Tack

Spectator 1 – Shoes

Using their specific object(s), the groups were given ten minutes and tasked with creating a visual way to represent the character's journey. Matt Harrison described this as a creative heart monitor for the character.

This exercise allows the group to start exploring the arcs in the play whilst also throwing up some interesting creative responses that might feed into the staging of the play. It is a playful way to explore the story of each character and an effective way to chart the emotional demands of each character.

A variation on this can be to cast the play using fruit and vegetables, describing how the chosen fruit or vegetable is the right choice for a role by comparing the texture, tastes and look to that of the characters in the play.

Miram Battye commented on the variety of wants the characters experience in the play. She talked about how Sam M can be complex – he can simultaneously love someone and also have a competitive drive to want to win. This messy place is interesting as both things can be true and that gives the performer real texture and richness to play with.

Character starting points

The following exercises were referenced as useful ways to begin developing character:

Physical lead – Working with performers to identify which part of the body their character leads with, particularly when working with archetypes. How does the whole physicality of a person change when they lead with their nose/chin/chest/knees/forehead, etc.?

An extension of this can be to think of character tells – physical gestures that are part of who the character is or how they cope in a certain situation; e.g. unable to sit still when nervous or playing with their hair when thinking.

Relationship to time – How does time affect each character? Are they concerned with time?

How has their past informed their current situation? What do they hope their future will be?

Which vector of time do characters sit in? Past, present or future? Which are they most influenced by/connected to? How can this influence the performance of each character?

Emotional connection – To unlock the feeling and truth of each character
Matt Harrison set up an exercise using Sam F's speech on page 198 that begins 'I. I mean I *like* him, I want to hang out with him . . .' The group read through the text and then used this as a springboard. This exercise can be used for any speech in the play.

Comic book of the heart

Each person was invited to person to take a page of A4 paper and to divide it into six squares. Each square was then to be filled with an image connected to the text that was drawn from the individuals' memory that related to particular moments in the speech. Moments that felt important or significant in the text.

For example: On the line 'I really *like* him', Matt Harrison shared a memory from when he was in Year 5 and left a Valentine's card in the tray of another pupil as a time he remembers being aware of what it was to like someone else.

The group were given time to take themselves through this process. This is the chance to connect their own experiences and understanding to help inform their understanding of the characters in the play. There is the option to share back moments they feel comfortable to offer to the room but the primary purpose is to recognise similarities between their own experiences and those of the character.

A note on working with young people

Miriam Battye mentioned that some young people might not have first-hand experience with relationships or love in the way that is described in the play. She suggested it is useful to invite them to reflect on TV shows/films/plays where they can recognise these feelings too, so the onus isn't placed on having to have had the same experiences as the characters.

Text exercises

Facts, questions and events

Using the Prologue and Act One, teams investigate how to apply initial text exploration exercises. They were asked to look for the following:

Facts – something that is given in the text – names, times, places, specific items

Questions – things that the text brings up – Why is someone doing this? How are they doing a certain action? Who is in control? Who is leading this moment?

Events – what are the moments that change the course of the action – e.g. they could be big things such as people being killed and people choosing a new partner or smaller things such as the way someone reacts to a moment. How do these events alter what happens next?

These are a way to find clarity. It shows you the gifts that the writer has given in the text – so much will already be contained within the words and these are the foundation to draw from. These are the clues that the writer leaves us.

Punctuation

Matt Harrison talked about punctuation as a way to explore the rhythm of how a person speaks. This can be a gateway to unlocking character. Punctuation is a link to breath, breath is a link to emotion.

How does the way they speak reveal who they are? How does the way they speak feel different to the way the actor speaks?

The group were asked to select any monologue from the play to explore this. They were invited to walk around the room, reading the speech out loud. Every time they hit one of the following punctuation they were to use the related action.

Full stop – a definitive change of direction

Comma – suspension in movement

Question marks – a clap

Exclamation marks – a stamp

Ellipses – a lean (to represent an incomplete thought)

Dash – a sidestep (to represent a connecting or interrupting thought)

Capitals – a bolder marking of the steps (to represent greater emphasis and an increase in volume)

Interruption – a slashing motion with your hand in front of you

Speech marks – marking air quotes in the space

Italics – upper-body tension (to represent something more than the capitals and a greater emphasis but not related to volume)

This exercise is a way to physicalise the ways in which each character speaks, and to encourage the performers to connect to this in a way that takes them out of their heads and into their bodies.

What did these actions feel like to play alongside the text? What do they unlock in the rhythm of the speech? What do these vocal habits reveal about each character? How does it relate to the ways they think?

Matt Harrison reminded the group to trust the text as it contains so much to work from.

Variation – Earth and sky

An alternative version of the exercise is where the performers are asked to highlight moments that ground a character and moments that transcend them or take them outside of themselves.

Reading aloud, performers either sit on the floor or stand and deliver the text to the sky in accordance with when they feel grounded or transcended.

Questions to ask:

What has happened to make a character say these words?

What has happened just before? Why are they saying this *now*?

Why are they saying these words – what do they want? What is their purpose or intention?

Characters shouldn't stop speaking until they've made their point or have been interrupted. Matt Harrison suggested encouraging performers to play the questions above and not the emotion – the emotion will be unlocked from the questions and find a more textured performance.

Thought by thought

This exercise is designed to allow performers to understand the thinking patterns and habits of their character.

Using the scene between Jess and Andy on page 196 starting:

Andy   Jess, don't leave. We don't know what happens if we leave.

Jess   I know.

Andy   If we leave. Then. What happens to us?

Each performer was given a pile of Post-it notes. These represent the thoughts of the character. They were asked to read the scene aloud and every time their character expressed a thought, they use a Post-it note to determine if the thought is about:

Me – stick the Post-it note to themselves

You – stick the Post-it note on the other actor

The place – stick the Post-it note in the space

They can also consider the energy of the thought; e.g. is it placed gently or forcibly? And where is it placed? E.g. on the head to appeal to thinking, on the heart to appeal to love etc.

This should be a playful and accessible way to begin unveiling the nuance of each character. It also creates a very visual representation of what takes up most of a character's thoughts.

Initial staging – thoughts in motion

An exercise for the point in the process where you are bridging the gap between reading the play and starting to stage the play.

Begin by populating the space with lots of chairs.
Decide a scene to be explored.
Performers for this scene walk into the space, look at each other and then sit.
As soon as they sit, they begin to read the scene.
Using the chairs in the space, performers move between chairs when they have a change of thought, moving closer or further away from the other people in the space depending on how much they are trying to connect to the other person or to get away from them.

Matt Harrison talked about how scenes naturally begin to find a physical life and relationships begin to emerge. As a group, a company can reflect on what they discover and what they would like to carry forwards in staging the play as a whole. These exercises are intended to create a container for exploration to begin and through action you can begin to learn more about the material.

Out of context: Speaking to a child

The group was invited to use one of their belongings as though holding a baby (a rolled-up jumper, a bag, a water bottle) and to deliver the Sam F speech on the bottom of page 198 as if speaking to the baby.

Matt Harrison mentioned it can be useful to take a speech out of context to find new perspectives and ideas on it. It can allow us to hear the speech afresh and to reacquaint ourselves with words we've become overly familiar with and deliver on autopilot.

'Every time we speak, it comes with some level of cost – this shifts in scale but we risk exposing something of ourselves every time we speak. By talking to a baby, it strips away the performance and invites intimacy in.'

The group commented on the sense of responsibility that came through, the words taking on a new importance.

'When you're talking to someone who can't judge you, it changes the sense of how honest you can be.'

Direct address

Matt Harrison flagged the moments of direct address in the play.

What is the speaker's relationship to the audience in these moments? What is it flavoured with?

It can never just be talking into a vacuum. It needs a dynamic or purpose. The choices made don't need to be laboured in the performance but, by making a choice, it will automatically change the delivery of the text.

Question and answer with Miriam Battye and Matt Harrison

Q: Do the contestants know they might get shot?

MB: Yes, the contestants know. They are willing to roll the dice and put both feet in. It is high stakes! It might mean that they win everything their heart desires. People are willing to risk everything – we do this every time we enter into a new relationship. We forget that it might end in heartbreak because we are willing to focus on what it might bring.

Q: Are the Spectators accountable?

MB: The Spectators haven't taken a risk yet. The point of them is that they haven't risked what the contestants have. They are quick to judge but don't know what it's like to be in the game.

Q: The play is broken up into different parts – do these sections need to be shown?

MB: They are chapters or episodes of the story. They are new rounds with a new energy. The titles at the top can help you to focus on what the next part of the story is about. They are the management of the story and how it escalates. The gaps between can be as long or as short as you like.

Q: Why aren't there any LGBT characters?

MB: The play is reasonably elastic. When it was originally conceived I was interested in the 'heterosexual carnage' as described in one scene. The play doesn't represent the entire world but, having said that, there is space in the play for a group to explore what they think is interesting. I don't think there is anything particular about a heterosexual relationship or a homosexual relationship that can be defined, so I really hope that these characters can be embodied and found by anybody. I offer this play to the companies and if it's of interest to a group to explore a particular relationship, then find it in the way that is best for you. What is important is to make a choice and define it.

MH: Let your company meet the text in the way they want to.

MB: A play is a brief offer into the universe. The offer is for the group to make their version of it, as each group will have their own make up, the play can be stretchy to what the group needs.

Q: It is great to hear you talk about fitting the play to the group but is there anything that needs to stay really true?

MH: A key thing is to decide whether you are keeping the pronouns as written – and then the level at which the performer embodies the gender of the character as written. At one end of the spectrum is full transformation and at the other end is more of a focus of drawing from masculine or feminine energies. Another option is to adapt the pronouns to the identity of the performer playing the role.

Or all the pronouns become neutral, to remove gender. My instinct is that retaining some of the pronouns is important to this piece – but this might be wrong.

MB: I would encourage you to focus on communicating the choices you make, so the audience is able to accept what is there as true as opposed to being unsure and then can't understand it. Don't be obscure, define it. The stereotypes of the characters might be useful for you in this instance and might be the most communicative way to convey the story to the audience. Don't be afraid to work with it – see everything with creative potential, not as a problem. Make sure the performers are clear and that will convey to us.

MH: The characters have defined energies and this feels very strong. These can be found within anyone and there is a whole spectrum available for each character. Grab the energy of each character and work with that.

MB: I wrote it with particular binaries in mind but I always intended for it to be flexible – and that is what I am finding more and more as I see more young people coming to the text – there is a need for it to be flexible. Find as much stretch as you need – and work with as much or as little as you need for your group. You can absolutely do it as written or work with stretching it.

MH: There is value and merit to both takes on it – do what is right for you.

Q: Can we change character names?
MB: Yes, make it work with any gender changes.

Q: When someone dies, can they then become one of the Spectators?
MB: It is intended for this to be the case. How they leave the space is up to you – it can be a movement sequence or they can be reabsorbed into the space. What is important is that that person is gone – forever. When they come back as a Spectator, it is a new energy; this should be defined.

Q: What is the scope for editing the text and changing the lines that feel inappropriate for younger people to say?
MB: I would say it needs to meet the group. The piece is there for you to deliver a play. Please don't butcher the text either – but the play is there to be used. The rhythm is really important, as is punctuation. If you are cutting or changing a line, make sure it all still reads in the same way. Don't move things around because it's written really finely for performers.

Q: Can lines be changed if we are finding the rhythm tricky?
MH: My instinct would be to lean into the difficulties and to not be afraid of it. This play is caustic and beautifully sharp and we have to lean into that.

MH: We should notice the difference between it jarring with the performer or where it is asking us to engage with more knotty ideas. Don't edit to avoid these moments.

MB: The whole play is written with intent – see the thought under the 'Language' section for further explanation.

Q: Who are the Spectators? Are they a studio audience? Are they Gogglebox people? Are they the same age as the group?
MB: I saw them as specific people – I'm throwing it out to the actors to find who they are. I saw them as people with individual wants and needs but if you'd rather them represent something bigger than that is up to you and how to communicate that.

Q: If working with a bigger cast, can it work as the Spectators being a bigger group of people?
MB: Absolutely, if that works for your show. They can be mercurial and a big beast – as long as when they speak they embody someone so the text is rooted in something. Text that exists anywhere in the world or online has come from a person with a body and thoughts – so when they speak, we ask why would someone say that about someone? It's more about that than it is about giving the Spectators names and backstories.

Q: Can archetypes work for the Spectators too so they become mini-choruses?
MB: Yes, choral speaking could be good.
MH: There is definitely something in the game of them wanting to be heard. You could find some lovely moments of through lines amongst the voices of the Spectators. It can be a concentration of something that then bubbles up. I've always hoped someone would do it with a colossal chorus of people, so they are a terrifying group. The main thing is that they are a person saying it, not a discombobulated voice. Enjoy the theatrical possibility that you are getting to see this person saying this. Someone might be the saddest meekest person saying the nastiest cruellest thing. It isn't always cruel people who say cruel things. I always think everyone should have the chance to say a good line!

Q: Are the overlords a character?
MB: No, it is my way of saying it is the unknown force controlling things.
MH: To see them diminishes their power; they are unseen.

Suggested references

Squid Games – Netflix
The Lobster – 2016 film starring Colin Farrell and Rachel Weisz
Love Island – ITV
The Love Trap – Channel 4 dating show

From a workshop led by Matt Harrison
With notes by Matt Hassall

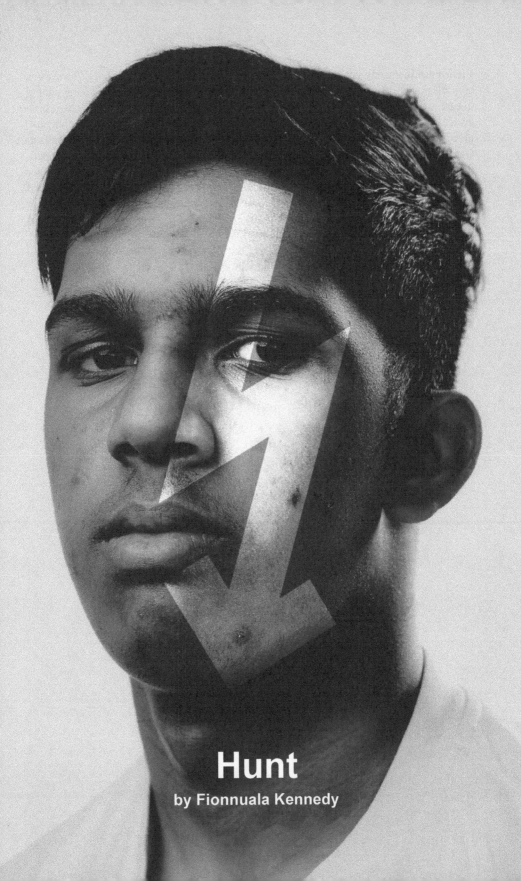

Hunt

by Fionnuala Kennedy

Fionnuala Kennedy is a writer and theatre director from Belfast. Her play *Removed*, a commission by Prime Cut Productions to explore the lived experience of young people in care in partnership with VOYPIC, has toured across Ireland and won the 2020 Zebbie award for Best Play. Most recently, she was commissioned by Replay Theatre company to write *Thaw*, a new show for PMLD audiences performed in The MAC Belfast, October 2021. She is currently under commission with NI Opera to write a new opera for young people about housing rights. Writing credits include: *Hostel*, based on her own experience of homelessness (produced by Kabosh, 2010 and 2012/Macha Productions, 2017); *Entitled*, looking at the impact and inequality of welfare reform (produced by Macha Productions, 2017). Fionnuala Kennedy was one of five directors selected for the Headlong Origins programme 2020. Most recently, she has directed *Sweeties* by Jo Egan, as part of *Body Politics* with Macha Productions. Fionnuala is one of the writers in the BBC Drama Room 21/22.

Characters

Jo
Lisa
Niamh
James
Fra
Peter
Steve
Carly
Eugene
Danielle

Set can be minimal possibly with objects or props to suggest action. Scenes can be conveyed through lighting and sound.

Scene One

The action takes place in the streets, gardens and alleyways of the estate. It's February. It's cold, windy and, importantly, dark – perfect for remaining unseen.

Eugene *is talking to his mobile phone, recording a video for his YouTube channel.*

Eugene   Hey, guys! It's Eu-Eu- (*His voice goes funny so he stops the video and clears his throat before starting again.*) Hey, guys! It's Eu-Eu-Eugene! I know I said I wasn't uploading any videos over mid-term because I'm supposed to be studying. But. I'm walking to meet my friends for something really exciting and I'm taking you with me. I'm going to give you an insight into the primal behaviour of post-millennial Generation Z without social media and technology, mostly! Please like, share and subscribe below! Now lower the lights, strap in, because it's gonna be one bumpy (*drops his phone*) – shit!

Scene Two

Jo   This is the box.

James   The box?

Jo   The electric box. This is where we meet.

James   Why here?

Jo   What do you mean?

James   Why an electric box?

Jo   Just. It's just where we've always met. I've never really thought about it. It's just our box.

James   Right.

Jo   Do you not have one of those places?

James   Places?

Jo   You know, where you and your mates gather or meet? We have the box, the corner, Pat's Shop, the Magic Tree . . .

James   What's magic about it?

Jo   Nothing. That's just what it's called.

James   We have a park?

Jo   We had a park. About an hour after it was opened, the swings were stolen and it was set on fire. It kinda *melted*.

James   Will you miss it?

Jo   This shithole? No chance.

Niamh *enters.*

Niamh   Is Lisa here yet?

Jo   What's the big secret?

Niamh   Just wait until everyone gets here. (*Texts on her phone, then looks at* **James**.) Who're you?

James   I'm James.

He waits on a response, **Niamh** *ignores him.*

Niamh   I haven't told you! Mad Danielle is back!

Jo (*unsettled*)   Who said?

James   *Mad Danielle?*

Jo   Did someone see her?

Niamh   Heard my ma whispering about it this morning.

Jo   What'd she say?

Niamh   I couldn't hear so I asked and she slapped me and said (*mimicking her mum pointing*) 'Mind your own business'. I think she was in jail.

Jo   They don't put children in jail.

Niamh   They do when you're as mad as her.

Eugene *enters.*

Eugene   Who're you gossiping about now?

Niamh   Mad Danielle is back!

Eugene   No!

James   Why is she called Mad Danielle?

Eugene (*to* **Jo**)   Who's this?

Niamh   Jo's *friend.*

Eugene   Danielle was lifted for breaking into somewhere. Or was it stealing something? I can't remember which but it was *definitely* one of those things.

Jo   Now who's gossiping!

Niamh   No her mum's *boyfriend* was lifted. For drugs.

Jo   Who told you that?

Niamh   Lisa. Her da put him out of the estate.

Eugene   For being a dealer? Was he doin' him out of business?

Niamh (*guessing*)   I know why they locked her up! The kitten!

Eugene (*hands over his ears*)   I don't wanna hear about that!

Jo   She wasn't locked up! She had to stay with her aunt.

Niamh (*jealous*)   So you're still best friends?

James   What happened with the kitten?

Eugene   La la la la la la la la la la la la laaaaaaaa.

Niamh *slaps him.*

Niamh   This . . . (*looks at* **Eugene**) *thing* happened last year. With a kitten. Then nobody was allowed to hang around with her. She's a crazy bitch.

Jo   She's crazy. He gets it. Will you just tell us why we're here?

Eugene (*jumping with excitement*)   Can I tell her?

Steve *and* **Carly** *enter.* **Steve** *is hyper and excited,* **Carly** *is the opposite.*

Steve   Here, do you remember the time we played and Baldy Des caught us scaling his fence and threw a basin of bleach over us!

Carly   Bastard. It went all over me, not you!

Steve   There was a big white blotch on my track bottoms!

Carly   My jeans literally turned four different colours. I had to tell my da it was a fashion statement. He made me wear them into town!

Steve (*laughing*)   Too funny!

Jo   No. Niamh. Is *that* why we're here? We're not playing.

Niamh   You have to!

Jo   No way.

Niamh   Yes way.

James   Play what?

Jo   Nothing. We're not playing.

Niamh   Two Man Hunt. It's the Best. Game. Ever.

Jo   Why didn't you tell me?!

Niamh   Because you wouldn't have come.

Carly   Are we not too old for this?

Steve   Come on! For old times' sake.

Carly   It's gonna rain tonight!

Niamh   Please! Jo moves on Monday and we're never gonna see her again.

Carly   You're so dramatic.

Jo   I'll come back and visit.

Niamh   You know you won't. You'll be miles away. (*Beat.*) You're leaving. Carly's got her course. Fra's never out any more. We used to be out all the time, for the entire day and now it's . . . *different*.

Jo   I swore I would never play again.

Steve   It's just a game.

Jo   It's not! You and her (*to* **Niamh**) do anything to win and we all end up in trouble! Play something else. Red Rover?

Carly   We're *definitely* too old for Red Rover.

James (*to* **Jo**)   Two Man Hunt sounds fun, let's play.

Steve   Who's he?

Jo (*before* **James** *can answer*)   James. James, Steve, Carly, Eugene.

Steve   What school do you go to?

Jo   Mind your business.

Niamh   C'mon, one last game before you go!

Eugene   Tell her, James, make her play.

James *looks at her.*

Jo   Whatever. Let's play.

Eugene   Why is it Two *Man* Hunt?

Niamh   Because that's what it's called.

Eugene   It's a bit problematic.

Niamh (*impatiently*)   What does that mean?

Eugene   Shouldn't it be something more gender-neutral.

Steve   Such a snowflake thing to say.

Niamh   What's a snowflake?

Carly   Two *Woman* Hunt because the men had their turn!

Niamh   It's just *man* as in *man*kind.

Jo   Two *Person* Hunt?

Niamh   Sounds crap.

Steve   Two 'non-binary LGBTQZ+-1' hunt?

Jo   Wise up, Steve.

Eugene   I just meant something simple like 'Hunt'?

Niamh (*over the discussion*)   Fine.

Steve   You sure you want to play again, Eugene?

He pretends to cry, mocking **Eugene**, *who keeps his eyes down.*

Poor wee Jess!

Carly   Don't mention the kitten.

Niamh   No phones allowed except for the chat. (*To* **Eugene**.) No filming us!

Eugene   Trust me, my followers would want something more interesting.

Steve   Your followers? Who? Your ma, and an old pervert waiting for the day you get your dick out?

Eugene   No, had to block your da.

Steve   What'd you say?

Lisa *enters, full face of make-up and dressy clothes.*

Lisa   It's Baltic!

Niamh   Lisa, do you have eyelashes on?

Lisa   I was practising my make-up when you *bribed* me to come out. (*She shivers.*) It's *freezing*!

Steve   It's February. Put some clothes on and you'll be warmer.

Lisa   Shut up, Steve!

Carly   Storm Ciara is to hit tonight. Is this a good idea?

Niamh   They always hype it up and it ends up being a bit of wind.

Lisa   Why are storms always named after women?

Steve   They're not, just the bad ones.

Niamh   Speaking of bad ones, did you hear? Mad Danielle's back!

Carly   No!

Lisa   My da gave me a lecture to (*mocking her dad*) 'keep well away from her'.

Niamh *scans the group, counting in her head.*

Carly   Where was she?

Jo   Not our business.

Carly   Calm your ham.

Lisa   She escaped from prison.

Jo   She wasn't in prison.

Lisa   That's what I heard.

Jo   You're full of shit.

Niamh   Where's Fra?

Steve   He's coming.

Niamh   We're not waiting. Let's just start. Items.

Steve   Clothes from a washing line!

Niamh   Good.

Carly   No baby clothes! We have morals.

Lisa   And nothing too expensive.

Steve   Fuck's sake, you're ruining the game!

Fra *enters with his younger brother* **Peter**.

Niamh   Fra, Peter? Really? He's too young.

Fra   It was take him with me or not come at all. He'll stay with me. My granny's not well. (*Warning.*) Our house is a no-go area.

Niamh   Fine. We've got clothes. What else?

Jo   Something metal.

Eugene   A rubbish bin?

James   Isn't that illegal?

Jo   They'll get it back, it's not like we're setting it on fire.

Steve (*sniggers*)   A family pet?

Carly   Not funny.

Steve   Come on, that cat was a dick.

Peter *whispers something to* **Fra**.

Fra   A football?

Niamh   Great idea, Peter. A football, tennis ball, any kind of ball.

Steve   Saint Susie's statue?

Lisa (*to* **James**)   Mrs Gregory's a Holy Joe who reeks of piss.

Eugene   She has this creepy statue of some saint or something.

Carly   It lights up.

Lisa   You can hear her praying to it. She's a psycho.

Fra   She's religious. Big deal.

Lisa   Calm down.

Fra   I am calm.

Niamh   Right – star item?

Steve   Something from Fat Davy's *den of iniquity*.

Lisa   Den of what?

Steve   His *man* cave.

Eugene   His shed.

Carly (*knowing what he's going to say*)   Don't even think about it, Steve.

Steve   Come on! We have to go big for the star item.

Jo   Spit it out.

Steve   His *rifle*.

Niamh   No!

Steve   It doesn't even work!

Lisa   No way!

Jo   Wise up, Steve.

James   He has a rifle?

Steve   He's ex-army. Does drills with it in his back garden. (*Laughs as he mimes it.*)

Lisa   He'll kill us if he catches us.

Steve   Don't get caught.

Niamh   Rifle it is. What have we got? (*Marking with her fingers.*) Star item: the rifle; gold items: statue, ball, clothes, something metal, rubbish bin. Random objects as wild cards, hunters decision. Everyone got that?

All agree – **James** *looks confused.* **Peter** *and* **Fra** *are whispering to each other.*

Niamh   Good. Now, the two hunters.

She sees **Fra** *and* **Peter** *continue talking a bit louder now.*

Niamh   Fra, is there something you want to share with the entire group?

Eugene   Don't be a dick, Niamh.

Fra (*reluctantly, slightly embarrassed*)   Peter's worried about The Man.

Steve   What man?

Fra   It's just a stupid rumour.

Lisa   It's true! My mummy's friend's sister's daughter almost got snatched by The Man last week.

Niamh   He drives about in a white van looking for girls to kidnap.

Lisa   Jo saw him!

All look to **Jo**.

Jo (*relishing the attention*)   It's true.

Carly   What'd he look like?

Jo   He has a long black coat.

Lisa   He hides a machete in it!

Danielle *enters unnoticed by the group.*

Niamh   I heard he chopped off his wife's head and flushed it down the toilet.

Fra (*for Peter's benefit*)   It's just a *story*!

Jo   It's not! My uncle works for the police. They can't tell everyone yet because they don't want to worry the public. *That's* why we're moving.

Carly   How do you flush a head down a toilet?

Steve   See, Peter, don't worry, it's just girls he murders.

Niamh   Enough! Time to play the game.

Danielle   What game?

Her presence inspires fear, the group go quiet for a moment. She stares at **Jo**.

Danielle   Joanne Joanne Frying Pan.

Steve (*to* **James**)   We're very sophisticated with nicknames round here.

Danielle (*aggressively*)   What?

Steve *freezes. She* *turns to* **Jo** *and* **James**.

Danielle   Who're you?

James (*slightly nervous*)   James, a friend of Jo's.

Danielle   You might wanna be careful.

She aims that at **Jo**.

Lisa   Where've you been Danielle because we heard –

Niamh *elbows* **Lisa's** *side.*

Lisa   Ouch!

Danielle   You should learn to mind your own business.

Niamh   She didn't mean anything by it.

Danielle   What are you, her ma?

Beat.

Are you playing Two Man Hunt?

Steve   No. Hunt.

Danielle   You trying to be funny?

Niamh   We changed it.

Danielle   Why?

They all turn to **Eugene** *to explain.*

Eugene   Because . . . we thought it was more gender neutral.

Danielle   Thought nobody (*mocking them*) *was allowed to play* after last time.

Niamh   We're doing one last game before Jo leaves.

Danielle   Where you going?

Jo   We're moving.

Beat.

Danielle   When?

Jo   Tomorrow.

Danielle   Why?

Jo (*sheepishly*)   Just.

Danielle   Who's on?

Beat.

Not me.

Steve   Not me!

The rest of the group collectively shout 'Not me!'

Lisa   Me and Niamh will do it.

Niamh   We were on last time!

Lisa   I'm not getting my clothes ruined, my da will kill me.

Niamh   Fine! We'll count to twenty then the hunt begins. Everyone ready?

All except for **Lisa** *and* **Niamh** *run offstage.* **Lisa** *and* **Niamh** *begin counting down from twenty.*

Niamh/Lisa   Twenty, nineteen, eighteen, seventeen –

Lisa *stops and looks around her – then texts on her phone.*

Niamh   What's wrong?

Lisa   I'm not playing if Danielle's playing. My da will murder me.

Niamh   Maybe Danielle will do it first.

Jo *and* **James** *enter.*

Jo   What's wrong?

Carly, **Steve**, **Fra** *and* **Peter** *enter.*

Steve   What's going on?

Lisa   We can't play with her. She's mental.

Carly   Lisa's got a point.

Lisa   Jo, tell her she can't play.

Jo   Why me?

Steve   You were besties.

Jo   She hates my guts.

Lisa   Someone needs to tell her.

Fra   You volunteering?

Lisa (*looks around*)   I'm gonna text Eugene and say he has to tell. (*She texts.*)

A text comes back.

Niamh   What'd he say?

Lisa   Not a fucking mission.

Lisa *continues to text.*

James   Can't we just let her play?

Lisa   No offence – you're new. You don't get an opinion.

James   Is she that bad?

All   Yeah.

James   What will she do?

Steve   What *won't* she do?

Thunder sounds; they all look up.

Carly   The storm's coming.

Jo   If nobody's willing to say it, just let her think she's playing and stay away from her.

Niamh   Right, go!

Thunder sounds get louder.

Scene Three

Eugene (*whispering*)   Hey, guys! The big reveal! Tonight, you're joining me on a game of *Hunt*. It used to be called *Two Man Hunt* but my friends of course are woke so they changed it.

Danielle *enters unseen by* **Eugene** *and watches him.*

Eugene   It's sort of like *The Hunger Games* except nobody round here looks like Liam Hemsworth, and nobody gets killed . . . *hopefully.* (*Proudly.*) I'm the reigning champ so I shall be defending my title, with your help!

Danielle   Ha! The reigning champ? You ran crying last time.

Eugene *is so startled his phone goes flying in the air and drops.*

Danielle   You're fuckin' jumpy.

Eugene   Thought you were The Man.

Danielle   Do I look like a man?

Eugene   The Man that's going around murdering everyone.

Danielle   What are you talking about, weirdo?

Eugene   The man the peelers are looking for. Wanted for murder. He's been spotted round here trying to snatch people.

Danielle   Says who?

Eugene   Everyone.

Danielle   Nah.

Eugene   Jo saw him.

Danielle   She's full of shit.

Eugene   Her uncle's a peeler. She knows for a fact.

Danielle   Know what I know for a fact? Jo's a fucking liar. Bet she's not even moving. She's a spoof.

Eugene   She is. Her mum even said.

Danielle   Yeah, well, her ma's a liar too.

Eugene *gets a text, reads it and* **Danielle** *sees the fear in his face.*

Danielle   Is that about me?

Eugene   No!

Danielle   Let me see your phone.

Eugene   It's not about you.

Danielle *grabs his phone from him.*

Danielle   Who's Glamour Babe fire-crying laughing face-heart-flower?

Eugene   They wrote that!

Danielle   I know how Snapchat works, Eugene. Who is it?

Eugene   I don't want to say.

Danielle   It's Jo, isn't it? (*Mocking baby voice.*) *Nobody wants me to play*? This is MY game. Want your phone back?

Eugene   Yes. Please.

Danielle   I'll give you it as long as you don't tell anyone that I've seen this message.

Eugene   I won't.

Danielle   I mean it. I'll find you if you do. It won't be your phone I smash. Got it?

She lobs his phone at him and storms off. **Eugene** *attempts miserably to catch it, picks it up and wipes it, relieved that it still works.*

Scene Four

Lisa *and* **Niamh** *are standing at the post looking out.* **Niamh** *is competitively bored.* **Lisa** *is cold and slightly afraid of the dark.*

Lisa   Mad Danielle is . . . *mental.*

Niamh   Clue's in the name, brains.

Lisa   She just joined the game. We didn't even have a choice.

Niamh   Would you have said no to her? I think it makes the game more interesting. Ups the stakes. Adds a bit of risk.

Lisa   I don't want risk. I wanna be in the house. In my jammies. Watching Netflix.

Niamh   Well, you're not.

Lisa   Look at those clouds. It's gonna lash. We're definitely even now.

Niamh   Dead on. Your da finds a quarter bottle in your bag and you say it's mine? Even, ha!

Lisa   It's not a big deal. Your mummy wouldn't care if you were drinking.

Niamh   *What*?

Lisa   If my da finds out I'm playing with Mad Danielle, I'm dead.

Niamh   I feel sorry for her.

Lisa   I don't.

Niamh   Do you ever see the state of her ma? She's a zombie.

Lisa   Doesn't give Danielle a free pass to be a maniac. Thought her ma was clean?

Niamh   Is she definitely off them?

Lisa   Heard my da say.

Niamh (*aside*)   I'm sure it's hit his business hard.

Lisa   *What*?

Niamh   Do you think Jo will come back and visit us?

Lisa   Who cares.

Niamh   I'd hate to leave here.

Lisa   It's a hole.

Niamh   But it's *our* hole.

Lisa   You're a paedo.

Niamh   This is boring. We need to go out and search.

Lisa   I'm not moving.

Niamh   Hunting is literally the point of the game.

Lisa   Who's that?

Niamh *'s on alert*

Niamh   Where?

Lisa   There!

Niamh   That's a man. You need your eyes tested.

Lisa *doesn't take her eyes off him.*

Lisa   *I know* but what's he doing?

Niamh   Nothing.

Lisa   *Exactly*. He's just . . . staring at us.

Niamh   Just a random weirdo, mate. Place is full of them. Probably off his head or steaming.

Lisa   He's freaking me out.

Niamh   Just be glad he's not touching himself.

Lisa   What?!

Niamh   I'm goin' out to hunt.

Lisa   You can't leave me here!

Niamh   Someone has to man the post.

Lisa   He's gone! What if that was The Man?

Niamh   I'll be back in a bit.

She exits. **Lisa** *takes her phone out and texts. SX – thunder followed by huge gusts of whistling winds.*

Scene Five

Peter and Fra are crouched down with hoods up. A message comes through to Fra's phone.

Peter   Is it Granny? Does she want us in?

Fra   It's Lisa.

Peter   What did she say?

Fra   Nothing.

Peter   You think Granny's OK?

Fra   She's fine.

Peter   Maybe we should check on her.

Fra   She needs to rest.

Peter   Fra?

Fra   What?

Peter   Is Granny gonna die?

Fra   Don't say that, Peter!

Peter   She's really sick.

Fra   She'll be fine.

Peter   What'll happen to us if she dies?

Fra   She's not going to die! If you keep talking, you're gonna get us caught! This is why we don't let you play!

Beat.

Peter   It's really windy.

Fra   Pull your hood up.

Peter   My hands are freezing.

Fra   I told you to bring your gloves.

Peter   Can we go back and get them?

Fra   It's too late now. You should've listened to me.

Peter   It's really dark now, Fra.

Fra   You are the most annoying person ever. You need to grow up!

Peter   I am grown up!

Fra   Then stop acting like a baby! I have to take you out with me. With *my* friends. I have to bring you everywhere. All you do is moan.

Fra spots **Niamh**.

Fra   Sssshh!

He points and mimes 'Niamh'. **Peter** *is afraid.*

Fra   She's seen me. I have to run. Stay here.

Peter   Please don't leave me.

Fra   You'll be fine. Stay down. I'll come back for you when the coast is clear.

He bolts offstage being chased by **Niamh**.

Peter   Fra!

He looks around him and crouches down, afraid. He hears a gentle tapping in the wind. As it picks up, he hears a sharp bang. He jumps, shaking. With another bang, he runs off.

Scene Six

James   What are the rules again?

Jo   Sssshhhhh!

James   What do we do now?

Jo   We find an item.

James (*beat*)   What did Danielle do to the kitten?

Jo   You don't wanna know.

James   Who lives here?

Jo   Mrs Duffin. She's nuts.

James   So glad we're in her garden.

Jo   My mum found her wandering the streets in her nightie.

James   Creepy.

Jo   She was looking for her husband.

James   Was he wandering too?

Jo   Not likely, he killed himself five years ago.

James   I feel bad stealing from her now.

Jo   We'll bring it back. Just find something she doesn't use.

James (*lifting it up*)   A clothes peg?

Jo   Can't. That's a penalty.

James   Please explain the rules again!

Jo   Ball, bin, clothes, metal.

James   What about this? (*Picks up a compost bin.*)

Jo   Is there food in it?

James (*opens it*)   Ugh, God, smell it! It's full of . . . *maggots*.

Jo   Yuck, put it down!

James   *Technically* it's a bin.

Jo   Just keep it away from me.

James   Is it wrong that I'm really enjoying stealing something?

Jo   It's a career round here.

James   We never play anything like this where I live. It's exhilarating.

Jo   No!

James   What?

Jo   You can't be saying things like *exhilarating*.

Her phone beeps

Lisa. 'Beware, The Man is watching us'.

James   Ooohh, The *Man*. Did you really see him?

Jo (*trying to impress*)   Loads. One day, I'm walking home from school and this dirty white van starts driving along slowly beside me. I look right at him. His eyes are *really* dark. He has this big scar on the side of his face. He rolls his window down and asks me if I want a lift. I say no. He starts shouting, *get in the van, get in the van*! I start running. He speeds after me. But I know this place inside out. I run down the alley and hide behind the bins. (*Beat.*) He doesn't scare me.

James   You're not just a tiny bit afraid?

Jo   Not one bit.

James   Because I'll protect you if you are.

Beat.

Jo   It's starting to rain, let's find cover.

They run off. **James** *runs back on to grab the bin.*

Scene Seven

Peter *is alone crouched down, holding his hood tight. He's looking around waiting on* **Fra** *until a gust of wind bangs a nearby gate.*

Peter   Fra?

Danielle *enters. She watches* **Peter** *in his terror for a moment until he discovers her.*

Peter   Have you seen Fra?

Danielle   This is a terrible hiding place, Peter.

Peter   Fra's gonna come back for me.

Danielle   What if he doesn't?

Peter   He will.

Danielle (*irritated by his childishness*)   You can't be a baby all your life, Peter.

Peter   I'm not a baby.

Danielle   There'll be a time when Fra can't protect you. You'll have to look after yourself.

Peter   I wanna go home.

Danielle   Aren't you having fun?

Peter   This ground is all wet. I'm cold.

Danielle   Go! Go home then! Run off back to your granny.

Peter *visibly jumps when she shouts but doesn't move*

Danielle   Didn't think so. I know a really good hiding place. Come with me.

Peter   I wanna wait for Fra.

Danielle   What if he doesn't come back, Peter? Do you know there's a murderer on the loose?

Peter   Fra says The Man isn't real.

Danielle   Oh but he is, Peter. I saw him once. I couldn't see his face, but he was holding a long, sharp knife. Just turning it about in his hand waiting to find someone, anyone to use it on. What if he finds you before Fra does? The rain's getting heavier now, you'll get soaked. Don't worry, I'll tell him where to find us, OK?

Peter *reluctantly takes her hand and they walk off before* **Fra** *enters.*

Fra (*whispering*)   Peter, I'm back. Peter? Peter! Where are you, I can't see anything? If I turn my torch on they'll see me. If you can hear me, just whistle, or cough or make some sort of noise so I know where you are. (*He pauses for a moment to listen, then turns on his torch, worried now.*) Peter?

The wind really picks up followed by rain.

Scene Eight

Carly *and* **Steve** *enter with hoods up and stand under a porch.*

Carly   Another text from Lisa. (*Putting on a serious voice.*) 'The Man has been spotted again. Remain vigilant.' What is she like?

Steve I love it. We're playing Hunt but who is the real hunter? Oooohhh.

Carly Don't move.

Steve Why?

Carly Security light. What are we stealing from here?

Beat.

Steve Come on.

Carly What?

Steve We're in *Tracey's* back garden.

Carly So?

Steve Has to be something (*putting on an accent*) *saucy*.

Carly You got a bra once and haven't fucked up about it since. So immature.

Steve Jealous?

Carly You and your da are obsessed with her.

Steve You still don't believe it.

Carly That she's – how did he put it? A 'lady of the night'?

Steve She is! She's a hooker. My da saw her one night.

Carly Very coincidental.

Steve He was driving past the big clock in town /

Carly / Oh he just happened to be driving past.

Steve My da wouldn't go near her!

Carly Your da fancies her!

Steve No he doesn't!

Carly All the men round here do.

Steve How else does she have all this stuff?

Carly Yeah cos a woman couldn't possibly be successful without selling her body.

Steve She's a hooker! Lisa's da's always in and out of her house.

Carly She's probably getting a bit of green.

Steve Maybe she deals for him!

Carly She's not a hooker. Or a dealer. Jesus, you'd get someone hung with that mouth. What are we taking?

Steve   What about those funny scissor things?

Carly   Shears. What's wrong with you?

Steve   That's a fancy way of saying scissors.

Carly   Why does she have shears? Her entire garden's concrete. Not even a plant.

Steve   Maybe she –

Carly   I don't even wanna here what you're about to say. How are we gonna get over there without the security light coming on?

Steve   Lucky for you, I'm a bit of an expert at this. (*Cracks knuckles.*) Watch, learn, maybe hum the *Mission Impossible* theme tune?

Carly   Or, I go on my phone, you get the shears and we get out of here before we get caught.

Steve *moves closer to the shears as if he's competing in the Olympics; maybe he tries to grab them with his foot.* **Carly** *remains bored and scrolls on her phone.* **Fra** *makes a noise offstage to get their attention – 'Pssst!'*

Carly   What was that?

Steve   What?

Carly   Did you hear that? Someone's there!

Fra *enters.*

Fra   Have you seen Peter?

Carly   For God's sake, Fra, you nearly gave me a heart attack!

Steve   The sightings of *The Man* has got her spooked.

Fra   Have either of you seen Peter? I can't find him.

Steve   That's sort of how the game works, Fra.

Carly   Shut up, Steve. We'll keep an eye out for him, Fra, don't worry. I'm sure he's just hiding out of the rain. Maybe he went home?

Fra   I checked. My granny is raging at me for leaving him. I told her he was in Jo's house. Text me if you see him OK?

They nod. **Fra** *exits.*

Steve   Maybe he was taken by 'The Maaaannnn'.

Carly   Don't say that, Steve.

Steve   So you do believe?

Carly   Just get the bloody shears.

Just as **Steve** *gets the shears, the security light turns on and they run.*

Scene Nine

Eugene *is holding a long coat.*

Eugene   OK, guys. I'm currently in the back garden of The Rottweiler. He's not a dog, he's actually my friend Lisa's dad. He's called Rottweiler because he once bit a man's ear off for scratching his car. Talk about toxic masculinity! I've found this coat hanging over the fence. It's actually kind of gross, it smells of cigarette smoke or old socks or something, but this will get me a triple bonus and put me in the lead. *This* is why I'm the reigning champ. Let's get this to base.

Lisa*'s text comes in –* **Eugene** *turns his camera back on.*

Eugene   Shit just got real. My friend Lisa just spotted The Man – an actual murderer on the loose. It's not just a rumour. My friend Jo was almost snatched by him. They say he wears a *long black coat.*

We hear the sound of a door opening and a man shouting 'Who's out there?!' as **Eugene** *runs offstage losing his shoe.*

Scene Ten

Fra *enters the stage,* **Danielle** *is standing still staring at the religious statue.*

Fra (*whispers*)   Danielle?

She glances at him for a moment then turns back to the statue trancelike.

Fra   Have you seen Peter?

Danielle   Are you religious, Fra?

Fra   No. My granny is. I read the Bible to her.

Danielle   Does it help her?

Fra (*shrugs*)   She's not getting better.

Danielle   It's fucking weird-looking, isn't it?

Fra   St Agnes.

Danielle   St Agnes?

Fra   My granny's obsessed with saints. We pray to St Anthony when we lose something. Pray to St Jude when we're worried. Padre Pio when the shit hits the fan.

Danielle   What does St Agnes do?

Fra   Dunno. I do know there's a patron saint for dentists. Which is odd because all dentists are evil.

Danielle   You believe in evil?

Fra   Maybe.

Danielle   Do you think I'm evil?

Fra   No.

Danielle   Don't lie.

Fra   I'm not.

Danielle   I saw your faces when I walked in.

Fra   What do you mean?

Danielle   You jumped like a little bitch.

Fra   I didn't.

Danielle   You're all afraid of me.

Fra   We're not.

She takes a few steps towards him threateningly.

Danielle   You're not afraid of me?

Fra   No.

Danielle   You should be afraid of me. Get out of this garden.

Fra   OK, but Danielle please, if you see Peter . . .

Danielle   What? If I see Peter, don't hurt him?

Fra   That wasn't what I was gonna say.

Danielle (*sarcastically*)   Maybe you should pray to St Anthony to find Peter. Tell everyone if they touch this statue, they're dead!

As **Fra** *hurries off,* **Danielle** *lifts the statue.*

Scene Eleven

Lisa *is standing with an umbrella,* **Niamh** *enters and goes under it.*

Lisa   Where have you been?!

Niamh   Do you actually understand how this game works?

Lisa   You've been away ages.

Niamh   I chased Fra. Thought I spotted Steve but it was his ma, not even lying. Almost jumped on her until I saw the handbag. Saw someone in Mrs Duffin's, which turned out to be Mrs Duffin, and she threw an orange at me! An *orange*. Checked behind the factory fence down to the corner wall. They must be round the backs. We need to go together to draw them out.

Lisa   Niamh, something *weird* is going on. We've already got shears and a bin full of maggots.

Niamh   Lisa! Why did you leave base?

Lisa   I didn't!

Niamh   I told you to stay here!

Lisa   I did! I swear.

Niamh   Then how did the objects get there?

Lisa   I think Danielle's using black magic again.

Niamh   Her and Jo made that up.

Lisa   Jo *swore* to me. They did the Ouija board, summoned the ghost of Roald Dahl and a book flew across the room. I think she made them objects fly over here with her mind like Matilda.

Niamh   Why *Roald Dahl*? Like of all the dead people . . .

Lisa   She freaks me out. Who knows what she's capable of.

Her phone beeps.

Fra says to keep an eye out for Peter.

Niamh   Is he not with Peter?

Lisa   He can't find him.

Niamh   *Oh . . . very* clever, Fra. It's a trick! He's trying to lure us away from the box with a stupid story. Well we're not gonna fall for it!

*We see a figure approaching the box unseen by **Lisa** and **Niamh**.*

Lisa   I don't think it's a trick.

Niamh   You're so gullible.

Lisa (*sudden realisation*)   Oh my God!

Niamh   What?

Lisa   I bet The Man has got him!

Niamh   Oh for God's sake!

Lisa   Creepy weirdo hanging about as children play, child goes missing!

Niamh   Catch a grip.

The figure takes the shears then exits.

Lisa   I can already hear my TV interview. 'I knew as soon as I saw that man that something wasn't right, but nobody would believe me.'

Niamh   One five-pointer and we lose the game. Wait – I thought you said there were shears?

Lisa   Yeah, they're right – they were there!

Niamh   Are you sure?

Lisa   They were right there beside the bin!

Niamh   Why would someone go to the effort of leaving them at base and then go get them again?

Lisa   I swear they were right there.

Niamh (*a realisation to herself*)   I've got it! What *if* Fra and Steve are in cahoots?

Lisa   In ca-wha?

Niamh   Clever. But they can't get the star item if the star item isn't there?

Lisa   Wouldn't that be cheating?

Niamh   Then we'll know who the real champ is.

Lisa   Are you even listening to me?

Niamh   Exactly. Let's go.

She walks off followed by a confused **Lisa***.*

Scene Twelve

We see the light from **Jo***'s torch on her phone before they enter. We can hear the rain pelting on a roof.*

Jo   Quick!

James   It's really coming down now!

Jo   I'm soaked.

James   Me too!

Jo   They'll not find us here.

James   What is this place?

Jo   Just a hole in the wall.

James   It must have a purpose.

Jo   Nope. It's been here for years. It's my secret hideout.

James   I like your friends.

Jo (*disbelieving*)   Oh really?

James   Yes! They're . . . *interesting*. Fun. I suppose.

Jo   They're not really my friends.

James   What do you mean?

Jo   We live in the same area so we play together. But they're not my *friend* friends.

James   Why?

Jo   We're just . . . different.

A flash of lightning reveals **Danielle** *hiding by the entrance holding the statue, unseen by* **Jo** *and* **James.**

Jo   I think that was lightning!

Beat.

James   Am I your *friend* friend?

Phone beeps.

Jo   Fra. Says keep an eye out for Peter.

James   Which one's Peter again?

Jo   The youngest one. Fra's his older brother.

James   The one who lives with his grandmother?

Jo   Yeah. She never leaves her bed.

James   Where's his mum?

Jo   In a hospital for crazy people.

James   What about his dad?

Jo   He doesn't have a dad.

James   Oh.

Beat.

Jo   Yes you are.

James   What?

Jo   My *friend* friend.

Beat.

James   What did you do when you came here?

Jo   Nothing.

James   You just sat here in silence?

Jo   I used to come here when my parents were arguing. It's a good wee place to escape from everything. But then my dad left and everything was OK.

James   That must've been hard.

Jo   Nope. I still see him and all, like. Almost everyone's parents are split round here. I always had both my parents, then I became like everyone else.

James   I don't think you're like everyone else.

Jo   What do you mean?

James   You're unique.

Jo   Is that a good thing?

James   Definitely.

Jo   I don't think so. I wish I was like you.

They go to kiss. **Danielle** *jumps out.*

Danielle   I'm gonna throw up.

Jo *and* **James** *jump.*

James (*like he's been caught*)   Danielle!

Danielle   Little Jojo. What would your mum say if she knew you were in here alone with a boy?

Jo   We were getting in out of the rain.

Danielle   Yeah because you're so innocent.

She stares through them.

Thought you'd forgotten about this place. We used to come here all the time, remember? We came here after we set the caretaker's shed on fire. Remember that, Jojo?

Jo   Yes.

Danielle   We couldn't stop laughing at Mr Quigley. He actually started crying!

James *looks at* **Jo.**

Jo (*apologetic*)   He really wasn't a nice man.

Danielle   He was an *asshole*. He deserved what he got. Hope you're not one of those people, James.

James   Sorry?

Danielle   People who walk around thinking they're better than everyone else, can say and do whatever they want and people just let them.

James   No . . .?

Danielle   Do you know who this is? (*The statue only with the head.*)

Jo   Is that Mrs Gregory's statue? What happened?

Danielle   St Agnes. I googled her. All the people who tried to hurt her went blind. They chopped her head off in the end. She was *too* powerful.

Jo   Did you chop her head off?

Danielle   It was too heavy to carry.

James   Is that blood?

Danielle   I must've cut my hand.

James   Are you hurt?

Danielle   I tried to cut it off with garden clippers. That didn't work. So I smashed against a wall feet first.

Jo *receives a text and replies back.*

Danielle   Are you texting about me!

Jo   No! Look. I'm just texting the group.

Danielle   Why am I not in the group?

Jo   I didn't have your snap.

Danielle   Liar.

Jo   Peter is missing.

Danielle   Fra can't protect him forever.

James   Everyone's a bit freaked out because of The Man.

Danielle   You made that up, Jo.

James   She didn't. She saw him.

Danielle   She's a liar.

James   She's not.

Danielle   You don't know her like I do.

James   Tell her, Jo.

Jo   It's true, Danielle.

Danielle   When did you see him?

Jo   Last week.

Danielle   What did he look like?

Jo   He had really dark eyes. And when he smiled his teeth were all rotted, black and yellow.

Danielle   I don't believe you.

Jo   You don't have to. The peelers are looking for him. My uncle told us to be really careful, make sure we lock all our doors.

James   That's why she's moving.

Danielle (*softer*)   Is that why? I thought it was . . .

Jo   My mum's terrified.

Danielle   Swear on St Agnes you're not lying?

Jo   What?

Danielle   Put your hand on her and say you swear you're telling the truth.

Jo   No!

Danielle   You're a liar. I knew it.

James   She's an honest person.

Danielle   Swear on the statue.

Jo   Fine.

Danielle   If you're lying, something really, *really* bad will happen to you.

Jo (*hand on the statue*)   I swear I'm telling the truth.

Danielle   Time will tell. You better hope you're not lying.

She exits.

James   She scares me more than The Man.

Jo   She's not really scary.

James   She's terrifying!

Jo   You don't know her like I do.

James   Were you actually best friends?

Jo   Yes. Until the kitten thing.

James   Just tell me already!

Jo   Let's get out of here.

Scene Thirteen

Niamh *and* **Lisa** *are in Fat Davy's shed.*

Niamh   You're chicken shit.

Lisa   *We're* not supposed to be getting objects.

Niamh   But if *we* have the rifle, Steve can't get it.

Lisa   It's cheating.

Niamh   Where's the rifle?

Lisa   I don't know.

Niamh   Well, look!

Lisa Will I put my torch on?

Niamh So Fat Davy can see us snooping about his shed?

Lisa I'm just trying to be helpful!

Niamh It's up there. Climb up.

Lisa Will I fuck!

A shadow of a man passes outside the shed window. They freeze.

Niamh Sshhhuush!

Lisa Is he coming in?

Niamh Be quiet!

Lisa I'm so dead. If he doesn't kill me, my da will.

Niamh *Shut up!*

They cling to each other as we hear the sound of someone trying to open the shed locks.

Lisa Oh God!

A moment passes.

Niamh They're gone. Lisa, look!

Lisa What?

Niamh On the floor. The coat.

Lisa What about it?

Niamh Isn't that Peter's coat?

Lisa It couldn't be.

Niamh It's hardly Fat Davy's. That's the coat Peter was wearing.

Lisa What do we do?

Niamh I'll get the coat, you get the rifle.

Lisa I'm not climbing up!

Niamh But I have to?

Lisa It was your idea!

Niamh Rock, paper, scissors?

Lisa *loses.*

Niamh Too bad. I'll give you a heave-up. One, two, three!

*As **Lisa** leaps, the lights come down and we hear the sound of tins and tools crashing to the ground.*

Scene Fourteen

Fra *is searching furtively for* **Peter**. **Eugene** *limps in on one shoe, freezing when he sees the figure of* **Fra**.

Fra   Oh it's you.

Eugene   I'm having the worst night. Lost one of my shoes and stood on broken glass or something.

Fra   I actually don't give a flying piss, Eugene. My brother is missing.

Eugene   He's just hiding.

Fra   That's what everyone keeps saying. We all know it's not true. He hates this game. I never should have made him play in the first place.

Eugene   It'll be OK.

Fra   Just shut up! I wish everyone would shut up and stop saying these stupid things. I left him on his own. Even if he's hiding, he'll be afraid. I did that to him.

Eugene   But you didn't do it on purpose/

Fra   That doesn't make it better! Are you stupid? Piss off.

Eugene   Just trying to help.

Fra   What would you know? You live in your stupid camera prancing around talking about things nobody cares about. You've no idea what our life is like.

Eugene   You don't know anything about *my* life.

Fra   It's all make-believe, la-di-da. 'I'm Eugene, I don't have any friends. I have robot friends on the internet because they're the only people who like me.'

Eugene   'Oh I'm Fra. I'm so hard, I have to make other people feel bad about themselves so I can look like a big man.' I'm standing here in front of you offering help.

Fra   I don't need your help.

Eugene   Fuck off then.

Fra   What's your problem?

Eugene   You're the one being an asshole.

Fra   I don't have time to waste arguing with some muppet like you.

Eugene   Go find the brother you abandoned. You don't need my help. Better still, let The Man find him.

Fra   What did you say?

Eugene   I'm just saying . . . we all thought it was a rumour, now everyone's seeing him about the place. Hope he doesn't get to him before you.

Fra   You nasty piece of shit!

Fra *lunges towards* **Eugene** *and tackles him to the ground.*

Scene Fifteen

Steve   I'm telling ya, we should've waited.

Carly   For Fat Davy to come out of his shed and shoot us.

Steve   What if it wasn't him and someone else is getting the rifle? They didn't look fat.

Carly   Then we'd still win.

Steve   But *I* wanted to get it. And rub it in Niamh's face.

Carly   Too bad.

Steve   What can we take from here?

Carly   Danielle will kill us.

Steve   We'll take something small.

Carly   Such as?

Steve (*pointing*)   Empty cans.

Carly   A beer can?

Steve   Something metal.

They peer out towards the audience.

Careful. Her mum's in there. Is she sleeping?

Carly   Her eyes are open.

Steve   She's not moving. Maybe she's dead.

Carly   She's not. Her fingers are tapping.

Steve   She's off her face. I thought she was clean?

Carly   Just grab the can.

Steve   What's wrong with you today? You're so grumpy.

Carly   Nothing!

Steve   Is it your . . .

Carly   My what?

Steve   Your . . . *thing* . . .

Carly   My *thing*?

Steve   You know . . . your *time* . . .

Carly   You can't even say it. So immature. *Period* is the word you're looking for.

Steve   Ugh, that *word*!

Carly   Wise up!

Steve   So it is . . . *that* . . .?

Carly   I'm gonna slap you in a minute.

Steve   Don't poke the bear.

Carly   Are you calling me fat?

Steve   Jesus, why are you so touchy today?

Carly   It's my dad's anniversary today.

Steve   I totally forgot.

Carly   One year.

Steve   Do you miss him?

Carly   It still doesn't seem real. I just keep expecting to come home from school and find him in the kitchen. With a glass of vodka and coke, obvs. Singing along to the radio.

Steve   He was good craic, your da.

Carly   Most of the time. I feel bad for Danielle.

Steve   Your da was nothing like Danielle's mum.

Carly   I know what that's like, to live with an addict. It's not just that. I feel guilty for moving away to do this course and leaving my ma on her own.

Steve   She'll be fine. I'll call round and see her, your ma loves me.

He is suddenly distracted.

Carly, look!

Carly   What?

Steve   Did you see?

Carly   Where?

Steve   There's someone in there with her.

Carly   I don't see anybody.

Steve   I'm telling you, I saw someone.

Carly   It's probably Danielle.

Steve   No it's a man.

Carly   It's just a shadow.

Steve   Come here. Look.

They huddle close.

Carly (*turns to him*)   I don't see anything.

Steve *goes to kiss* **Carly**.

Carly   What are you doing!

Steve   Sorry . . . I . . .

Carly   Asshole!

Steve   Carly, wait!

Scene Sixteen

Lisa (*freaking out*)   I'm so dead.

Niamh   Can't *believe* we left the rifle.

Lisa   Oh so-*rry*! I was too busy getting drowned in red paint!

They move towards base to see more items placed on the box including the statue.

Niamh   No rifle yet. We're still in play.

Lisa   My life is over.

Niamh   Steve must have the rifle. Who got the statue? It's in half! Whoever left it should get half the points!

Lisa   Do you think if I pray to this thing my da won't kill me?

Niamh   I want to say yes . . .

Lisa *kneels down in prayer.*

Lisa   Dear . . . *Jesus* . . .

Niamh   That's not Jesus.

Eugene *enters with a black eye/bloodied face.*

Niamh   What happened to you?

Eugene   I'm going home. This game's the worst.

Lisa   Did The Man get you?

Fra *enters looking as bad as* **Eugene**.

Fra   Guys, game's over. Peter is missing. I need everyone to look for him. It's been too long now.

He sees the statue.

What is that?

Lisa   A statue . . . *not* of Jesus.

Fra (*horrified*)   Is that blood?

Niamh   It's paint. Lisa's covered in it.

Lisa (*stands*)   I never touched it.

Niamh   Fra . . . we found this. (*Indicating the coat.*)

Fra *lifts it up.*

Fra   It's on Peter's coat.

Niamh   Let's not jump to conclusions.

Fra   Get everyone back here.

Lisa *texts on her phone.*

Niamh   It's paint. It's got on it somehow. It was everywhere.

Fra   It's not on you.

Niamh (*to* **Lisa**)   You must've touched it.

Lisa   I didn't.

Fra   Are you sure?

Lisa   I don't know.

Steve *enters.*

Steve   What the hell's happened?

Fra   What if it's not paint?

Niamh   Of course it's paint!

Steve   I've heard about these things. Statues crying blood.

Niamh   It's not blood!

Steve   Who got it?

Eugene   It was gone when I went in earlier.

Steve   Wasn't me or Carly.

Fra   Danielle. She wouldn't let anyone touch it.

Steve   She probably killed another kitten with it.

Jo *and* **James** *enter.*

Jo   What's going on?

Fra   I need everyone to look for Peter!

Steve   There's blood on the statue.

Jo   Danielle had it.

Niamh   It's paint! We spilt paint in Fat Davy's shed.

Eugene   How would the statue get into the shed?

Jo   Is that Peter's coat?

Fra   Let's go now!

James   I think we need to report him missing.

Fra   No! No police.

James   They can find him a lot quicker than us, Fra. They're there to help.

Fra   What would you know?

Jo   My uncle's a policeman, he could help us.

Fra   In *my* experience, the peelers don't help. They take away the people you love. If we phone your uncle, he'll tell social services that my granny can't look after us. They'll take us away from her. They'll take Peter away from me.

Lisa   Where's Carly?

Steve   She went home.

Lisa   Why?

Niamh   Lovers' tiff?

Steve   Shut up, Niamh.

Niamh   It's about time you were both honest about it.

Steve   Is this really the time?

Jo   Has anyone seen Danielle?

Niamh   Ring her!

Jo   I don't have her new number!

Eugene   I only saw her when we started.

Jo   We saw her a while ago with the statue.

Niamh   Has anyone else seen her?

Fra   Ages ago, when she told me not to touch the statue.

Lisa   So Danielle put the statue here . . . it may or may not have blood on it and Peter is missing –

Niamh   Don't say it, Niamh. She's mad but she wouldn't . . .

Lisa She did it to the kitten.

James What *did* she do?

Lisa She bashed its head in with a brick.

Eugene Lisa!

Next exchange is a flurry of shouts building into an argument at the same time until **Eugene** *takes charge.*

Jo We need to focus!

Lisa Maybe The Man has both of them!

Fra (*to* **Lisa**) What are you saying?

Jo Don't say that, Lisa! Don't even think it.

Steve This is mental. I'm going home.

Eugene Yeah, run away and leave us to deal with it.

James I think we should all try to calm down and think rationally.

Fra I'm gonna punch him in a minute.

Jo He's just trying to help.

Niamh (*to* **Lisa**) See what you started!

Lisa How did I start it?

Fra (*really freaking out*) What am I gonna do? I've lost him . . . my granny won't be able to . . . how will I . . . what will I do? What am I gonna do?

Eugene Stop! This is what we're gonna do. Me and Fra will take Corrib Avenue. Steve, get Carly back out and search Dunville Crescent. Jo, James, do Mountpottinger. Lisa, Niamh, Frank Street. If you see anything, put it on the group chat. Once you're done, move to another street, put it on the chat so we're not covering the same area. We're gonna find him. Go!

Scene Seventeen

This scene is a snapshot of the pairs out looking for **Peter**. *They might be at different points of the stage only lit when they're speaking. The storm is at its worst, blowing gusts of wind, blowing objects around, knocking things over, slamming gates*

Jo Peter!

Lisa Peter!

Steve Peter!

Niamh Peter!

Fra   Peter!

Lights up on **Jo** *and* **James**.

James   Maybe we should tell your mum.

Jo   No way.

James   This isn't a game any more.

Jo   We'll find him.

James   There's blood on the statue!

Jo   We don't know it's blood.

James   I don't like this, Jo.

Jo   Peter!

Lights up on **Steve** *and* **Carly**.

Steve   Thanks for coming back out.

Carly   Poor thing must be freezing in this weather.

Steve   He's out here somewhere.

Carly   Are you sure it was blood?

Steve   Looked like it.

Carly   I hope to God he's not badly hurt.

Beat.

Steve   Carly, listen . . .

Lights up on **Lisa** *and* **Niamh**.

Lisa   I'm in so much trouble.

Niamh   Fuck up, Lisa.

Lisa   You don't understand.

Niamh   We've a bloody statue and a missing child and all you're worried about is paint on your clothes!

Lisa   Do you know how much they cost?

Niamh   We all know where your da gets his money from.

Lisa   What?

Niamh   Why don't you just tell him I threw it over you? You blame me on everything anyway.

Lisa   I don't.

Niamh   You do. What was it you said? My mummy wouldn't care anyway.

Lisa   I didn't mean it like that.

Niamh   What *did* you mean?

Lights up on **Fra** *and* **Eugene**.

Fra   Peter! Where the hell is he?

Eugene   Maybe he's just . . . taking a break.

Fra   A break?

Eugene   Have you never done that?

Fra   What?

Eugene   Just go hide somewhere quiet.

Fra   No. That's weird.

Eugene   I have.

Fra   Why?

Lights up on **Jo** *and* **James**.

Jo   Where could he be?

James   How mad is Mad Danielle?

Jo   She wouldn't hurt him.

James   Do you think The Man has got him?

Jo   . . . Maybe.

James   What did he look like again?

Jo   Why?

James   You'll need to describe him to the police.

Jo   We won't. We'll find Peter.

James   You're uncle's hunting for The Man. You might have to do one of those police sketch things.

Jo   He was wearing a hat. I couldn't see his face.

James   You didn't mention the hat before.

Jo   Didn't I?

James   What kind of hat?

Jo   Does it matter?

James   Jo, this is important.

Jo   Let's just find Peter.

James   There is a murderer on the loose and a child missing, we need to –

A gust of wind blows.

Jo   I made him up.

James (*can't hear her*)   What?

Jo (*shouting*)   I made him up! OK! There is no man.

James   *What?*

Lights up on **Lisa** *and* **Niamh**.

Niamh   Tell me what you really think about my ma?

Lisa   She's just . . . more focused on other things.

Niamh   What's that supposed to mean?

Lisa   You never get in trouble for stuff. She doesn't go on at you about homework or how late you stay out. You never really get new clothes . . . or anything.

Niamh   She's on her own with four kids, Lisa. She's got enough on her plate!

Lisa   Calm down.

Niamh   All you ever think about is what a person has or looks like. At least she's honest and doesn't pretend to be something she's not like your family.

Lights up on **Fra** *and* **Eugene**.

Eugene   Sometimes you just want to be alone.

Fra   Peter's not like that.

Eugene   Are you sure?

Fra   I know my own brother. He wouldn't want to be alone.

Eugene   Maybe you do it because you want to see if anyone will notice that you're gone? If anyone will miss you or worry about you.

Fra   That's horrible. Why put someone through that worry?

Eugene   You don't know they're worried until you do it. Some people mightn't worry.

Beat.

Fra   About before. I'm sorry, mate. I was a dick.

Eugene   Yip. So was I.

Lights up on **Steve** *and* **Carly**.

Steve   I'm sorry about earlier. I should never have done that.

Carly   No you shouldn't have.

Steve   I was out of order.

Carly   It's OK.

Steve   It's not. It's just . . . I'm really gonna miss you when you leave. You're my best mate.

Carly   I'm not going forever. I'll be back.

Steve   Why would you come back here?

Carly   This is my home. I'm gonna come back with my certificate, get the youth centre opened again and . . . (*joking*) teach all the kids how to play Hunt.

Lights up on **Lisa** *and* **Niamh**.

Niamh   That was a shitty thing to say. I'm sorry.

Lisa   I'm sorry too.

Niamh   What if we don't find him?

Lisa   Let's not think about that.

Niamh   One good thing to come out of tonight though . . .

Lisa   What?

Niamh   Technically . . . we won.

Lisa   Are you havin' a laugh?

Lights up on **Jo** *and* **James**.

James   Why would you make up something like that?

Jo   It was just a joke.

James   It's not funny. You need to tell everyone the truth!

Jo   Why?

There is a strike of lightning and a gunshot hidden under the sound of thunder. Lights are up on all characters as they freeze when they hear it.

James   Was that –

Steve   It couldn't be the – it doesn't work . . .

Eugene   Maybe it was a firework?

Carly   It was thunder!

Fra (*grave*)   It was a gunshot.

Lisa   This is the worst night of my life.

Niamh   Worst night of someone else's more like.

After a moment, we hear **Peter** *calling out for* **Fra**.

Carly   Ssshhh!

Jo   What's that?

Carly   Can you hear that?

Niamh   Peter!

Lisa   Are you sure?

Fra   Peter!

The characters all shout 'Peter' as they run off to look for him.

Scene Eighteen

Peter *is centre stage as the pairs come in one at a time.*

Fra   Are you hurt?

Peter   I wanna go home, Fra.

Fra   Where have you been?

Peter   What was that noise?

Fra   You've been missing for three hours!

Peter   I was hiding.

Fra   I've been looking for you everywhere!

Peter   But you're not a hunter.

Fra   Why did you move?

Peter   Did I win?

Fra   Where were you?

Danielle *enters with a rifle.*

Peter   Danielle put me in a shed because my coat was wet.

Fra   Did she hurt you?

Peter   No she gave me biscuits.

Jo   Where is Danielle, Peter?

Peter   I don't know.

Danielle   Turns out it works after all.

They all turn and freeze.

Did you really think I would hurt him?

Fra   I heard the gunshot and I panicked.

Danielle   I was testing it. Next time, I might just take aim. That's what you all think anyway, don't you?

Carly   No!

Steve   Of course not.

Danielle *turns the gun towards* **Steve**.

Danielle   Really? You're not afraid?

Carly   Danielle, please be careful.

Danielle   You don't call me Mad Danielle?

Niamh   That's just a nickname!

Danielle   Liars! (*Turning to* **Jo**.) It's all because of you.

James   Jo's your friend.

Danielle   What the fuck do you know?

Jo   I'm sorry for everything that's happened.

Danielle   Like what?

Jo   Just . . . everything.

Danielle   Everyone thinks I'm the crazy one you can do no wrong.

Jo   Nobody thinks that.

Danielle   I swear to God if you keep lying I'm gonna fire this thing. Just be honest!

Jo   I am.

Daneille   I told you something bad would happen if you lied.

Jo   I don't think you're crazy. I know you.

Danielle   Tell everyone the truth.

Jo   What do you mean?

Danielle   Tell them what you did.

Jo   Danielle, please.

Danielle   Say it in front of everyone, in front of your new posh friend, tell them all the kind of person you are.

Jo *remains silent.*

Daneille   Everyone listen up, I'm gonna tell a little story. One day, Jo and I are climbing the sheds. Little Jess curls up on the wee spot of sunshine on the ground below. Jo says, do you dare me to push this brick off the shed? No, I say, only a fucking monster would hurt an animal, let alone a wee kitten. She smiles and pushes the brick off the shed. The wee thing couldn't move and was making this *noise*. *Howling*. I never knew cats howled. I jumped down and hit it again to put it out of its misery. You were still laughing. Even then. Until Mrs Gregory saw us. Then you ran. Her mum is moving so she, the kitten killer, will be away from me, let's be honest.

James   Is that true, Jo?

Daneille   Tell them!

She goes to lower the rifle and accidentally fires it. It hits **Jo** *in the thigh. Everyone screams.* **Jo** *writhes in pain,* **Danielle** *is visibly in shock and throws the rifle down.*

Danielle   I didn't mean it!

Lisa   She's hit!

Carly   She's bleeding!

Danielle   It was an accident! I swear!

Steve   You shot her!

Niamh   What have you done?

Danielle   No . . . Jo . . . I didn't . . . I swear . . .

James   Someone phone an ambulance!

Eugene   I'll get her mum!

Jo *steels herself for a moment.*

Jo   Wait!

Takes a deep breath.

The Man shot me.

Niamh   What?

Jo   The Man. Was hunting us all night. The Man. Shot me. Danielle, *run*!

Danielle   No!

Jo   Go! Everyone! James, go! I don't want you to lie for me.

James   No!

Jo   There's people coming!

James   I can't leave you!

Jo   You have to! Go! Go now!

Eugene, **Fra** *and* **Peter** *hurry off;* **Lisa** *and* **Niamh** *run off together;* **Carly** *and* **Steve** *pull* **Danielle** *and* **James** *away;* **Jo** *drops to the ground as we hear people approaching.*

Scene Nineteen

This scene takes place several years later, perhaps projected onto a screen.

Eugene   Hey, guys! Welcome to my channel! We're almost at 200,000 subscribers so please smash that button. I've been thinking a lot about my early videos. There's one I didn't share, for reasons I cannot say. But it reminded me of games we used to play when we were young. On the street where I lived, we had this game called Hunt. Did anyone else play it? To me, it was the scariest but most exciting game in the world. I'm not even sure where it came from or who made it up . . .

*At another part of the stage, a young **Danielle** enters followed by a young **Jo** looking around. This scene takes place years before but can be played by the same actors. **Eugene** can keep talking silently then disappear gradually.*

Jo   What is this place?

Danielle   I don't know. I found it by accident.

Jo   You always know the best places to hide!

Danielle   You can't tell anyone about it. I'm only telling you cos you're my best friend.

Jo   Cross my heart and hope to die.

Danielle   See! I told you I would cheer you up!

Jo   I love it!

Danielle   Nobody will ever find us here.

Jo   Not even kidnappers.

Danielle   Nobody. It'll be our secret hideout.

Jo   What'll we do now? Wanna play a game?

Danielle   I just played the best game in my cousin's street but we need more people.

Jo   What game is it?

Danielle   It's called Two Man Hunt.

Jo   Wow!

Danielle   So, you pick two people to be the hunters. Everyone else has to run and hide. It's like hide and seek but you can move around different hiding places. And you have to steal all these things from different places. Everybody has to decide what you have to steal.

Jo   A treasure hunt!

Danielle   Sort of. No. But they all have different points. So, you can have a star item, which has to be something hard to steal. Then you can pick random things like a stone, or pick a colour and find something of that colour –

Jo   Green! Green's my favourite colour!

Danielle   So something green like a tree, well, not a tree because that's too big, but you can pick a . . .

Lights go down as **Danielle** *keeps describing the game.*

End.

Hunt

BY FIONNUALA KENNEDY

*Notes on rehearsal and staging, drawn from a workshop with the writer,
held at the National Theatre, October 2021*

How the writer came to write the play

When Fionnuala Kennedy was asked to write a play for Connections, she thought about the enormity of the opportunity. She would be writing for young people – she remembered when she was younger, there were very few plays on offer for a young cast. She wanted to write something young people would really enjoy performing.

Fionnuala Kennedy began writing this play in 2018 following the #MeToo movement in Ireland. She said she noticed push-back from the theatre industry, and noted that it was while talking to her sixteen-year-old daughter that the need to write this play crystallised further. Kennedy described how her daughter started to notice how societal expectations impacted on girls her age: even when her daughter was younger, she was told she had to wear a dress at school, rather than being able to wear trousers or shorts. It meant she wasn't able to join in the rougher games with the boys. The headmaster's excuse was 'tradition'.

Alongside this, Kennedy discussed how Northern Ireland is a post-conflict nation. She grew up in a very nationalist, Republican community, and noticed a fiercely protective attitude to the community's history and narrative. For example, at the centenary of the Easter Rising, the community re-enacted the event. She said many people disagreed with the traditions – but that it was hard to voice dissent when they were guarded by such an intimidating male presence in the community.

She noted that in this regard, nothing much had changed since her own childhood – and this is where the initial spark of the play came from.

Then she had the idea to structure it around a game, to give the story shape: 'Two Man Hunt', which she used to play herself in Belfast. 'It was hide and seek on a whole other level.'

She discussed how she wanted to use the game as a tool to explore the wider discussions mentioned – and also to write a play that had some really good parts for young girls.

Introduction

Exercise: Scavenger hunt

Lead director Alix Harris and writer Fionnuala Kennedy began the day with a scavenger hunt. The purpose: to get the group thinking about the mindset of the characters in *Hunt*. Alix Harris read out a list of objects, and the group had five minutes to search for something blue, a piece of paper, something with a scent and a random object about which to tell a story.

Exercise: Make a play

The group was asked to take ten minutes to put together a short play featuring each of the gathered objects.

Alix Harris talked about how much she enjoys using simple objects in theatre-making. She stressed how important it is to encourage teenagers to play, and unlock that sense of their inner child. For example, you could run an exercise where you ask your young people to choose a random object in the room, and invent a game that involves that object.

The reading

The group read through the entire play.

Before the reading began, Alix Harris handed out Post-it notes. She encouraged the group to write down any questions that cropped up during the reading, to address at the end. She also noted this is a useful exercise if you're running short of time. Post-it notes can be left behind, and unanswered questions can be read, considered and followed up later.

Exercises for use in rehearsals

Alix Harris led the group through some exercises that could be useful in the rehearsal room. She explained she tries to develop a physical language when she's directing. It can be easy to get tied up intellectually and forget our bodies. She asked the group to think about how they could tell this story with their bodies as much as the text. Young people can be awkward in themselves – how do you in your process help them feel comfortable, but also lean into how these characters feel awkward in their own bodies.

Exercise: World of the play

The group was split into teams, and each team was handed a big piece of paper and a pen. Harris asked each group to draw the map of where the characters live. Harris asked them to consider what facts they know about the place. For example, from the text, they know that Mrs Johnson has a house on their street. She also encouraged them to invent their own facts about the world, and add those to the map.

Then she encouraged the groups to take their maps into more fantastical territory. If you were to draw Mrs Johnson's house in number 15, what does it look like in the children's heads? Is it spiky? Is it made of candyfloss?

She asked the groups to also consider *senses*. Is there a house that is the 'smelly house'? Is there a house that is the 'noisy house'? Is there a house that needs a lick of paint?

Alix Harris discussed how it was a good technique to get everyone talking about the play, and getting everyone to create the world together. It also moves you away from everyone thinking about *set*, which productions might not have a budget for.

Another good way of using this exercise is to get the actors to do it individually. What does Mrs Johnson's house mean to each character? Perhaps different things to different people.

Exercise: The doorway

Everyone was asked to choose a character from the play.

Alix Harris asked them to take a piece of paper, and draw a door. This would be the door on the *inside* of that character's house. Around the door, she asked the group to write words, or draw images, that explore how their character feels inside this house.

For example, it might be a safe space for them. Or it might be a scary place. What are the different things going on for this character behind closed doors?

She noted how it's important to remember that although characters don't go home in the play, they still have homes. Maybe there's something they're proud of in here? Maybe an award from school? Or maybe they still sleep with a blanket. They might have an older sibling. They might be responsible for cooking dinner.

Then she asked the group to turn the paper over and draw a door on the other side. She asked them to imagine that the character is stepping outside. What words would you write around the door on the outside? What's their outside persona? What characteristics do they have when they are outside, with others? She encouraged the group to make clear connections between how these 'outside' emotions link to a character's 'inside' emotions.

When everyone was finished, they were asked to stand and work on a personal performance.

The only text everyone was allowed to use were the words, 'My name is [character name]'; e.g. 'My name is Eugene'.

Harris asked them to look at the words on their *inside* door. To repeat the phrase and begin to take on the physical attributes of the character.

After a while, Harris asked everyone to visualise the door in front of them. She asked them to think: 'Is it *easy* to open that door, or difficult?' She asked them to perform attempting to open the door.

Once the door was open, she asked the group to step through and explore the 'outside version' of their character, using the same repeated phrase, 'My name is . . .'.

She noted that with some characters, like Peter, there might be a big change from inside to outside; but for other characters, like Jo, there may be less of a change. She said this is interesting, and a useful talking point with your cast – not all teenagers need to be dark and lonely inside.

Exercise: Physical actioning

Alix Harris asked the group to choose a character. Then she asked them to choose a phrase from this list that best suited their character:

- I am heavy
- I am light
- I am fizzy

- I am punchy
- I am floaty
- I am flicky

The group moved around the space, repeating one of these phrases over and over, focusing on representing their phrase with their movements, connecting up the body and the voice.

Then she asked them to return to the text, and find a line that their character speaks. Then she asked them to repeat their phrase (I am light, or I am heavy, etc.), building up to a line delivery.

For example, Alix Harris chose Danielle. She repeated 'I am punchy' over and over, matching up her body and her voice; then when she had built up her energy, she swapped to the line, 'Are you texting about me?'

Exercise: Physical actioning in pairs

The groups paired up and chose a conversation in the play between two characters. They repeated the exercise, starting with an action from the list, and then swapping to dialogue.

Alix Harris noted that often as directors we can think – 'Oh, that's just not working' – but not have the answers to solve the problem. An exercise like this, where you are simply encouraged to try new things, really helps.

She also suggested that performers don't have to enact these actions with their entire bodies. You can easily make these ideas smaller. For example, just put the sense of lightness in your left hand, or your heaviness in your feet.

Q: Do you tend to use these kinds of actions, rather than more traditional 'actioning', i.e. I press, I convince, etc.
Alix Harris: I prefer to use things like this. Admittedly, you are asking people to be weird, which teenagers might feel uncomfortable about, but the more repetition you do, the easier it is to be bigger in your actions. It's also useful as a 'refresh', say before opening night or something.

Discussion

Alix asked the group to consider three things:

- What excites you the most about this play?
- What scares you about this play?
- If budget wasn't an issue, what's your dream version of this play?

Everyone spent five minutes thinking about this, jotting down responses and discussing their groups.

Alix Harris reminded the group of how useful a central metaphor can be to a production. Is there a ticking clock running all the way through? Does the storm regularly grow with each scene change? What takes this play beyond just scene following scene? What central metaphor could unite it as a piece?

Exercise: Provocations

Each group chose a scene to work on. They were handed a piece of paper with a 'limit', a 'provocation' or a 'framework' to explore within the scene. The groups were invited to stage a scene from the play with one of these provocations in mind:

1 The dialogue must be delivered to the audience
2 The scene must use either soundscape or music or both
3 The audience are part of the scene
4 Characters in this scene are constantly moving
5 The scene is in the round

The group watched each scene, and discussed how the provocations informed the text.

1 The dialogue is delivered to the audience

The group discussed how scenes like this engage the audience in a different way, how they can break up the action. They also felt Jo was a character that interacted well with the audience.

Alix Harris suggested that a technique like this can really make an audience listen to a text. It can also help to place locations and ideas at specific points in the audience. For example, if you talk about the man with the van, do you pick a corner of the audience to always deliver dialogue about him to?

She also asked the group to consider using this technique for one or two characters. What happens if everyone talks to the audience aside from Jo and Danielle? Or what if Peter is the only person who can talk to the audience? Rather than just 'opening up to the audience', she asked, what happens if you make the audience an active participant?

2 The scene must use either soundscape or music or both

The group discussed how naturalistic sound really helped to imagine the space, and non-naturalistic sound helped emphasise the emotion. They also noted how sound can inform the performance of the actor. For example, a tense sound effect in rehearsal might encourage the actors to deliver their lines with more urgency.

Alix Harris noted that sound can really open up our sense of the world of the play. She also suggested making 'character playlists' to think about each part in the play. What music does each character listen to in their bedrooms?

3 The audience are part of the scene

The group discussed how making the audience part of the scene can give a greater sense of the world of the play. They also considered who they were casting the audience as: The houses? The storm?

Alix Harris suggested it's a really great way to bring an audience on board with the play. She also noted the presence of adults can be quite useful in this piece in particular.

4 Characters in this scene are constantly moving

The group discussed how movement delivered a sense of urgency.

Alix Harris noted that the movements didn't all have to be huge – some were quite small; which successfully communicated anxiety. She discussed how useful it can be to throw a provocation in and let the cast play, rather than giving everyone overly specific instructions.

5 The scene is in the round

The group discussed how challenging it can be to perform in the round, but also the reward it can give an audience – how it can really welcome them in.

Alix Harris suggested that in this play, the idea of a 'game' fits very nicely with being in the round.

She noted that often limitations can be really helpful when working on a play. On one day you might just look at sound, on another you might restrict yourself to trying it out in the round.

Question and answer with Fionnuala Kennedy and Alix Harris

Q: How do we begin to engage with some topics that could be triggering to young people?
AH: It matters how much you amplify some of these topics. If you unpack the entire script, there will be things in here that could be triggering for everyone. You can choose the most important thing in each scene and work on that, rather than digging into everything. We should also be careful of imposing/assuming what will be triggering. Just be open to what's happening in the room, and what comes up. It also helps to channel discussion through the notion of *character*. If you're worried, often using different forms and styles can create emotional distance between the character and the actors.

Q: For younger actors, i.e. years nine and ten, how much freedom is there to adapt swear words?
FK: You can have freedom with swear words and locality. I'm happy with swear words being cut if you can't say them in your context, and also for you to change the place this is set. Also, the young people will let you know if a word isn't working – they'll say, 'We don't say that'.

Q: Are there any further exercises to use when rehearsing this play?
AH: Games are useful. There are lots of standard drama games that you can play and then hook into the text. For example, to investigate a moment in the play where characters are scared, you could use a game where there is a sense of fear, like Grandmother's Footsteps. How does the game help you discover more about the scene? Games are a good way of avoiding doing too much sit-down work with your cast.

Q: If I cast different genders, are there any parts that specifically are girls or boys?
FK: It's flexible. But if it jars with the text, then it probably won't work. Fra and Peter could be female. Niamh could be male. But, for example, it feels like Lisa probably has to be female, and Steve probably has to be male.
AH: Try thinking past gender, and focusing instead on amping up specific characteristics to that character; e.g. if Fra was female, she could still be tough.

Q: If we changed genders, could you change lines, i.e. Fra 'hard man' to 'tough girl'?
FK: Whilst I'm OK with it being adapted locally, and male and female actors playing different characters, I think with changing lines like this there's a danger of it becoming a different play. Apart from swear words, locality and genders, I don't think you should change or take anything out.
AH: As long as you're really nailing the characterisation, an audience will accept what you present. Giving the student confidence to do that, rather than being concerned about the precise language, is the way forward.

Q: How old is Peter? And in the flashback, how much younger do you think Danielle and Jo are?
FK: Peter can be between eight and eleven, or older. He has been babied by Fra. Fra can be younger too, could be as young as thirteen. In terms of Danielle and Jo, I'm thinking they are about eight years old in the flashback at the end of the play.

Q: Do you have any thoughts on having more characters?
FK: There is the potential to double up some of the larger parts, like Danielle and Jo, on alternate nights.
AH: Or, you could think of more stylised ways to represent characters. For example, with Danielle, you could have her as a chorus. The children have made her into a monster, and so you could represent her that way. You could have, say, five actors play her in a monstrous way, then you could gradually decrease the number of actors as she becomes more human. Perhaps there is also a similar sort of exploration to have with Jo.

Alix also noted there's lots of room in this piece for a physical and non-verbal chorus. How do you represent the storm, or the community around the characters? What do you do between scene changes? You could create non-speaking parts that are pivotal to the mood or tone of the piece. Think big – perhaps Peter could be a puppet?

Q: Does Peter know about the kitten when he meets Danielle?
FK: He would know about it. But in the scene with Danielle, he has no choice but to be with her, and that's why he begins to open up. Peter's generally a fearful kid, and in the end Danielle has an affinity with him. They're both vulnerable, and they're both outsiders. There are often moments in the play where Danielle is nice, or kind, but it comes out of her in a forceful way.

Q: How much should we lean in to Danielle being a villain character at the beginning?
FK: Loads. Danielle *is* really scary. That's part of her method of survival. She and the storm are very linked in this text. There are lots of terrifying elements circling the kids: the man in the van, the storm, Danielle. What's interesting about Danielle, however, is

she's still so loyal to Jo, and she still won't tell anyone about what really happened. Danielle and Jo likely had a real loyalty to each other in the past, and Danielle feels that trust has been broken.

Q: What is Fra short for?
FK: Frank or Francis.

Q: Can you tell us more about Jo?
FK: In terms of her killing the kitten, Jo's not a bad person. Children do terrible things all the time. Sometimes they think it's funny, but then can still carry the guilt of it years later. Adults really harshly judge children, but as children you don't think through consequences. Perhaps when killing the cat, she was showing off.

Q: What is Jo's relationship with lying?
FK: For me, Jo's lying all the way through. She's showing off, and trying to impress James. The man in the van is a fib that runs away with her – which happened to us all as kids. The ending, when she tells the group to say the man shot her, for me this is an apology. It's admitting to the fact she made him up. It's also her opportunity to say sorry to Danielle.

Q: How did Jo meet James?
FK: In a previous draft he was in her music class. But it could be anything. I wanted to look at class with these two characters, so James can't be part of the estate. Jo is showing James the life of the estate, but also protecting him from it, like when she corrects him for saying 'exhilarating' – you can't say that on the estate, especially if you're a boy.

In terms of Jo's family, it's about aspirations. There are people in council estates who are worried about the bins, washing your car, etc. I'm interested in Jo's family as an *aspirational* working-class family.

Q: Jo is moving away. Is she moving far? Where?
FK: As long as it's out of the estate, it doesn't matter. When you're out, you're out, and when you do go back, you're not part of the gang any more.

Q: How old is Carly?
FK: She's probably seventeen, maybe turning eighteen.

Q: In Scene Eleven, who is the 'shadowy figure behind them'?
FK: That's Danielle. But it's written like that to create a sense of spookiness and fear.

Q: Why does Eugene go through such a change in personality?
FK: Eugene changed so much in each draft. For me, he is way ahead of the game in terms of social awareness and politics. He speaks like that on his YouTube, but with his friends he tries to do that and gets a lot of pushback.

Q: How would you feel about taking the technology out?
FK: I think it's a key part of this piece, and setting it in a different time period wouldn't work. In terms of the stage directions, where I have suggested, for example, projection, you don't have to follow those.

Q: Could you talk more about Eugene's YouTube persona?
FK: He's trying to be very cool. Eugene has a turning point when Fra challenges him.
He takes charge and stands up for himself.

Q: Can we change place names in the play to local areas?
FK: Yes!

Q: What are the rules of Two Man Hunt?
FK: You are supposed to be confused about the rules. Don't worry, and don't get hung
up on them. They're deliberately obscure – and you can lean into it and play for laughs.

From a workshop led by Alix Harris
With notes by Jack Bradfield

Like There's No Tomorrow

by the Belgrade Young Company with Justine Themen,
Claire Procter and Liz Mytton

Like There's No Tomorrow was created with the Belgrade Young Company, through a process of discussion, research, improvisation, scripting and revision. They first performed this play on Monday 9 March 2020.

Justine Themen (director) is a theatre director and change-maker. She was Deputy Artistic Director of the Belgrade Theatre and Co-Artistic Director for its City of Culture 2021 programme. During her time at the Belgrade, she has built a small participatory programme into a broad-reaching ethos across the work of the building. The programme provides access to arts activity to some of the city's least arts-engaged communities, shapes talent development opportunities that strongly promote diversity across the sector and creates new work for the theatre's stages. Her co-created work includes *Rise* (Belgrade Young Company), *Walk for Your Life* (Belgrade Black Youth Theatre), *Hussan and Harry* (Belgrade Youth Theatre with Coventry Refugee Centre) and *The First Time I Saw Snow* (Belgrade Theatre). Her directing work focuses on new work from female writers of colour – *Red Snapper* (Liz Mytton), *Under the Umbrella* (Amy Ng), both Belgrade Theatre. She played a key role in Coventry winning its bid to become UK City of Culture 2021, and was Co-Director of its Signature Event. She is also a Clore Fellow (2012–13). Prior to working at the Belgrade, she worked for six years in Senegal and Suriname co-creating theatre (*Hia Maun*, Stiching Botopasi) and documentaries (*Abigail*, VPRO), and using the arts as a tool in development and cultural diplomacy.

Claire Procter (co-director) is the Belgrade Theatre's Creative Producer for Education. She has over twenty years of experience working with children and young people, both as a class teacher and theatre practitioner. Prior to joining the Belgrade, Claire Procter worked for renowned Theatre-in-Education (TiE) company Big Brum. She has written and co-created a number of original plays for and with young people, including *The Impossible Language of the Time* (Belgrade Youth Theatre/Chris O'Connell), *Room to Grow* (Belgrade TiE) and *On the Line* (Belgrade Youth Theatre/ Jennifer Farmer). Her work to integrate TIE methodology into the making of the Belgrade's youth theatre work has been central to the development of the theatre's participatory practice.

Liz Mytton (wordsmith) is a playwright and poet based in the North West of England. She took part in the Critical Mass writing programme at the Belgrade Theatre in 2014, which led to the production of her first full-length play, *Red Snapper*, a runner-up for the 2016 Alfred Fagon Audience Award. In 2018 as a Bristol Old Vic Open Session writer, Liz Mytton wrote *Across the River*, about Marcus Garvey and the KKK, which featured in Bristol Ferment Fortnight. She has also developed a piece of work exploring hate crime, *Southside Stories*, which premiered at the Tobacco Factory in February 2019, and recently her own musical project, *Shame Shanties*, which uses seas shanties to explore women's mental health. She regularly works as a writer and lyricist with Talking Birds Theatre Company in Coventry, most recently on a commission for the Shakespeare Birthplace Trust. She has worked with the Belgrade's Young Company on two occasions in the role of wordsmith – firstly on *Rise* in 2017, and again in 2020 on *Like There's No Tomorrow*.

The **Belgrade Young Company** was established to give young people showing particular talent/ability from across the Belgrade's participatory programme an opportunity to grow their skills and abilities in a semi-professional context. Past work has included Frank Wedekind's youth classic *Spring Awakening*, rarely performed by young people of the same age as the characters; a physical production of *The Tempest* with Frantic Assembly; and *Rise*, co-created with a company of ten young women aged thirteen to twenty-three about their experiences of discrimination and rising beyond it.

Like There's No Tomorrow was devised by the Belgrade Young Company between October 2019 and March 2020.

The basic narrative of human beings failing to live well with the natural world, with a global crisis as the inevitable consequence, was conceived before the outbreak of Covid-19. As we filled in the details, of course, we were influenced by events happening around us, able to draw on real-life responses to the unfolding pandemic as we scripted and improvised to our story. The show was first performed on 9 March 2020, with the run ending on Saturday 14 March, the last day of performances before the Belgrade closed to the public in response to the government announcement that people should avoid attending theatres. All through the week of performances, audiences asked us how we had managed to foreshadow so closely the circumstances of the pandemic. Our answer is twofold. Firstly, the world is 'knowable' – evidence is out there for all who choose to listen that the resources of the earth are finite, and that our constant draw on them is creating crisis on a massive scale that may eventually end our very existence. Secondly, the joys of devising and of working over a longer period of time (as is usually the way with youth theatres) include the ability to draw in material influenced by the world around us right up to the last moments before performance – Trump, Johnson, politicians, campaigners, friends, parents – all are in there, feeding the words of our characters, the situations they find themselves in. And working with young people, the drive is always to be responsive, to want to make change in the real world.

'We conceived of ourselves as separated from nature, we felt cunning and almighty . . . We usurped nature, we dominated and wounded it. We incited Prometheus, and buried Pan. So much haughtiness made us lose our sisterhood with the butterflies, the flowers, the trees and the roots. So much outrageous greed made us lose the harmony and the care, the connection and the belonging.'
                              Alessandro Michele, Creative Director, Gucci (May 2020)

Performance notes

Central to this play is the relationship between capitalism and environmental decline, with a focus on the tension between the West and the developing world. During our process, we chose to locate part of our story in Zimbabwe as this reflected the origins of some of our company members, but there is flexibility in this – future companies may choose another country in place of Zimbabwe, and to amend elements of the text accordingly (the Shona language used in the Prologue and by Asha in Scene Ten; the story in Scene Three; Asha's narrative about the substitution of crops for tobacco in

Scene Ten). This is entirely feasible provided the story reflects the truth of communities at risk of environmental damage and disaster.

All characters have gender-neutral names and can be played by performers of any gender. Pronouns used in the script reflect the gender of the original company and can be adjusted accordingly.

Wherever possible, it is our intention for the action to flow seamlessly from one location and one scene to the next. These transitions are marked by the stage direction '*Into*'.

Characters

Maru
Maru's **Parent 1**
Maru's **Parent 2**
Luca <, *Maru's older sibling*
Georgie, *Maru's younger sibling*

Fin, *Maru's best friend*
Bobby Brunt, *campaigning to be Mayor*
Asha, *emerging from the* **Crack** *(a singer)*

Community Elder *(a singer)*
Teens 1 and 2, *at school with* **Maru**
Teacher *at Maru's school*
Campaigners 1 and 2 – Brunt's *team, supporting his campaign*
Neighbours 1 and 2
Brunt's Aide
New Parent *and baby*
Child and Parent, *stuck in traffic*
Chancer, *selling T-shirts*
YouTuber, *filming the* **Crack**
Parkour Movers, *jumping the* **Crack**
Negative Nelly
Journalist
Camera Person
Pastor
Fly-Tippers 1 and 2
Child and Mother, *escaping the city*
Parent, *searching for lost child*
Crowd 1, 2, 3 and 4
Village Community/City Dwellers/Storybook Villagers/Children/Crowd
Crack

Like There's No Tomorrow was first presented by the Belgrade Young Company at the Belgrade Theatre, Coventry, on 9 March 2020, with the following cast:

Maru	Oluwasemilore Kaji-Hausa
Fin	Femi Themen
Asha	Seyi Olomolaiye
Bobby Brunt	Sachin Sharma
Mum	Ifeolu Olomolaiye
Dad	Tillmann Osici
Luca	Emma Gibson
Georgie	Georgie Gibson
Campaigner/Neighbour	Jess Lake
Elder/Journalist	Kimberley Musa
Student/Fly-Tipper	Luqman Mwalim
Campaigner/Fin's Mum	Yolande Thompson

All other parts were played by members of the company.

Director/Devising Facilitator	Justine Themen
Co-*Director/Devising Facilitator*	Claire Procter
Assistant Directors	Jules Chan, Sebbie Mudhai
Dramaturg	Ola Animashawun
Wordsmith	Liz Mytton
Songsmith	Unamay Olomolaiye
Designer	Janet Vaughan
Lighting Designer	Adam Warren
Sound Designer	Oliver Howard

Thanks to Frances Marks for making it possible to put on a production of the play as part of the development process for the final script.

Prologue: Balance

We are part of a **Community**, *a community of warmth, generosity and light. The scene is rich with colour and rhythms and the air is thick with expectation.*

The **Community** *sings a ritual libation giving thanks to Mother Earth. The ritual is led by an* **Elder** *of the* **Community**, *and supported by a child,* **Asha**. *The* **Elder** *carries some water in a calabash, and one of the* **Villagers** *wafts some incense amongst the crowd. The* **Elder** *pours a portion of the water with each verse, showing* **Asha** *how to pour. By the end of the song, the* **Elder** *hands over to* **Asha** *to pour.*

The audience need to be captivated, so that when this world is gone, they too feel the loss.

Elder   Great Mother!

Community   Great Mother! We thank you, Great Mother!

Elder   You, who with loving hands, sculpts the clay from your earthy womb

Community   Form us!

Elder   Who, from your verdant sanctuary, yield both root and fruit

Community   Feed us!

Elder   Who, in your ancient wisdom, sends both storm and flower

Community   Teach us!

Elder   Who, with graceful force, forges rocks and continents

Community   Shield us!

All (*singing*)
    You are the Mother, we are the children,
    Hear our prayer!
    Ndini mai vacho, isu tiri vana
    Hear our prayer!

Elder
    To those who came before
    Those who lit our way
    Let us honour your memory
    Let us carry your stories.
    (*Singing.*) You are the Mother . . .

Community
    . . . we are the children,
    Hear our prayer!
    Ndini mai vacho, isu tiri vana
    Hear our prayer!

Elder
    For we who are blessed to be here and now
    May we be mindful of our legacy

Consider those who are yet to come
And tend the gardens of tomorrow

Elder (*singing*)   You are the Mother . . .

Community
 . . . we are the children,
Hear our prayer!
Ndini mai vacho, isu tiri vana
Hear our prayer!

Asha
For the children of our future
We pray you have the confidence
To stand strong in the gale
But yet the humility to bend in the breeze

(*Singing.*) You are the Mother . . .

Community
 . . . we are the children,
Hear our prayer
Ndini mai vacho, isu tiri vana
Hear our prayer!

The singing draws to an end. Through the smoke of the libation comes the reality of the toxic air of a city, a perversion of the tendrils of the incense.

Into:

Scene One: City

This is the same Earth, but what is different is us. Through a movement sequence, we see that we have the power to transform something that is beautiful into something that is destructive. Earth's resources have become a commodity, the balance has tipped. We no longer live for the meaningful, but for the material.

We see the people of the city driving cars, being wasteful with our resources, polluting our world with chemicals, rushing from one place to the next with no time for reflection.

The pollution that we pump into the air is also taken into the air we breathe. The inhabitants of the city struggle to catch a breath. They struggle to breathe in chorus. They are straining, reaching for a lungful of clean air . . .

The city clears into a school scene.

Some **Teens** *are walking into a school classroom, one holding a textbook.* **Maru** *is sat reading a book. There are two bins – an ordinary bin and a recycling bin.*

Teen 1   I'm so tired of being treated like a machine!

Teen 2 (*turning the pages of her textbook*)   Yeah! How can we answer all these questions by tomorrow?

Teen 1 *suddenly reaches over and tears the pages out of the textbook.* **Maru** *notices and winces.*

Teen 2   What are you doing?!

Teen 1 *screws the paper into a ball and points at the bin.*

Teen 1   Solving all our problems!

Teen 2   Bet you can't!

Teen 1   Watch me!

Teen 2   OK . . .

Teen 1 *throws a piece of paper, and misses the target.*

Teen 2 (*laughing*)   What was that?!

Teen 1   You try then!

Teen 2 *tears more pages from the book.* **Maru** *pointedly moves her chair away from the* **Teens***, banging it on the floor.*

Teen 2   You need to try and get a bit of a flick into it. Now watch!

Teen 2 *aims more specifically, making the sound of the 'flick' to give focus, but still misses.*

Teen 1 (*laughing*)   It's all the way over there! The bin's here!

Maru *disapproves.*

Teen 2   You try again!

Teen 1 (*pulling back to take aim, and so getting closer to* **Maru**)   Let me try to get a 'flick' into it!

They are laughing louder now. **Teen 1** *misses again.*

Maru   What are you doing? Tearing up a textbook is one thing, but you're not even throwing the paper in the recycling bin! I mean it's literally just there!

Teen 1   It's a game.

Teen 2   Yeah, calm down, Maru!

Maru   But, why would you . . .?

The **Teens** *ignore* **Maru***. A low groaning sound can be heard by the audience, but not by the* **Teens***.* **Maru** *senses it as unease, rather than as a sound that can be heard. It lasts until* **Maru** *asks them to stop again.*

Teen 2   I'm gonna film it.

Teen 1   Go on then.

Teen 2   Five pounds that it won't go in.

Teen 1   Alright, a fiver!

Teen 1 *throws and it goes in.*

Teen 1   Told you!

Teen 1 *dances a victory dance, with* **Teen 2** *filming. They are laughing and jostling, while* **Maru** *eyes them disapprovingly, shaking her head.*

Teen 2   What?!

Maru   Look at all the paper on the floor!

Teen 1   What don't you get about having fun?

Maru   What don't you get about not wasting paper? Are you fuckin' stupid?

Teen 2   What? What did you call me?

Teen 1   She called you fuckin' stupid! Don't have it!

The **Teens** *square up, ready to fight, and* **Maru** *jostles with them to get out of their way.* **Teacher** *approaches.*

Teacher   Excuse me!

Teen 1   Miss, Maru tried to hit us!

Teen 2   Yeah, she started shouting and 'effing' at us for no reason!

Maru   Miss, I did not! Look at the paper all over the floor!

Teacher   Maru, we do not tolerate swearing in this school!

Maru   I was just reading! And they were ripping up a book – destroying school property – then throwing paper all over the floor!

The **Teens** *stand behind the* **Teacher** *imitating her.*

Teacher   And I will deal with them later. But swearing is completely unacceptable.

Maru (*coughing*)   But, miss –

Teacher   Enough, Maru! (*To* **Teens**.) Don't you have a class to go to?

Teen 1 *and* **Teen 2** *leave, looking smug.* **Maru** *is angry, and is coughing heavily.*

Maru *notices a* **Crack** *on the floor/wall, as does the* **Teacher**.

Teacher   Where did that come from? What on earth have you been getting up to?

Maru   Nothing. Maybe it was the class before us. (*Coughing.*)

Teacher   Are you OK? Do you need some water?

Maru   No. I'll use my inhaler. (*Looking in bag, but not finding it.*) I'll be fine.

Teacher   Good. And Maru, I'm disappointed in your behaviour.

Teacher *hands* **Maru** *a slip of paper.* **Maru** *reads it – it is a detention slip.*

I'll see you in detention on Monday.

Maru *and* **Teacher** *go in opposite directions, with* **Maru** *looking back at the* **Crack** *suspiciously.*

The city crosses through the space, clearing the school and leaving the **Mayoral Campaigners** *in the city centre, handing out flyers. They try to attract the attention of passers-by, drawing them into conversation where they can.*

Campaigner 1   Vote Bobby Brunt for Mayor.

Campaigner 2   Hi . . . hi . . . vote Bobby Brunt. Thank you.

Campaigner 1   Bobby Brunt for Metro Mayor. Here, if I could just give you . . . (*Hands over a flyer.*)

Campaigner 2   Bringing car manufacturing back to the city. Yes, you heard right, your ears did not deceive you! Bobby's going to open the factories and get us all working again!

Maru *and* **Fin** *enter. They're busy laughing at something on* **Fin**'s *mobile phone.* **Campaigner 1** *walks in front of them, trying to hand a flyer to a passing shopper, causing* **Fin** *and* **Maru** *to stop in their tracks.*

Campaigner 1   End to the proposed congestion zone. Free access to the city centre for all.

Campaigner 2   Nice jacket, madam. I bet you'd be interested to hear about our exciting new plans for the shopping centre . . . the world's biggest Trimark!

Campaigner 1   The proposed Green Park housing development will create 142 new homes for families moving into the city by . . .

Fin   What?

Campaigner 1   Excuse me?

Fin   You just said they're building on Green Park . . .

Campaigner 1   Oh . . . (*Beat.*) Here, take one of these for your parents. (*Handing over flyers.*) It's all in there . . . (*Returning to previous conversation.*) By utilising green space in prime development locations right here in the city centre –

Maru   You want to build on our park?

Campaigner 2   Well, it's everyone's park, not just yours. It's our plan to invest in local infrastructure –

Fin   You can't do that!

Campaigner 2   Let the people decide, eh? It's called democracy. Parks are expensive things to run (*patronisingly*). Where's all the money coming from?

Maru   But where will we go after school? (**Maru** *is starting to cough.*)

Fin   And where's my mum going to walk our dog?

Maru   And what about the music festival?

Campaigner 2   Money doesn't grow on trees, you know. Which is why we need to cut them down and replace them with something that generates wealth. Breathing life back into the city.

Campaigner 1 (*reading from the flyer*)   'By investing in new homes we're making the city centre a more attractive place in which to live'! (*Points to the flyer.*) See? Nice houses attract nice people, producing a tidy profit.

Fin   But there's no other park for miles –

Campaigner 2   You've got to see the bigger picture here. A housing development really is a win-win for everyone.

Campaigner 1 (*placating them*)   Why don't you have a pen? Here, take two (*Hands the pens to* **Fin**.) Nearly forgot, pen for your friend! (*To* **Campaigner 2**.) Kids love pens. (*To* **Maru** *and* **Fin**.) Now if you don't mind . . . (*Awkward beat before* **Campaigner 1** *moves off.*) Hello, sir, have you got a minute? I'd like to tell you about Bobby Brunt's stance on immigration . . .

Campaigner 2   Vote Bobby Brunt for Mayor!

The **Campaigners** *continue their mission to engage passers-by, leaving* **Fin** *and the coughing* **Maru** *alone, looking at their gifts.*

Maru   Well, that sucks.

Fin   Come on, let's go to the park – make the most of it while we still can.

Maru   I'm sorry Fin, but I can't be late home tonight – it's Friday, you know what my parents are like.

Fin   Just for a bit – it'll do your breathing good.

Maru   OK, but only for ten minutes, then I'm gone.

Maru *and* **Fin** *are once more absorbed into the city on the move until it clears again and we find them in the park beneath a large tree.*

Maru *takes in a lungful of air and then exhales, with no sign of any coughing or wheezing.*

Maru   It's so beautiful here.

Fin   Told you it'd help with your breathing.

Maru   It never fails.

Fin   How can they even think about destroying this place?

Maru   Chopping down all these trees and flattening the earth.

Fin   All the times we played hide and seek in those bushes.

Maru   I've still got scars on my knees from all the scratches I got!

Fin   It was worth it though wasn't it?

Maru   Course it was!

Beat.

You know, they didn't even ask for our opinion.

Maru *'s coughing starts to return.*

Fin   They don't need to – we can't vote!

Maru   But it's our future they're shaping. And our children's future! Imagine that swing – gone!

Fin   All the times we've swung on it!

Maru   And all the children still to come, who'll have nowhere to play!

Fin   I think my dad's going to vote for him.

Maru   No, he can't. You've got to stop him.

Fin   He won't listen to me. He likes Bobby. Everybody likes Bobby.

Maru   Why?

Fin   Because Bobby's going to make everything grow again. Least that's what he says.

Maru *starts coughing sharply now.*

Fin   Where's your inhaler?

Maru (*looking through her bag*)   I can't find it – I must've left it at home.

Fin (*rubbing* **Maru** *'s back*)   Breathe, Maru, breathe! You have to carry your inhaler.

Maru   I just want to be able to breathe without it!

Fin   Relax. In and out. (*Pause.*) Guess what?

Maru   What?

Fin   My mum bought another 'bag for life' yesterday!

Maru (*laughs, triggering the cough again*).   Don't make me laugh! How many lives is that now?

Fin   Well, this is probably her twentieth – it was the blue swirling patterns, too pretty to resist!

Maru   At least you know what to get her for her birthday!

Fin   Talking of birthdays . . . how does it feel to be almost a teenager?

Maru   Not much different, to be honest.

Fin   But it is different. You'll be able to do more stuff, and people will start treating you differently, listening to you.

Maru   Not my parents – and if they don't listen, why should anyone else?

Fin   Well, I wish it were me!

Maru   Five months will pass quickly.

Beat.

Fin   We should mark it!

Maru   Mark it?

Fin   I mean, it's important, isn't it?

Maru   I suppose so.

Fin   Have you got some paper?

Maru   I've got my detention slip!

Maru *tears off a blank section from the bottom, whilst* **Fin** *gets the pens they were given by the* **Campaigners** *out of her pocket.*

Fin   Might as well use the pens!

Maru *tears the blank paper in two, gives one half to* **Fin** *and stuffs the detention slip back into her schoolbag.*

Fin   Write down your biggest wish.

Maru   OK!

Fin   And I'll write what I wish for you.

They turn away from each other and write.

Fin (*turning back*)   I'm done.

Maru (*turning back*)   Me too!

Fin   You go first.

Maru   I wish for the freedom to breathe!

Fin   And I wish for your voice to be heard.

Maru   What, by my teacher, you mean?

Fin   Yeah, but not just her, others too, like the people who want to build on our park.

Maru   Yeah. Thank you!

They hug.

Fin   Now, we bury them.

Fin *digs with her fingers.*

Maru   Dig deep, so no one finds them.

Maru *places the papers in the hole and* **Fin** *covers them over.* **Fin** *looks at her dirty hands, laughing. They prompt another idea.*

Fin   Have you got your water bottle?

Maru *gets out her water bottle.*

Fin   Pour some here.

Fin *indicates the area that has been dug up, mixes the soil and water into a paste and then turns to* **Maru** *with muddy fingers.*

Fin   Sit still.

Fin *starts to hum as she uses the mud to carefully paint marks onto* **Maru***'s face. At the end,* **Fin** *takes* **Maru***'s hand and clasps it, holding tight* . . .

Fin   I hereby mark you with the soil from beneath our tree . . . that you may be rooted in the earth, whilst reaching out with your branches to breathe . . .

The ritual is interrupted by a text arriving on **Maru***'s phone.*

Maru   It's my mum – she's nearly home!

(*Heading off.*) I'd better go. (*Turning back.*) Thanks, Fin! (*Exits.*)

Fin   See you tomorrow!

The city once more crosses, driving **Fin** *from the park. When it clears, we are in the family living room.*

Into:

Scene Two: Home (before)

Parent 1 *enters with* **Georgie***, who is full of energy.* **Parent 1** *has shopping bags, and* **Georgie** *has school bags.* **Georgie** *drops coat, hat, bag as they run around the table several times. They're in an open-plan living room. During the following,* **Parent 1** *puts down bags, looks through mail, puts a parcel to one side, takes off coat.*

Georgie   Maru! We're home! (*To* **Parent 1**.). Can I play Nintendo?

Parent 1   Shoes off!

Georgie (*taking off shoes*)   Now can I?

Parent 1   You know the drill! Ten . . . nine . . . eight –

Georgie *is running round, hanging up coat, emptying bag, wiping down table, tidying chairs round table.*

Parent 1   Seven . . . Maru? Sandwich box!

Georgie *arrives with homework diary.* **Parent 1** *looks through.*

Parent 1   You've got a lot of homework!

Georgie   I can do it tomorrow!

Parent 1 (*giving back the book*)   I want to see it when you're done . . . six . . . sandwich box? . . . five . . . you're running out of time . . . four –

Georgie   I'm getting it!

Parent 1   I'm putting the dish washer on! . . . three . . . two . . . one.

Georgie   Here. (*Handing over the sandwich box.*) Nintendo now?

Parent 1   Go on! Alexa – set the timer for ten minutes!

Parent 1 (*checks the sandwich box*)   Why didn't you eat your sandwiches? I even cut the crusts cut off!

Georgie   I wasn't hungry.

Parent 1   You've managed to eat the chocolate bar. And some crisps! I didn't even give you crisps.

Georgie   Susan had two bags, so she gave me one.

Parent 1   And you want to end up looking like Susan?

Georgie   She's really nice!

Parent 1   Susan is a girl who eats nothing but crisps. I don't want you turning out like her. Eat your sandwiches!

Georgie   Yes, Mum.

Parent 1   Good. You've got eight minutes left.

Georgie *rushes to the floor and starts playing a computer game.*

Parent 1 (*tidying kitchen*)   Maru! I hope you're doing your homework?! I want to see some good grades!

Luca *arrives home, throwing coat on the floor.*

Parent 1   Coat. Hang it up!

Luca *picks coat up, drops it on chair.*

Parent 1   Hang it up!

Luca *hangs up coat, then heads for cupboard in search of food.*

Parent 1   What are you doing?

Luca   Getting something to eat!

Parent 1   Another snack.

Luca   I'm hungry!

Parent 1   It's Friday – you know food will be here in twenty minutes.

Luca   OK! (*But still sneaks a snack as soon as* **Parent 1** *isn't looking.*)

Parent 1 (*waving parcel*)   Oh, and another package came for you!

Luca   Thanks!

Parent 1   Thought you were saving for driving lessons?

Luca   I still need clothes to wear!

Parent 1   You don't wear half the clothes you've got hanging in your wardrobe.

Luca   S'alright, none of the stuff I buy is expensive. (*Goes to play with* **Georgie** *on the Nintendo.*)

Georgie   Do you want to play Mario Cart?

Luca   200cc . . .

Georgie   200cc? No, that's too fast!

Luca   . . . and Rainbow Road . . .

Georgie   Rainbow Road?!

Luca   Three, two, one, go!

*They settle into playing, making a lot of noise. Shouts of 'Get out of the way, Luigi!',
etc.* **Maru** *tries to creep in, signalling to* **Georgie** *and* **Luca** *not to let on to* **Parent 1**
that she's only just got home. **Georgie** *stops playing, trying to understand* **Maru**'s
gestures, so **Luca** *stops, too. The silence draws attention to the situation and* **Parent
1** *turns round and sees* **Maru**. **Georgie** *and* **Luca** *become avid spectators.*

Parent 1   Where have you been?

Maru   I lost track of time.

Parent 1   I thought you were up in your room! It's nearly six!

Maru   I got distracted –

Parent 1   Did you walk home again?

Maru   Yes.

Parent 1   Maru, how many times?! You're not well –

Maru   Mum, I'm fine.

Parent 1   I pay money for you to get a bus pass so you can stay away from the
fumes from all those cars . . .

Maru   I walked through the park..

Parent 1   Did you have your inhaler?

Maru   Yes! And Fin looked after me.

Parent 1   So you had an asthma attack!

Maru   Yes! No . . . yes

Parent 1 (*hugging* **Maru**)   Are you OK? (*Holding* **Maru**'s *face.*) Darling, your
health is not to be messed with. And what's that on your face?

Maru   It's just a bit of mud.

Parent 1   Oh, please don't tell me you walked past Janet's house with that mud on
your face!

Maru   I walked past quickly . . .

Parent 1   Oh Lord! She'll be walking around with those dogs of hers, telling
everyone how my daughter had mud on her face.

Maru   Mum – calm down!

Parent 1   Give me your sandwich box!

Maru *digs in the bag for her sandwich box and the detention slip falls out.*

Parent 1 (*unfolding it*)   What's this?

Georgie   You got a detention!

Luca   Maru!

Parent 1 (*reading slip*)   What happened?

Maru   It wasn't my fault! It was these kids . . .

Parent 1   And have they got detention slips as well?

Maru   No.

Parent 1   Just you?

Maru   Yes.

Parent 1   Maru – keep your head down and get on with your work!. We can't afford to be drawing attention to ourselves.

Parent 2 *arrives home with bags full of takeaway food and fizzy drinks in single-use packaging.*

Parent 2   Hello, family! Who's ready for takeaway?!

Georgie   Dad! (*Runs to hug* **Parent 2**, **Parent 2** *hugs* **Georgie** *with bags in hand.*)

Parent 2   Traffic was terrible – hope the food's still hot. (*Kisses* **Parent 1**.)

Luca   I'm starving!

Parent 2   As usual!

Everyone stands around the table expectantly.

Parent 2   Georgie – meat feast pizza for you – your favourite. Luca – there's your kebab.

Luca   Georgie, get some forks.

Parent 2   I brought plenty of the little plastic ones!

Maru *quietly goes to get a metal fork.*

Parent 2 (*to* **Parent 1**)   For you, Singapore fried rice with extra beef, some pork balls and sweet and sour sauce. And a side of ribs just in case. That's my Singapore fried rice and some chicken wings. Maru, you've been a bit picky recently, so I bought you a mega super box with a bit of everything. And drinks for the kids (*takes out cans of fizzy drink*).

Parent 1   Luca – do you want to say grace?

Luca   Good food, good meat, good God, let's eat!

The family unpack and dive in hungrily. The groaning sound returns, but only **Maru** *notices – and still just as a sense of unease, rather than as a sound that can be heard.*

Luca   Pass the remote.

Georgie   Put on the movie channel.

Parent 2   Hang on. I want to hear the news first.

During the news report, **Parent 2** *stares at the TV as if what is being reported is normal.* **Parent 1** *surfs the internet on a mobile.*

Reporter   . . . Quake-like cracks have appeared in several rural villages in the north of Zimbabwe. Geological and climate specialists from across the world are gathering in the capital Harare to discuss their response, in the wake of similar cracks in Bangladesh, Greenland and Papua New Guinea. The conditions in Zimbabwe are particularly –

Luca (*looking for person with the remote*)   It's boring!

Parent 2 (*turning the TV over*)   Why do they always have to share bad news?

There is canned laughter coming from the TV from the new programme, a comedy.

Parent 1   Oh, look at that little dog on a bicycle!

They all laugh, except **Maru**, *who is playing with her food.*

Maru   Maybe we should do something to help?

Parent 2 *turns the TV off.*

Parent 1   Unfortunately in countries like that, these things happen. There's nothing we can do about it.

Parent 2   You're just picking.

Maru   I don't really like the food.

Luca   It's because Maru's turned vegan.

Parent 2 *laughs. No one else does. There is silence.*

Parent 2   You're not joking?

Parent 1   What do you mean you turned vegan?

Luca *and* **Georgie** *sneak off to watch TV on the floor.*

Maru   I just decided not to eat meat any more.

Parent 2   I work hard to earn the money to provide you with good food and now you're vegan, you're not going to eat it all of a sudden? Maru, there are kids in this very city who barely have enough to eat.

Georgie   Can we talk about this later?

Parent 2   You can be vegan in your own time, not in this house.

Georgie   I want to watch the film!

Parent 1   You know she got a detention today?

Parent 2   Detention?

Parent 1   Maru – explain to your father.

Maru   These kids were playing around with all this paper and they put it in the wrong basket – so I calmly tried to encourage them to consider using less paper and to recycle what they had used . . . and the teacher –

Parent 2   So now you're a vegan – and an activist as well?

Parent 1   Next she'll be joining Extinction Rebellion and lying down in the street.

Luca   Detention Rebellion more like!

Parent 2   I learned the hard way, Maru. Standing up for yourself gets you nowhere in life. Tomorrow they'll still be throwing rubbish in the wrong bin and what are you going to do? Get yourself excluded?

Maru *clearly starts to get agitated and starts breathing heavily.*

Maru (*getting up abruptly*)   I've got homework to do . . .

Parent 1   Good, do your homework, but listen to your father – what he's saying is true.

Maru   I will.

Parent 1 (*calling after* **Maru**)   And take your inhaler – I can hear you wheezing from here.

Maru   OK.

Maru *exits. The family transform the furniture of the living room into the furniture of* **Maru**'s *bedroom.*

Into:

Scene Three: Bedroom

Maru *goes to the bed, takes out her inhaler and looks at it – then puts it to one side and, instead, takes out a book from under the pillow. She sits on the floor and starts to read. As she reads, the story calms her, and the world of the story starts to come to life in the bedroom.*

Maru   Once there was a girl who wanted to plant a garden. (**Maru** *breathes deeply.*)

She was born in a village, where life was precious, and in a land that was plentiful, but where seasons could be fierce. (**Maru** *takes another breath, becoming calmer.*) Her Mother showed her how to plant vegetables – rich roots, succulent fruits and fresh leaves.

And in the centre of the garden, she planted a beautiful tree.
She watered and tended the tree every day, singing as she worked.
And sometimes, the tree sang back to her:

Tree
  If ever it may seem
  Like there may be no tomorrow,
  Plant one small seed
  It may grow to feed a village.

Maru   And as she grew, so did the tree.

And when it was grown, Mother and Daughter would sit under its wondrous branches, grateful for the shade it provided from the hot summer sun and the shelter from the rain.

Over the course of time, the girl's village suffered a drought, one that devastated much of her country and the hearts of her people.
There was barely enough water to drink and slowly the girl's garden withered away.
Before long, they were down to their last calabash of water.

Mother
  Drink, Daughter, for you have all your life to live and mine is nearly at its end.

Maru   So the Daughter drank, and they sat under the tree. And in the morning, the Mother did not wake.
They buried her body under the tree, and the girl watered the ground with her tears.

The following year, the rains returned and with the rain the tree grew to become a mighty and wondrous memorial to the Mother. For the first time, it bore fruit and the whole village came to gather its juicy flesh.
The girl was happy for the villagers to eat their fill, provided they watered the tree after each visit:

Daughter
  Eat, but please – remember my mother who cares for the roots.

Maru   To begin with, the people did as she asked.
But as time wore on, they began to neglect this simple request.

Villager 1
  The roots of that tree are too thirsty.

Villager 2
  I have just enough water for myself.

Villager 3
  I didn't even know her mother!

Maru   Before long, people were coming from far and wide to take fruit from the tree. Some even set up stalls to sell what they had picked, trampling over its drying roots without a thought as to how it would survive.
The earth became dry as a desert and as hard as a rock.
The fruit became scarcer and scarcer.

Until one day, the earth was so dry that it split in two and a giant crack tore through the centre of the village. (*Inhalation.*)

Luca (*from outside the room*)   Maru!

Luca *knocks and the village scene evaporates.* **Luca** *enters.*

Luca   You've got to clear the draining board!

Maru   But I hoovered the whole living room yesterday!

Luca   Still your turn to do the draining board!

Maru   Leave me alone!

Luca (*shrugging*)   You'll have Mum to answer to if you don't.

Luca *leaves.* **Maru** *is pensive. She hides the book again.*

The family reverse the previous transition – back from bedroom into living room.

Into:

Scene Four: Transitions

Bobby Brunt *is having tea with* **Maru***'s* **Parents** *in their living room.*

Brunt   . . . and I've always believed that the working man must come first! Jobs for British workers, investment in car manufacturing – make this city great again!

Parent 2   That's what I've always said!

Brunt   Of course you have, and you're 100 per cent right! Which is why I'm *personally* visiting factory workers like yourself to give you some assurances – like I always say, 'There's no front with Brunt!'

Parent 1   Cup of tea, Mr Brunt?

Brunt   Nothing like a good cup of English tea.

Parent 1 *goes to pour it.*

Brunt   No, please, allow me – it's what this campaign is all about – me serving you!

Parent 1   Ooh, thank you! Some cake?

Brunt *pats his waistline and shakes his head as if to say, 'I couldn't possibly!'*

Parent 2   She's hands down the best baker on this street!

Brunt   You've twisted my arm! (*Taking a bite.*) Oh now, that's amazing – what a woman!

Parent 1 *is coy but proud.* **Brunt** *stands to leave.*

Brunt   Right, I'm afraid I have to drag myself away – got lots of other hardworking people to see this afternoon. But it's been an absolute pleasure to meet you both.

Parent 2   You too – you're a breath of fresh air, Mr Brunt!

Brunt   Please – call me Bobby – we're friends now!

Parent 2   Thanks, Bobby!

They shake hands enthusiastically. As **Brunt** *prepares to leave,* **Maru** *and* **Fin** *come through the door and are stunned to see him.*

Maru   What's he doing here?

Parent 1   Darling, this is –

Maru   Bobby Brunt.

Parent 2   Yes – and he's going to be the new mayor!

Brunt   So I can count on your votes then?

Parents   Yes!

Brunt *shakes their hands again, and puts his hand out for* **Fin**.

Brunt   Hello! (**Brunt** *forms a fist bump which* **Fin** *reluctantly reciprocates.*)

Brunt *then tries the same with* **Maru**, *who ignores the fist altogether.*

Parent 1   Maru!

Maru   He's going to destroy our park!

Fin   Digging it all up to make houses!

Brunt   Workers need places to live. Plenty of parks on the outskirts. We need to make compromises to move forward.

Parent 2   More jobs coming – good news for your dad, Fin, down at the car plant!

Maru   So more cars polluting the city!

Brunt   Ah, but these are electric cars!

Maru   Electric cars still need energy to power them!

Brunt   I care as much about the environment as you do – but I've been to China and the pollution is terrible. There's really no point in doing anything about it here until they do . . . in 2050, say . . .

Maru   By that time half the country could be under water!

Parent 1 (*embarrassed and trying to lighten the mood*)   Turning thirteen today, lots of opinions!

Brunt   Ahhh! Happy birthday – I think this calls for a 'Bobby Brunt for Mayor' lollipop.

Maru (*disgusted*)   It's got your face on it!

Brunt   So it has! Kids . . . are our future! Best be off! (*As he disappears.*) Lobby for Bobby!

Brunt *leaves.* **Parent 1** *looks disappointed at* **Maru** *and is about to say something but* **Parent 2** *stops them.*

Parent 1   Time to celebrate someone's birthday! (*Opens arms to embrace.*) I can't believe my little girl's thirteen!

Parent 2   Georgie, Luca! Maru's home!

Georgie *runs in.*

Parent 1   A new chapter, fresh responsibilities!

Luca *runs in.*

Maru   Thanks, Mum!

Georgie   You've got presents to open!

Luca   Happy birthday, Maru!

Parent 1   And we've got a special surprise for you upstairs.

Maru   Seriously?!

Parent 1   Close your eyes!

Parent 1 *covers* **Maru***'s eyes, whilst the family once more set up the bedroom in front of her. This time, however, the bedroom is different. It is now a modern room, with new matching units and a fresh, cool colour scheme.*

Parent 1   You can open them now!

Parents   Surprise! / Ta dah!

Parent 1 *takes her hands from* **Maru***'s eyes.* **Maru** *is stunned.*

Maru   Oh my God!

Parent 1   You love it, right?

Fin   This is sick!

Fin *starts moving around the room, checking all the new features.* **Maru** *is adjusting to the new space.*

Parent 1   Everything matches now – curtains, bed covers, new wardrobe, bigger desk for studying, bigger bookshelf for your books –

Maru   I liked my old bookshelf.

Parent 2   Yes, but this is all from that massive new Swedish shop –

Parent 1   Cost a small fortune –

Parent 2   Been doing overtime for weeks –

Parent 1   But you deserve it! Happy birthday!

Luca   I never got this for my thirteenth!

Parent 2   Well, you had a big party!

Fin   I wish my room was like this!

Maru   It's . . . wonderful!

Parent 1   You've got a mirror now so you can do your hair and things! And there are lights in it!

Maru   I can see that.

Parent 2   Much more grown-up!

Maru   I love it!

Parent 1   We knew you would!

Maru (*looking for her book in the usual place under her pillow*)   My other things. What did you do with them?

Parent 1   You'll be pleased to know we listened to your advice –

Parent 2   Reuse, recycle, reduce –

Parent 1   Nothing wasted!

Maru   But my book – I had a book, with a red cover?

Fin   Your storybook?

Maru   Yes!

Parent 2   Didn't think you'd want it any more now you're growing up . . .

Parent 1   Got to focus on your studies . . .

Parent 2   We gave it to a charity shop. Some other child will get to enjoy it, just like you did.

Maru   Right. (**Maru**'s *breathing is starting to get difficult again.*)

Parent 2   Can see you're overwhelmed. We'll leave you two to chat!

Parent 1   Don't be too long – there's cake downstairs!

Parents *leave and* **Maru** *collapses in a heap. She is devastated, panicking and struggling to breath.*

Fin   What's wrong?

Maru   My whole room has gone!

Fin   But this is so cool!

Maru   But I didn't *need* any of it!

Fin   They wanted your thirteenth to feel special.

Maru   I get that, but I can't believe they got rid of my book!

Fin   They probably just thought you'd grown out of it.

Maru   Whose side are you on, Fin?

Maru *'s crying and coughing gets worse.*

Fin   I didn't realise it was that important to you!

Maru   Not that important?!

Maru *produces a massive barking cough, as a* **Crack** *opens up in the new bookcase.*

Fin   What the . . .?

Both **Maru** *and* **Fin** *'s eyes watch as the* **Crack** *splits the bookcase in two. They are shocked and frightened.* **Fin** *looks at* **Maru** *and is spooked. She starts to back out of the room.*

Fin   I – I need to go! I'll see you later!

Fin *leaves.* **Maru** *is curious about the* **Crack** *and approaches the bookcase. She runs her finger along the* **Crack** *out of curiosity. The* **Crack** *seems to groan softly.*

Parent 1 (*shouting*)   Maru! Time for birthday cake!

Maru *leaves her room and goes to meet the rest of the family.*

Parent 2 *is holding a birthday cake.* **Parent 1** *is excited.*

All (*singing*)   Happy birthday to you! Happy birthday to you!
Happy birthday, dear Maru! Happy birthday to you!

Parent 1   Blow your candles out! Make a wish! Right, plates everyone!

Parent 1 *starts cutting and serving the cake.* **Maru** *is distracted by what just happened upstairs.*

Parent 2   Fin left in a hurry.

Maru   Oh, her mum called.

Parent 1 *serves* **Maru** *a piece of cake.*

Maru   What kind of cake is it?

Parent 2   We remembered that you're vegan –

Parent 1 (*serving* **Luca** *a piece of cake*)   So no eggs!

Georgie (*disgusted*)   It's a vegan cake?

Maru   Great. And what did you use to replace the butter?

Parent 1   Replace the butter? You can't make a cake without butter!

Maru   But butter isn't –

Georgie   So it isn't vegan! (*Digging in.*)

Parent 1   I've messed it up haven't I?

Maru   No, no, I'm sure it's lovely!

Parent 2   Butter isn't vegan?

Maru   Don't worry!

Everyone goes to take a bit of their cake, and there's a sudden 'crack' from upstairs, from the direction of **Maru***'s bedroom. Everyone pauses and looks up, lowering their cake.*

Maru (*to self*)   Not again.

Parent 2   Wait here, I'll be back in a second.

Parent 2 *departs to investigate.*

Parent 1 (*looking at* **Maru**)   What do you mean 'again'?

Into:

Scene Four: Papering over the cracks

Parent 2 *enters* **Maru***'s room with a bucket of wallpaper paste, some brushes and a roll of wallpaper.*

Parent 2   This is a right mess, Maru (*shakes head*). What happened?

Maru   I'm sorry. I don't know . . .

Parent 2 (*indicating the newly decorated room*)   Look at the state of it! You've barely had the stuff for five minutes! Do you know what this cost us?

Parent 2 *starts to paste the back of the wallpaper.*

Maru   It wasn't me.

Parent 2 *sighs in response.*

Parent 2   Cracks don't just appear for no reason, Maru.

Parent 2 *continues to work at the pasting of the paper.*

Honestly, the stuff you kids take for granted. You think I had this kind of luxury when I was your age?

Maru   I'll fix it. (*Pause*) . . . If it helps I could get the old bookshelf back from the charity shop you donated it to.

Parent 2   Right . . . (*Continues working.*)

Maru (*continues talking awkwardly*)   Fin and I could go and get it if you tell me where it is. We could get Georgie and Luca to help us –

Parent 2   And why would I pay good money for the old stuff I've just given away?

Maru   I liked it. And you wouldn't need to, I've got money saved up.

Parent 2   From your pocket money, right? The money that your mum and I work hard to give you?

Parent 2 *starts to hang the wallpaper.*

Maru   Maybe I could just get my book back then?

Parent 2   What book?

Maru   The storybook you and Mum gave me, it was on the bookshelf. Do you know which charity shop –

Parent 2   You want me to traipse halfway across town for a children's book? When I've got this mess to fix?

Maru   But it's . . . sentimental.

Parent 2   Sentimental! You're far too young to understand what that word means!

Maru   It's like the watch Granny gave you.

Parent 2 (*looking at the watch on his wrist*)   Granny's watch is completely different. This is actually worth something.

Maru   But I need it. It's important.

Parent 2   No, Maru, it's not!

There is the sound of groaning and creaking. The papered **Crack** *rips open.*

Parent 2   No, no, no, no, no! Maru, what have you done?

Maru   I didn't touch anything!

Parent 2   Well it's starting to look wilful to me. What's wrong with you? Any normal teenager would love to have a bedroom like this.

A loud 'crack' is heard from downstairs.

Georgie (*from off*)   Dad, you'd better come quick, there's a crack in the living room now as well!

Parent 2 *looks at* **Maru**, *shakes his head despairingly and then leaves.* **Maru** *is mesmerised by the* **Crack**.

Maru   It's just like the story!

Suddenly a sound like an inhalation comes from the **Crack**. **Maru** *looks into it.*

Maru   Hello?

The **Crack** *answers back with a breathy exhalation.*

Into:

The bedroom clears and we see **Maru** *looking for her book in a charity shop. She can't find it.*

Into:

Scene Six: Home (after)

Parent 1 *enters with* **Georgie**. **Parent 1** *has shopping bags, and* **Georgie** *is keen to play a game. There is now a huge* **Crack** *down the centre of the living room. The family have to walk carefully around it, wary of making it worse. Each are mindful of it in their own way –* **Georgie** *afraid,* **Parent 1** *anxious,* **Luca** *resentful/curious,* **Parent 2** *undermined. This is important in colouring the scene differently from Scene Two.*

Georgie *circles the crack and goes straight to sit at the Nintendo.*

Parent 1   Have you done your homework?

Georgie (*evasively*).   Yes!

Parent 1   What about your chores? (*Silence from* **Georgie**.) Ten . . . nine . . . eight –

Georgie *is running round, hanging up coat, emptying bag, but is having to be careful around the* **Crack**.

Parent 1   Seven . . . Maru? Downstairs! . . . Six . . . Lord! That child! Five . . . four –

Georgie   Mum, I can't do it! (*Looking at the* **Crack**.) It's too hard now!

Parent 1   I know, baby. But it's just the way things are at the moment. Best not to make a fuss. We'll work round it.

Luca *enters and is about to dump coat.*

Parent 1   Coat! And before you ask, there's nothing to eat. I've not been to the shops. Couldn't face . . . all those people outside our house, pointing and staring . . . making up excuses for walking past here . . . to judge . . . Your dad will be back soon, so you'll have to wait.

Luca   Aw, Mum –

Parent 1   Look, there's some stale cake on the kitchen counter if you're that desperate! Now leave me be! And you (*To* **Georgie**.) – sandwich box?

Georgie *hands over full sandwich box then goes and sits in front of the TV to play their game on one side of the* **Crack**.

Parent 1   Er . . . what's this?

Georgie   I had a few packets of crisps . . . I was too full to eat it. Susan gave me –

Parent 1   I don't want to hear it!

Luca   Anything arrive for me?

Parent 1   On the table. You better still have enough savings for those driving lessons –

Luca   OK, Mum!

Luca *backs away and goes to sit with* **Georgie**, *but on other side of the* **Crack**.

Luca   OK, Rainbow Road, 10cc?

Georgie   Again?

Luca   Ready?

They begin to play the game. There's a good-natured competitive rivalry between the siblings and **Georgie** *is glad of the distraction from the* **Crack**.

Georgie   Why do you always do this?

Luca   What? Win?

Parent 1 (*calling off*)   Maru!

Parent 1 *takes out her laptop and starts reading.* **Luca** *opens package and examines the new purchase, an item of clothing, fast fashion, she can take it or leave it. She discards it, indifferent to her wastefulness, and starts playing the game with* **Georgie**.

Maru *creeps in.* **Georgie** *and* **Luca** *stop playing.* **Maru** *gestures to them to keep making a noise, but they don't understand.* **Parent 1** *notices.*

Parent 1   Maru! Late again!

Maru   I'm sorry –

Parent 1   Were you ill? Sit down! How's your breathing?

Maru   Honestly, I'm OK!

Parent 1 *sighs and rummages for* **Maru**'*s sandwich box.*

Maru   Mum – stop! – I can do it . . .

Parent 1 (*taking kitchen implement out of bag*)   What is this? (*Outrage.*) British Heart Foundation?

Maru   I thought it might be useful – Dad dropped ours down the crack.

Parent 1   Stop buying things at charity shops! People will think we can't buy new!

Maru   I just want to find my book –

Parent 1   Did you walk?

Maru   Yes I walked and I'm fine!

Parent 1   What is wrong with you? You know how I worry and yet you seem determined to drive me crazy!

Parent 2 *arrives home with takeaway boxes and soft drinks in plastic bottles.*

Parent 2   Hello, family! Help me please!

Georgie   Dad!

Georgie *runs to hug* **Parent 2**, *jumping over* **Crack**. **Parents** *share a perfunctory kiss.* **Parent 2** *hands out the meals – first to* **Georgie**, *who runs to sit by the Nintendo.* **Luca** *takes their own food and joins* **Georgie**.

Parent 1   Maru was late again. Walking through smog to find some rubbish in a charity shop.

Maru   It's not rubbish!

Parent 2   It's been a long day. I can't cope with this at the minute.

Parent 1   Did you get my sweet and sour pork and special fried rice?

Parent 2   As always. And for us (*referring to* **Maru**) – I thought I'd try being vegan too – I got us fish and chips.

Maru   Oh . . .

Maru *takes the food in silence.* **Maru** *and* **Parent 1** *sit at the table to eat their supper.* **Parent 2** *leaves their supper on the table, gets some plaster out of a bag and starts inspecting the* **Crack** *under the table.*

Parent 1   Darling . . .?

Parent 2 *looks up, bumping their head on the table.*

Parent 1   Please come and eat your food.

Parent 2   I will. But I need to do something about this first.

Parent 2 *starts filling the* **Crack** *with plaster, patching it up.*

Parent 1   Ignore it for now. It'll be fine.

Parent 2 (*from under the table*)   It won't fix itself.

Parent 1   But your dinner is –

Parent 2 *stands up and almost topples the table. The rest of the family steady it.*

Parent 2   You scrimp and save for a new house, you believe all the stuff those developers say, and then this! Right out of the blue!

Parent 1   Well, banging around and shouting isn't going to help. I don't want the neighbours thinking we've got problems!

Parent 2   We have got problems! And they don't come much bigger than having a massive crack right through the middle of your living room floor!

Parent 1   Tone it down! Kids, eat your food! Maru, you've haven't even touched yours!

Maru   It's fish.

Parent 2   I can't keep up with you – I thought you were a vegan?

Parent 1   No more meat – that's right isn't it?

Maru   No animal products at all. I can maybe eat the chips.

Parent 2   Oh, that's very kind of you – haven't completely wasted my hard-earned cash!

Maru   Dad! I'm standing up for what I believe in – don't you want me to have values?

Parent 1   Of course we do, but this is not the way! You living on veg isn't going to change the world. Best you can do is keep your head down. Believe me, there are worse things than eating meat.

Luca *throws a napkin down the* **Crack**. **Maru** *starts wheezing.*

Parent 1   You OK, love?

Maru *coughs.* **Luca** *notices, looks puzzled and throws another piece of rubbish down the* **Crack**, *watching* **Maru** *carefully.* **Maru** *coughs more.*

Parent 1   Where's your inhaler?

Maru *points at her coat.* **Parent 2** *runs and grabs the inhaler from the pocket. Both* **Parents** *help* **Maru**, *and her breathing calms.*

Luca *takes the packaging from her parcel and throws it down the* **Crack**. **Maru** *starts wheezing again.* **Luca** *knows there is some connection.* **Maru** *and* **Luca** *lock eyes.*

Maru (*getting up*)   I just need to find my book.

Parent 1   Nonsense, you can't breathe, you need to lie down and prop yourself up.

Maru   Please, I need it!

Parent 1   How's a kids' book going to make you better?

Maru (*searches for an explanation*)   I can't explain it. Once I've found it, I'll show you.

Maru *grabs her coat and heads for the door.*

Parent 1   Maru, come back this minute. (**Maru** *leaves.*) You've left your inhaler!

Into:

Scene Seven: The crack spreads to the city

Maru *continues her search for the storybook in another charity shop, but still does not find it. She is becoming desperate.*

The people of the city continue in their wasteful ways, oblivious to their role in creating the **Crack**.

Into:

A bake sale on the street outside **Maru***'s family home. Two* **Neighbours** *stand next to a small cake stand. They are gossiping about the recent appearance of the* **Crack,** *which is now visible from the outside of the house.*

Neighbour 1 (*admiring their handiwork*)   Your red velvet looks delicious!

Neighbour 2   Not as good as your Black Forest gâteau!

Neighbour 1   It'd be absolutely perfect, if it wasn't for one thing . . . (*They look at the* **Crack.**)

Neighbour 1 *and* **2**   . . . that crack!

Neighbour 1   I mean, who wants to come to a cake sale on Crack Street?!

Neighbour 2   And what if it spreads down the street? I don't want my house devalued because they can't afford to do repairs!

Neighbour 2   I know! I mean, I'm not a nosey person, but I was doing my morning jog and I couldn't help but see into the house . . . and the crack . . . .it's so big!. . . (*Looks over her shoulder.*) And they've got yellow wallpaper!

They both laugh.

And you should see the carpet!

Neighbour 1   You never know what's behind closed doors. Oh, did I tell you? My Sophie wanted to donate some money to that village in the Philippines – the one with the tornado . . .

Neighbour 2   Bless her little heart!

Neighbour 1   Well, she also wants the new iPhone . . .

Neighbour 2   . . . and you know what they cost!

Neighbour 1   I said, 'Sophie, it's either iPhone or tornado'.

Neighbour 2   I mean you can't do everything can you?

Bobby Brunt *and* **Aide** *arrive on the street.* **Brunt** *makes a beeline for the group.*

Brunt   Good afternoon, lovely people!

The group spots **Brunt** *and immediately stop talking. It's as if they're in the presence of a celebrity. They smile and laugh, ready to hang off* **Brunt***'s every word.*

Brunt (*shaking hands with each of them*)   Bobby Brunt . . . Hi, Bobby Brunt . . . Nice to meet you – Bobby Brunt. Nice cakes! They smell divine!

Neighbour 1   Please, have a cookie.

Neighbour 1 *offers* **Brunt** *a cookie.* **Bobby** *takes a bite from it.*

Brunt   Mmm, delicious. (*Pocketing the cookie and brushing the crumbs from their hands.*) Now, can I tell you lovely ladies about my plans to . . .

A **New Parent** *carrying a baby appears.*

Brunt   One second . . . (*Rushing over to the* **New Parent** *and baby*.) What a lovely baby! Do you mind if I hold it?

The **New Parent** *is hesitant but has no choice.* **Brunt** *takes the baby and poses next to the* **New Parent***, as the* **Aide** *hurries forward to take a photograph. As soon as they have the picture* **Brunt** *dumps the baby back in the arms of the parent, and hurries off to their next official engagement.*

Into:

Fin *and* **Parent** *trying on clothes in a shop.* **Fin**'*s* **Parent** *holds up a jacket. It's a very trendy piece of clothing, something that is unlikely to be worn for more than a few weeks.*

Parent   I do quite like it . . .

Fin   You bought a coat last week.

Parent   I'm gonna try it on. (*Puts on the jacket, which is clearly too small*.) What do you think?

Fin   Er, maybe you should get a slightly bigger size?

Parent   They don't have a bigger one, but I really like it . . . I reckon I can lose the weight! (*Looks at the tag*.) It's so cheap.

Fin   But do you *need* it?

Parent   I'm going to get it!

Fin'*s* **Parent** *goes off to the cash desk.* **Fin** *goes to follow, then makes a quick decision to slip off to look for* **Maru***.*

Into:

Parent *and* **Child** *sitting in the front seats of a car. They are stuck in traffic.*

Child (*impatiently*)   Why did we have to drive?

Parent   I'm not walking around in this cold weather.

Child   I know, but it's like five minutes away, and now we're stuck in all this traffic.

Parent (*beeping the horn at the car in front*)   Move, you wanker!

Driver (*winding down their car window*)   Do you mind?!

Child   Wait, is that Tilly's dad?

Parent (*embarrassed*)   I'll speak to him in church on Sunday!

Parent *waves at the* **Driver***, to hopefully placate them. Traffic starts to move.*

Into:

Maru *continues the search for the storybook in another charity shop – but still doesn't find it.*

Into:

There is the sound of a huge 'crack'. Bigger than any that have gone before.

The whole stage splits in two as the **Crack** *spreads from the house to the city.*

Into:

Bobby Brunt *is with a bunch of* **Young Children***, at a library, reading them a book. There is a* **Camera Person** *present recording the event.*

Brunt   . . . so she took it to the garage in the village, where Paddy fixed the engine – but what happened? That's right, the little red car got stuck in the mud again! We can't be having that can we?

Children   No!

Brunt*'s* **Aide** *gets a call and is flustered.*

Brunt   Well, you'll be pleased to know, my young followers, that as Mayor, I will be directing our investment –

Aide   Sorry, Mr Brunt. Something is happening in the centre. It seems a massive crack has appeared – some kind of disaster!

Brunt *looks awkwardly to the* **Camera Person** *who is capturing the moment.*

Brunt   So the dwarves all lived happily ever after. The end. Got to go!

Brunt *throws the book at one of the* **Children** *to catch and struts off with the* **Aide***, leaving the* **Children** *behind.*

Into:

Scene Eight: Exploiting the crack

The **City Dwellers** *are going about their day-to-day lives, either ignoring the* **Crack***, or exploiting it for their own gain.*

A **Chancer** *is trying to sell T-shirts and tours of the crack.*

Chancer   Come and get your original 'CRACKING UP' T-shirt! One-time special offer, ten pounds with every ticket booked for the exclusive 'Crack' tour!

A **City Dweller** *crosses, unperturbed by the* **Crack***.*

Chancer   Not to be missed, get your tickets now!

A **City Dweller** *crosses, completely uninterested – they've got places to go . . .*

A **YouTuber** *is filming a post about the* **Crack***.*

YouTuber   What's up, guys! Welcome back to the channel. Today we're at 'the Crack'. Wow! It's really deep and dark – it feels like it could go through to the other side of the world! We're going to have a look around and chat to a few people. Remember click 'like' and 'subscribe'!

Chancer (*to* **YouTuber**)   Can I interest you in a 'CRACKING UP' T-shirt? Only ten pounds with a ticket for the exclusive 'Crack' tour!

YouTuber   'Crack tour'? Yes, please!

A group of **Youths** *arrive to explore the possibilities of the* **Crack** *for parkour. They put pay to* **Chancer***'s 'Crack' tour. They take it in turns to do daring leaps over the* **Crack***, cheering each other after each leap.* **Chancer** *joins the cheers, offers T-shirts.* **YouTuber** *films.*

A **Negative Nelly** *approaches the* **Crack** *and susses out its possibilities for an insurance claim. When the others are cheering the* **Youths***, she walks over the* **Crack** *and pretends to trip.*

Negative Nelly   You saw that didn't you? I just damaged my ankle! Get me the council's number! I'm contacting 'Injury Specialists dot com' – I'm suing! I've had an accident and it wasn't my fault!

The **Youths** *help her up.* **Chancer** *offers her a discounted T-shirt.* **Chancer** *and* **Negative Nelly** *exit.*

A **Journalist** *enters and is practising lines in front of a* **Camera Person***. The* **Youths** *notice and try to sneak into shot.*

Maru *enters and watches the way the* **Crack** *is being treated.*

Journalist   'Environmental crisis . . . or local neglect?' Not snappy enough!

The **Camera Person** *notices the* **Youths***.*

She indicates to the **Journalist** *to change position so that they are no longer in shot.*

A **Drunk** *comes in and uses the* **Crack** *for a quick pee.*

Journalist   'Climate catastrophe or domestic disaster' – what do you think?

Camera Person *indicates to* **Journalist** *that there is a problem.*

Journalist *turns to see the* **Drunk** *in shot.*

A **Pastor** *enters wearing a sign with 'THE END IS NIGH'.*

Pastor (*to the* **Drunk**)   Change your ways before it's too late!
The Devil, he is coming up through the depths of hell!
So, get your place in heaven!

Camera Person   Hey! Could you be quiet – we're trying to film!

Journalist *indicates to* **Camera Person** *to find a different angle.*

Pastor (*to* **Maru***, warning*)   Turn your life around! (*Exits.*)

Journalist   Whilst parallels are being drawn with the freak cracks appearing in countries across the globe, this crack seems to have originated with just one family located in the northern suburbs of the city. Authorities are requesting that people with more information should contact them immediately.
OK – that should do it. Let's go and grab a beer!

Journalist *and* **Camera Person** *exit.*

Maru *is fearful of the news she has just heard, but mesmerised by the* **Crack** *and begins to move closer.* **Fin** *appears and spots* **Maru** *leaning over the* **Crack***.*

Fin   Maru! What are you doing?

Maru *turns, spots* **Fin***. A moment of uncertainty passes between them. They embrace.*

Maru   I really missed you.

Fin   You OK? (*Beat.*)

I missed you too. I'm sorry about your bedroom, and your book. And . . . for walking out like that. I was scared.

Maru (*indicating the* **Crack**)   I did this, Fin. Everything that's happening is because of me.

Fin   It's not your fault, Maru . . . it's not.

Maru *looks doubtful.*

Fin   OK, so let's think about it. You were in your room, you noticed your book was gone, you were coughing . . . your asthma came . . . you coughed and . . . it happened.

Maru   So I did cause it.

Fin   You didn't. It's a coincidence. These cracks have been appearing all over the world, we've all seen them.

Maru   Yes, but there weren't any here until the one in my bedroom and now they're all over the city. And everyone's saying it's my fault!

Fin   Well, they're wrong. They should be trying to do something about it instead of just going around blaming people.

Maru   Exactly. And that's why I need to find my book.

Fin   You think the answer to all of this is in your book?

Maru   If you're not going to take me seriously . . .

Fin   Sorry!

Maru   Look, I know this might sound a bit weird, but whenever I read it, I feel, I don't know, I feel like me. I can breathe again. And in one of the stories a large crack suddenly appears in the earth.

Two **Fly-Tippers** *appear carrying a large load of rubbish.*

Fly-Tipper 1   It's good and wide over here, Stevie.

Fly-Tipper 2   Excuse me.

They move **Fin** *and* **Maru** *out of the way and tip the rubbish down the* **Crack***.*

They exit.

Fin   Right, and then what?

Maru *starts to struggle to breathe again.*

Maru   I don't know, I haven't finished the story because my parents gave the book away!

Fin   So you think if you could read the end of the story, it might have the answer to how to get rid of all the cracks?

Maru   Exactly! But I've looked everywhere.

Fin   Let's keep trying.

Maru *is wheezing now.*

Fin (*to* **Maru**)   Are you OK?

The **Fly-Tippers** *re-enter and attempt to barge past* **Maru** *and* **Fin**.

Fin   Hey! Can't you see she's not well?

Fly-Tipper 1   Can't you see I've got my hands full?.

Maru *is still struggling to breathe.*

Fly-Tipper 2   Bleeding kids!

Impatient, **Fly-Tipper 2** *drags a plank out of the wheelbarrow, puts it over the* **Crack** *and indicates to* **Fly-Tipper 1** *to cross over to the other side.*

Fly-Tipper 2   Here – try this!

Fly-Tipper 1   OK – three, two, one . . .

They empty the container into the **Crack**.

Maru *'s breathing becomes suddenly worse, as if she has something lodged in her throat. The* **Fly-Tippers** *exit.*

Fin   Maru, where's your inhaler? Shall I get someone?

Maru *shakes her head, reaches into her pocket and pulls out the inhaler. After a few moments her breathing begins to ease.*

Fly-Tipper 1 *returns, armed with more rubbish and again tips it into the* **Crack**.

Maru   What are you doing?

Fly-Tipper 2   What does it look like?

Maru   Stop it. It's not a rubbish dump.

Fly-Tipper 1   Really? (*Looking down at the* **Crack**.) That's not what it looks like to me. Why don't you mind your own business?

Maru *begins to cough again.*

Fin   Don't speak to her like that.

Fly-Tipper 2 *dumps their rubbish into the* **Crack**.

Fin   You should take better care of the environment!

Fly-Tipper 2   Why? What's the environment ever done for me? (*To* **Fly-Tipper 1**.)

Honestly, little kids that don't know when to mind their own business . . . it pisses me off, Dave!

Maru *coughs and the* **Crack** *opens up into the auditorium.*

The **Fly-Tippers** *gawp and look panicked.*

Fly-Tipper 2 (*to* **Fly-Tipper 1**)   You saw that right?

Fly-Tipper 1 (*points to* **Maru** *and* **Fin**)   What the – *you* just did that! We . . . we saw it . . . with our own eyes . . . right, Stevie? (*To* **Fly-Tipper 2**, *who takes out his phone and is taking photos.*) Stop that! Call the police or something!

Fly-Tipper 2   Wait a minute – I know you! You're the one on the news – the one from that house in the north of the city – they're calling you the 'Super Cracker'!

Fly-Tipper 1 *starts to phone the police.*

Maru *and* **Fin** *look shaken and quickly leave.*

Fly-Tipper 2 *is glued to his screen.*

Fly-Tipper 1   The line's jammed. Must be something going on. What you doing?

Fly-Tipper 2   Just updating Twitter – I can't believe what I just saw!

Fly-Tipper 1   I know, mate (*taking selfie*) – weird!

Into:

Scene Nine: Chaos in the city

The **Crack** *is getting bigger, causing chaos in the city.*

A sequence of **Worried People** *enter, all observing their phones closely and tapping out messages.*

Worried 1   Oh my God – crack's getting bigger – first cracks, next wars! – hashtag 'World War 3'!

Worried 2   Lord save us! My dog just fell into the crack – hashtag 'It ain't safe on these streets'!

Into:

A **Mother** *and* **Child** *trying to escape with all their worldly belongings packed into a few suitcases.*

Child   Mum – these are heavy – where's the car?

Mother   I could have sworn I parked it right here!

She presses the automatic unlock button on her keys and hears a beep. It's coming from the **Crack**. *They approach and look into the* **Crack**. *The car has fallen in.*

Child   Now what will we do?

Mother (*determinedly*)   We'll have to go with the Wilkinsons. Quick – they were leaving at 3!

They run off as quickly as their luggage will allow, looking back at where the car should have been.

Into:

Worried 3   Oh, there goes the school! And there goes Greggs!

Worried 4   My city's being destroyed!

Worried 3 *and* **4** (*together*)   Hashtag 'Scared for my life'!

Into:

Maru *and* **Fin** *enter as if pursued and hide behind a convenient wall. Their* **Pursuers** *run past them. They are relieved as they are tired from running.* **Maru** *looks at her phone.*

Maru   There's a photo of us!

Fin   What?

Maru   We're trending on Twitter!

Fin   Those guys with the rubbish . . . never mind, we can't think about that now . . . (*dragging* **Maru** *away*) we need to find somewhere safe.

Maru   Where? Everyone's looking for us!

Maru *starts coughing and tries her inhaler but it's empty. She carries on coughing.*

Fin (*referring to the inhaler*)   Take some more, Maru. Come on, deep breaths.

Maru   No use, it's empty.

They hear **Bobby Brunt** *arriving.*

Fin   Come on, there's only one place we can go.

Fin *and* **Maru** *exit in the opposite direction.*

Into:

Brunt *enters with a* **Journalist** *and* **Camera Person** *in tow, and a small* **Crowd** *including* **Maru**'*s family.*

Brunt   Of course, we are incredibly concerned. Citizens are rightly worried about the cracks appearing across our fine city, and about the potential impact on homes and jobs. I assure you that all possible resources will be ploughed into protecting the property of honest, working local people.

And a message to this so-called 'Super Cracker' and her friend – we will not bow down to terrorists. We know who you are and we're coming to get you.

Luca   Maru isn't a terrorist! She isn't responsible for this!

Parent 1 (*pulling her away*)   Don't draw attention, Luca.

Brunt   We have our best people looking into this. I can assure you that –

Luca   How can you blame one individual?! There are cracks like these all over the world!

Brunt   Er . . . we need to move on. Rest assured I am leading the charge to restore our fortunes.

Another group of **Citizens** *fleeing the city cross the stage carrying suitcases and looking desperate – a contrast/parallel to the* **City Dwellers** *in the opening scene.* **Brunt** *moves away with the group.* **Luca** *wrestles free of* **Parent 1** *and runs off.* **Parent 1** *follows them.*

Into:

Scene Ten: Tree (after)

The park. **Maru** *and* **Fin** *enter, running, though* **Maru** *is clearly weakened.* **Fin** *supports* **Maru**, *and both look edgy, checking over their shoulders.*

A voice offstage through a loudhailer.

Brunt   Maru! Fin! We've got you surrounded. There's no escape.

The girls shrink into the tree, trying to make themselves as small as possible. **Maru** *covers her mouth with her hand to try and prevent a cough.*

Fin   He's bluffing – no one saw us come here.

Brunt (*off*)   You're not in trouble. We just want to talk to you.

Maru   I don't trust him.

Brunt (*off*)   You need help, Maru. Why don't you let us help you? (*Getting closer.*) Fin! Maru!

Fin (*whispering*)   What are we going to do?

Maru *doesn't answer.*

Fin   Maru?

Maru   I don't know! . . . I don't know how the story ends!

Fin   Then make it up!

Maru   What?

Fin   You know most of the story . . . find the ending yourself.

Maru *hesitates for a moment, but* **Fin** *encourages her to start.*

Maru   Once there was a girl, who planted a garden, and it was beautiful. One day she grew a tree, a massive lush tree, but then there was a famine . . .

Fin *nods to encourage* **Maru** *to continue.*

Maru   Even though there was a famine her mum always managed to find some water to give to the tree, and the tree always provided them with fruit. But when her mum died, people started to just help themselves to the fruit to make money from it without watering it. Without giving anything back. Until everything got so dry a crack appeared . . . and . . .

Fin   And?

Maru *shrugs as if to say I don't know.*

Fin   And then one day . . .

Maru   The tree . . .

Fin   Yes, the tree . . . it . . .

Maru   . . . it . . . spoke.

Fin   It spoke and it said to the people of the village . . .

Maru   . . . to change their ways! It warned them and they listened. The people made peace with the tree?

Suddenly there is the sound of rupturing. A human hand appears from out of the **Crack***, covered in dust and mud. Slowly a figure emerges, hauling itself up onto the other side of the* **Crack** *to* **Fin** *and* **Maru***. The figure is a young person about the same age as* **Fin** *and* **Maru***. This is* **Asha** *– we recognise her as the young singer from the Prologue. She coughs, clearing her lungs, and wipes the grit from her eyes. She recoils in fear at the sight of* **Maru** *and* **Fin***, who are equally shocked by* **Asha***'s sudden appearance. Silence. They look at each other.*

Fin (*in disbelief*)   What is going on?

Asha *takes in her surroundings and spots the extent of the* **Crack***. She looks alarmed and becomes agitated.*

Asha (*shouting*)   *Kwete, kwete zvakare! Izvi azvisi izvo!* ('No, not again! This isn't right!')

Fin   Shhh . . . be quiet! They'll hear you.

Asha (*almost angrily*)   The people made peace? You think that's how this ends?

Fin   Who are you?

Asha   I come from a village like the one in your story. I would pick fruit every day with my family, there was enough for each of us. Great Mother looked after us well.

But one day, men from far away places came. They offered our leaders money to grow tobacco on our land. So we cleared the fruit trees to make way for fields of leaves that no one could eat. When it came to harvest, the company would not pay what the tobacco was worth. We complained, over and over again, but our cries were ignored.

Then, the weather changed, a drought hit us and our remaining crops failed to produce. The earth was broken, groaning for help, until one day, it split! A crack appeared, just like this one. (*Pointing.*) It got so large that it started to consume everything. Homes. People. I was swallowed up by the splintered ground. But it seems the earth took pity on me . . . at least I am alive.

Maru   I'm so sorry. I don't know what to say.

Brunt   Come out, Maru! We can fix this.

Asha   Who's that?!

Fin   One of our brilliant leaders!

Asha   Then make them see how this might end.

Maru   We . . . we should tell them your story.

Asha   My story? My own people wouldn't listen to me, so why would anyone here take notice of what I've got to say?   ·

Fin   Maru, I'm scared.

Maru   So am I.

Crowd (*off*)   I can hear them – they must be nearby!

Parent 2 (*off*)   Maru!

Asha, **Maru** *and* **Fin** *are startled and afraid. The voices are coming from* **Asha**'s *side of the* **Crack**. **Asha** *looks around and spots a nearby plank. She places it over the* **Crack**. **Asha** *crosses over the* **Crack** *to join* **Maru** *and* **Fin**, *pulling the plank up behind her. She is just in time.*

Crowd (*off*)   Let's get them! They're over there, yes! Quickly! Come on!

Bobby Brunt *approaches with his* **Aide**, *and* **Maru**'s *family. A* **Crowd** *gathers quickly and there is tension with boos and shouts of confusion as they discover* **Fin** *and* **Maru** *on the other side of the* **Crack**.

Crowd   There they are!

Brunt   Good citizens, I come to you tonight not as your leader, but as a neighbour, a parent and your friend. Let me begin by expressing my deepest condolences to those who have suffered as a result of these cracks. Family members have been lost. Homes have been destroyed. Businesses have disappeared.

The **Crowd** *calms down and begins to listen.* **Brunt**'s **Aide** *is sipping from a branded fast food paper cup.*

Brunt   There will be a time for grieving. But right now, we need to take back our city from those who would seek to harm us.

Eco-terrorists are capturing the minds of our young, exploiting their naivety. Do not be fooled by their 'facts' and statistics – these people do not share our values! They are weeds, intent on choking the life out of our future. And where do weeds reside? In the cracks!

Rest assured that these weeds will be identified, rooted out and destroyed.

We say: 'Let our children be children, and leave the politics to us!'

The **Crowd** *claps and starts to cheer.*

Brunt   Elect me as your Mayor, and I will fill in the cracks! We will use concrete, concrete mixed and poured by local labour! Yes, we will create opportunity where they planned ruination! We will build over these cracks – shopping malls to rival the best, housing for our workers, support for local families –

Asha   What about *our* families?! What about *my* family?!

They all turn and look at **Asha**. **Asha** *walks forward.*

Asha   I've lost my father, my grandmother, my brother! Others have lost their homes, their livelihoods. My life is not a fairy story, in a book for children. You live your lives, without any sense of what the choices you make might mean for people like me, living on the other side of the planet!

Brunt   People like you? Other side of the planet?

Crowd 1 (*smoking*)   If you don't like it, go back to where you came from!

Asha   I would love to go home. But my home no longer exists.

Brunt (*turning to* **Aide**)   Who is this child?

Asha   My name is Asha. My family died just trying to survive.

The cigarettes you smoke, the clothes you wear, the food you eat, the coffee you drink. Where do you think they come from? You take and you take and you take and you buy and you take yet more again until we . . . until the earth that we all live on, can't give any more.

Brunt   Young lady, I can assure you that my plans have got nothing whatsoever to do with wherever it is you come from!

Asha   The decisions you make impact on the future of us all.

Brunt   You can't see the future! Certainly not the future of our fine city!

Beat.

(*To* **Crowd**.) I always say, everyone is welcome here, but we will not have negative attitudes undermining British values!

The **Crowd** *claps and starts to cheer.*

Asha *stands her ground.*

Brunt   We will rebuild. We will welcome a new wave of multi-national partnerships, the likes of which has never been seen before! We'll improve transport by investing in car manufacturing – electric cars to support *our* environmental objectives, *our* local needs and *our* future prosperity!

Maru (*walking out onto the plank*)   You're not listening to what she's saying! It's not the earth that's dying, we are!

The **Crowd** *gasp.*

Parent 2   Maru, it's going to be alright!

Maru   No, it's not, Dad. Everything is *not* alright! There are cracks all over the world, in places like Asha's village and on every other continent.

Parent 1 (*under her breath*)   Maru! Get back over here!

Maru   No. We need to *do* something!

Parent 1   You can hardly breathe without the help of an inhaler, what are you going to do?

Maru   That's exactly why we need to act, Mum!

Crowd 2   Haven't you been listening? He's already said – electric cars!

Parent 2   We've got to trust the people in charge, Maru. They know what they're doing.

Maru   No, Dad – the people in charge aren't doing enough. We need more than electric cars!

Crowd 1   Alright, little Miss Perfect!

Fin   It's not about being perfect, it's about starting to change how we behave . . .

Maru   I think we are scared. Our city is fragmenting before our eyes.

Crowd 3   Only because of people like you! With your doom and your gloom!

Maru   Why aren't you listening? It's not people like me – it's all of us – we need to work together!

Brunt   Why can't you just shut up, go home and let us clear up this mess, so we can get back to normal and get on with our lives?

Maru   That's just it – we close our eyes and carry on as 'normal', filling the cracks – in our homes, our families, our lives – with things. A new iPhone, the latest clothes, takeaways on a Friday night. And another crack appears, and we close our eyes and carry on, round and round and round, filling the cracks again and again and again! Until there's nothing left to fill the void . . .

Helicopters are circling overhead.

The **Journalist** *returns with their* **Camera Person.**

Parent 1 (*desperate*)   Maru. You're risking your future! Please!

Crowd 3   It's your generation that insists on having everything brand new!

Maru Listen!

Aide I've saved for these trainers – you saying I shouldn't have nice shoes?

Crowd 2 Yeah, we all work hard!

Maru You're not listening!

Crowd 3 And we all pay our way.

Crowd 2 You saying we don't deserve a holiday? It's only once a year!

Maru No. I'm not saying –

Crowd 4 Why shouldn't I have the latest iPhone?

Crowd 2 They wouldn't make them if we didn't need them!

Maru *wavers.*

Crowd 3 If I start recycling now, what difference is it gonna make?

Crowd 1 No one else bothers and it all ends up in the rubbish tip anyway!

Asha *joins* **Maru** *on the plank.*

Asha (*singing*)   If ever it may seem
Like there may be no tomorrow,
Plant one small seed
It may grow to feed a village.

Aide What's she singing for?

Brunt's **Aide** *drops their takeaway cup in the* **Crack***.*

The earth groans, the plank shakes, **Maru** *and* **Asha** *teeter over the chasm.*

Everyone gasps.

Maru Listen.

Crowd 2 We've heard what you've got to say.

Maru No – don't listen to me. Listen to the earth.

Aide Now they've really lost it.

Maru Can't you hear it? It's sobbing so hard, it's flooding our towns and cities.

It's shouting so loud, that fires rage though our forests and woodlands. The earth is cracking up and melting down. Right before our eyes. It's desperate to be heard. But you can't hear it. Whatever it does, we just carry on the same, giving it not even the slightest sign that we're willing to change.

Maru *turns, defeated, and walks back to where* **Fin** *is standing.*

Luca *approaches the opposite end of the plank and very carefully starts to cross. The* **Crowd** *gasp and object.* **Maru** *turns to watch.*

Luca (*arriving at the other side and grabbing* **Maru**).   I am. I'm willing to change. I could try meat-free Mondays from now on?

Maru *and* **Luca** *hug.*

Parent 2 (*calling from the other side of the* **Crack**, *with the* **Crowd** *continuing to object*)   It wouldn't hurt me to start walking to work.

Parent 2 *starts to cross the plank, pauses to look back at the crowd, then continues.* **Maru** *is grateful.*

Parent 2   And maybe we could cook together on a Friday night.

Crowd 3 (*rushing to the middle of the plank and then stopping to regain her balance as the* **Crowd** *object most to one of their own abandoning the cause*)   Yeah, OK, I guess I could take the kids to Margate this year, for their summer holidays, instead of Marbella.

Asha   We all need to work together.

Parent 1   What about it, Bobby? What if your factories made electric buses . . . get us all out of our individual bubbles?

Pause as **Brunt** *tries to appear composed and unflustered.*

Brunt   Well, obviously, I have a five-stage plan . . . (*looking at* **Aide** *for support.*) . . . No one cares about the environment more than me . . .

The **Crowd** *turn on him, hostile and full of questions such as, 'Why shouldn't I have a new phone?', 'You promised us jobs!' and 'What you gonna do, Bobby?'* **Brunt** *is overwhelmed and tries to pacify them.*

Maru *and* **Fin** *speak over the hum of the general hubbub.*

Fin   Is this how it ends?

Maru   No, this is how it starts.

Asha *draws a calabash from the folds of her cloth and starts to sing the libation to Mother Earth from the start of the play.*

Others are drawn to her – first **Maru** *and* **Fin**, *then* **Luca**, **Parent 2**, *then* **Crowd 3**, *one or two others – but they don't know how to join in.*

Asha *starts to feed them, the new community, the lines as the rest of the* **Crowd** *are slowly silenced, whilst remaining resistant to joining in.*

Asha   Great Mother!
Great Mother! We thank you, Great Mother!
You, who with loving hands, sculpts the clay from your earthy womb
(*Singing as if to indicate the others should join, but they don't understand.*) Form us!
Who, from your verdant sanctuary, yield both root and fruit
(*Quietly and to those gathering.*) Feed us!

Maru/Fin (*tentatively*)   Feed us!

Asha   Who, in your ancient wisdom, sends both storm and flower (*Quietly and to those gathering.*) Teach us!

Maru/Fin/Parent 2/Luca (*building confidence*)   Teach us!

Asha   Who, with graceful force, forges rocks and continents (*Quietly and to those gathering.*) Shield us!

Maru/Fin/Parent 2/Luca/Crowd 3+ (*with full commitment*)   Shield us!

End of play.

'Great Mother' (Prologue)

Great Mo-ther,__ Gre - at Mo-ther,__ we thank you Great Mo-ther__

You__ who with lo-ving hands__ sculpts the clay__ from your ear-thy wo-

mb, Form u - us!

Who__ from your ver-dant sanc-tua - ry, Yield both root, and frui -

t, Feed u - us!

Who__ in your an-cient wi - is - dom, sends both sto - rm and

flower, Teach u - us!

Who with grace-ful force,__ For - ges rocks and con - ti - ne -

ents, Shield u - us!

You are__ the mo - ther, we are__ the chil - dren, Hear our prayer!
N - di - ni mai va - cho, i - su ti - ri va - na, Hear our prayer!

'If Ever It May Seem' (Scene Three)

If e - ver it may seem like there may be no to - mor - row, plant just

one small seed, It may grow to feed a vil - lage.

Like There's No Tomorrow

CREATED BY THE BELGRADE YOUNG COMPANY WITH
JUSTINE THEMEN, CLAIRE PROCTER AND LIZ MYTTON

*Notes on rehearsal and staging, drawn from a workshop led by
Sally Cookson held at National Theatre, October 2021.*

How the company came to make the show

The Belgrade Theatre's young company work with 200 young people each week. For this particular project, the Belgrade team wanted to make a full-length piece of work. *Like There's No Tomorrow* was made with a company of twelve young people living in and around Coventry, alongside co-directors Justine Themene and Claire Procter, and writer Liz Mytton. At the start of rehearsals, they didn't have a story in place; they just knew that they would be making a show about the environment. This meant that each of the young people involved felt a really strong sense of ownership of the play. At the time of making the show, the Friday school strikes were in full swing and it felt important to everyone involved that they made something that speaks to young people around the country.

As well as the themes, the company felt that they were connecting to one another through the medium of storytelling; the idea of telling stories, and particularly of folk stories, is central to the piece. The company who made the show were very diverse, with people from European, African and South Asian backgrounds, and although the prologue is set in Zimbabwe in the text, the company feel that it can be set anywhere – for example, the funeral held for the Okjokull glacier in Iceland was one of the key inspirations for the play.

Throughout the making of the show, the company found themselves becoming increasingly aware of small acts they could do themselves to help the environment – going round their homes switching off the lights, not using tea bags – but also thinking more and more about the structural problems in Western society and how these take us away from our natural environment. The biggest responsibility we have as citizens is to hold those in power accountable.

Beginnings: Making work now

Lead director Sally Cookson noted that, as a director, you don't have to solve all the problems on your own, that there's a joy in discovering things collaboratively. She acknowledged that the pandemic months have been really destabilising and that we can feel anxious when we come to making a play, with self-doubt often being part of the creative process. Cookson shared that for every play she does, she puts a Sylvia Plath quote in her notebook, 'The worst enemy to creativity is self-doubt'. She discussed how theatre-making involves exploring the world, asking questions and sharing other people's perspectives – which is amazing but a hard business too, emphasising the power of collective discovery.

Exercises for use in rehearsal

Sally Cookson led the group through a series of ensemble exercises which she uses in her devised, ensemble-led productions as a useful way to explore play beginnings – for example a cityscape or whole group scene, as in *Like There's No Tomorrow*.

Exercise: Light on, light off

The practical work began by checking in with the physicality of what it means to be present and to be an ensemble. Cookson asked the group to:

- Find the part of you that shines. Invest yourself, feel like a light is shone on you and out of you – open body stance. 'I'm here, this is me and I'm ready to go'.
- Move between 'closed-off' and upright stances.
- Notice that immediately there's an energy that's palpable when you turn the 'light on'. Keep that light on, allow your body to lift you up – a foot taller, connected to the floor (supporting you, giving you a base) and body lifting you up beyond the ceiling.

Exercise: Moving in the space as an ensemble

Sally Cookson developed the ensemble work with the following tasks:

- As we walked around the room, Sally Cookson gave us different prompts to respond to: play, stop, start, *Keep the light on*. Find an interesting path through the room; find an interesting pattern as a whole group using all of the space – the corners of the room, not just middle. Think about the tempo you move in. Negotiate when you're going to bump into someone, find moments of play as a pair. Now find a shared group tempo together, so that you end up walking in this dynamic pattern but at the same tempo.
- Walking in the space at a particular tempo; the leader calls a rhythmic count 1-2-3-4 go and 1-2-3-4 stop. It's important to move sharply, dynamically on the 'go'. When you're still, it's as if you can't wait to move (without over anticipating the 'go' moment and moving too early). When still, keep the energy going internally.
- With one person moving: the leader calls 1-2-3-4-stop and all become still except for one lone walker. It's the group's job to silently negotiate this together. The rest of the group give the singular walker all of your focus and energy before rejoining after 1-2-3-4-go. Next: two people walk following the '1-2-3-4-stop' call. Now there's a duet – you have a playmate: what's the relationship between the two people?

- With music: allow yourself to be inspired by the music, informed by the music. Don't ignore the music – find the rhythm and tempo.

- Variations on numbers of people walking: *one person, two people, five people, seven people.* Each time the group standing still give the 'movers' their whole energy and focus before rejoining them moving through the space on a 1-2-3-4 count called by the leader.

Approaching the play

Image exercise

The group brought images that related to the play and set them out on the floor. With some music on in the background, Sally Cookson asked the group to take the images in.

The group was then asked to find the courage to speak what comes into their minds while looking at the images. Some reflections included:

'suffocation, lack of breath, finding it hard to breathe', 'time running out', 'connection, neglect, greed', 'a unified force', 'stories, theatre', 'strangulation, fragility', 'trapped, voicelessness, industry,', 'frustration, capitalism, community', 'vulnerability, time running out', 'it's cheap so I don't care, guilt, it's not my fault, shame', 'melting, shirking responsibility, race a against time', 'someone else's responsibility', 'life and death', 'the physical surface of the earth', 'our relationship with the natural world', 'time, taking responsibility, climate denial', 'the next generation', 'a living breathing being', 'no future'.

Sally Cookson encouraged the group to allow themselves to be vocally affected by the emotion that each word brings out and to work with the principle of repetition. She encouraged the group to work with their 'light on' and to get their thoughts out into the space.

Sally Cookson reflected with the group that the play is such a gamut of all the ideas shared that when making a production about climate change, you can feel scared of doing anything other than a serious or didactic production. She offered that the best way to engage an audience is to get them having a good time – through joy, theatricality, entertainment – rather than it being an hour of doom. Find ways of bringing energy to this piece, which has a lot of humour in it.

Co-writer and co-creator Justine Themen added: you know how funny young people are, the play really came from a point of satire – they were laughing at the characters they were creating.

Exercise: Why the play?

Sally Cookson asked the group to think about why they each wanted to direct *this* play and led the following reflective exercise:

- We had five minutes to think about and/or write an answer to that question in the form of a short paragraph that we could remember and learn. It didn't need to be clever – it could be simple and it *had* to be honest.

- Once we had each written our paragraph, we had to repeat it in our own head. Check it felt right.
- We walked into the room, saying our phrases out loud but to ourselves. *I want to direct this play because . . .*
- We stood in a line across the room.
- Sally Cookson then numbered the group and called out numbers (out of order with the line), to create a seemingly random pattern. She encouraged the group to work with big voices – try to be heard, want to be listened to, make it a clarion cry.

After hearing everyone's responses, Sally Cookson led a final stage in the exercise in which she asked the group to share again, as if they were collectively staging a performance, creating a dynamic theatrical picture, speaking their words with belief and conviction that they each have the *right to direct this play*, trusting that *your reason is the right reason*. This part of the exercise was underscored with music.

Challenges

The group talked through the biggest challenges the play presents with Sally Cookson and the writing team from Coventry Belgrade.

The crack

First think about what the crack represents before you think about how to make it. The group offered that it could be:

- A puncture in the earth that's slowly deflating the Earth.
- An onion, a layer peeling off for the next layer: a positive force. An opening.
- The Earth trying to breathe again.
- Once you have a crack there's nothing you can do to take it back to new, as in the Japanese art of *kintsugi* (filling cracks in pottery with gold making the damage beautiful). There is hope in the fracture.
- As something gets older you get cracks – a sign of wisdom.
- An embodiment of Maru's (and so many young people's) frustration at not being heard.

The group shared real life examples of cracks and earthquakes which could be referred to in the process: coal mines collapsing, subsidence, earthquakes.

Practical exploration of how to stage 'the crack' in groups

Sally Cookson introduced a focus/energy device for sharing back work in rehearsals in which the 'audience' do a drum roll on their knees culminating with three sharp claps together to introduce whichever group is sharing back their idea.

One group: at first running on the spot, as if affected by what was happening (the world cracking) then becoming the crack itself.

Reflection from the group: there's richness in the fluidity between responding to the stimulus of the crack and embodying the crack itself.

Another group: interlinked arms and legs; breathing together, with the ensemble shape rising and falling with the group's inhale/exhale.

Reflection: a way to get in and out of this ensemble shape is to get 'sucked into it' one at a time, so there is a build-up.

Sally Cookson suggested that the named character (Maru, Fin) should always stand apart from those shapes.

A final group: lying on the floor representing the crack through scrunching and tearing big sheets of paper.

Sally Cookson's observations: There's a liveness in working with bodies to create the crack: it's then something you can invest a feeling or intention in, rather than material which just sits on stage (and isn't manipulated by actors); e.g. if you used physical design only to represent the crack.

Maru's breathing/cough

Elements to consider:

- Relation of the cough to the crack.

- Coughing on stage isn't good for someone's voice (and anxiety inducing in the context of Covid-19).

- Finding a language that the ensemble can be part of to elevate that idea – to make it more theatrical and have more weight.

- Connecting to ensemble movement – a silent cough found in the body, with the ensemble mirroring/responding to Maru physically and vocally.

The prologue: Making the prologue with groups of varying levels of cultural diversity

The original production: Sally Cookson and Justine Themen talked through the nuances of staging the prologue. The prologue is a libation or offering to Mother Earth led by Asha which, in the original production, draws on Zimbabwean culture and the Shona language.

Justine Themen: we worked with a group of young people with roots from all over the world. One young woman had a particular connection with Zimbabwe and knew something of the traditional heritage that she came from.

It's about our story here (in the UK) and how we are connected with another culture *on the other side of the world*. We did research into societies that had a more harmonious connection with nature than our own. You might discover links you didn't know about – ties of friendship with other cultures perhaps, if not blood ties. It's an opportunity for people to connect with their own and/or other people's cultures.

You can set the play in your location but the key is finding a country far away that has suffered a similar or linked climate crisis event or issue. For example, Greenland, where traditional cultures are being erased; or Scotland and the Highlands; or linking worldwide subsidence problems, in places like northern England and Australia, to mining. The impetus behind this is about having more in common with a country across the other side of the world than with the political elite of our country.

Justine Themen added that you could rewrite the tobacco speech (when Asha emerges from the crack, p. 317) in relation to the cultural context of their group. The context is the robbing of the global south to resource the global north.

Casting and representation

A linked question was around cultural representation in presenting a culture or ethnicity on stage which is different from that of the majority of the company's cultural background (e.g. in a group which is predominantly or all white).

Sally Cookson acknowledged that this was such an important discussion in the industry about who has the right to tell what kind of stories.

Justine Themen put to the group that if ninety-eight per cent of the company is white, who are the other two per cent? Is that an opportunity for their story or narrative to come through?

She articulated that National Theatre Connections is a learning opportunity to build connections with the world and with other cultures. In that sense, it's different from the wider professional industry and that if the choice and process is handled with sensitivity, a white company member can play the Asha role. You could explore a culture from within the group or another culture that isn't Zimbabwe but is also not present within the group.

Process

Justine Themen contextualised the process the Belgrade Young Company undertook to reach this choice.

Justine Themen: it's important to give ownership to the group in this choice. In the original production we had one session that was just about researching traditional cultures that the group had connections with (even though you will choose only one).

In the Belgrade group, the young company member who played Asha (the character of Zimbabwean origin) was herself of Nigerian heritage. She and the whole company had to learn the Shona-language parts of the script.

In the prologue the libation phrases are spoken in English and Shona. Seyi Olomolaiye (Young Company Member) explained that it's important to try to incorporate a community or country's language into the play. Language is something that's quite integral to a community – it's how they communicate and transfer things.

Characterisation and acting style

Another challenge that arose for the group was the question around acting style and ensuring that the adult characters (e.g. the parents and Bobby Brunt) aren't played in a pantomime/clowning style in contrast with the realism of the main young characters.

Sally Cookson talked about the importance of finding the theatrical style of the ensemble. If something is done with proper investigation – exploring why people behave as they do – the character is not just presented as a clown but has a real intention behind that outward presentation – e.g. Bobby Brunt – to hold onto power.

Justine Themen added that the mother's lines were in fact real stuff found through improvisation. Belgrade Young Company member Seyi Olomolaiye talked about developing this character through thinking about the people around her, her mum's friends and her friend's mums, things that feel close and familiar.

The links into scenes (transitions)

Sally Cookson suggested that it's important to see how transitions can enhance the story overall and not to leave work on them until the last minute.

Units

Sally Cookson took us through her process of breaking a script up into units, giving each unit a title as a method for scheduling rehearsals and having a grasp of the whole play. For this play in particular (in which the environment changes fluidly) this task can clarify and bring precision about where you are in each scene.

Cookson's titles for the first few sections of the play:

- The Prologue
- Metropolis 1
- School (Maru's cough is introduced, the crack appears for the first time)
- Metropolis 2 (Campaigners)
- Metropolis 3 (The Park)
- Metropolis 4

Staging transitions

Sally Cookson shared that at the beginning of any performance you have *eleven golden minutes* when an audience will typically be really with you and generous in their attention – that's your chance to get the audience on side using techniques such as changes of rhythm and working with music.

Prologue to Metropolis 1
The group then explored practically how to move from the Prologue to Metropolis 1. The performers began close to the earth – imagining themselves as clay and over a count of twenty slowly pulled themselves up from the surface of the earth. *Feel the sun on your body, the warmth of the air, the environment support you.*

The group physically explored the natural fluidity of the organic world contrasted with the angular, sharp, mechanical repetition of the urban world. Counting to twenty, Cookson directed all but one performer to stay in this slower organic energy from which one performer emerged (at count fourteen) into the new quick, angular urban energy, joined one by one by the others (beyond the twenty count) travelling around the room. One of the group remained in the slow organic prologue mode.

The group then explored the same movement dynamics rooted to the spot, standing closely together with heightened facial expressions and character intentions alongside unified breath, physical suspension (pause).

Metropolis 1 to School

The group then explored how to shift between the city into the school. Sally Cookson directed the transition working with a *harsh cut* – an immediate change in scene/ scenario and rhythm. The performers tried popping out from the city space into the classroom with a snap, with two of the ensemble jumping straight into the student characters (who have the opening lines of dialogue in the classroom scene) piercing through into a new atmosphere. The rest of the company took on the other background student characters to support.

This way of approaching the link/transition could set up a convention then used throughout the play.

Themes of the play

Free-writing exercise on identity

Sally Cookson ran an exercise in free writing as a model for a rehearsal exercise to use with your company to initiate discussions about identity.

The exercise ran for around seven minutes, accompanied by music. The exercise was taught to Cookson by choreographer Dan Canham, who uses this to trigger choreography.

The exercise was set up in the following way:

On format/technique

This exercise is about not censoring what you're going to write. To help you do that there's a phrase you can use as many times as you want: *I come from*. What you write on the page has to be a response to that: it can be literal, poetic, non-naturalistic. However you want to respond to that trigger phrase is up to you – there's no right way or wrong way to do this exercise.

On theme

You can write about the places in which you've lived and come from, the culture, family, city or country you've experienced. You can return to that phrase and write it as many times as you want: *I come from*.

The exercise is based on continuous writing – don't allow yourselves to stop and think, so you aren't editing yourselves; you have to keep writing.

On working in a safe way

Put down anything – don't censor yourself – but choose what you want to share (in terms of looking after yourself). Share things that are about you but aren't going to make you feel hugely vulnerable.

Sharing back the writing

The group then sat in a circle and a number of the group shared back their full 'free-writes'.

Sally Cookson noted that it feels a real privilege to be let into someone's story. It's a great way of giving everyone a voice in the room, for someone to tell their story. It's a relatively simple exercise but actually a deeply complex one to allow everyone to tell their story.

Justine Themen added that, in their original process, it was important that people only shared back what they wanted to.

Belgrade Young Company member Femi Themen commented that in the original process they did a similar exercise in which they wrote down ten key moments from their lives, exploring how they impacted on them and who they are now. There were a few tears. Fellow company member Ife Olomolaiye added that the group also used free writing too, with different stimuli.

Justine Themen and Claire Procter had also set independent research tasks throughout their process – both to do in the session and out of the session. They got the group to bring things back in and a shared library of books was created.

Sustainability in staging and design

Sally Cookson opened up the question of how you can make a play in a way which is sensitive to the central ideas that the play is trying to address, namely the climate crisis.

The group talked through ideas, including:

- using recycled materials for design
- using the constraints of working with only sound and lighting
- borrowing items from within the local theatre/school community

The group shared theatre companies or organisations making waves in this space:

Theatre Green Book Initiative: https://theatregreenbook.com

Julie's Bicycle (organisation): https://juliesbicycle.com

Staging Change: Sustainable Theatre Network: https://www.stagingchange.com

Pigfoot Theatre (theatre company): https://www.pigfoottheatre.com

Set Exchange initiative: https://www.set-exchange.com

Question and answer with the writers and young company members

Q: What was the process like for you, the Young Company Members? Can you tell us about the journey that you went on through the process of making a play from scratch?

Ife Olomolaiye: I remember how much fun we had with it, creating stuff and improvising. We came in with preconceived notions of climate change and how we aren't related to the movement or can't find our place in the movement. When we got into it, we saw it from a new lens, a new perspective.

Seyi Olomolaiye: It's so much trial and error. Trying things from new perspectives.

Femi Themen: Having prompts to start our exploration – such as 'what is crisis?' – was really helpful. Building a team in the cast was a really important part of it.

Sally Cookson: Give time to explore the backgrounds within the group, what they think of the subject matter, where they stand on it, who they are.

Femi Themen: For youth group members, climate change was not part of their priorities in relation to other factors in their lives – from youth violence which impacted very personally, to class and ethnicity.

Q: In the original script there are offers such as 'they create the bedroom' – was that done literally or slightly more stylised?
Sally Cookson: Create the world in an imaginary space that allows the audience to fill in the gaps. If you bring on the set literally, e.g. all of the bedroom furniture, that's an extraordinary amount of stuff.

Claire Procter: If some of the stage directions are ambiguous that's intentionally so, your company can make creative decisions that work for you. You interpret it as you choose.

Q: How did you encourage your actors to find their theatrical voice?
Femi and Justine Themen: We worked with a practitioner – a former youth theatre member, who had since trained at drama school, and who came in to do some peer-mentoring – who ran an exercise which was about holding/owning the space with each actor standing forward on stage with a particular phrase. Plus each rehearsal session began with a check-in and a warm-up.

Claire Procter: Our aim was to thread vocal work through the whole process.

Q: Can you change the characters' names (e.g. to a Scottish name)?
Justine Themen and Claire Procter: The framing of gender neutral names came from the group and was a deliberate and careful process to facilitate the characters being played by any gender. We would feel open to changing names but this has been taken into consideration.

Q: I'm fearful of not having enough time to lead a reflective and rich ensemble rehearsal process with limited rehearsal hours (in a school context). Any tips?
Sally Cookson: Use the time in between sessions – time for you and time for the cast to absorb what's happened. Be disciplined and quite strict with your expectations of them.

Justine Themen: A small injection of the exercises explored can have a big impact. For example, a reflection task to do within the week on impact of climate change in your week or a short five-minute exercise in rehearsals.

Ife Olomolaiye: Limiting the time on exercises to as little as three minutes works really well creatively.

Claire Procter and Ife Olomolaiye: In our production, the group was attuned to the themes of the play and carried it around in their day-to-day lives.

Suggested references

Seaspiracy, a Netflix documentary, which shows other white communities affected by the climate crisis

Anthropocene, a film about how humans are now controlling geological shifts rather than the earth itself: https://theanthropocene.org/film/ – specifically, this film shows a village which is being decimated by palladium mining to use for mobile phones.

From a workshop led by Sally Cookson, with Justine Themen and
Claire Procter, along with Ife Olomolaiye, Seyi Olomolaiye
and Femi Themen of the Belgrade Young Company
Notes by Nathan Crossan-Smith

The Ramayana Reset

by Ayeesha Menon

Ayeesha Menon's adaptation of *The Jungle Book*, re-imagined in the concrete jungle of present day Mumbai, is a finalist for Best Adaptation at the BBC Audio Drama Awards 2022; her adaptation of *A Tale of Two Cities* won Best Adaptation in 2019. Her *Midnight's Children* won the Outstanding Achievement Award in 2018. She has won Sony Awards for her adaptations of *Q&A (Slumdog Millionaire)* and *The Cairo Trilogy*.

Ayeesha Menon's original detective drama *Undercover Mumbai* has run for three series on BBC Radio 4. She also wrote *Into the Maze* for the Riot Girls series. Her adaptations for radio include *Girl with a Pearl Earring*, *Oliver: Lagos to London*, *A Tale of Two Cities: Aleppo and London*, *A Fine Balance*, *The Seventh Test*, *The Mumbai Chuzzlewits*, *Six Suspects* and *My Name Is Red*.

Ayeesha Menon's adaptation of Agatha Christie's *The Mirror Crack'd*, reimagined for an Indian audience and directed by Melly Still, was performed in Mumbai in 2020.

Hofesh Shechter OBE (Choreographer) composes atmospheric musical scores to complement the physicality of his choreography and movement. He is Artistic Director of the UK-based Hofesh Shechter Company, formed in 2008. The company are resident at Brighton Dome and Shechter is an Associate Artist of Sadler's Wells.

Work for Hofesh Shechter Company includes *Uprising* (2006), *In your rooms* (2007), *The Art of Not Looking Back* (2009), *Political Mother* (2010), *Political Mother: The Choreographer's Cut* (2011), *Sun* (2013), *barbarians* (2015), *Grand Finale* (2017), *Show* (2018) and *Political Mother Unplugged* (2020). *Grand Finale* was nominated for an Olivier Award for Best New Dance Production.

Shechter has also staged and choreographed works for leading international dance companies including the Alvin Ailey American Dance Theater, Batsheva Ensemble, Candoco Dance Company, Cedar Lake Contemporary Ballet, Nederlands Dans Theater 1, Paris Opera Ballet, Royal Ballet and Royal Ballet Flanders.

He has choreographed for theatre, television and opera, notably at the Metropolitan Opera (New York) for Nico Mulhy's *Two Boys*, the Royal Court on *Motortown* and *The Arsonists*, the National Theatre on *Saint Joan* and for the Channel four series *Skins*. As part of #HOFEST, a four-week festival celebrating Shechter's work across four London venues, he co-directed Gluck's *Orphée et Eurydice* with John Fulljames at the Royal Opera House. In 2016 he received a Tony Award nomination for his choreography on the Broadway revival of *Fiddler on the Roof*.

In 2018, Hofesh Shechter was awarded an honorary OBE for Services to Dance and the company's first dance film, *Hofesh Shechter's Clowns*, was broadcast by the BBC in September.

In 2020, Hofesh Shechter Company was named the winner of the Fedora – Van Cleef & Arpels Prize for Ballet for *Light: Bach Dances*, in collaboration with Royal Danish Opera and co-directed by Hofesh Shechter and John Fulljames. Hofesh Shechter's new creation *Double Murder* premiered in 2021.

Author's note

This script is not an instruction manual. Think of it as a starting point to a creative process. Take the words, move them around, discard them, use them as you wish. Feel free to create something from it that means something to you.

The play within the play, the *Ramayana*, is an ancient Sanskrit epic that was orally passed down from one generation to the next. It's a story that has travelled and mutated over time. It has been translated and adapted in different languages and for different cultures and has changed with every retelling.

This is the spirit with which I approached this play. My hope is that with each production it will change and grow from the creative input of everyone involved. I hope that, with each staging, new themes and new meaning will be found. At its heart, the *Ramayana* is about real life – decisions, duty, relationships, love and choices. It's about the here and now.

I wouldn't want the Indian-ness or the 'epicness' of the original to be a deterrent in the production of this play. When we workshopped it, we incorporated Maori Haka dancing in the war scenes, techno house music for the wedding celebrations and American folk music for the murmuration of starlings. Elaborate costumes and special effects are brilliant, but not at all essential. There are stage directions about characters growing in size, flying, walking through fire, getting swallowed by the earth – I hope these directions will not frighten you away but serve as a springboard for creative expression. Don't feel restricted by a sense of realism or logic. Make it whatever you want it to be. Make it whatever works for you.

Characters

Zara *(fourteen), cool, fun, popular*
Seth *(seventeen), sarcastic, always ready with a witty comeback*
Leah *(seventeen), clever, thoughtful and a feminist*
Parker *(seventeen), uptight, doesn't like change*
Nina *(fourteen), Zara's school friend, shy*

Ram *(twenty-three), a noble, brave prince*
Sita *(twenty-two), a beautiful, strong-minded princess*
Lakshman *(twenty-one), Ram's faithful brother*
Ravan *(twenty-five), king of demons, sports ten heads*
Hanuman *(twenty-one), the friendly, brave, flying monkey*
Jambhavan *(thirty-five), king of the bears*
King Janaka *(fifty), Sita's father*
King Dashratha *(fifty), Ram's father*
Kaikeyi *(forty), Ram's evil step-mother*
Vishvamitra *(seventy), sage, Ram and Lakshman's teacher.*
Agastya *(seventy), sage, giver of weapons and vital information*
Sugriva *(fifty), the monkey king*
Lord Shiva *(seventy), god of all gods*
Vishnu *(sixty), god who reincarnates himself as Ram*
Luv *(twelve), Ram and Sita's son*
Kush *(twelve), Ram and Sita's son*

A school bell rings. **Zara** *(fourteen), in school sports kit, sits on a bench tying her shoelaces.* **Nina** *(fourteen), wearing school uniform, approaches tentatively.*

Nina   Hi.

Zara *(under her breath)*   Hi.

Nina   Are you going to the lunch hall?

Zara   Ya.

Nina   Can I sit with you?

Zara *(hesitates)*   Thing is . . . I told the girls I'd sit with them.

Zara *gets up and walks a few steps.*

Nina   Why don't you tell them to stop, Zara?

Zara *stops.*

Nina   They are all over my Instagram page . . . making fun of me – abusing me.

Zara   They just like to joke around. It's a joke.

Nina   We've known each other since we were three. When I changed schools and came here I thought –

Zara   – They are my friends, Nina.

Nina   If they are your friends then tell them to stop.

Zara   I can't.

Nina   Yes you can.

Zara   No.

Nina *(stomps the ground)*   Who are you, Zara? Who have you become?

Nina *storms off, the earth begins to shake.* **Zara** *looks confused. It gets dark.*

Zara   What's going on?

Shaking stops, sun shines. A bird flies towards her. It dances. Then another bird joins in and then another.

DANCE. Soon they form a murmuration of starlings swirling across the stage, forming beautiful patterns.

Zara   A murmuration of starlings. Reminds me of my friends and I when we go dancing. All doing the same moves. Someone watching would find it impossible to know who's the leader. Sometimes even we don't know. That means something right? Being in tune with each other. Knowing that, no matter how ridiculous your moves are . . . someone will be right there, being ridiculous with you . . .

The birds fly away to reveal a book lying on the ground. She picks it up and examines it. **Seth** *(seventeen) and* **Leah** *(seventeen) enter squabbling.*

Seth   That's cause you live in another world –

Leah   Oh, I live in another world? Wait. Look.

Leah *gestures towards* **Zara**. **Seth** *approaches* **Zara**.

Seth   Oh great. You have it. I thought I'd lost my book.

Leah   Your book? How is it yours? (*To* **Zara**.) Can I have it please?

Zara *looks inside the book.*

Zara   There's no name in it.

Seth   That's because it belongs to everyone. But it's my story to tell.

Leah   Who said so? Look, Zara, woman to woman –

Zara   How do you know me?

Seth   Seriously? 'Woman to woman'? That's all you have in your armour, Leah.

Parker *(seventeen), wearing glasses, shirt buttoned up right to the top, enters from the other direction.*

Parker   Ah wonderful, Zara! You found my book.

Seth/Leah   Oh no.

Zara   You guys don't go to this school . . .

Parker   Could I have my book please?

Leah   Don't give it to Parker. He's the boring version.

Zara   Version of what?

Seth   The book.

Zara *looks at the book in her hand.*

Leah   His version has dominated for centuries. If you give it to him, this will remain a misogynistic story forever.

Parker   If you give it to her she'll impose her feminist slant and it won't be the truth. The truth, Zara. Isn't that what you want?

Seth   With either of them it will be boring as hell. I can speak to generations to come. I'm accessible.

Zara   I don't understand. What's in the book?

Seth   It's not easy to understand – the *Ramayana*.

Zara   The what?

Seth   *Ramayana*. The book. There are over 300 versions in existence.

Zara   So . . . what are you? An academic?

Seth   I'm one version of the story.

Zara   Look, I don't know what you want but . . .

Leah   You are freaking her out, Seth.

Parker   We can tell you what's in the book, then you decide who it should belong to.

Seth   I'll keep it . . . interesting.

Parker   I'll tell you the truth.

Leah   But you'll *get* my version, Zara.

Zara   How do you know me?

Leah   Everyone knows you, Zara. You're one of the girls.

Zara   Am I dreaming?

Parker   Many, many years ago in a land far away . . .

King Janaka *appears on stage and starts ploughing a field.*

Leah   King Janaka was ploughing his field when he found a baby girl in a furrow.

Zara   Is this some kind of joke?

Seth   Hang on! Why was a king ploughing a field?

King Janaka *stops thinking about it.*

Parker   It was a part of his yagna . . . an offering to the gods.

King Janaka *notices something in the ground ahead of him. He picks up a baby from a hole.*

Zara   What the . . .?!

Leah   So, he found this girl, adopted her and named her Sita, which means furrow.

Zara   This is crazy. I'm calling a teacher.

Seth   And what will you tell them? I met these guys in the school grounds who decided to tell me a story?

Zara   No, I'd tell them about some weirdo dressed like a clown trying to bury a baby in the sports field.

King Janaka   Excuse me?!

Leah   He's not a weirdo, he's King Janaka.

Parker   And he's not burying the baby. He's bringing her into the world.

Zara   I can't do this. I'm late for lunch.

She is about to leave. They crowd around her.

Seth   Wait, wait. It's just a story.

Leah *holds her hand.*

Leah   I know you have other things on your mind. Decisions to make about loyalty and friendship . . .

Zara   What –

Leah   – But don't you want to know what's in that book?

Zara   How do you . . .?

Seth   I always say, if you prefer to think of something as a dream then knock yourself out.

Leah   Now let's get back to the birth of Sita!

Parker   Wait a minute.

Leah   What?

Parker   Are we narrating the *Ramayana* starting with Sita?

Leah   You ruin everything, Parker!

Parker   Do you know how much trouble you can get in for starting the *Ramayana* with Sita? You'll be murdered by Hindu nationals.

Zara *(to self)*   I'm going mad.

Parker   It's called the *Ramayana*. You have to start with Lord Ram.

Lord Ram *walks proudly onto stage.*

Seth   But the thing is, in order to start with Ram, you kind of have to start with Ravan.

Ravan *appears, taps* **Ram** *on the back and gestures for him to leave.* **Ram** *leaves despondent while* **Ravan** *sits on a hill meditating.*

Parker   No, Seth, no one starts with the bad guy.

Seth   Bad guys are more appealing to the masses.

Leah   And why should appealing to the masses be our priority?

Seth   Because, Leah, we live in a world of social media influencers and advertisers convincing us to eat cereal because it's healthy. If you don't appeal to the masses –

Parker   Anyway, he was not just an ordinary bad guy. Ravan was a brilliant scholar. He meditated for a thousand years just for the gods to grant him one wish.

Lord Shiva *magically appears before* **Ravan**. **Zara** *lets out a yelp.*

Leah   It's OK. It's just Lord Shiva.

Zara   Of course it is.

Lord Shiva   *Ravan, you have proved your devotion to the gods. What is your wish?*

Ravan *I wish to be the most powerful creature in the universe.*

Lord Shiva *Bit much, don't you think?*

Ravan *I wish never to be defeated by any god or demon.*

Lord Shiva *I can do that. Your wish is granted.*

Leah And then all hell broke loose, right?

DANCE. **Ravan** *sprouts ten heads and cackles, dancing on stage with other demons.*

Seth Yes, quite literally . . . he grew ten heads, weapons in all arms. He invaded hell and unleashed a race of demons that terrorised, destroyed and plundered.

Zara *starts backing away.*

Leah Where are you going?

Zara It's lunch break. I have to . . . Anyway . . . This is not real.

Seth What's 'real', Zara? Really?

Leah Please. If you still want to leave in five minutes, we won't stop you. We know your friends are waiting for you. You'd rather be with them. Who wouldn't? They're a cool bunch.

Zara *is about to say something when* **Vishnu** *enters.*

Vishnu Excuse me. Can we please move on? Ravan is destroying the universe. We need damage control . . .

Parker Apologies, my Lord. So then . . . all the gods approached Lord Vishnu.

All the gods congregate around **Vishnu** *who is deep in contemplation.*

God 1 *This madness has to end, Lord Vishnu.*

Vishnu *Ravan made one mistake. He asked for immunity against gods and demons but not mortal men.*

God 2 *What mortal man can destroy Ravan?*

Vishnu *They can't. However, I will reincarnate myself as a human and rid the world of Ravan.*

Seth That's kind of cheating but hey . . . he's a god so . . .

Parker So Vishnu was reincarnated and born as Ram.

Lord Ram *enters with his bow and arrow and practises hitting a target.*

Parker He was born to the King of Ayodhya, King Dasharatha, who had three wives and four sons. Out of all the brothers it was Lakshman who was the closest to Ram.

Lakshman *runs out with his bow and arrow and hits the target too.*

Parker They were taught prayers and archery by one of the most venerated sages of India, Vishvamitra.

Enter **Vishvamitra** *who instructs the boys.*

Vishvamitra   *I am proud of you both. You will achieve much greatness. But remember to use your skills in the pursuit of the truth. With great power comes great responsibility.*

Seth   Really? We're quoting Spiderman?

Parker   That was Churchill.

Zara   It was Voltaire, actually.

Vishvamitra   Could we move on please? It is time to journey to Mithila.

Seth   Yes of course. And on they went to Mithila.

Ram *and* **Lakshman** *approach the palace with* **Vishvamitra**. *A celebratory atmosphere surrounds the palace.*

Vishvamitra   *This is the palace of King Janaka.*

Ram   *What are they celebrating?*

Vishvamitra   *Today is King Janaka's daughter's swayamvara. Today she will choose a husband.*

Zara   Sorry. I don't know where this is going but –

Leah   Does his name sound familiar to you, Zara?

Zara   What?

Leah   King Janaka?

Zara   Yeah, he's the clown who found the baby in the ground.

Leah   Yes. Good. You're listening.

Seth   Can you not talk to her like she's a child, Leah?

Leah   Can you not talk . . . period?

Parker   Look – Sita!

Sita *appears at the balcony of the palace.*

Parker   And then Ram saw Sita. And Sita saw Ram.

DANCE. They look at each other and then everything moves in slow motion. They are drawn together but the world seems to be pulling them apart. **Sita** *climbs down the balcony and moves towards him but is interrupted by her maids dressing her up.* **Ram** *moves towards her but is blocked by dancers.*

Sita   *The moment I saw him, it happened. Mother Earth dancing as if to tell me that this moment will change everything. The birds singing . . . and suddenly I understand their song. This is him. The one I have known in other lifetimes.*

He is within reach of her when she is whisked away to sit by her father.

Zara   Look, this is just not my scene. This means nothing to me.

Seth   Are you sure? Because we are tuned into your news feed. Advertising only what you need.

Zara   What?

Seth   All the messages you get on a daily basis are carefully selected according to your interests.

Zara   I don't need your messages.

Leah   It's no use, Seth. Coming from us, this means nothing. If her friends were telling her this story, she would listen. She always listens to them.

Zara   I don't . . . I don't always listen to them.

Leah   Don't you? You are going to do what they asked you to do, right?

Zara   I . . . I don't know.

Leah   I can hardly blame you. They're the popular kids. Who wouldn't want to be a part of that?

Zara   I don't do everything they tell me to.

Leah   But this Instagram thing . . . this new girl . . . Nina?

Zara   I don't want to talk about it.

Seth   Don't talk. Just listen.

Inside the palace, in the presence of **King Janaka** *and* **Sita**, *numerous strong men line up to lift a heavy bow but none succeed.*

Vishvamitra   *That is the bow of Shiva. King Janaka will offer his daughter's hand in marriage to whoever is able to lift it.*

Ram *walks forward and touches the bow.*

Seth   And yes, of course, you guessed it . . .

Ram *lifts it high above his head but as he strings it, it breaks in his hands. The palace erupts into celebration.*

Janaka   *Who are you, young man, who has done what no mortal has done before?*

Leah   Hang on. No mortal?

Actors stop and look towards them.

Leah   Are we forgetting why he set up this test in the first place?

Seth   Here we go.

Leah   When Sita was a little girl, a ball she was playing with bounced into the box that held the bow of Shiva and she lifted it with one hand.

Parker   Not in my version.

Leah   Oh come on, Parker.

Parker   My version is the purest.

Seth   Also . . . boooorrrring!

Leah   A sage saw this and said to the king, you must marry her to a man who can lift that bow and prove he is as strong and special as she is. So could we rephrase that, please?

Janaka   Yes of course . . .

(Back to **Ram***.) Who are you, young man, who has done what my extraordinary daughter did as a child but no mortal has done since?*

Leah   Much better.

Ram   *I am Ram. Prince of Ayodhya.*

Janaka   *I give you the hand of my daughter in marriage.*

DANCE. **Sita** *garlands* **Ram**. **Ram** *garlands* **Sita**. *A priest blesses them, puts her hand in his and they walk around a fire seven times. Celebrations ensue. Everyone dances in a euphoric manner.*

Leah   And they lived happily ever after.

Seth   Excuse me?

Leah   Can't we end when everyone is happy?

Seth   That's the dumbest thing I've ever heard.

Parker   And it's not the truth. What do you want Zara . . . the truth or the fantasy?

Zara   The truth . . . I guess.

Parker   Fine, in that case . . . They came back to Ayodhya and lived happily for a while until Ram's manipulative stepmother Kaikeyi decided to hatch a plot against Ram.

Kaikeyi *appears looking evil.*

Leah   Excuse me, but I take objection to this whole manipulative stepmother thing. Kaikeyi had her own issues. She grew up without a mother and her mind was poisoned by her maid. It's easy, isn't it, Zara? To listen to what people say, to believe it and think those are your thoughts, your feelings . . .

Zara   I . . . guess so.

The chorus creates **King Dashratha**'s *court. We see him playing with his sons.* **Kaikeyi** *watches them. He seems to love* **Ram** *more than the others.*

Seth   Fine, Ram's stepmother, who would have been quite nice if she had had a good psychotherapist, wasn't too keen on her husband's love for her stepson.

Parker   Basically she wanted *her* son to be crowned king.

The boys leave. **Kaikeyi** *approaches* **Dashratha**.

Kaikeyi   *My king, when I saved your life on the battlefield, you promised me two wishes. I would like to cash in on them now.*

Dashratha   *Ask anything of me, my queen.*

Kaikeyi   *I wish for my son Bharata to be crowned king.*

Dashratha   *What about Ram? He is the oldest.*

Kaikeyi   *I was getting to that. My second wish is that Ram be exiled to the Dandaka forest for fourteen years.*

Dashratha   *I can't do that. There are dangers there. Demons, monsters . . . he won't return alive.*

Kaikeyi   *You made me a promise.*

Dashratha   *Please, Kaikeyi. Don't take him away from me.*

Kaikeyi   *Does your word mean nothing?*

King Dashratha *holds* **Ram** *close and speaks into his ear. He is sobbing.* **Lakshman** *and* **Sita** *are present.*

Parker   So with a heavy heart, King Dashratha said goodbye to his favourite son and exiled him to the jungle.

Ram   *You gave my stepmother your word. And I will honour it.*

Lakshman   *I refuse to be separated from Ram. I will go with my brother.*

Ram   *Sita, you must stay here and wait for me.*

Sita   *No. My place is with you.*

Ram   *I can't . . . I won't allow you to come.*

Sita   *Then I must disobey you.*

Seth   And eventually Ram realised he was not going to win an argument with his wife and off they went into the jungle.

Ram *leads* **Lakshman** *and* **Sita** *through the jungle.*

Parker   And then they set up home at various ashrams. Defending the inhabitants from the resident demons. And winning favour with some pretty important sages.

Leah   Like Agastya.

Agastya *pops up and gives* **Ram** *and* **Lakshman** *weapons.*

Parker   Like Agastya. Who gifted Ram with the miraculous bow of Vishnu.

Seth   Why are we wasting time with Agastya? He's not important.

Agastya   I am very important. When I come back later, you will realise I'm by far the most important.

Leah   Thank you for coming, kind sage.

Agastya (*pause*)   I shall leave now.

Agastya *leaves.* **Ram** *is cutting wood.* **Soorpanaka** *emerges from the trees watching him.*

Parker   And then . . . Enter Soorpanaka. The shape-shifting demon.

Seth   Who was also . . .

Leah   Ravan's sister!

Zara   Oh. Trouble.

Leah   She falls in love with Ram and transforms herself into a beautiful woman to lure him to her.

DANCE. She transforms into a beautiful woman and dances before **Ram**.

Seth   And Ram is not tempted? Even in the slightest? I mean, look at her.

Parker   No. He's a god among men.

Seth   But not actually a god.

Parker   A godly man.

Seth   A manly god.

Sooparnaka   *Come to me, you beautiful man.*

Ram   *I'm sorry, dear lady. I'm devoted to my wife. But I have a brother who is unmarried. If you wish I could –*

Soorpanaka   *– No, it's you I want.*

Sita *enters carrying a pot and sees them just as* **Sooparnaka** *drapes a leg around* **Ram**.

Sita   *Ram . . . would you like to introduce me to your new friend?*

Ram *pushes* **Soorpanaka**'*s leg away.*

Soorpanaka   *I can introduce myself.*

Soorpanaka *transforms back into a demon and explodes in a demonic rage.* **Sita** *throws her pot on the ground and stares at* **Soorpanaka** *who is advancing towards her.* **Ram** *intervenes.*

Ram   *Stop. If you leave us alone now I will spare you. But if not . . .*

Soorpanaka *laughs.*

Soorpanaka   *If not . . . What will you do?*

Suddenly **Lakshman** *enters with a sword and rushes towards her.*

Ram   *Lakshman, no!*

Sooparnaka *lunges forward.* **Lakshman** *cuts off her nose with his sword. Blood flies across the stage.* **Soorpanaka** *cries in agony.*

Soorpanaka   *Curses on you. On your marriage, on your future, on the life you dreamed of. You will have no happiness from this day forth.*

Lakshman   *Go away. Leave us alone.*

Soorpanaka   *I will tell my brother. He will destroy you.*

Soorpanaka *runs away.*

Parker   But it was fate, right. All this had to happen. If it hadn't, Ram would not be able to fulfill his destiny . . . what he was put on earth to do.

Zara   To destroy Ravan?

Seth   Bingo! But this incident with Sooparnaka had instilled fear in Sita's heart.

Lakshman *is cutting wood.* **Sita** *emerges from the hut.*

Sita   *Lakshman, where's Ram?*

Lakshman   *Hunting in the woods.*

Sita   *Why aren't you with him?*

Lakshman   *He asked me not to leave your side.*

Sita   *I could swear I heard him calling my name.*

Lakshman   *I didn't hear anything.*

Sita   *There's something wrong. I can feel it.*

Lakshman   *Sita –*

Sita   *He's in danger. I know it. Please, go to him.*

Lakshman   *He gave me his orders.*

Sita   *If you won't, I'll go myself!*

Seth   Bit of a rock and a hard place, eh Lakshman?

Lakshman   You said it. (*To* **Sita**.) *OK, so this is what I'll do.*

Lakshman *draws a circle with his sword in the ground around* **Sita** *and their hut.*

Parker   He draws the magical Lakshman Rekha of protection around the hermitage. If anyone besides Sita crosses this line, they will burst into flames.

Lakshman   *Do not, under any circumstances cross this line. It will protect you against harm.*

Sita   *Go now. Go to my husband.*

Lakshman *exits.*

Seth   And as soon as he's gone . . .

Ravan *dressed as a minstrel enters playing a drum and singing a song.*

Zara   Oh, Ravan!

Parker   Disguised as a humble minstrel.

Zara   Excuse me, but the ten heads are a bit of a giveaway.

Ravan *removes his extra heads and continues playing.*

Zara   Ya, that's better.

Sita   *What is that beautiful music?*

Ravan *approaches* **Sita** *at her hut.*

Ravan   *Kind lady, do you have some food for a hungry musician?*

Sita   *I'm sorry. I can't step over this line while they are gone. It's for my protection.*

Ravan   *Will you deny a poor man food?*

Zara   Don't do it, Sita!

Sita *picks up some food. She hands it over to* **Ravan**.

Ravan   *My eyes are weak. Come closer.*

Sita *steps out and* **Ravan** *grabs her.*

Sita   *No, no! Let me go!*

Ravan *transforms back to himself as a chariot approaches.*

Sita   *Ram! Ram!*

Ravan *pulls her into his chariot and it flies into the sky.* **Sita**'*s screams reverberate through the sky.*

Parker   When Ram and Lakshman return they realise she is gone.

Ram *and* **Lakshman** *run to the hut, they look for her.*

Seth   And then they see the monkeys and bears.

DANCE. Enter bears and monkeys dancing. **Ram** *and* **Lakshman** *approach the monkey king* **Sugriva** *and tell him what has happened.* **Sugriva** *calls for their attention.*

Sugriva   *My brothers, friends, this is Ram. His wife Sita has been abducted. I've promised that we will help him find her. We'll send our forces in all four directions and we will not rest till she is found.*

The monkeys and bears cheer. The monkey **Hanuman** *steps forward.*

Hanuman   *I will go south with Jambavan.*

Zara   Who's Jambavan?

Jambavan *steps forward.*

Jambavan   Hello, hi, that's me. King of the Bears.

Zara   Hi. Sorry. Carry on.

Hanuman   Thank you. (*Clears his throat.*) *Don't worry, brother. We will find her.*

Ram   *What's your name?*

Hanuman   *Hanuman.*

Ram   *Hanuman . . . If you see her, tell her I'm coming.*

Hanuman *kneels before* **Ram**.

Hanuman   *As you wish, my Lord.*

Zara   Wait . . . an army of monkeys and bears? Really?

Seth   It's a metaphor.

Zara   For what? They could have been an army of tigers and elephants.

Seth   Yes but a half-monkey, half-human race might have existed at the time of the Ramayan. The last existing of the Homo Erectus species.

Parker   Are you saying the modern human is superior to Lord Hanuman? It's not, Seth. We've de-evolved! Modern humans have destroyed the earth!

Leah   OK, enough with the theology.

Hanuman   Shall I go south then?

Parker   Yes of course, my Lord. Who are we to stop you?

Hanuman *and* **Jambavan** *lead an army to the sea. They stop at the water's edge.*

Hanuman   *Look, Jambavan, an island. We must investigate.*

Seth   But then they are, like, wait a minute, none of us can swim or fly or anything so what do we do now?

Parker   And then the mighty Jambavan revealed a secret to Hanuman . . .

Jambavan   *Hanuman, you possess extraordinary powers.*

Hanuman   *Who? Me?*

Jambhavan   *When you were young you used them to play pranks on sages so you were cursed. They made you forget your powers. You are the son of the Wind God.*

A great wind starts to blow.

Parker   And suddenly his magical powers came flooding back to him and the most extraordinary thing started to happen.

Hanuman *starts to grow tall like a giant.*

Zara   Seriously, he waited this long to tell him?

Parker   Hanuman hadn't needed to use his powers till now.

Hanuman *lifts his hand to shield his eyes.*

Hanuman   *I see Lanka. Ravan's palace.*

Hanuman *squats and flies into the air. He lands on a tree in Lanka and returns to normal size. He sees* **Sita** *in a clearing being guarded by demonesses.*

Leah   And there she was. In a forest clearing guarded by demonesses. Sita.

Enter **Ravan**.

Ravan   *Why do you grieve for Ram? I am your husband now.*

Sita   *My heart will always belong to Ram.*

Ravan   *There is an ocean between you and him now.*

Sita   *Even if there was an ocean of stars between us, Ram would still come find me.*

Ravan   *I can do whatever I want to you, but I haven't. Because I love you! Look at my face . . . my faces. Can't you see there is love in my heart?*

Sita   *I cannot return your love.*

Ravan   *I will wait for you.*

Ravan *exits throwing some scraps of meat to the demonesses.* **Hanuman** *sneaks up to her.*

Hanuman   *Sita, don't be scared. Ram is coming.*

Ravan *turns around and sees* **Hanuman**.

Ravan   *Guards! Get me the head of that monkey.*

DANCE. The guards and the demonesses surround **Hanuman**. *He dodges them while they try to attack him with spears.*

Zara   This would be a good time to grow in size, wouldn't it?

Parker   Hanuman was free from ego. He will only use his powers when he is in dire need.

The demons have captured **Hanuman**.

Zara   It's looking pretty dire to me now.

Ravan   Set his tail on fire!

They set fire to his tail. He chants to himself in prayer.

Hanuman   *Ram, Ram, Ram, Ram . . . (cont'd).*

Zara   I can't watch this.

Parker   It's alright. He feels no pain. Look his tail is growing.

His tail grows and he flies into the sky setting the city on fire.

Parker   And with his burning tail he set the city of Lanka on fire.

Zara   Really? With Sita in it?

Leah   He was careful not to cause a flame anywhere near Sita.

Seth   Yup, he was a gentleman among monkeys!

Parker   And he returned to Ram to deliver the good news.

Hanuman *returns to* **Ram** *and the troops.*

Ram   *Let us march forth to Lanka!*

Ram *leads the others to the ocean's tip.*

Seth   Then it was déjà vu! They reach the sea and they are, like, wait a minute, we can't swim or fly so what do we do now?

Jambavan   *We must build a bridge to Lanka!*

The monkeys and bears start gathering stones and building a bridge.

Leah   Days and days turned into weeks.

Seth   Actually, Leah, it took five days.

Leah   Five long days they toiled day and night to build the Great Bridge of Ram.

Ram, Lakshman, Hanuman *and their armies march into Lanka.*

Parker   And when the bridge was built they marched into Lanka until they stood face to face with the army of demons.

Seth   And then there was war.

DANCE. **Ram**'s *army clashes swords with the demons. They fight.*

Leah   And Sita, who could hear the sounds of clanking swords and deathly screams wept for the lives that were lost.

Seth   That's not a part of any of the versions of the *Ramayana*.

Leah   It's a part of mine.

Sita   *I had visions of timeless evil. Of battles older than the earth which have been fought before in countless worlds. And after the war of Lanka, it will be fought over and over again. And lives will be lost and hearts will mourn. It will be the same. From the beginning till the end of time.*

Parker   Ram's army was more powerful than the demons.

Seth   And then Ravan was, like, wait a minute, this is not going well. It's time to take matters into my own hands.

The armies part while **Ravan** *gets into his chariot. A hush falls as* **Ram** *and* **Ravan** *move towards each other.* **Ram** *salutes* **Ravan**, *joining his palms and bowing to the King.* **Ravan** *bows too.*

Zara   Bit unfair that Ravan has a nice chariot and Ram has nothing.

Hanuman   Oh yes.

Hanuman *approaches* **Ram**.

Hanuman   *Lord Ram, sit on my shoulders. Let me be your chariot.*

Ram *does so. A horn is blown.* **Ravan** *attacks* **Ram** *with a battery of weapons.* **Ram***'s arrows shoot them all down.*

Parker   And then Ravan was only left with one weapon. The trident that could burn up the universe!

Seth   And Ram picked up his brahmastra, which had the power to end all creation.

Two weapons collide. The earth shakes.

Parker   Both mighty weapons cancel each other out.

Leah   And then Ram heard a voice in his head.

Agastya *pops up next to* **Ram**.

Agastya   *Good Lord Ram . . .*

Zara   Who's he?

Agastya   I told you I was important.

Zara   There have been quite a few characters.

Agastya   Remember, I gave Ram and Lakshman some cool weapons when they were banished to the forest?

Zara   Not really.

Agastya   But I need to be here now, OK? I mean I'm not really here. Ram can hear my voice in his head.

Zara   I guess that's acceptable.

Leah   And then Ram heard the voice of Agastya in his head.

Agastya   *Good Lord Ram. Ravan's weakness lies in his belly. Aim at it and you will destroy him.*

Seth   Handy he came along, isn't it?

Parker   Wait, Leah. This whole aim for the belly thing is not in Valmiki's version of the Ramayan.

Leah   I like it. It's about intuition winning the war against ego.

Seth   That's cheesy.

Leah   It's deep.

Seth   Deeply cheesy.

Leah *shoots* **Seth** *a murderous look.*

Ram *shoots at* **Ravan***'s belly. As the arrow hits him,* **Ravan***'s scream shakes the universe.*

Parker   And in the moments before he died, Ravan could see that Ram was an avatar of Lord Vishnu.

Ravan   *Oh. God.*

Ravan *falls.* **Ram***'s army erupts in cheers.* **Sita** *arrives.*

Sita   *I knew you would come.*

Ram   *You are free, Sita. You may go wherever you want now.*

He turns his back on her.

Zara/Sita   Excuse me?

Ram   Well, she's been in another man's house. I don't know whether he has touched her.

Zara   Then ask her.

Parker (*nervous laughter*)   Zara, calm down.

Zara   I will not calm down. Tell him to ask her.

Seth   Well . . . we can't really –

Zara   Leah, say something.

Leah   I have tried, Zara. I've tried to stop this but it will happen. Over and over again.

Ram *turns away.*

Sita   *I AM pure, Lord Ram.*

Ram   *But how can I believe you?*

Zara   Because she's telling you.

Sita   *Did you rescue me because your honour was at stake or because you loved me?*

Ram   *I had a duty to rescue you.*

Sita   *Is that all it was?*

Ram   *I'm sorry. I cannot accept you as my queen any more.*

Zara   Don't be ridiculous. You are a god! You can't just turn your back on your wife.

Sita   *Lakshman, build me a pyre.*

Zara   What?

Lakshman   *Sita . . . I can't . . .*

Sita   *Do as I say.*

Zara   What is she doing . . .?

Lakshman *builds her a pyre and sets it alight.*

Sita   *I am pure. I am innocent. I submit myself to Agni, the God of fire, and I ask that the flames do not harm me if I am pure.*

Lakshman *tries to stop her but he is no match for her strength. She steps into the pyre and is engulfed by flames. Everyone reacts.* **Zara** *storms off, throwing the book at* **Parker**. **Leah** *goes after her and brings her back to see* **Sita** *emerging from the pyre unharmed.*

Leah   She is pure and she walks out of the fire unscathed.

Ram *collapses in tears.*

Zara   I'm done with this story. She had to prove her fidelity?

Seth   The rules were different in those days.

Parker   And he is very sorry. I mean . . . look at him.

Ram   *I'm sorry, Sita.*

Zara   Don't forgive him.

Sita   *I forgive you, my Lord.*

Ram   *Come home with me. It is time to return to Ayodhya and for you to take your place by my side as queen.*

They hug.

DANCE. **Ram** *and* **Sita** *return to Ayodhya. Fanfare and celebrations. Crackers bursting in the sky.* **Ram** *is crowned king.*

Leah   And they lived happily ever after.

Seth   Well . . .

Leah   Let's end here, Seth. Many versions of the *Ramayana* end here.

Seth   OK.

Zara   What? You two are agreeing with each other?

Parker   'Ramayana' translates to Ram's journey. So it wouldn't hurt to end when they return to Ayodhya.

Zara   But it's not the end . . .?

All are silent.

Zara   Why aren't you saying anything?

Leah   It's the end.

Parker   Technically it's the end of the journey so . . . it's the end.

Leah   And it's hopeful. Sort of.

Zara   You're keeping something from me.

Parker   Anyway, thanks for the book.

Leah (*pulling it from him*)   No! it's mine.

Seth   I'm the voice of the future. It belongs to me –

Zara (*pulls the book out of* **Leah**'s *hands*)   Tell me what happens next.

Leah   Why do you need to know?

Zara   Because how do you know how to feel about something unless you know everything. Those tailored ads you were talking about . . . I don't want them. I don't want bits of information. I need everything. Only then can I decide how I feel . . . OK?

They all look at each other.

Seth   OK, fine. So they return to their kingdom and everything is good for a little while. And then Sita discovers she is pregnant.

Zara   And . . .?

Seth   And Ram is totally onboard with it. But the people of his kingdom begin gossiping.

Whispers around the kingdom. **Ram** *in the centre as they talk to each other.*

Man 1   *Did you hear Queen Sita is pregnant?*

Woman 1   *So soon after her return from Ravan's palace?*

Man 2   *Will the King ignore the fact that her child might not be his?*

Woman 2   *Will our kingdom be inherited by the sons of Ravan?*

Ram *approaches* **Sita**.

Zara   Don't listen to them!

Leah   So many voices, Zara. How can you block them out? You know what it's like.

Ram   *Sita, I must ask you one more time to walk through fire but this time we'll do it for the whole kingdom to see. Then there will be no doubt in their minds that you are carrying my child.*

Zara   You're kidding me, right?

Sita (*pause*)   *I have always remained true to our love. Do you believe that?*

Ram   *I do.*

Sita   *That's all that matters to me. I'm not concerned with what people think.*

Ram   *I need my people to trust me.*

Zara   Really?

Ram   Yes. I need them to trust me, believe in me. I need them to 'like' me!

Zara   What about Sita? You love her.

Ram   You won't understand. You can't comprehend the duties of a king.

Zara   Oh please.

Ram   Isn't it important, Zara? What people think? We're not that different you know . . . you and I.

Zara   I stand up for the people I love.

Ram   Really? Are you going to like that post on Instagram? The one where your gang have bullied the new girl? Your oldest friend, Nina.

Zara   Don't bring her into this.

Ram   You have to 'like' it, don't you? If you don't stand by them then . . . who are you? What becomes of your reputation?

Silence.

Zara   It's not the same thing.

Ram   Isn't it?

Zara   You can change this. (*To herself.*) We can change this.

Sita   *I'm sorry, my Lord. With all due respect . . . I don't need to make a performance out of my faithfulness.*

Sita *walks away.* **Ram** *approaches* **Lakshman**.

Parker   And so he was left with no choice

Ram   *Lakshman, take Sita to an ashram in the forest. She cannot be my queen if the people of my kingdom do not trust her.*

Lakshman *and* **Sita** *walk through the forest.* **Ram** *addresses* **Zara** *who looks angry.*

Ram   I have a duty to listen to my people.

Zara   What about love?

Ram   I'm doing this for her too.

Parker   He is a king and a god. We must trust that he has his reasons.

Sita   *It's so nice to go away for a while. Away from all the rumours and suspicions. Lakshman . . . why are you crying?*

Lakshman   *Sita, Ram has asked me to leave you here.*

He cries. She comforts him.

Zara   So, what? She's going to give birth in a forest all by herself?

Lakshman *leaves and the sage* **Valmiki** *appears.*

Parker   No, she is looked after by the kindly sage Valmiki. Also the author of the first *Ramayana*.

Seth   And she has her twin sons there. Luv and Kush.

Two boys **Luv** *and* **Kush** *appear.*

Parker   Valmiki educated the boys. He even told them the story of Ram and the kingdom of Ayodhya.

Seth   And then one day, the boys decide to capture one of the king's horses.

A horse gallops into the forest where **Luv** *and* **Kush** *stop it.* **Ram** *and guards come out from the woods.*

Ram   Young men, by capturing that horse you challenge me. The King.

Luv *and* **Kush** *draw their swords and fight* **Ram** *and guards.*

Zara   Oh no, they didn't.

Leah   Yes they did.

Boys defeat **Ram**.

Seth   And, the great Lord Ram is defeated by them. And he's like . . .

Ram   *Who are you both?*

Sita *enters.*

Sita   *Luv, Kush, let them go.*

Parker   And then Ram saw Sita. And Sita saw Ram.

They look at each other and everyone freezes.

Sita   The moment I saw him, I knew. This will change everything. It was him. The one I have known in other lifetimes. But this time the birds weren't singing.

Ram   *Sita . . . ?*

Sita   *They didn't mean any harm.*

Ram   *The boys . . . are they . . . ?*

Ram *looks at them and realises.*

Ram   *My sons.*

Ram *rushes to* **Sita** *and falls at her feet.*

Ram   *Sita, forgive me. I see these boys and I know they are mine. Come back to the palace and be my queen.*

Suddenly thunder rumbles and lightning strikes the earth.

Parker   Then all of a sudden, the earth begins to crack.

Leah   When the king is without mercy, the earth loses its essence.

Parker   Just as the earth cracks when it's dry . . .

Leah   Without moisture, without love.

Sita *is being swallowed up by the earth.* **Hanuman** *appears on the periphery. No one notices him.*

Sita   *My Lord, you have acknowledged your sons. That's all I wanted. From the earth I was born and to earth I shall return.*

Ram   *No, Sita!*

Sita   *Take care of them.*

Zara   Why is she doing this?

Parker   Ram had accepted his sons and she could not go back to the palace. There was no other way.

Luv   *Ma, don't go. Please.*

Kush   *Don't leave us.*

Sita   *I'll always be here. In the earth, in the trees. I'll be in the air, the flowers, in your laughter and tears . . . I will be with you always.*

Luv   *That's not enough.*

Sita   *Be strong, my children. This is my destiny.*

Sita *is gone. Everyone mourns.* **Ram** *comforts the boys.*

Leah   But she lived again. She has lived so many times since.

Parker   So many Sitas everywhere.

Zara (*to* **Ram**)   You didn't stand up for her.

Ram   It was a different time. I couldn't then. But you – you can stand up for her.

Zara   But you are a god and a king and *you* couldn't . . . I'm a nobody. I'm just one small person in this vast universe.

Hanuman *speaks up.*

Hanuman   Now would be a good time to grow in size, right?

Everyone turns to look at him.

Zara   What?

Hanuman   That's what you said to me. Now would be the time, Zara. To grow in size.

Zara   I don't have . . . powers.

Hanuman   That's what I thought too.

Leah   All it takes is one person.

Parker   Then others will follow.

Seth   Every time we don't stand up . . .

Leah   For our peers, lovers, families, countries . . .

Parker   Every time we shy away from telling our truth.

Leah   We condemn another Sita. Will you stand up for Sita?

Parker   Keep the book. You tell the story, Zara . . . tell it your way.

The earth shakes. Darkness sets in. Blackout.

Zara   What's going on?

When the lights come back on, **Zara** *is alone on the bench. She looks around.*

Zara   Leah, Parker, Seth . . .? Was I . . . dreaming?

She gets up to look for them but only finds the book. A starling flies across the stage. DANCE. Other starlings join in.

Zara   I saw the starlings again. I thought of the children of war who were afraid to look to the sky in case they saw a bomb falling down on them. I thought of the women who were swallowed up by the world and don't have a voice. I have a voice. I can speak for them. I can stand for the truth.

Zara *gradually gets up and starts to dance – a different dance from the starlings. The starlings watch her and gradually join her in her dance.*

Zara   I will not follow when I can lead. I can grow in size, I can fly, I can walk through fire, I can fight my demons and I can dance to my own tune. That is my superpower. That is my magic.

A school bell rings and the starlings fly away. **Nina**, *wearing school uniform, approaches tentatively (same as beginning).*

Zara   Nina. Hi.

Nina   Hi.

Zara   Are you going to the lunch hall?

Nina   Ya.

Zara   Can I sit with you?

Nina   You . . . you sure?

Zara   I'm sure. I've never been more sure of anything else.

Zara *approaches and puts her arm through* **Nina***'s.* **Nina** *smiles. The girls walk off stage together.*

The End.

The Ramayana Reset

BY AYEESHA MENON, WITH CHOREOGRAPHY BY HOFESH SHECHTER

Notes on rehearsal and staging, drawn from a workshop with the writer and choreographer, held at the National Theatre, October 2021

How the writer came to write the play

The inspiration for *The Ramayana Reset* came through a conversation between Ola Animashawun (National Theatre Associate and Connections Dramaturg) and Ayeesha Menon. They spoke about how people were aware of Greek tragedies, of epic pieces from different cultures, but were less familiar with those from Asia.

They spoke about the *Ramayana* and its significance. Growing up in India, Menon's cultural reference points for the story were of grand epic productions, performed every year around Diwali and of a cheesy TV version filmed in the 80s. It had always been so formal and mechanical because it was a part of a ritual, and she'd always wished there was a version that she could relate to better. Ayeesha Menon began to think about how the themes and messages could relate to now, in a different country, and how it could be made accessible. She discovered that there were different takes on the *Ramayana*, including one from Sita's point of view, and another that focuses on Ravan's journey; versions that she had not known about when she was younger.

Ayeesha Menon started to think about the overload of information young people faced today and the pressure they have to know who they are. She noted that the mythological story of the *Ramayana* can't be changed but that we can have our own view and interpretation of it. Ayeesha Menon hopes this play sparks young people to think about where they are getting their information from, to have their own opinions and to stand up for what they believe in. They Menon hero of their own stories and an agent for change.

Themes

Ayeesha Menon noted the main themes of the original *Ramayana* are: duty, honour and loyalty. In the present day these words have very different meanings. Young people are given so much information from online, from family members, teachers and friends; they are having to decide what they are going to be loyal to, what makes them an honourable person and what their duty is. It's a confusing world to be living in, especially if you are young, so it's about how you negotiate all this information and work out how to make your own decisions from it.

Approaching the play

This play is an offering, it's an invitation to learn, explore and create. It's important that people feel ownership over the story no matter what their culture. Ayeesha Menon doesn't want anyone to be afraid of taking on this piece. She doesn't see it as an 'Asian play' and therefore would discourage people from putting on accents or wearing specific clothing. Instead it's about exerting an energy and passion and working together as a company.

The same is to be said when approaching the movement sections in this piece. Choreographer Hofesh Shechter reiterated the importance of being open. The best way to create movement is to dive in head first. You can only learn if something works by doing it. Not everything will work, but it's about giving yourself the time and space to experiment and play. The skills you have as a director will only help you when approaching movement. Instead of seeing it as a scary concept, think of it as a creative extension of your role.

Movement and choreography

Language and movement

So much of dance and choreography is about the words that you use. Hofesh Shechter suggested that 'you get what you ask for as long as you know what you want'. When working with his own company he doesn't use dance terms such as *pas de bourree* or *pirouette* but instead uses directives that will evoke an energy. It's important to understand what each section's energy looks like; for example, with the Starlings, this dance could be a number of things: it could be hectic, messy, light or floaty. Once you know what feeling you want to evoke, name it.

Exercise: Starting points

The following exercise could be used as a starting point, to help you consider the language you use to get a company moving.

Hofesh Shechter invited the group to stand. They all faced the same direction and followed a list of simple actions:

Place your arms out in front of you.

Imagine the room is full of water and your arms are lifting up, floating up, they are weightless. Now push the water back down, your arms move down.

Feel the water underneath your armpits as you repeat this movement.

Water rises, arms come up, water falls, arms come back down.

Imagine the water pushes up, reaches and covers your head. Allow the feeling of the water to move every part of you as your arms continue to rise and fall. Knees bend and straighten, waist shifts.

You are moving in water.

Now let that go.

Push your hands forward, away from your body and then bring them back in.

Push forward a big cloud; it is thick and soft at the same time.

As your arms move back imagine that they are being pulled by elastic strings.

Pushing clouds out, elastic strings pull your arms back in.

The group were then invited to join movements together, to create a small sequence:

Push the cloud forward, let your leg step and push the cloud to the left.

Imagine there is a breeze from the sea as it goes to the left – how does that affect your arms? It is light and airy.

Repeat this a few times.

Now try the same sequence with a different energy.

Imagine you are pushing someone away.

(Try this in time together. 1, 2, 3 PUSH!)

Imagine you are holding a ball and throw it away.

Throw the ball to the front and the side.

What does the energy of throwing look and feel like?

Next the group was invited to move randomly around the room with different energies.

- Float around the room.
- Now imagine water trickling on your body.
- Move in a messy way.
- Move with a very focused energy, with a clear sense of direction.
- Now try moving in small jumps.
- Freeze.
- Move on every click. Let your body do whatever it wants.
- Now let your palms lead the movement. It could be smooth, it could be quick and shaky. Allow your body to follow wherever the palms go.

Exercise: Creating energies

Hofesh Shechter then set the group a task:

Take two of the dance sections from *The Ramayana Reset* and write down a list of words that represent the energy of these moments. Once you have them, narrow it down to three words, so you have a clear idea of what you want these sections to be.

These words were then tested on dancer Kim Kohlmann.

The group saw how she responded, what she chose to do.

More performers were invited to get involved so they could see how an ensemble reacted to the director's words.

(You could take this task and try it with different numbers of people.)

Examples of words the directors used:

- Frantic, float, whoosh
- Magnets, oppose, attract, resist

Shechter noted that the words do not have to literally describe the story but can be quite abstract. It can be a chemistry or an energy that supports the scene. He talked about how making dance is like archaeology: 'you start with something you know, then you start experimenting and you discover more and more. It might be abstract (you find a little bone) but then it grows in different directions.'

The group had another go.

- Hypnotised, fluid, enchanted
- Unaware, urgent, magnetic
- Rhythm and bounce
- Glide, expand, flicker
- Punch, stomp, confront

Hofesh Shechter stepped in and played with formation.

He asked two people to follow the movement of the third dancer.

Following can be a very useful tool.

He asked the dancer leading to try and move quickly, to surprise the others.

The leader then becomes a fluid role, so it is less clear to the audience who is following who. Think about how the dancers interact and interweave with one another.

Be aware of words like 'rhythm' and 'bounce' as they are more technical and structural, rather than portraying an energy. Bounce could be loose, it could be stiff. You need words that are more to do with an energy. This also relates to words like 'confront'; they could be played in so many ways. Once you find a word that shows and represents the energy you want to perceive, you can still be flexible and keep exploring its meaning and how it manifests in the body. Hofesh Shechter talked about playing with where it is in the performance or rehearsal space, what part of the body you are using – do you show sharpness in your whole body or is it just with your hands or your head?

A participant asked about working with a young company with varying physical needs, and if synchronicity is important. Hofesh Shechter responded by saying that having people with different bodies only adds to the richness of the movement, and that it's about sharing an energy rather than all moving identically. The action can be very simple, something recognisable like being moved by a breeze. It's not about being too technical but instead about how, as choreographers or directors, you can free them from a level of self-consciousness to access movement.

Structuring movement

Hofesh Shechter talked about how constructing choreography is a very instinctive process and that 'the only way to do it is to do it'. Although you may want to plan in advance by sketching out patterns, using geometry, considering how many people you want on stage, it is only once you see it and try it that you will know if it works. It can be tedious and hard, but you must just try – if it grows in the right direction, expand it, if it doesn't, try something else. It won't always work the first time, so keep experimenting.

He also talked about the need for everything to feel connected, that it all comes from somewhere and that all movement, however seemingly distant, is connected to the heart of the story.

Lead director Mina Barber reiterated that the movement is not random, that it's all underpinned by the play. It's important when you are structuring the movement sections you remember what has happened before, during and after. Remember that you have the story as an anchor, and if you get stuck use bitesize quick exercises to help yourself get out of a rut. For example, get the company into groups, give them five minutes to create a moment, come back together and watch. Work with your students to crack the problem.

Exercise: Structuring movement

Looking at the three words that have already been created (e.g. flicker, slice and float), make a list of ways you could structure these energies.

How do you want it to look in the space?

Keep it simple.

Once you have this other list, try it out.

One person choreographs, and the other participants will act as the dancers.

You are combining the energies, creating a structure, and on top of that it should include one moment of contrast, which can happen in either the energy or the structure.

The room were put into groups and they played with energy, structure and contrast.

They jumped in head first.

If they had music in mind, they were encouraged to play it.

The groups generously shared their work.

Feedback from the sharing:

- Hofesh Shechter noted that contrast works so well in dance. It is a magical choreographical tool.
- The group spoke about the beauty of seeing the individual within the ensemble.
- It was lovely how bodies were used to create the set.
- The use of repetition was very effective. You become familiar with a sequence and then are surprised when it's broken.
- Ayeesha: Menon flagged that we should be aware of Ram and Sita's repeated scene (when they look at each other). It's important that these two moments contrast but feel connected.
- Hofesh: Shechter advised that we be careful with slow motion; it really reveals the details. For example, you need to think about where the performers' focus is. Make sure there is clarity in the intention.

The room split up into groups again. They made and shared their work.
Feedback from the second sharing:

- You can use time and speed as a tool to create anticipation.
- It was brilliant how the performers' attention changed – how it can shift from the performers looking at each other, to looking at the audience.
- Hofesh Shechter advised that sometimes technical elements, like rhythm, really need time to be rehearsed.
- It was interesting to see different formations and variations. Knowing that a routine doesn't have to be symmetrical, but you can play with having pairs and trios around the space.
- There were really beautiful moments of finding ways for images to appear and disappear. How can it happen without us having to see the mechanics behind it?
- Hofesh Shechter commented on the importance The importance of feedback, having people watch the work, who aren't a part of the process is really helpful to understand what people are seeing, what it is that you are creating.
- Shechter encouraged us to think about how production elements could support the movement. How do you light it? Backlighting can simplify the image whilst with a front light you can see all the detail.

Music

Hofesh Shechter talked about the importance of paying attention to music and musical choices when choreographing. Playing with music that can support or goes against the movement can really help to enhance an energy or contrast it.

Q: Could we have live musicians in our production?
HS: From a choreographer's point of view, that's a brilliant idea!

Q: How do we go about finding the music for our production?
HS: Go with your own flow. It would be hard to construct this in silence, so even if you don't know what to use, try with one track and then another. You might try Britney Spears, classical or heavy metal, but to set the energy, to give it fuel, music is very important.

Transitioning from text to movement

Mina Barber asked the group to work out ways to transition from the text before the movement section, into the dance. How can you make it a fluid moment?
Feedback:

- It's really important to look at the connections that hold it together.
- How can the starting image of the dance already exist, so that they go seamlessly into one another?

- Mina Barber: How can you create clear stage pictures that direct the audience's attention, so they know where to look?

- The use of voiceover could be very effective – think about how you can incorporate audio with movement.

- How do you use the ensemble so it doesn't become confusing as to who they are if they are multi-roling? Maybe it is about establishing a physical language for specific characters; for example, there is a recognisable movement that the demons do.

- The use of the stomp before the starlings is very powerful. Ayeesha Menon mentioned that the stomp is important, you need something as Nina is the catalyst for this moment.

Question and answer with Ayeesha Menon and Mina Barber

Q: How would you feel about gender-swapping roles?
AM: There are some characters, like Parker, where swapping their gender isn't a problem. It might be different for other characters like Sita and Leah, where their gender is an integral part of their identity.

Q: Do you have any suggestions as to how to break up the script for rehearsals – are there natural breaks you would suggest?
MB: You're right, when reading it feels like one long scene. For preparation I would sit down and break it up into scenes. So, for example, the first scene is Zara and Nina, then the starlings have their own moment. Movement is not a separate section, it is part of the scene, but I would tackle it separately.

I would then break it down further, so separate your scenes into events. An event is when something shifts or changes or where someone enters or exits. There is no exact science to it but breaking a scene up into events will help with rehearsing, then you know where the change is coming and how to achieve a shift.

Q: Are we able to shorten any of the longer names?
AM: Many of my family members, who have moved from India to places like Canada, have changed their names to fit in. I think it would be great to honour the culture and keep the names longer. If it's pronounced slightly differently then that's fine. Try, and if you're having problems refer to the audio track we have provided with pronunciations.
MB: If you can say supercalifragilisticexpialidocious you can absolutely say Vishvamitra.

Q: Where do you feel the comedy is in the script? What made you laugh?
AM: I suppose it comes from watching the *Ramayana* as a child. The whole thing was so bizarre to me; seeing Sita walking through the fire, my whole body was screaming. It comes from a place of: what the hell is this?! The voice of Seth and Leah is what goes on in my head all the time; most of the comedy happens between these two characters and when the action is stopped to be commented on.
MB: For me the comedy comes from the breaking of the fourth wall, around the juxtaposition between the modern day and the past. When Sita has to walk through fire

for the second time. Think about the rules of each world, and how does the audience know that we are switching – is there a sound or a movement, what takes them back? What are the parameters of each world?

There's something very Monty Python about it. Even with the magical realism you could think about the stage directions – could they be given to the students to speak as text? There are opportunities to support your movement and to give lines to lots of different performers.

Q: Did you have a specific idea of what the narrators are wearing? Who are they and where are they from?
AM: In the beginning they were birds. I do imagine them in modern dress, so they fit into the real world. I saw them as people of this world, but when they start talking they become something else. Play around with it.
MB: They slip between worlds. As they talk, you slowly realise they are something else. Think about how you can show the slip of who they really are. You need to decide who they are. You have to work out what they represent.

Q: Could you give some more information about Zara's character?
AM: She is a good person at heart. She's probably quite sporty and smart. She's slightly lost herself and her identity. This is the moment she finds herself. It is a growing up story. She's full of life but doesn't know how to speak her mind, but she will gain power.

Q: What is the significance of the lines in italics?
AM: It is when characters in the *Ramayana* are speaking that story.

Q: Do you envisage that the cast is split into a movement group and an acting group, or are they together?
AM: I saw it as a very fluid thing.
MB: That is a directorial choice, but really they need to be one and the same thing; the movement is an expression of the story. The characters are still moving in dialogue, but in those movement sections, it allows it to turn into a grander gesture.

Q: It's such a generous offer to allow us to make it our own – is there anything for you that shouldn't be changed?
AM: I can't imagine the play without Sita walking through the fire. As long as the story works, I don't mind cutting down lines, but the narrators are strategically placed in the story for moments where the audience might be lost, might need some clarification or even just need a break from the story within the story.
MB: As long as it makes sense and you can still follow the characters' narrative then that's fine. If you do choose to cut lines, make sure to read the cut version of the play the whole way through with your group so that you can see if it makes sense.

From a workshop led by Mina Barber and Hofesh Shechter
With assistance from dancer Kim Kohlmann
With notes by Grace Gibson

Remote

by Stef Smith

Stef Smith is a Scottish multi-award-winning stage and screen writer working to international acclaim.

Work for stage includes: *The Pack* (Wonder Fools' 'Positive Stories for Negative Times'); *The New Tomorrow* (Young Vic); *Nora: A Doll's House* (Glasgow Citizen's Theatre and Young Vic Theatre); *Enough, Girl in the Machine, Swallow* (Traverse Theatre); *The Song Project, Human Animals* (Royal Court); *Acts of Resistance* (Headlong / Bristol Old Vic); *Remote* (National Theatre Connections Festival); *Smoke (And Mirrors)* (Traverse Theatre and Dot Istanbul for Theatre Uncut); *Back To Back To Back* (Cardboard Citizens).

Audio/Digital work includes: *Tea and Symmetry* (BBC Radio); *The Deadlift* (Earwig, Tron Theatre); *The Present* (NTS); *Love Letter to Europe* (Underbelly); *How to Build A Nation* (Young Vic).

For screen, Stef has taken part in the BBC Drama Writers Room and her six-part digital series *Float* was released on BBC iPlayer.

Stef has won numerous awards; these include three Scotsman Fringe First Awards for *Enough, Swallow* and *Roadkill*. *Roadkill* has also won an Olivier Award and the Amnesty Freedom of Expression Award. Stef was also shortlisted for the 2020 Susan Smith Blackburn Prize for *Nora: A Doll's House*.

Stef is under commission from several theatres and is developing new projects for both television and film. She is an Associate Artist at Playwrights' Studio, Scotland.

Characters

Antler	*Female*
Oil	*Male*
Crystal	*Female*
Blister	*Male*
Skin	*Female*
Finn	*Female*
Desk	*Either gender – he has currently been written as a male but if this character is played by a female, the production simply changes the gendered pronouns in the [square brackets] to female*
Dashed lines	*Any gender/number of performers (minimum of two)*
Blister's crew	*They have no lines but should be represented on stage when **Blister** is in a scene – until they disband half way through the play*

*The characters can be any age. The only suggestion the writer makes is that **Blister** appears to be the oldest and **Desk** the youngest.*

Writer's note

The smallest number of performers this play could be performed with is nine; there is, however, no maximum number due to the use of a chorus.

The lines denoted with a dash '–' can be said by any performer.

Lines may also be altered, where appropriate, to suit the dialect of the performers. References to high school can also be changed to college, if needed.

This play can be set in any park, anywhere in the UK. The staging can be simple or complex and is open to the interpretation of the group. There are no scenes, but rather this play is one long moment, flicking back and forward between other moments.

Ultimately the writer wishes for the group to imagine their own world within *Remote*.

- Lock
- Open
- Handle
- Door
- Push
- Step. One foot
- Then the other
- Onto the front step
- She closes the door behind her
- Fresh air hits her face
- Smell of clouds and cold. All that autumn stuff
- She pulls out her phone
- Places it on the second step
- Lifts up her foot and slams it down
- Again
- And again
- And again
- Screen. Buttons. Circuit board. Everywhere
- That little piece of plastic
- Broken into smaller pieces of plastic
- And her chest is suddenly free and full
- And she stands for a moment

Antler   Good riddance.

- Good riddance she says
- And it's one foot in front of the other
- It sounds like an easy task
- And most of the time it is
- And it's steps
- No, not steps, strong strides
- Strong strides forward, always facing forward
- She pulls her hood up over her head

- But it isn't that cold

- It's more for, like, an atmosphere

- A mood

- Determined

- Yeah, a mood best described as determined

Antler   I've got somewhere I need to be. Simple as.

- The park, mostly it's the park she needs to be at

- It's only a few minutes' walk from her home

- Her parents, home

- She used to come here often

- When she was kid

- Swings and roundabouts. All that kid stuff

- Tarmac and iron

- Faded painted

- Mums with prams

- Eight-year-olds with adventure in their blood

- The rest of the world ahead of them

- Tarmac and iron

Antler   Huh. It looks the same as it ever did.

- She steps into the park

- Walking with purpose

- Like she is listening to loud headphones

- But she isn't

- Nothing is blocking those ears

- Just those heavy thoughts sitting in between them

- Swirling around her mind like a magic eight-ball

- And in the middle of this park is a tree

- A big old rustic looking one

- Been there since always

- Always been there

- Got names carved into it

– Chewing gum stuck to it

– Holds the snow in the winter

– Back when it used to snow

– And she stops at the bottom. Looking up

– It's been a long time since she looked at it

– And for a moment she recognises

Antler   Nature is pretty cool.

– And with that thought she takes one last look behind her

– The park at eye level

– And then she reaches for the nearest branch

– Grabs it and begins her climb

– Upwards, onwards.

– Branch after branch

– Heaving herself up it

– One foot then the other

Antler   Those gymnastic classes when I was six are really paying off

– She climbs amongst the autumn leaves

– Flakes of orange and brown

– Falling like snow flakes

– Like back when it used to snow

– She finds a branch, solid and strong

– She has never been good with heights

– But then she has never been bad with them either

– Breathe hard

– Breathe deep

– Taller now

– The height of a second-floor window maybe

– Maybe even third

– No other trees about here, not any more

– This tree stands alone

– Surrounded by a world of cars and street lamps

– Of tall buildings and people talking

– Of coasts and cliffs

– Surrounded by this country

– A piece of land

– And after all a piece of land is only a piece of land

– And she shouts

Antler   My name is Antler. And I will not be part of the world. Not this world. Not any more.

– And so we cut to the other side of the park

– A boy called Oil takes his phone out of his pocket

– Three bars of reception

– No new calls

– He shuffles from foot to foot

– Got new trainers for his birthday

– They look pretty good but don't fit quite right

– Clicks contacts

– Clicks call

Oil   Pick up.

– His phone does a double ring

– Goes to voicemail

Oil   Hey, Antler, it's Oil. Where you at? I got your weird text. What's up with you? Where in the park are you? Why the park? Anyway. I'm out. Call me back.

– Somewhere not far from here a girl knocks on her sister's door

Crystal   Antler – you in? I'm coming in.

– But there is no one there. Not a note. Not a sign. Not a nothing

– Just a well-made bed and a weirdly tidy room

– She pulls out her phone

– Compose new message

Crystal   Yo. Sis, exclamation mark. Mum says you're to get washing-up liquid from the shop. You out, question mark. Crystal, kiss. Face with its tongue sticking out.

– Checks her phone again. Nothing

– She grabs her jacket

– Opens the front door

– Crunch

Crystal   What was that?

– Broken pieces of plastic

– Smashed screen

– Tiny pieces of circuit board

Crystal   Antler's phone.

– Back in the park a group of shrugs and sighs collect

– Checking pockets

– Look in their bags

Skin   Nobody got any cigarettes?

Blister   What about cash?

The whole group shakes their head and pats their pockets.

Skin   Nothing.

Blister   You lot are worse than useless. Well. We better go find some then.

– Antler sits. In silence

– Looking out for change

– Listening out for change

Desk   What you doing up there?

Antler   What?

Desk   I said what you doing up there?

Antler   I'm thinking.

Desk   Can't you just think down here?

Antler   Can you leave me alone please?

Desk   It's dangerous being up there so high. At least without ropes. I mean if you had ropes it would definitely be more safe. But you don't have ropes, so it really isn't safe. I'm Desk. Who are you?

Antler   Your name is Desk?

Desk   Sure.

Antler   Weird name.

Desk   What's your name?

Antler   Antler.

Desk   Antler? Why you called Antler?

Antler   It's a long story.

Desk   Have you got somewhere else to be?

Antler   Can you just go. I'm having a private moment here.

Desk   I'll go once you tell me.

Antler   Why are you called Desk?

Desk   Because it's my name.

Antler   Not much of a name is it?

Desk   Works for me.

– [He] looks up at her

– She looks down at [him]

– They pause in that moment

Antler   What? Stop watching me. Just move along.

Desk   You just seem a little old for climbing trees.

Antler   No age limit on climbing trees – is there? No age limit at all.

Desk   How long are you staying up there?

– Antler doesn't know how to answer that question

– Not yet

– Images of screeching cars

– And flags in the air

– And police throwing gas canisters

– And homeless people

– And exam results

– All flick through her head

Antler   It's a protest. You're not meant to know how long a protest is.

Desk   A protest?

Antler   Yeah.

Desk   Have you just decided that?

Antler   No.

Desk   What's it about then?

Antler   It's private.

Desk   I don't think protests are meant to be private.

Antler   Well, this one is.

Desk   Shouldn't people know why you are protesting so they know what it is you want done?

Antler   It's not that kind of protest.

Desk   Don't you want something done? Like something changed or fixed?

Antler   Yes.

Desk   Well. What is it then?

Antler   How many times do I need to say it's private.

Desk   I don't think you're very good at protesting.

Antler   And I don't think you're very good at listening. This has nothing to do with you.

Desk   Can I come up then?

Antler   Look. I am sorry but go find something else to climb.

Desk   Well. You don't own the tree. No one can own trees. They're just, there.

Antler   Yeah? So?

Desk   So I'm coming up.

–   [He] tries to put one hand on the branch

–   Lifts [himself] up

–   The branch snaps

Desk   *Merde*!

Antler   What?

Desk   Means shit in French.

Antler   Well, get you.

Desk   Can you help me up?

Antler   I'm doing this solo, kid.

Desk   Is there a nice view? I'd like to see.

Antler   You can see the whole park from up here. I mean sure. It's pretty.

Desk   Can you help me up?

Antler   Sorry but there is only room for one up here. Only room for me.

–   The wind whips around them both

–   It's suddenly very cold where Antler stands on the branch

Desk   It's a giant tree. There must be room for me.

Antler   You should go home now. Your mum or legal guardian or whatever will be worried.

Desk   What about your mum?

Antler *sits down on the branch.*

–   Antler cuts Desk in half just by looking at [him]

Desk   I best be going. (*Joking.*) Same time, same place tomorrow?

Antler   Bye.

–   The [boy] zips up [his] jacket

–   Takes one last look at the girl in the tree

Desk   You're bonkers you are.

Antler   See you later, Chair.

Desk   It's Desk. My name is Desk.

–   Just north-west from here a boy called Oil also zips up his coat.

Oil   Freaking freezing.

Checks his phone again. Nothing.

–   His mum says he is addicted to checking his phone

–   But he isn't

–   He can stop any time he wants

–   And he is starting to feel a fizz in his throat

Oil *bites his nails.*

–   Oil can taste blood in his mouth

–   He chews his fingers till they bleed

–   He never used to

–   He just started doing it this year

–   And now he can't seem to stop

Oil   Just call me back.

–   Just as he says that

Oil   Aw crap.

–   A herd of chants and chewing gum arrive

Blister   Oh! Oil-spill. Where is your girlfriend at? Not like your mum to let you out alone.

Oil   Hi, Blister.

Blister   What you got for me then?

Oil   Excuse me?

Blister   Can I borrow a fiver?

Skin   Better give him a fiver.

–   This girl called Skin chips in

–   She might be Blister's cousin but no one is sure and no one dare ask

Oil   I'm still waiting on that fiver you borrowed last week.

Blister   I spent it. Need another lend.

Skin   He needs another fiver.

Blister   Anyway the price of smokes has gone up. Inflation, or something.

–   Blister didn't know what inflation meant but it didn't matter

–   He looked much older than his age

–   This was due to a mixture of smoking

–   And wearing jackets that were three sizes too big

Blister   Me and my friends here are desperate for a smoke. We get in a real bad mood if we don't have a smoke after a hard day.

Skin   And it's been a real hard day.

Blister   Really hard.

Skin   Really really hard.

–   Blister has a gaggle of groupies who follow him around

–   None of them say much

–   Minus the occasional shout of something about someone's mother

Oil   I haven't got any money, Blister. I only got my phone on me.

Blister   Well, then, give us that. I'm in need of a new phone, about time I got an upgrade.

Skin   You heard the big guy.

Oil   You're joking?

Blister   Do I look like a comedian?

Oil   I mean you're funny looking /

Skin   / What did you say?

Blister   Phone.

Oil I got it for my birthday. My mum forked out a fortune.

Skin 'My mum forked out a fortune.' Whatever.

Blister Now it's your present to me.

Oil No. I'm not giving you my phone.

Blister What did you say?

Oil What I'm saying is I'm not giving you my phone.

Blister You want to rethink that?

Skin You're probably gonna want to rethink it.

Oil Why? What are you going to do?

Blister Why don't you imagine what we'll do and then times that by a hundred.

Oil Why can't you times it by a hundred yourself?

Blister I'm dyslexic.

Oil No you're just dumb and there *is* a difference.

Blister What did you say?

Oil I mean, what I meant it is . . .

Skin Do you want to repeat that for us? Oil-slick.

– At this point the group is silent

– Blister clenches his fists

– Skin doesn't blink

– And Oil just felt his stomach do a high kick into his throat

– He instantly regretted everything he just said

– Oil had a problem with opening his mouth and just letting the words fall out

Oil Look. Blister. I'm sorry. I'm just messing. I didn't mean to say those things . . . I'm waiting on Antler calling and I've got all up tight is all.

Blister Your girlfriend? You guys going on a date are you?

– The good thing about Blister is that due to his overuse of Facebook and Twitter, he was distracted easily

– No thought or person held his attention too tightly

– And being the oldest of five siblings, Oil knows how to play a distraction to an advantage

Oil Yeah, something like that. But I mean we're not actually going out.

Blister She'll be angry you're late. For your date.

Skin   Tut. Tut. Girls don't like lateness.

Blister   And she should know. She's a girl.

Oil   You know. You guys are right. I better go . . . thanks for the advice.

– And just like that

– Oil slips around the group

Blister   See you around.

Skin   See you around.

Oil   Yeah see you around.

– Disaster narrowly averted

– Oil gnaws at his nails again

– He dare not look back as the group walks away

– And Blister shouts

Blister   Enjoy your date!

– And Skin follows up in the distance with

Skin   Oil and Antler up a tree, K-I-S-S-I-N-G.

– Just as they disappear

– Oil bumps into this [boy]

– Walking at the pace of a snail

– Which is incorrect because snails don't actually walk

– But still

– But still

– All the while Antler had been watching Desk

– Like a bird perched following a mouse

Desk   Sorry.

Oil   Watch where you're going

Desk   I said sorry.

Oil   Oi. You might want to turn around.

Desk   Why?

Oil   Bunch of idiots around the corner.

Desk   That's OK. I can look after myself.

– From high up in that tree in the middle of the park

– A voice yells

Antler   Oil!

– She shouts it loudly but she is too far up

– And he is too far away

– From down here she just sounds like birds

– Or the wind

– Or a car in the distance

Oil   It's your life.

Desk   Thanks anyway.

Oil   Whatever.

– The two of them collide only for a moment

– And pace off in different directions

– Meanwhile Crystal paces the street near her home

– She doesn't want to tell her mum, doesn't want to get Antler in trouble

– Even she knows something has happened

– Meanwhile Oil paces the paths of the park

– I mean it isn't that big but if someone wants to get lost

– There is always some way to get lost

– Meanwhile Antler sits in the tree. Colder now

– Staring across the skyline

– She whispers to herself

Antler   My name is Antler and I won't be part of this world. Not any more.

– But there is a slight crack in her voice

– As if from seeing her friend

– She isn't so sure any more

– Her strength loosens

Antler   It's fine. I'm fine. You're doing this for a reason. You're doing this for a reason.

– And she is fine

– As she thinks about earthquakes

– And flooding

–   And fires tearing down forests

–   And she looks back up at the sky

Blister   Oi! You.

Crystal   What do you want?

Blister   We saw your sister's boyfriend kicking about the park. (*Sarcastic.*) Bet you're jealous of her getting a stud like him.

Crystal   You saw Oil?

Blister   You jealous?

Crystal   No, I'm looking for Antler.

Blister   Well, we haven't seen her.

Skin   Seen nothing of her.

Blister   She probably sucking the face off that numb nut Oil. I mean they really suit each other. Both total losers.

Crystal   Which way did he go?

Blister   Round that way, in past the swings.

Skin   Off on his date.

Crystal   Right. Thanks

With that **Crystal** *goes to walk past* **Blister** *but he grabs her by her arm.*

Blister   Now. Now. We need payment for that information. That information wasn't free of charge.

Skin   No free passes here.

Crystal   I haven't got any money.

Skin   She says she hasn't got any money, Blister.

Blister   Tut. Tut.

–   He twists her arm

–   Everything closes in

–   Blister can be real brutal when he wants to be

–   Everyone knew that

–   Crystal's arm burned

–   And Blister's eyes lit up

Crystal   That hurts!

Blister   You've gotta have something.

Skin   Someone always has something.

Crystal   I don't have nothing. You're hurting my arm.

Finn   Careful. That's a girl you're hurting.

Blister *lets go of* **Crystal***'s arm.*

—   What was that?

—   Who said that?

—   No one, especially not those in this group, question what Blister is doing

—   Not on Blister's watch

Blister   What did you say?

Finn   It's just not . . . .

Skin   Tiger got your tongue?

Finn   It's just manners!

Blister   Since when have you cared about manners?

Finn   You always said manners are important

Blister   Right. But it isn't manner-ful to question what I am doing.

Skin   The man has a point.

Finn   She's younger than you and a girl. She didn't do anything. No disrespect /

Blister   / No disrespect?

Skin   You got an eye for her?

Finn   What?

Blister   Do you fancy her?

Finn   No. No! It's just . . . I've got a little sister about her age. It's like you're doing it to my sister.

Blister   But I'm not.

Skin   But he isn't.

Finn   But it's like you are. I'm sorry Blister, but you just gotta be . . . you know . . . when it's a girl . . . I think . . .

Skin   Not so mouthy now – are you?

Blister   Did I open this up for discussion? For a big chit-chat about manners? Or was I just after some money so I could buy you some fags? Shut up, Finn. Or you can see what happens when someone really has no manners.

For a moment there is silence.

– This girl called Finn never said anything to anybody

– But when she imagined her sister being there

– Blister with his big hand around her little arm

– Finn didn't like imagining that

– She didn't think it was manners at all

– And all the while, Antler was watching

Antler   Don't you dare hurt her!

– It was too far to hear them

– Too far to see the details

– And she had no idea what to do

Antler   I said don't you dare hurt her!

– But she was shouting into the air

– And she couldn't help but feel totally powerless

Finn   I'm outta here. See you guys later.

Blister *grabs* **Finn**'s *jacket.*

Blister   Where do you think you're going?

Skin   Have you suddenly got somewhere else to be?

– And just like that all the sides change

– Friendships, allies, enemies, unknowns, the powerful, the voiceless

– Everything changes

Skin   Go on then.

Finn   Go on what?

– Suddenly Finn sees a part of Skin that she has never seen before

– Eyes close in on her

– Like a predator

– Tigers

– Lions

– Panthers

Blister   Run.

Finn   What?

Skin   He said run.

Finn   Blister. Don't be a /

Blister   / You turned on us.

Skin   Now we're turning on you.

– So quickly, everything switches

– But no one said any of this would be fair

– No one said anything about fairness

– Finn's nerves make her taste sick

– And her guts make her heart race

And with that she grabs **Crystal**'s *hand.*

Finn   Come on!

– One foot in front of the other

– One foot in front of the other

– Blister and his sidestepping crew just stand there

– Watching

– Cruelly giving them time to run into the park

– And up that tree Antler is suddenly starting to feel very stupid

– She is suddenly starting to feel very pointless

– I mean if she got down

– No one would have to know she was ever there

Blister   What do you think, fellas? Time to set off after them?

Skin   I say we give the little puppies a head start. You know. I never . . . really . . . well . . . trusted her.

Blister   Oh yeah? What did she do to you?

Skin   I just never had a good feeling about her. You know that way? When your gut twists?

Blister   No. But, yeah.

Skin   Right. That's enough time, let's head after them.

Blister   You calling the shots now?

Skin   No. Of course not. I'm not calling the shots . . . I'm just doing as you would do. Aren't I?

Blister   Yeah. Yeah. We better go after them.

– The heavy footsteps of Blister trail off into the park

–   I don't think I like him much

–   I think that's the point

Antler   Keep running!

–   Panicked, Antler is stuck

–   She thought it would be easy

–   Easy to stay up in the clouds

–   But she forgot stuff would keep on happening on the ground

–   She hadn't really thought this all through

–   If you ask me, it's a stupid thing to do

–   But she's done it, hasn't she

–   I mean no one would have to know she was up there at all

–   She just has to step down off the tree

Desk   You coming down then?

Antler   What? No. No . . . I'm just . . . why are you back?

Desk   I've lost a glove. It was in my pocket and now it's not. My mum is gonna be as mad as a bag of cats if she knows I lost a glove. She says I go through gloves like dogs go through bones. Which, if you ask me, is a weird thing to compare it with. Because I don't eat the gloves . . . I just lose them. So you given up on your protest? It didn't last very long did it?

Antler   No I haven't . . . I wasn't . . . I'm just getting comfortable.

Desk   It's more comfortable down here. I can promise you.

–   Antler feels a wash of embarrassment over her

–   She didn't want to seem so weak

–   Because this wasn't a phase

–   All of this – it wasn't just a phase

–   It was delayed buses

–   And milk prices

–   And the age of consent

–   It wasn't just a phase

Antler   Did you see a group of guys messing with a girl?

Desk   What?

Antler   A guy called Blister. Face like a bag of smashed crabs.

Desk   Blister? Why is he called Blister?

Antler   Back in primary he gave this boy a Chinese burn so bad it blistered his arm. Name stuck like chewing gum on new Converse. You should stay away from him. He'd eat you alive.

Desk   Well, I haven't seen them. How come?

Antler   You see it's just my little sister is. . . . never mind.

Desk   Your little sister what?

Antler   It doesn't matter.

Desk   Don't suppose you can see it from up there?

Antler   What?

Desk   My glove.

Antler   Your glove?! No. I've got more important things to see than your glove.

Desk   Well. It's important to me and that means it is important.

Antler   Why care so much? It's only a glove. Go to cornershop, get 16 of them for a quid.

Desk   I don't have that kind of money.

Antler   You don't have a pound to buy some gloves?

Desk   No.

Antler   Just ask your mum then. It's only a quid. You shouldn't stress the small stuff. Plenty of big stuff to be stressing about.

Desk   My mum doesn't have that type of money.

Antler   Yeah right. She doesn't have a pound? Whatever.

Desk   She doesn't work.

Antler   Then you should get a job.

Desk   How am I suppose to get a job?

Antler   Do I look like a careers advisor?

Desk   I don't have time for a job. I look after her.

Antler   Oh.

–   With that Antler delves into her pocket

Antler   Here. Catch.

–   She throws down a pound coin

–   Which was nice of her

–   I think we'd all agree that was a nice thing to do

Antler   You can buy a new glove with that.

Desk   Really?

Antler   Don't look at me like that. I'll give you another pound if it makes you go away.

Desk   No. You don't have to . . . thanks. For the loan.

Antler   You don't have to pay me back. I don't need your life story either. Just move along.

Desk   If you ever need . . . a pal.

Antler   I don't need another friend. I don't need anything from *you*. Best be moving, yeah? Why don't you go and see if you can find that other glove . . . keep the pound for something else.

Desk   Yeah. Yeah. Good idea. See you. I'll give the pound back if I find it.

Antler   Whatever. See you.

– Desk wonders off with [his] eyes to the ground

– Looking for [his] lost glove

– And Antler looks back but she can't see her sister

– Can't see Blister

– Just the sky slowly turning dark

– And her stomach grumbles

– And her teeth grind

– Listening out for her sister

– Listening out for change

Crystal   What was that?

Finn   Hey, I helped you.

Crystal   He wasn't going to hurt me. Not, like, really hurt me.

Finn   You don't know him. I've seen him pin kids up to walls and turn them upside down.

Crystal   Then why hang out with such a /

Finn   / Protection. You know how in the ocean little fish hang out with big fish so they don't get eaten.

Crystal   No.

Finn   Well, they do. That's what I'm doing. I know I'm a little fish. Just trying not to get eaten.

Crystal   Sounds like you're being a coward.

Finn   Would a coward do that?

Crystal   It's not like you saved me.

Finn   You looked like you needed saving.

Crystal   I was fine. I would have been fine.

Finn   I was just . . . I've seen enough folk get ploughed through. Between Blister and then there's my brothers . . . well . . . you get bored of watching people get hurt. It gets boring after a while.

–   Unexpected

–   That's the word you'd use for right now

–   Unexpected

Crystal   What's your name?

Finn   Finn.

Crystal   I'm Crystal. You don't go to my school do you?

Finn   I don't go to any school.

Crystal   Oh yeah?

Finn   Nah. Don't see the point.

Crystal   Oh, you're right. Hanging out with Blister is a much better plan.

Finn   Better than nothing. In fact, in my life it's better than anything else.

–   Both of them stood there

–   Knowing nothing and everything about each other

Crystal   What's your plan then? They just gonna chase us around the park forever?

Finn   They'll get bored soon. We just gotta stay one step ahead. That's all. You coming?

–   Just like that Crystal takes Finn's hand

–   Crystal realises in that moment she hasn't held anyone's hand since she was a kid

–   Like, really a kid, younger than now

–   She takes it and they walk further into the park

–   Crystal likes the small fish, so it seems

–   And small hands. She realises Finn has remarkably small hands

Antler   What am I doing . . .

– Now Antler was starting to think about this choice she had made

– It seemed like a simple choice

– A choice of strength

– A choice of courage

– But now she wasn't so sure

– To be honest I'm not entirely sure either

– Maybe she was too old for this

– Because she wasn't a little kid any more

– She wasn't a child any more

– The world had made it very clear there was nothing childish about her

– Exams

– Pounds

– Euros

– Holidays with just friends

– Saving up for a flat

– Saving up for a car

– When you turn old enough

– But just maybe this was a rash thing to do

– I mean what teenager sits up a tree?

– All of a sudden it felt like a childish thing to do

– A grown woman wouldn't do this

– Would they?

Oil   Pick up your phone.

– Oil's walked half the park

– Can't see his friend

– Can't call his friend

Oil   Look, Antler, it's Oil. Has your phone ran out of charge? I mean. I know there is no point in leaving this voicemail if your phone's died but I mean . . . if it hasn't and you get this. Can you call me back? I'm waiting for you. It's not cool to leave me just waiting . . . hope everything is alright. Call me.

– Somewhere else in the park, feet are shuffling the leaves

– Eyes focused on the pavement

— Sunken into thought

Desk Excuse me? I was wondering if any of you guys had seen a glove.

Blister A glove?

Desk Yeah, it looks like this one, because it's a pair. You know?

Skin Do we look like we've seen a glove?

Desk I don't know . . . what does someone look like when they've seen a glove?

— Silence falls on the group

— All of them a bit confused by Desk's distinct lack of fear

— I mean let's face it, they aren't the sharpest pencils in the pencil case

Blister Where you going?

Skin Did you hear him? Where you going?

Desk I'm just looking for my glove.

Blister Where you been?

Skin Where you been?

Desk Just in the park . . .

Blister Bit old for parks.

Skin Yeah, bit old.

Desk Do you have to repeat everything he says?

Skin No. I can say what I want.

Desk Then you should.

Skin What?

Desk Say what you want.

Skin I do.

Desk Good.

Blister Hold on, what is happening here?

Desk Nothing. Excuse me . . .

Skin Hey, wait. We are looking for these two girls, they were running that way.

Desk I've seen a girl up a tree but not two girls running.

Blister Girl up the tree?

Desk Sure. The tree up the top of the park.

— Like a mouse who walks through an alley way filled with stray cats

– Desk disappears

Desk   Thanks anyway.

Blister   What do you say we go and help that girl down?

Skin   What is that supposed to mean?

Blister   Well . . . From up by the tree we can see the whole park. Might be able to spot your friend.

Skin   She isn't my friend.

– Doesn't sound good does it?

– I'm with you on that

Antler   It's fine. I'm fine. Buck. Up. Get yourself together.

– Antler knew it wasn't madness

– She knew it came from deep inside her

– But she also knew somewhere in that park her sister was looking for her

– And she missed Oil.

– Missed his jokes

– It was that familiar balancing act of what your skull wants

– And what your rib cage wants

– Caught in between what came before

– And what comes next

Antler   Another sixty years?

– If she doesn't smoke or take up an extreme sport

– She's got another sixty years of this

– And that was the problem

Crystal   Is it true what they say about Blister?

Finn   About what?

Crystal   About those pills. At that house party.

Finn   Dunno. Depends what people are saying. It's more his big brother's thing.

Crystal   Is it your thing?

Finn   I mean . . . not really. Why?

Crystal   Just wondering.

Finn   Is it your thing?

Crystal   Are you kidding? My big sister would kill me if I went anywhere near anything like that. She's all protective of me.

Finn   There is no way I'd let my family run my life.

Crystal   You don't know my big sister. And I'd rather take her advice than your best friend Blister.

Finn   Can you just drop all that Blister stuff . . . He isn't really a friend. Like, not any more.

Crystal   Then why bother. You'd be better off just locking yourself in doors than hanging out with him.

–   What Finn wanted to say is that she had been stuck with them

–   For two years she had stood at the back of that crew

–   But they had been there when her mum kicked her out for a night

–   Or that time that her brothers took her wallet

–   But she had grown up quicker than them

–   More than them

–   But it was better to have them than no one, she thought

Finn   You know they're not that bad, just immature.

–   Even Crystal knew that wasn't the truth

Skin   This is taking too long. They'll be out of here before we get half way to them.

Blister   Just go home. The rest of you. Just split.

–   The group pause and look at Blister

Skin   Yeah. He's right. We can do this alone. We don't need your dead weight.

Blister   Alright, Skin. Cool it. No need to get nasty on the ones who do stick around . . . but yeah. The rest of you can split. We'll see you tomorrow. And bring cash. No empty pockets tomorrow. Unless you want another day without fags.

–   Just like that, the group starts to fade away

–   Nobody else wanted to chase two girls around the park

–   Nobody else really cared

Blister   Just us then.

Skin   Looks like it.

–   Antler can see this.

–   She sees the group break up.

–   She could feel sweat in her palms

- Could feel her eyes twitch

- Everything had switched

- And she had no idea what to do

Antler   Screw this.

- It's much so harder than she thought it would be

- Because no one had warned her how hard it would be to change

Skin   You should be worried, Blister. Finn leaving us. Don't want anyone else getting ideas, you know. Ideas like that can be contagious. Can be poison. When people get busy making their own ideas of how things should be, well, that's when it gets dangerous for big fish like us.

Blister   Big fish? I'm allergic to fish.

Skin   Big tigers. Lions. Whatever. You know back in the day there would have been wolves here. And that's us. We're the wolves now. And it's important people know that.

Blister   I thought there used to be a Tesco here?

Skin   Before that. Before all the humans. Wolves have real sharp teeth. And they aren't afraid to use them.

Blister   I've never been afraid, Skin. Even with everything that's happened, I've never been afraid.

Skin   That's why you're my friend, Blister. That's why all that lot respect you.

Blister   Yeah. Yeah you're right. Better go then.

Skin   You lead the way

- And with that Skin could hear her brother's voice ring in her head

- Protect yourself

- The world is filled with wolves

- Protect yourself

Oil   You have got to be kidding me. Antler? Is that really you?

- The two of them just look at each other

- Connected in silence and confusion

Oil   What are you doing up there? You hate climbing trees.

Antler   Oil, you gotta go after Crystal. Blister is after her.

Oil   What?

Antler   You gotta go.

Oil   What's wrong with your legs?

Antler   I can't come down, Oil.

Oil   Are you stuck?

Antler   No. . I just . . . /

Oil   / I tried calling you.

Antler   I smashed my phone up.

Oil   What?!

Antler   Don't need it.

Oil   You don't need it?

Antler   I don't need it.

Oil   You're not going to /

Antler   / Not any more.

Oil   Not any more?

Antler   Is there an echo? Look, can you just go and check and see if Crystal's OK?

Oil   Why don't you come down and we can go and look together?

– No words found Antler

– She felt this strange double feeling of shame and strength

– And her mind flicked to news broadcasters

– And trashy magazines

– And size zero

– And kissing boys

– And not kissing boys

– And definitely not getting pregnant before you're twenty

– And turning off lights when you leave the room

– And recycling

– And all she could mutter out was –

Antler   I can't.

Oil   Look. Come on. Enough of this. Let's go see what's happening.

Antler *shakes her head.*

Oil   Look I'm not going after Crystal without you. This is stupid. Just get down.
Blister is rolling around the park looking for trouble. You want to be up there when he
comes?

Antler   I don't care if Blister wants me.

Oil   Are you being a hero all of a sudden?

–   The truth is Antler had never felt less like a hero

–   She takes a deep breath

–   Like the kind you take before you dunk your head under water

Antler   I'm not being a 'hero' . . . but I don't want part of any of it any more.

Oil   Part of what?

Antler   Anything. Everything.

Oil   School?

Antler   No.

Oil   Something at home?

Antler   No. And yes. All of that. All of everything. I mean take a look around. This . . . well. . . it's a protest.

Oil   A protest? Can you have a protest with just one person?

Antler   It's a protest against all of that.

–   Both Antler and Oil take their eyes off each other

–   And they look at the ground

–   Look at the sky

–   Look at everything they know

Antler   It's all turning to shit.

Oil   I don't . . . since when . . . can you just come down?

Antler   No. Not any more.

Oil   It sounds like you're being a bit . . . Look. It doesn't matter. Come on. Protest on the ground or something.

–   Her hands were shaking

–   Her eyes were welling up

Antler   Can't you see? Everything matters.

Crystal   Look. Thanks for . . . well . . . I dunno . . . but I'm gonna split. I gotta find my sister.

Finn   Just like that? Gone?

Crystal   What do you want?

Finn   I can't leave you to wander off by yourself . . . you don't know where Blister is.

Crystal It's fine. I don't think he is half as tough as you think he is. You've got some idea of him in your head. He's just a guy . . . whatever.

Finn You kidding? A couple of weeks ago he found this little dog. This little three-legged thing. It was old, more scabs than fur. Skin pinned the dog down to the ground – it was yelping and crying, and then Blister picked up this big rock and dropped it on its head. And it stopped yelping but he didn't stop. He just picked up the rock again and smashed it into the dog and he smashed and smashed and smashed. Until . . . well, until the dog was nothing.

Skin said it was kinder to put it out of its misery but the dog had seemed fine to me. And they just left it there. It's just the other side of the park. And they've still got blood on their shoes. All dried in their laces. I haven't ever seen something like that before . . . and I don't want to see it again.

Crystal Why didn't you stop them?

Finn What was I suppose to do? When they get their mind on something . . . I mean look at us. I'm not gonna just let you go wandering off into the park.

Crystal I can look after myself.

Finn I got you into this mess.

Crystal But I'm not a three-legged dog. I'll be alright.
Honest.

Silence.

Finn That boy you were looking for

Crystal Oil?

Finn Yeah. He was walking up to the top of the park. Towards the tree.

Crystal Thanks.

– And with that she leans forward and kisses her

– Right on the lips

– It was a short kiss

– No tongues

– Crystal knew she didn't have to be saved but she didn't mind the gesture

– And both were a little surprised by the kiss

– But neither were particularly scared

Crystal See you.

Finn See you.

– One foot in front of the other

– One foot

– Then the other

– Different directions

Oil   Look. Come down. We'll find Crystal and sort this out.

Antler   How many times do I need to say it?

Oil   Come on. It's getting dark. And I don't have a torch. My phone has ran out of battery, yours is smashed. Your sister could be lost in the park for all we know. It's not just you here! Stop being so stupid. I'm gonna walk away, Antler . . .

– The sky dims

– Clouds move in

– Right enough, it was getting dark

Oil   Your mum will be worried

– It was a cheap shot but it was enough to make Antler's heart jump up to her tongue

Antler   I told her I was staying at yours.

Oil   I'm not sure she'll buy that excuse when you don't come home for a week.

Antler   I just can't do it. Not any more. It's too hard. My mum cries. A lot. My room is next to the bathroom and I hear her cry. I don't know why, Oil. She just cries. And you know it isn't good when your mum cries.

Oil   How long has she been crying?

Antler   Long enough. And my dad has taken up smoking again.

Oil   So? You smoke at parties.

Antler   But it's different. He's quiet. He looks . . . well . . . and I hate school. I hate it. I don't care about some revolution that happened eighty years ago. And there is no way I'm getting into uni with my grades and it's not like I have the money to move out and I don't have a job and I don't want to be, like, forty-five and still living with my mum.

Silence.

Oil   Is this all like . . . a hormone thing. . or something?

Antler   I'm not on my period, Oil.

Oil   Ew. Gross. Look. Come down. And we can talk about it. I'm getting a right sore neck look up at you and soon you won't be able to see where the branches are. Come down. It's just getting dangerous.

Antler   Good. Let it get dangerous.

Oil   You got a death wish?

Antler   No. But at least something would change. It's just grey. Look at all that grey.

– And Antler felt a twinge in a muscle just left on her heart

– As she looked out at the greyness

– And she knew it wasn't about that stuff

– Not really.

– Go on then

– Tell him.

Antler   That's not really why I'm here. It's just . . .

Oil   Spit it out.

Antler   I learnt a word the other day. In English. She was going on about some old book about something and she said – it was about people being apathetic . . . it was about apathy.

Oil   Oh yeah. What does that mean then?

Antler   It's people not caring. People not wanting to care about anything.

Oil   Can you tell me how you sitting up a tree is you not caring?

Antler   No. That's not the point. After she said the word, I saw it everywhere and I can't stop seeing and feeling it everywhere. And I don't think that's right. People not caring. It's frustrating . . . it's . . . hard . . . it's . . .

Oil   Are you gonna start going on about starving kids?

Antler   Stop trying to make it small. This isn't small. These thoughts aren't small.

Oil   Look. Sort all that stuff out when we're out of high school. Keep it small. It's like a survival thing. Just got to keep that kinda thing in the back of your mind until you can actually do something about it.

Antler   What? Like everyone else around us?

Oil   You're not exactly volunteering are you?

Antler   No. It's not that!

– Antler grabs her chest

– And tears fill in her eyes but none of them drop

– She didn't like the world much

– And she didn't know what do with that feeling

– Didn't know where to put it

Oil   Look. Don't get all wrapped up in it. You can save the world another day. Just come down. Yeah?

Antler   But that's it, isn't it? I can't change the world and I definitely can't save it. I can't do nothing.

Silence.

– The two friends look at each other

– Oil started biting his nail again

– And Antler felt like her lungs might burst

– It's been years since they fought

– They might only been feet away but they felt also worlds away

Oil   What about your sister?

– Antler felt a double twang of guilt and sadness

Antler   I can't come down.

– I mean she wanted to come down

– She wanted to find her sister

– And shout at her

– Tell her off

– And then hug her

– The way that big sisters do

– But she didn't

– She was sitting there, in that tree

– Wishing for something better

– Wanting something bigger

– One foot

– Then the next

– Antler looks out at the grey, her eyes wet with wanting

– Oil looks at his friend and tastes blood in his mouth

– Skin paces up the hill, looking for wolves, ready to jump

– Blister walks two steps behind, uncertain of this change of sides

– Finn touches her lips, thinking of the kiss, wondering how she felt

– Crystal feels the power in her feet, in her hands

– Desk suddenly turns on [his] feet. Suddenly aware that [he's] sent a pack of animals to roar at a girl up a tree . . . what has [he] done?

Crystal   Oil! You seen /

Oil   Crystal! Look, your sister won't get down.

Antler   You're alright? You're OK!

Crystal   I've been looking for you! I've been worried sick, I've been . . . what are you doing?

Oil   She won't get down.

Antler   I was worried, I could see Blister coming after you. Did he hurt you?

Crystal   How did you know about Blister? What else did you see? Did you see me?

Antler   I could see him chasing you.

Crystal   And you didn't come help?

Antler   I mean . . .

Oil   She isn't coming down. She doesn't like the world.

Antler   So what happened with Blister? Why was he so mad?

Crystal   Hold the phone! What was that about the world?

–   Antler was lost again

–   Someone new to describe everything too

–   And somehow with these people who she was closest to

–   She found it hardest

–   She found it hardest to explain that ache

–   The ache in her chest, in her skull

Crystal   Is this about those sad adverts on the TV? I told you not to watch them any more.

Oil   I've already asked that – it's not about the sad adverts.

Crystal   Is it about school? Home?

Oil   No it's not about that either. But also kinda everything.

Crystal   You can't be that upset – we're having a roast for dinner, oh and Mum says you're to get washing-up liquid.

Oil   Maybe it would help just not paying attention to what the TV is saying, yeah? Just like forgetting about all of it.

Crystal   This better not be a joke. Cause it isn't funny. I can't believe I spent all afternoon looking for you and you've just been stuck up here. You know what, Antler, I don't even care. I'm going home with or without. Oil, you coming?

Oil *looks at* **Crystal***. He is tempted. He is turning on his feet.*

Crystal   Coming?

Antler   Just stop it!

- And in her head it was
- Images of screeching cars
- And flags in the air
- And police throwing gas canisters
- And homeless people
- And exam results
- And earthquakes
- Flooding
- Forests on fire
- Delayed buses
- Milk prices
- The age of consent
- Exams
- Pounds
- Euros
- Holidays with just friends
- Saving up for flat
- Saving up for a car
- News broadcasters
- Trashy magazines
- Size zero
- Kissing boys
- Not kissing boys
- Not getting pregnant before you're twenty
- Turning off lights when you leave the room
- And recycling

Antler   Recycling!

Oil   What?

Crystal   You're kidding me. Now I really am going.

Antler   No. It's not that. But it is that. It's not that simple. There is nothing simple about these thoughts, there is nothing simple about me, or you or this place, this town, this country. And people try to tell you it's easy. Simple. But really it's just that no one cares. No one cares enough to see what it's really like. How *hard* everything is. Because it's hard. It's hard knowing that you can't fix anything. You can't do nothing about anything. It's hard. And no one cares.

Silence.

Crystal   I care.

Antler   You care more about the shape of eyebrows than you do about what's happening in the world.

Crystal   That's just mean.

Oil   Why should we care?

Antler   Because it's ours as well.

This is what we'll get. This. Their mess. And I don't want it, Oil. I don't want any of it.

Silence.

– With that, silence falls on the trio

– It's painful to see the world

– Oil understood that now

– It's painful to see what the world really is

Oil   Well, hiding up a tree isn't the best way to . . . fix it.

Antler   Then what do you propose?

Oil   I've got no interest in proposing anything. Voting?

Antler   Do you think that does anything?

Crystal (*sarcastic*)   Oh sure. It's not nearly as useful as hiding up a tree.

– Minutes away Finn turns on her heels

– She knows that she's got to see that girl again

– Minutes away Skin and Blister march up closer to the tree

– Seeking out something to stir up, seeking out something

– Minutes away Desk runs towards the tree

– Wanting to make sure no trouble was caused

Antler   Then what else? I can't think of anything else to do.

Crystal   You're acting like a right idiot. You haven't even got a decent reason. I'm gone, I'm so gone.

Antler   You're the reason, Crystal! You're the reason I'm up here!

Crystal   It's my fault? Why is it my fault?

Antler   I didn't want to tell you because I didn't want to upset you, but . . .

–   And just like that, everything changed again

Finn   Crystal!

Crystal   Finn? What are you doing . . .

Finn   I needed to talk to you, about what happened /

Oil   / What you doing knowing this loser? She's pals with Blister.

Crystal   She isn't like that. She . . . helped . . . me earlier.

Oil   Leopard can't change its stripes.

Antler   Spots. Leopards have spots.

Finn   I didn't mean anything earlier. Like sorry about your phone and that. Blister was just joking.

Oil   Wasn't very funny.

Blister   I thought it was pretty hilarious.

Skin   Don't mind us, we've got a bit of business needed with our friend here.

Oil   Thought you weren't friends with these guys any more.

Blister   No one said anything about friends.

Skin   I did. I said friend.

Blister   Oh.

Crystal   Just leave us alone.

Skin   Oh we'll go, all in good time.

Oil   You just the sidekick, Blister?

Blister   You kidding? I'm still the boss around here.

Oil   Doesn't look like it

Skin   None of us have any bosses, not any more.

Blister   Oi. Skin. Watch your mouth.

Finn   Look, I'm sorry for before. I'm sorry. I was out of line.

Crystal   What are you saying, Finn?

–   Finn clocks the dried dog's blood on Blister's shoes

Finn   Look I've got some money at home. I'll buy your smokes for the rest of the week.

–   Crystal felt the knot of disappointment

–   Blister felt sweat in his palms

– And Skin just glared at Finn

– And I have no idea what is going to happen

Blister   I think that's fair, Skin. I could do with a smoke. We've all had a stressful day.

Skin   I don't. I don't think that's a good offer. I'm not soft like you, Blister.

Blister   Soft?

Finn   Look. Skin, what happened before, it didn't mean nothing.

– With that Skin reaches down

– She picks up the branch that Desk had snapped off

– From up above Antler can see

Antler   Watch!

Skin *swings the branch near* **Finn**.

Finn   You planning on putting that down?

Skin   Are you planning on staying still for me?

Skin *aims at* **Finn**.

Crystal   What are doing?!

Skin   Don't come near me!

Blister   This isn't funny. You could mess her up with that.

Skin   That's the point.

Finn   Look, Skin. I didn't mean nothing. I'm sorry. Alright. No need to do nothing drastic.

Skin   I know you like to kiss girls. I was doing you a favour, keeping it private. But then today . . . when I saw you run off with her . . . I think . . . well why I don't I just show you what I think about that.

Skin *steps forward. The branch in her arms. Ready to swing.*

– Now Finn sees the dried blood on Skin's shoes

– She thinks about that three-legged dog

– Thinks about what its head looked like after the rock

Finn   Stop! I'm sorry. OK? I'm sorry. I didn't mean nothing. I kissed a girl. OK? But I don't know . . . like . . . I'm just . . . .

Skin   Do me a favour and stand still. Will you?

Crystal   We kissed. Alright? Didn't mean nothing. Just a kiss. No need to give someone a decking just for a kiss.

Blister   Just put it down, Skin. You hit her with that, you'll get done. You don't want that. Trust me, my brother got put in a unit. And she isn't worth it. She isn't worth it.

– A tear creeps out of Blister's eye but he quickly wipes it away

– Oil is pretty sure his heart has stopped

– And Finn just stares into Skin's eyes.

Desk   Don't hurt her! I won't let you hurt her.

– Out of nowhere Desk rushes up to Skin

– He tries to grab the branch

– They tug back and forth

– Skin pushes [him] off

Skin   Enough! I oughta smash in all your skulls just for being cowards. Look at you. You don't have the guts to fight. You don't have the guts to do nothing about this, me. Scared of a stupid branch?! Bunch of cowards. Don't even know how to fight. You'll get nowhere if you don't know how to fight. You're just a bunch . . . of kids. Stupid kids, the lot of you.

Skin *throws the branch on the ground.*

– They stand there

– In silence

– Looking less like kids and more like adults by the minute

Silence.

Crystal   I'd rather be a coward than just plain stupid.

Crystal *quickly picks up the branch. She points it at* **Skin** *who barely flinches.*

Blister   Oi! Don't talk to her like that.

– Skin looks at Blister

– Relieved to have the responsibility of words taken away from her

– Blister steps in the middle

He pushes the branch down.

– No one is getting hurt today, he thinks

– No one is getting hurt

– I don't know about you but I'm relieved

– Shhh!

Desk   What has been happening here?!

Silence.

Antler   We're just trying not to fuck it up.

—   One by one they turn and look at the girl in the tree

Antler   You're wrong. It isn't about fighting, not in that way. I mean look at everyone around us. All the power in the world and they don't care about nothing, don't fight for anything. We aren't being cowards by not fighting.

—   It's just about choosing what to fight for

—   Antler realised that now

—   She did want to fight

—   But she wanted to fight for something better than this

Antler   Because when I fight. I want it to be for more than you holding a branch up to some girl because she kissed another girl. I've got better things to do with my time, better things to fight for, we all do.

Silence.

Skin   No need for the lecture.

Oil   Antler, it's time to come down . . . yeah?

Crystal   Hold on. What did you mean I caused you going up there?

—   With deep dark breaths Antler sighs

—   Exhausting

—   Antler knew one thing

—   Change was exhausting

Antler   It was that text.

Crystal   Text?

Antler   You sent me that message.

Crystal   What message?

Antler   I asked you if you wanted to go and see Gran this weekend or next and you said – 'I don't care either way and I don't need you to organise my life'. You typed that into your phone and sent it to me. In about thirty seconds. You said you didn't care. You said you didn't need me.

—   The group looks amongst themselves

—   No one is quite sure of her point

—   To be honest I don't know her point but I sense she probably has one

Crystal   I mean maybe it was a bit harsh but there is no need for all this. I just meant I'm free all weekend . . .

Antler   But you said you didn't care. You said you didn't need me. And I thought, if my own sister can say that. Then it really is messed up.

Crystal   But that's just what sisters do? That's just normal. You say stuff like that all the time.

Antler   No. I don't. I'm careful with my words.

Crystal   You're older.

Antler   Only by a year . . . It's apathy. It's everywhere. You said you didn't care. You said you didn't me. I mean what can I do? How can I change any of this? If I can't get my own sister to care about me.

Crystal   Look. I'm sorry. I was in a bad mood.

Finn   I think you're reading too much into it.

Antler   No. It was like. What's that saying?

Blister   The straw that broke the camel's back.

The whole group turn and look at **Blister***.*

What? I know stuff.

Antler   Exactly.

Oil   Is that why you stamped on your phone?

Antler   Texting seemed pointless. Facebook seemed pointless. Taking another stupid photo of my cat seemed pointless. It doesn't matter – does it? Any of that stuff.

–   It doesn't matter when there is better stuff to care about

–   That's what she wanted to say

–   That there was bigger stuff to care about

Antler   That stupid phone was just . . . just . . . a distraction.

–   It stopped her seeing from seeing world for what it really is

–   It stopped everything

–   She saw that now

Desk   If you ask me, Antler, you're the one who cares least . . . what's that word?

Blister   Apathy . . .

The group turn and look at **Blister** *again*

What? I was paying attention.

Desk   Apathy. Sounds like some weird disease. Us, down here, on the ground. We care. We've got no choice. Otherwise it's just . . . boring or pointless or whatever. You've got to care about something. Everyone knows that. And you're just up there. In that tree. It's one thing to count yourself out but it just seems stupid to count yourself out because others are counting themselves out.

Crystal   What?

Desk   She is doing the exact thing she hates other people are doing.

Crystal   Oh. Right.

Desk   I don't know how you fix people not caring. I don't know how you get people to notice all the things that need fixing. Because it's everywhere, the stuff that needs fixing. All of us can name three things in thirty seconds that need fixing, but you aren't going to fix it by not being part of it.

Skin   Talk about sugar coating something.

Blister   Shut up, Skin.

Oil   What you were saying before? You're right. This is ours. All of this is ours. But we can't make it ours, like truly properly ours, unless we're in it. Can't fix anything by being above it.

– There are shifts you feel

– Somewhere under your ribcage

– Somewhere just left of your heart

– Something happens

– Like something changes

– And it will happen plenty of times over the years

– Even I know that

– It's like a breathlessness

– Yeah, it's best described as a breathlessness.

– And Antler felt that. As she sat in the tree. Looking down

– Looking down at those people

– People who looked just as confused as she was

– It had been a hard autumn, she thought

– The autumn of what came before, and what comes next

Oil   Please, come down.

Crystal   I need you. I'm sorry I said I didn't. Like . . . I was wrong. Simple as. I care. I've always cared.

– And just like that. It all changes again

– Just when you get a hold of something

– Just when you decide

– It changes

Antler   Alright.

– An exhale

– A breath taken

Antler   On one condition. You all gotta come up here first.

Oil   What?

Antler   It's the sun. It's setting. You can't see it from down there. Too close to ground. But from up here. The reds and the yellows. It's beautiful.

– Antler looks at Blister and Skin

Antler   But first I think it's best you guys get gone now.

Crystal   You heard her.

– Blister and Skin look at the group

– Bunch of no ones

– Bunch of everyones

Blister   We know where we're not wanted. You coming?

– Finn shakes her head

Finn   Not this time.

Skin   Best we don't see you again, yeah?

Finn   Yeah.

– In silence the two march off

– They won't talk about what happened today

– Not ever

– But it changed them

– In the smallest of ways, it changed them

Antler   Look, I promise I'll get down, afterwards. Come on. See this.

– And just like that

– One by one they start climbing the tree

– Helping each other.

– Clambering upwards

Crystal   I don't think I like heights.

Finn   You'll be alright.

– Branch after branch

– One foot above the other

–   The group settle in the branches of the tree

–   Like crows

–   Or pigeons

–   Or seagulls

–   Or robins

–   All perched in the branches

–   Watching the light change

–   Watching the sun dip below this big lump of rock

Oil   It's cool how the light changes.

Antler   Desk! I can see your glove! Look! Over by there . . . oh no. It's just a crisp packet.

Finn   Everything looks so much smaller up here.

Crystal   What do they call it? Like, in a photo. We just learnt it in art. All the depth and that . . .

Antler   Perspective.

Crystal   Yeah. Perspective.

–   And then in a single moment

–   A spec of white falls from the sky

–   Antler holds out her hand

–   And catches it and it disappears

–   Was that snow?

–   Antler wasn't sure.

–   But she did know. The sun would most likely rise again.

–   Just as it would set again.

–   It's amazing what you can see if you look.

Antler   Nature is pretty cool.

–   As darkness and shadows fall on the group

–   They all sit in silence

–   Hold on to the branches a little tighter

–   And they are still, if only for a moment.

–   Antler smiles to herself as she wonders if the whole day was worth it

–   If it was worth the battle

– Just so she could see this sun set

– And she concluded it probably was

– It was always worth seeing another sun set

– She promised herself she'd look up more. So she didn't miss it

– Perspective, after all, is everything

– With that Desk broke the settled silence

Desk   Just one thought . . . How are we going to get down?

Blackout.

Remote

BY STEF SMITH

*Notes on rehearsal and staging, drawn from a workshop with the writer,
held at the National Theatre, October 2021*

How the writer came to write the play

For Stef Smith, growing up in a small village, ninety minutes from Glasgow, theatre began as a distant and expensive concept. Her first exposure to theatre was youth theatre, and as a fourteen-year-old she went to youth theatre every Saturday for three years.

Remote was inspired by the understanding that young people can be highly politicised and engaged with what is going on, and yet have no political structures within which to focus these frustrations; among other things, they cannot vote. It is also inspired by the way that teenagers' brains work; they make connections and have reactions that the post-adolescent brain does not. They are forming their identities and how they think and feel about the world as they interact with it.

The first draft of *Remote* was written in 2013 for the National Theatre Connections in 2014.

Stef Smith also wanted to write something that was accessible to a range of abilities; the ensemble nature of the play allows it to be approached by a young person with any range of experience.

In a post-Covid environment, the themes of isolation, separation and feeling disenfranchised with the political structures in place feels very resonant for young people.

Approaching the play

Lead director Tessa Walker divided the obstacles that a director might face with this play into four sections. In the exercises throughout the day, each of these areas were investigated for provocations and answers:

- THE ENSEMBLE
  - The challenges of different sizes of cast, and how that interacts with the ensemble element of the play
- THE STAGING
  - Particularly the tree
  - Levels
  - Capacity – if you have forty people on stage, what are they doing and how are they moving the story on?

- THE TEXT
  - ○ Looking at sections of the text and putting staging/ensemble together
  - ○ Looking at small sections in detail rather than attempting to tackle all of it
  - ○ Looking at flow and rhythm and how this plays out in the form of stream of consciousness
- DIALOGUE, RHYTHM, NAMED CHARACTERS
  - ○ Thinking about stream of consciousness
  - ○ To resist the temptation to dwell in moments
  - ○ Looking at moments of silence
  - ○ Looking at how you might approach the dialogue with your company

Chorus

Exercise: Exploring ensemble

We split into groups of five and Tessa Walker allocated a ten-page extract from the play to each group. Each group was asked to divide up the ensemble lines between them. Once allocated, the group then decided *what is being done* with each line:

- For example:
  - ▪ Is it being told to the audience?
  - ▪ Is it being told to the whole group of chorus?
  - ▪ Is it being told to a single person in the chorus?
  - ▪ Is it being given to one of the named characters and if so what are they doing with it?

Discoveries

The groups found that by allocating the lines, and by deciding where they were directed, the intentions of the lines started to create dynamics in the group: friendships started forming and the investment in the situation by the characters started to surface.

Tessa Walker discussed that the danger of this style of chorus work is that it can be repetitive. Being specific and detailed about the intention behind the line keeps the storytelling dynamic alive.

It was also discovered that the chorus can hold the story on their own – which will demonstrate to the young people how crucial the Chorus is, despite not being a 'named' character.

Tessa Walker encouraged the groups to make a few choices – and even if these go on to change, they encourage the Chorus to have tension, movement and communication. For example: you could decide with your company how much the Chorus knows of the story when they are telling it. And if you have a bigger company you can decide how many of the Chorus might tell one scene or event – are there just two of them on stage or six of them at any given time?

Text

Exercise: The objective of the line for the chorus

The groups were asked to decide on the objective of the line (e.g. 'to fit in', 'to persuade a friend', 'to show the audience I can control the situation') and then to identify a key relationship for each actor within the ensemble of the group (e.g. this is my best friend, this person I had a fight with yesterday)

The groups then shared their findings by showing the scene to the rest of the groups.

Discoveries

Setting intentions at the start of the play carries the audience through the whole scene because it is engaging to watch.

Each member of the ensemble can also discover their entire character arc for the play, as a narrator of the piece but also someone who is part of the unfolding events.

Each member of the ensemble can also have a relationship and dynamic with the named characters on stage – are they friends? Are they supporting Antler in her endeavour? Are they disagreeing with Crystal and Finn?

Staging

Exercise: Staging these objectives as chorus

Tessa Walker asked the groups to decide on how they might stage an extract featuring the chorus on its feet. The groups were asked to put some blocking and staging into the scene and present it to the rest of the group.

Discoveries

Opening images were powerful and important – they told the story from the start.

One group had a collective intake of breath which was powerful as a collective expression of suspense.

Questions that presented themselves as opportunities for artistic decision were:

How do you speak to the audience? Would you decide to not bring the lights down? Are you talking to one audience member of a number of them?

How do you direct focus within the group (e.g. at a pivotal moment when Antler is climbing the tree, the Chorus might all look at Antler)? How might it feel if one ensemble member looks away?

What comes first, the action of the named character or the Chorus' narration of it?

How does Antler relate to the Chorus? How might this change through the events of the story?

Named characters

Exercise: Inserting the named characters into the extracts, and exploring their purpose

Tessa Walker asked each group to look at a different named character, and put them in the scene. The aim of this exercise is to investigate what changes when a named character enters the dynamic of the Chorus.

Group 1 : Antler

Group 2: Blister

Group 3: Blister and/or Antler

Group 4: Desk and/Antler

Group 5: Crystal and Finn

Group 6: Blister/Oil/Finn/Desk

Discoveries

There are a number of options of different languages for the Chorus to use: moving away from the 'telling-showing-telling-showing' language, you could actually create character tensions and dynamics in the group which moved the story forward.

You can choose the moments you want to highlight, but it doesn't have to become over-saturated with showing every element of the story; e.g. can just show the lead-up to Crystal and Finn's kiss, or Antler arriving at the top of the tree, rather than every section of these events.

The Chorus is valuable to indicate the dramatic/pivotal moments of a piece – you can use their energy, points of focus and physicality to create moments of tension and catharsis.

The Chorus can be in control of the story, and yet still be surprised by elements that perhaps they didn't know were coming.

There is the opportunity of creating Blister's group of friends from the Chorus.

It was discovered that characters are often locked in a moment whilst the Chorus is finishing the story and vice versa. This is an artistic challenge: what do you do in those moments to fill space and time? Is it useful to explore focus and stillness?

For Crystal and Finn, there were options to use the Chorus to physically block the audience's view, e.g. of the kiss, or for the Chorus to interact with this moment with someone behind Crystal and someone behind Finn.

The Chorus could also be protective of Antler and provide a caring presence or an affronting one.

Staging

Exercise: Blocking and movement of chorus and named characters

Tessa Walker then asked the groups to return to the pieces and look at:

1   How the Chorus navigates space, and how to extend and expand the ensemble movement language, building on their decided dynamics.

2   How to stage Antler being up the tree: the central staging challenge of the play.

Discoveries

Blocking the Chorus first and then inserting the named character creates a shared investment in the Chorus for the young people in the play, which is important considering there might be a tendency towards dismissing a role if it isn't a 'named' part.

Other provocations that came out of the exercise were:

Is the tree static or is it mobile?

Can the tree be created by the ensemble, can it move around the stage?

Can the Chorus be used to move physical props around the stage?

What shapes/form of the tree best allows movement and scenes to take place?

It was also discovered that working in traverse can give length, perspective and distance to make the tree almost horizontal or for the company to stage Antler's feelings of isolation. Movement of the chorus away from Antler – closing distance and opening distance – tells us different stories.

Text

Exercise: Character investigation

Tessa Walker asked the groups to draw up a list of facts and questions around each of the characters, in order to start interrogating how you might go about constructing them. From this list, each group was then asked to decide on three facts and three questions to share about this character that feel revealing.

Examples of these included:

Antler

She has a little sister

What is her relationship like with her sister?

Her mum cries

What's going on at home?

Her dad has taken up smoking

Why does she climb the tree?

Oil

He started chewing his fingers this year

Why does he start chewing his fingers?

Antler sent him a weird text

What does he think about Antler?

He lent Blister a fiver this week, doesn't give Blister his phone

What is the history between him and Blister?

Crystal

She kisses Finn

Why is she drawn to Finn?

She sends texts that send Antler off

What is the relationship between Crystal and Blister?

She is only a year older than Antler

Why is Crystal so much more confident than Antler even though she is younger?

Skin

Skin hangs out with Blister

Would she have killed the dog without Blister being there?

She has a brother

Why does her brother say she has to protect herself?

She is involved in killing of the dog

Does she genuinely like Blister?

Blister

Blister is dyslexic

Why is he so interested in Oil and Antler?

His brother is insecure

What is his home life dynamic and is this why he spends time at the park?

He kills a dog

Is Skin his cousin?

Finn

She hangs out with Blister for protection

Why doesn't Finn step in at an earlier point, why was she silent during the killing of the dog?

She's got a little sister and brothers

Where was her family?

Finn never said anything to anybody

Who are her family?

Desk

He is a carer for his mum

What is going on at home/home life?

He doesn't have much money

Why does nobody seem to know him?

He thinks protests should be public not private

Does he ever find his glove?

Tessa Walker advised that starting your rehearsal process with questions can focus your character discovery: many of the questions are around what the conditions are at home and relationships with family. It would be a good idea to do some work with Crystal and Finn together – so they can make these decisions and discoveries together. The more people know about their characters, the more the text can come alive.

This exercise is great to use with young people: facts give structure and a jumping-off point for the questions.

Because the script gives lots of answers, Walker suggested it as a great place to start before asking questions that you *don't* have the answer to.

Tessa Walker recommended hot seating as a useful exercise for the young people in order to start filling in the gaps that might not be answered entirely by the script. Hot seating is an exercise that requires them to answer questions in the first person as their characters in improvisational response/role-play style, using conjecture from a foundation of knowledge informed by facts in the script.

Tessa Walker also suggested that it is useful to get a sense of the characters' home lives. Taking Blister as an example, you can understand his character around the history of his home life. He can be the same age and social class as your actor who plays him, but you can start weaving the story of what is behind the character with imagination and creative licence.

Question and answer with Stef Smith

Q: What is the thinking behind the abstract names?
SS: There is something about *Remote* being very specific and very open – names can often locate people either by class or geography. Giving abstract names leaves it open as to who these young people are. The hope is also to allow a discovery to take place for the young people, to find why their characters are called what they are called.

Q: Do you have a character that you particularly connect with?
SS: I like all of them. All of them and none of them are me! I really enjoyed writing Desk – they are not a character I would usually write!

Q: Are the characters fixed in their gender assignment?
SS: If you can follow the gender identities written in the play, that would be amazing. That said, if the ability of the young people doesn't match the genders, or there is too much of a challenge in whatever practical sense, then of course change it. The priority is staging the play, and it is at your discretion.

Q: Is it important that Finn and Crystal are the same sex?
SS: I am interested in a same-sex relationship on stage that isn't necessarily the centre of the play, but stays light and playful. It doesn't have to carry the trauma and adversity that we might associate with previous narratives around same-sex relationships, so it feels important that it remains same sex.

Q: I have young people identifying as non-binary, using they/them pronouns – would this be OK in terms of gender reassignment?
SS: Yes, absolutely.

Q: Are we OK to change outdated terms Twitter/Facebook for more current platforms?
SS: Yes! Updating to whatever is relevant to your young people is fine by me!

Q: Why were you drawn to the park and an outside setting?
SS: There is something in the open air that invites a different sort of thinking, and I'm interested in that. As a kid I spent a lot of time outside, and with lots of young people's stories set in schools, I wanted to explore a different environment and a different way of thinking.

I'm also interested in the atmosphere outside – the weather, the cold, the movement – that can feel very alive on stage. There is also a real danger to the outside; anything could happen in a park. As soon as you place it in a domestic setting, you change the stakes of that.

There is also a wildness to the outdoors. Somewhere wild, natural, elemental and it could also be late by the time the play ends. The passing of time is something you can do in an open-air space.

Q: Is it OK to reference current political events?
SS: Absolutely. In terms of production, and references, go for your life! The more alive and relevant it feels to the young people, the better.

Q: With the dashed/unassigned lines, did you imagine them only said by one person?
SS: That is the artistic decision of the director, it is up to you how you keep the clarity of who is who. I didn't write it thinking 'all these lines belong to one person'; it was much more a stream of consciousness.

Q: A question about Blister: towards the end he starts to show his intelligence and then he is shunned right at the last moment. Could you talk about that a little?
SS: Blister is particularly complicated. When you're young it is easy to attach yourself to an image, or set of qualities as an identity, and sometimes you might not get an

opportunity to reinvent yourself until much later. It is interesting that he did something years ago, and it followed him. And now he has built his own character around that moment. The play is about the capacity for change, and for Blister there is a flicker of that at the end but it is not yet fully formed. There is longer to go for him on his journey.

From a workshop led by Tessa Walker
With notes by Sammy Glover

Superglue
by Tim Crouch

Tim Crouch is an Obie award-winning playwright, director and theatre-maker. He was an actor before starting to write and he still performs in much of his work. Plays include *Truth's a Dog Must to Kennel* (Lyceum, Edinburgh); *Total Immediate Collective Imminent Terrestrial Salvation* (National Theatre of Scotland, Royal Court and tour); *I, Cinna* (*the poet*) (Royal Shakespeare Company and Unicorn Theatre, London); *Beginners* (Unicorn Theatre, London); *Adler & Gibb* (Royal Court, Center Theatre Group and tour); *what happens to the hope at the end of the evening* (Almeida Festival and tour); *The Author* (Royal Court and tour); *An Oak Tree* (Traverse Theatre, National Theatre, Off-Broadway and tour); *I, Malvolio, I, Peaseblossom, I, Caliban, and I, Banquo* (Brighton Festival and tour); *ENGLAND – a play for galleries* (Traverse Theatre/The Fruitmarket Gallery and tour); *Shopping for Shoes* (National Theatre schools tour) and *My Arm* (Traverse Theatre and tour).

As a director: *House Mother Normal* (New Perspectives/Brighton Festival); *Beginners* (Unicorn Theatre); *Peat* (Ark, Dublin); *Jeramee, Hartleby and Oooglemore* (Unicorn Theatre, London); *The Complete Deaths* (Spymonkey/Brighton Festival and tour); *The Taming of the Shrew, I, Cinna* (*the poet*) and *King Lear* (Royal Shakespeare Company). Tim created and co-wrote *Don't Forget the Driver*, a six-part series for BBC2, which won Best TV Comedy at the Venice TV awards, 2019.

Other awards include: Writers Guild of Great Britain, Best Play for Young Audiences (*Beginners*); John Whiting Award, Total Theatre Award (*The Author*); Scotsman Fringe First, Total Theatre & Herald Archangel Awards (*ENGLAND*), Prix Italia for Best Adaptation in Radio Drama (*My Arm*).

Tim is published by Methuen Books.

timcrouchtheatre.co.uk
@thistimcrouch.

The year 2078, I will celebrate my 75th birthday. If I have children maybe they will spend that day with me. Maybe they will ask me about you. Maybe they will ask why you didn't do anything while there still was time to act.

Greta Thunberg

Characters

Lily
Tam
Morgan
Mattie
Hadley
Reece
Clark
Joe

Notes

The characters in this play are all elderly. The actors in this play are all young.

The young actors play the elderly characters without playing old. No mimicry. No putting on voices. No funny walks. No talcum powder in their hair.

The young actors are themselves. They play the truth of an older character's situation.

The audience's understanding of this form happens in their head. The realisation comes not from a change in those young people's performances. There is no change. It comes from the text and the context. It also comes from the presence of real elderly people who gradually populate the stage.

This is the story of an elders' climate action group – performed by young actors.

The young actors' clothes are smart but slightly ill-fitting – as though they haven't worn them for a long time. Ties and overcoats. An incongruous feel. Young people who are not accustomed to dressing smartly.

If music and/or sound is used, use it subtly. I think it could be beautiful.

An empty stage except for eight chairs spaced out across it.

As the audience enter:

An elderly woman sitting on one of the chairs – facing out. Still.

*A young female actor (**Lily**) stands at the front of the stage and looks out, waiting.*

*Both **Lily** and the older woman wear an identical (and identifying) article of clothing.*

*When the audience is in, **Lily** speaks to the audience.*

1. LILY

Lily   Early.

Look.

No one else here.

No other bugger's early, are they, look.

Look.

Always early.

Premature baby, my mum said.

Can't kick the habit.

2. TAM

Tam *holding a furled banner, gently catching their breath.*

Lily *oscillates between super-still and super-wired. There's something not quite right about her. She's funny but as you begin to understand her state she's more devastating than funny.*

A sense that **Lily** *has been waiting for* **Tam** *to get their breath for a minute or more.*

Lily   OK now? OK?

Tam   A minute.

Lily *watches* **Tam** *get their breath back.*

Lily   Now?

Now?

Tam   That's some hill.

Lily   Yes, sir. (**Tam** *can be any gender.* **Lily** *still says 'sir'.*)

Tam   Worth it for this, though.

They look out.

The low winter sun breaks from behind a cloud.

Stillness.

Tam   The dead get all the best views.

A core of gentle sadness running through it all. Expansive.
When there is space between the lines, honour it.
Things can happen in that space.
When there is no space between the lines, things can move.
Fits and starts.
An exercise in rhythm, holding on and going deeper.

Tam   Anyone else?

Lily   I was here first.

Tam   When does it start?

Lily   –

Tam   When did you get here?

Lily   I'm always early. Premature baby, my mum said, can't kick the habit.

Tam   I remember your mum.

They embrace during:

Lily   You fancied my mum,

Tam   Lil.

Lily   You perv.

Tam   You thought I did.

Lily   You did.

Tam   I didn't.

Lily   You did.

Tam   Lily.

Lily   You did.

Perv.

The embrace ends. They stand back and look at each other.

Tam   I fancied *you*.

Lily   Bloody weirdo.

Tam   You never noticed.

Alright?

Lily   You bet.

Tam   You look –

Lily   New penny!

Tam   I mean – Thought you weren't coming / thought you –

Lily   Wouldn't miss this.

Tam   No.

Lily   Wild horses.

Tam   Yes.

Lily   One of us.

Tam   She was.

Lily   One of us.

Tam   The best of us.

Lily   The best.

Tam   The best.

It hits them both in different ways.

They look out.

Tam   Poor Mags.

Lily (*deadly serious*)   Poor old Maggie Moo-Moo did a poo-poo on the loo-loo.

Lily*'s erratic behaviour is new to* **Tam**. *It takes them a moment to absorb it and adjust.*

Quickfire:

Tam   On your own?

Lily   Yes.

Tam   That's OK, is it, I / mean –

Lily   I ran away.

Tam   Did you, now?

Lily   From home.

Tam   Right.

Lily   Took some pills and ran away.

Tam   OK.

Lily   Hopped it.

Tam   Right.

Lily   Legged it.

Tam   Nice.

Lily   Yes.

Tam   OK.

Lily   Took a taxi.

Tam   Is that right.

Lily   On my own took a taxi.

Tam (*firm*)   Lily.

Lily   What?

They search each other for different signs of recognition.

Lily   Did *you* take a taxi?

Tam   I'm sorry to disappoint you.

Lily   How d'you get here, then? Fly, did you? Fly in a helibopter, was it, well?

Tam   I came on the bus.

Lily   Bus?

Tam   I have a bus pass, Lily. I use the bus.

Lily   Yes.

A kestrel hovers above them.

Lily *struggles for coherence.*

Lily   Now you're up here.

Tam   I am, Lil.

Lily   On my own, yes, now you're up here.

Tam   Yes.

Lily   With me.

Tam   Yes.

They look out. They breathe the air.

Tam   D'your family know where you are?

Lily   Fuck 'em.

An elderly person slowly walks onto the stage and sits in a chair. They sit and face out. They do not interact with the young actors. They sit in silence and stillness.

This elderly person is, I suppose, the 'real' character of **Tam**. *This is what* **Tam** *would look like in the real world. (Just as the elderly woman sitting on stage from the start is the 'real'* **Lily**.*) This older person should be the same gender as the young actor playing* **Tam**. *The presence of these elderly people throws a reflection onto the performances of the young actors. They don't do anything. They sit in stillness. They are metaphysical. They are like the younger actors' daemons. They are smartly* *dressed. They wear approximately the same clothes as their younger avatars. Their onstage presence alone bleeds into the life of the young.*

Stillness.

Lily   They deeped a dug hole.

Tam   They did, didn't they, Lil.

Lily   Brought some seeds to go in.

Tam   Nice / thought.

Lily   When she gets here.

Tam   Yes.

Lily   When we tuck her in.

Tam   We will, / won't we.

Lily   Tuck-up time for tinies.

The seeds.

Daisies.

These seeds are daisies.

Will be daisies. Are daisies. Which? Will. One day. If things still grow.

Tam   If things still / grow.

Lily   Give-me-your-answer-do.

The sun goes behind the clouds. The temperature drops.

Lily *gets some clarity but struggles to express it.*

Lily   What was it was it like what they said it was what was it like?

Tam   It was a shit-show, Lillian.

A beat.

Lily   I would have been there.

Tam   I know.

Lily   Took a taxi.

Tam   Yes.

Lily   No one else here.

Tam   No.

Lily   What *was* it like?

Tam   Some idiot threw a stone. The horses came in and the barriers gave way.

Lily   She got smashed up.

Tam   Her heart gave out, Lil.

Lily *tries to process what this means.*

Lily   Anyone I know?

Tam   Who?

Lily   Some idiot.

Tam   Have a guess.

Lily   One of us?

Tam   Sadly.

Lily   Are we friends?

Tam   Yes, Lily. I'm Tam, d'you remember? We were at school together.

Lily (*deadly serious*)   You need to sort your face you do you messy pup wipe it with a hanky-panky.

Imperceptibly, **Tam** *'s heart breaks a little.*

Stillness.

Lily   I would have been there, you know that, don't you, do you, do you?

Tam   You were best off out / of it.

Lily   I still write letters.

Tam   You do.

Lily   Can still write.

Tam   Just as / important.

Lily   I write.

Tam   I know you / do.

Lily   Campaigns.

Tam   Yes.

Lily   I write-write-write-write.

Tam   That makes a difference, you know it does.

Lily   Look at the state of you, bloody weirdo.

Tam   It's a sad day, Lil, Mags is dead.

Quickfire:

Lily   I could have stood in the way.

Tam   Don't think / about it.

Lily   Could've stepped in between.

Tam   She lost her / footing.

Lily   Lost –

Tam   The shock of it.

Lily   Maybe it didn't happen.

Tam   I was there, Lily.

Lily   You were there.

Tam   At the protest.

Lily   With the horses.

Tam   Yes.

Lily   And now you're up here.

Tam   Here I am.

Lily   With me.

Tam   Early.

Lily   I was here first.

Tam   You were.

Lily   A premature baby.

Tam   I know.

A beat.

You going to sing today?

Lily   Will I?

Tam   If you want to.

Lily   Then yes.

Tam   I look forward to it.

Lily   You going to sing, buddy?

Tam   If I can.

Stillness.

You up for giving us a hand with this? (*The banner.*)

Lily   What's the plan?

Tam   There'll be photographers, Lily.

Lily   No, I don't think I can, you see, no, no, no.

Tam   That's fine.

Lily   I was the first one here.

Tam   That means a lot.

Lily   Sorry, I'm a bit all over the place.

Tam   It's good to see you.

Lily   What's your name again?

Tam *unfurls their banner and places it.*

'NO NATURE NO FUTURE'.

3. MORGAN

Lily *is upstage, amongst the chairs, in a world of her own. She can sit on empty chairs if she wants. Her relationship with life and death and nature is fluid.*

The empty chairs contain a sense of the trees they were made from, the trees they represent in the play and the human form they were designed to accommodate. In other words, they're just plain wooden chairs on an empty stage.

The main design feature of Superglue *is in the banners which become the provocations around which this play exists. They can be as big/beautiful/colourful/ simple as you like.*

Morgan *is with* **Tam** *at the graveside. They both look at* **Tam** *'s banner.*

Morgan   They won't be happy (*about the banner*).

Tam   *I'm* not happy.

Morgan   No one's happy.

They embrace.

Morgan   Who's coming?

Tam   Who's *not* coming?

Morgan   Jesus. (*A quiet expression of disbelief that everyone's coming.*)

Tam   He'd have some explaining to do.

Morgan   Who?

Tam   Jesus.

Morgan   I'd ask for my money back.

They take it all in.

> You spend your whole life saying there's no god and everyone's fine with that and says well done you, and aren't you something, you and your independent mind, so inspiring and rational. And then you die and everyone's 'GOD!' / 'GOD!'

Tam   GOD! / GOD!

Morgan   GOD!

Etc. (playfully).

Their voices echo through the woodland. Birds in the upper branches take flight.

The energy dissipates into the air.

Morgan   Yeah.

Tam   That.

Morgan   Yeah.

Tam   Yeah.

Morgan   Like we're incapable of possessing opinions of our own.

Tam   Yeah.

Morgan   Like who wouldn't believe in an invisible being who causes indescribable suffering?

Tam   And then judges everyone for no reason whatsoever.

Morgan   Yeah.

Tam   Yeah.

An elderly person walks onto the stage and sits in a chair. They sit and face out.

This person is, I suppose, something like the 'real' character of **Morgan**. *This is what the character of* **Morgan** *looks like. Wearing similar clothes to young* **Morgan**. *Smart clothes.*

Morgan   Got stopped coming here, dressed like this, asked if I knew where I was going. Yes, I said, yes, officer, yes. 'Do you need a hand?' he said.

Tam   You're on some database.

Morgan   I said, thanks, officer, I can look after myself.

Tam   Face recognition.

Morgan   Followed me for the next five minutes.

Tam   Jesus.

Morgan   Jesus.

You go in a shop and they start staring at you.

Tam   You go into a pub.

Stillness.

A reminder.

The performances give no indication that the characters are any different in age from the actors performing them.

4. MATTIE

Mattie *has made it up the hill. A furled banner in their hand.*

Between each 'scene', the configuration of the actors can change; some time has passed, the nature of the waiting has altered slightly.

Mattie   Killer this hill.

Morgan   They should have a thing –

Mattie   Didn't know this was here.

Tam   No.

Morgan   – a chair lift thing –

Tam   It's beautiful.

Morgan   – Funicular!

Tam   It's the knees.

Mattie   Don't talk about knees.

Morgan   Too much football.

Tam   A misspent youth.

Mattie   A *spent* youth.

A gust of wind.

Mattie   I'm down by the chapel.

Tam   You drove?

Mattie   So?

Morgan (*with a twinkle*)   Shameful.

Mattie   I still have a licence.

Tam   That's not the point.

Mattie   To the shops and stuff.

Morgan (*with a twinkle*)   Traitor.

Mattie   And if I were to offer either of you a lift back?

Morgan (*deadpan*)   Then I would have to accept.

They each embrace.

A moment of connection.

Tam   Lily's here.

Mattie   I thought she wasn't able to –

Morgan   She's up by the trees.

Tam   Ran away from home, she says.

Mattie   She did?

Tam Ran metaphorically.

Morgan They'll be looking for her.

Tam She said 'fuck them'.

Morgan Lily said 'fuck'?

Tam She did.

Morgan That's a first.

Mattie She alright?

Tam No.

Morgan Medicated.

Tam Yes.

Morgan Saw it with my dad.

Mattie I remember your dad.

Morgan Swore like a docker towards the end.

Tam So / cruel.

Morgan Funny.

Mattie (*calling*) Lil!

No response.

Mattie Here we are then.

Tam You alright standing?

Morgan You alright patronising me?

Amazed I still fit this stupid / thing.

Mattie I've shrunk.

Tam I think we look good.

Morgan Like gangsters.

Mattie Weekend gangsters.

Stillness.

Morgan *takes out a hip flask and drinks from it.*

The flask gets passed around.

Mattie   You didn't want to be at the chapel?

Tam   It's for the family.

Mattie   So?

Morgan   What would they do?

Tam   You got the email.

Morgan   They can't tell us.

Mattie   They think we'll kick off.

Morgan   I feel like kicking off.

Mattie   She spent more time with us than she ever did with them.

Tam   Family gets its claws into you in / the end.

Mattie   No escape.

Morgan   'You eating properly? You going out in that? Got your keys?'

Tam   Like we're / kids.

Morgan   Idiots.

Mattie   Kidiots.

Nice to get away from it all.

Everything feels hopeless.

Morgan   This is meant to be the happiest time.

Tam   What?

Morgan   This age. Our age. In the surveys, we're meant to be happiest.

Mattie   Who says that?

Morgan   Not if you're dead. Not happy if you're dead.

Mattie   Not anything.

Morgan *suddenly overwhelmed.* **Tam** *gives them a hug.*

Tam   Come on.

An elderly person enters slowly and sits on one of the chairs. This, I suppose, is what the character of **Mattie** *looks like. Stillness.*

Mattie See the van down there?

Tam Local news.

Mattie There'll be others, though, won't there, the papers.

Tam She'd want this, would she?

Mattie That's what we were there for, to raise awareness.

Tam She didn't die for nothing.

Morgan Everyone dies for nothing.

Tam Not true.

Lily *comes down to join the others.*

Mattie Hi, Lily.

Lily I brought some seeds.

Mattie Didn't think we'd see you today.

Lily You in the gang, then?

Mattie It's Mattie. We used to paint banners, Lily, remember?

Lily These are future (*the seeds*).

Stillness.

Mattie Are they coming up, then?

Tam A few.

Mattie Three thirty, I thought.

Tam It's late.

Morgan It's going to get messy.

Tam It's already messy.

Morgan It's like we killed her.

Tam That's what they think.

Mattie They can't stop us being here.

Morgan Let them try. .

A siren in the distance.

Lily   The nodding oxeye bends before the wind –

Mattie   Nice, Lil.

Lily   Learnt that at school. Can't member what I had for breakfast, but member that.

The sun breaks out again.

Mattie   You still living at home, then, Lily?

Lily   Am I?

Morgan   You're with your daughter, aren't you, Lily?

Mattie   That's nice. She looks after you?

Lily   Are we murderers?

Tam   You wouldn't murder anything, would you, Lil?

Lily   Meat is murder.

Tam   Exactly.

Lily   Am I in trouble?

Morgan   We're all in trouble, Lil.

Lily   I mean am I though?

Mattie   We did nothing wrong.

Morgan   Most of us.

Tam   All of us.

Mattie   Let's not start that again.

Tam   I hope he has the sense to stay at home.

Morgan   He won't show his face today.

Tam   He got the message.

Mattie   He knows he's not welcome.

Lily   Who?

Tam   Joe, Lil. Remember Joe?

Lily   Bad boy.

Mattie   Bad boy.

Lily   Are we communists?

Tam   We're just trying to save the world.

Lily   Like Batman?

Tam   Like Batman.

Mattie   You warm enough in that?

Tam   Like a summer's day.

Mattie   Isn't it.

Morgan   It's all wrong.

Mattie *unfurls their banner and places it.*

'TIME IS RUNNING OUT'.

5. HADLEY

Hadley *has arrived. A furled banner in their hand.*

They all look at each other.
Silence.
Broken by:

Hadley   I look like a prick.

Tam   You look fine.

Mattie   It's respectful.

Hadley   To look like a prick?

Mattie   In some cultures.

Hadley   Name them.

They embrace.

Tam   It's not about us.

Morgan   We all look like pricks.

Lily   They say never put things round your neck and so as if you could get strangled by it, and then they make you wear these, what is it, like a noose, it is, round and round and you're, argh, and that's supposed to be smart, is it, smartly does it, think you look so something, a noose around your neck!

Hadley   Hi, Lil.

Lily   Think you look so smart?

Hadley   I think I look like a prick.

An older person walks slowly onto the stage and takes their place on a chair. This is what **Hadley** *looks like.*

Hadley   I thought I'd missed it.

Tam   They're running late.

Hadley *places a banner:*

'SYSTEM CHANGE NOT CLIMATE CHANGE'.

6. REECE

Reece *is there, with a furled banner.*

Lily *upstage among the chairs – studying their occupants. The older do not look at* **Lily**. *They remain facing out.*

Reece *embraces everyone (except* **Lily***) in silence.*

Reece   I'm going to too many funerals.

Lily (*shouted*)   You can see the sea.

Reece   How do you know where anyone is?

Hadley   That's the whole point.

Tam   Just trees.

Lily (*shouted*)   You can see the back of your own head if you look hard enough.

Reece   I'd want something.

Hadley   Why?

Reece   You'd know where to find me.

Morgan You wouldn't be there.

Reece My remains.

Hadley Why?

Reece A place, I mean.

Mattie Remember you in here (*head*).

Hadley Or here (*heart*).

Tam Or in a tree.

Lily (*by a chair with an older person in*) This is a birch.

Tam They'd know with a tree.

Morgan When did you last visit your great-grandparents' grave?

Hadley They're just stones on the ground with the names of people nobody remembers.

Reece I love an old graveyard.

Tam It's vanity.

Mattie And you're dead so what's it to you.

Morgan When you're dead you're dead.

Lily (*calls*) All birches.

Hadley Exactly.

Morgan So, when did you last visit your great grandparents' grave.

Reece I suppose.

Tam When did you last look at a tree?

*They all look up (except **Lily**).*

Tam Crows.

Reece Rooks.

Morgan Same thing.

Reece No.

Morgan Yes.

Reece Rooks have a –

Mattie What?

Reece Paler –

Tam   What?

Reece   You know.

Tam   What?

Reece   Lips.

Tam   Lips?

Reece   Not lips.

Mattie   No.

Reece   My brain.

Morgan   They're beaks.

Reece   Beaks.

Morgan   Beaks.

Reece   Beaks *are* lips.

Morgan   Bollocks.

Reece   Bird's lips.

Morgan   They don't have lips.

Mattie   Hard lips.

Tam   Not good for kissing.

Mattie   Give us a kiss, clack-clack!

Tam   Clack clack!

Laughter. Into reflection.

An elderly person takes their place on a chair. This, I suppose, is what the character of **Reece** *looks like.* **Lily** *is by this person's chair and looks at them. (They do* not *look at* **Lily**.*)*

Lily   This is a hornbeam.

Hadley   Look up and I fall over.

Morgan   The state of us.

Reece   Amazed I'm still alive.

Lily *is by the elderly woman who was on the stage at the start (***Elderly Lily***).*

Lily   This will be me. Is me. Look. Look!

Reece   Hardly recognised Lil.

Mattie   She still at home?

Tam   On and off, she said. Good days and bad.

Morgan   Pretty bad by the looks of it.

Tam   I think this is a good one.

Mattie   Really?

Tam   She's on new medication.

Reece   She was sharp.

Tam   Sharpest of us all.

Morgan   Tragic.

Tam   Yes.

Morgan   The drugs don't work.

Hadley   What about her family?

Mattie   Have you met her family?

Hadley (*calls*)   Lil – how's your family?

Lily (*by a chair with an elderly person in*)   Another hornbeam.

Mattie   They're dicks.

Hadley   You met them?

Mattie   Her daughter works for an investment bank. Drives a BMW.

Tam   Flies around the world. Never lifts a finger for her.

Mattie   She just pays for the carers.

Reece   Poor Lil.

Morgan   Nothing worse than realising you don't like your own family.

The flask is passed around.

Tam   They're overrunning.

Mattie   This is wrong.

Morgan   All of this is wrong.

Tam   Don't set me off.

Lily *returns to the forestage.*

Reece   Alright, Lily?

Lily   These are how we all will be. Look.

Reece   Do you think?

Lily   I can see it.

Tam   You can, Lil.

Reece   You can.

Lily   You know the best time to plant a tree?

Reece   No, Lil.

Lily   Fifty years ago.

Tam   We blew it, didn't we, Lil.

Lily   We fucking blew it all up, you weirdos.

Mattie   Lily!

Morgan   Is anyone going to say anything?

Tam   Not me.

Hadley   Couldn't keep it together.

Lily   I've written it down.

Mattie   You've been great, / Lily.

Lily   I write-write-write.

Tam   You're the writer.

Hadley   Our best.

Lily   Something to say so so I so I so I write-write.

Tam   Something you want to say today, is it, Lil?

Lily   In my pocket here.

Tam   Have you?

Lily   In my paper.

Lily takes a piece of paper from her pocket.

Morgan   Cool, Lil.

Lily   Can't speak it with this fuzz in my head but my write-write-write and it sings like a birdy.

Morgan   Then you should let your birdy sing.

Lily   Make the bastards listen.

Morgan   Absolutely.

Tam   We'll wait till Mags is here, right, Lil.

Reece   I'm relying on this:

Reece unfurls their banner and places it.

'END OIL NOW'.

They admire it.

Lily   Who am I again?

Morgan   You're Lily.

Lily   And what are we doing here?

Morgan   We're here to bury Mags.

7. CLARK

Clark is there. The space is filling with older and younger.

Morgan   You bottled out. You bottled out!

Clark   No, I didn't.

Morgan   Yes, you bloody bottled out!

Mattie   Mags took over!

Clark   No she bloody didn't!

Tam   You have a selective memory.

Clark   Bollocks.

A pause.

I had psoriasis.

Morgan   So?

Clark   Do you know what psoriasis is?

Hadley   Yes.

Clark   Do you?

Hadley   Yes.

Clark   Really?

Mattie   We all know!

Clark   It flared up.

Morgan   Balls it did.

Clark   It did.

Reece   Balls.

Morgan   Glue your *balls* to the pavement.

Clark   You ever had psoriasis?

Tam   Eczema.

Clark   Not the same.

Tam   A bit.

Clark   Not the same!

Morgan   So?

Clark   It wouldn't've stuck.

Hadley   On the palms?

Clark   Yes.

Hadley   Never heard of psoriasis on the palms.

Clark   It gets flaky.

Reece   The palms?

Clark   Peely.

Morgan   It's called *super*glue.

Clark   But it would've flaked off.

Morgan   Nonsense.

Clark   I'd have put my hands down and it would've flaked off.

Morgan   You bottled out.

Reece   No one gets flaky palms.

Clark   Yes, they do.

Hadley   You said it was your knees.

Clark   No, I didn't.

Mattie   That's why you bottled out.

Hadley   Couldn't get / down –

Mattie   Couldn't move quick enough.

Clark   No, / I didn't.

Hadley   Couldn't get under the cordon.

Clark   *You* could have done it.

Hadley   It wasn't my job.

Tam   It wasn't Mags' job.

Hadley   I didn't have the glue.

Mattie   How did *she* get the glue?

Hadley   I had the D lock.

Morgan   You didn't even do that.

Hadley   I couldn't get to the gates.

Tam   No wonder the planet's dying.

Mattie   Can we not argue, please?

An elderly person enters and sits on one of the chairs. This is what the character of **Clark** *looks like.*

Clark   We're not arguing, we're reminiscing.

Reece   Good times.

Clark   The best.

Tam   Cold when the sun goes in.

Morgan   Have my scarf.

Tam   I'm alright.

Mattie   Catch our death.

The flask.

Hadley   This is getting stupid now.

Clark   Are you sure this is the right place?

Tam   There's only one woodland cemetery.

Morgan   Who did they dig the hole for?

Stillness. A shiver in the air.

Reece   You and that D lock, I remember.

Hadley   Are we too old for all that now?

Tam   Never too old.

Clark   She was something, wasn't she, Mags.

Morgan   Fearless.

Mattie   The look on that policeman's face.

8. JOE

An elderly man enters and sits. This is what the character of **Joe** *looks like.*

The eight chairs are all occupied now.

Young **Joe** *is there, a furled banner in his hands. (He might have been there a while and we didn't notice.) He keeps his distance from the group – amongst the trees.*

Tam   We didn't think we'd see you today.

Reece   We thought you'd stay away, Joe.

Lily   They said that shame would stick to you like shit to your shoe.

Tam   Lil.

Lily   They said you betrayed the movement.

Tam   Lily.

Lily   They said you should still be in jail.

Joe   I never went to jail, Lily.

Lily   Yes!

Joe   A police cell is not jail, Lil. Most of us here have been in a police cell. You've been in a police cell, Lil.

Lily   Have I?

Clark   You should leave, Joe, before they bring her from the chapel.

Mattie   Her family are here, Joe.

Reece   They'll know who you are.

Tam   Seriously, Joe.

Joe   I've come to pay my respects.

Hadley   Do you think that's appropriate?

Joe   Appropriate to show respect? Always.

Hadley   After what you did?

Joe   What did I do, exactly?

Clark   You started it.

Joe   Are we kids?

Tam   Joe.

Joe   Are we kids?

Reece   We should talk about this some other time.

An elderly person stands up from their chair.

The is the beginning of the final phase of the play. A slow merging of the older people into the action.

Tam   Three thirty, they said.

Joe   Four.

Tam   Three thirty.

Joe   Three thirty at the chapel. Four at the grave. This is the grave.

Tension.

Lily   Hold my hand.

Tam *holds* **Lily***'s hand.*

An elderly person stands up from their chair.

Joe   I didn't go armed.

Mattie   You threw a stone.

Joe   It wasn't premeditated.

Reece   Please, Joe.

Joe   You scared to have the conversation?

Morgan   It's Mags' funeral.

A beat.

Joe   Cobble shouldn't have been loose.

Tam   Joe.

Joe   Blame the council who left a loose cobble.

Clark   I can't believe this.

Joe   I didn't throw it very hard. Can't throw very hard. Not these shoulders.

Tam   You broke a window.

Joe   One window.

Tam   We talked about this.

Mattie   You were violent.

Reece   You could have hit someone.

Mattie   We're non-violent.

Tam   This is a non-violent group, Joe.

Joe   We can't afford non-violence any more.

Clark   You make us as bad as them.

Tam   Men.

An elderly person stands up from their chair.

Joe   They made twenty billion pounds last year.

Morgan   We know, Joe.

Joe   Profit.

Reece   Not now.

Joe   From fossil fuel. That's five billion trees they could have planted. Twenty wind farms. They could halt the crisis. But instead they give the money to their shareholders and they rob our grandchildren of their future. I think in that instance it's OK to be angry, don't you?

Tam   We were protesting against destruction and you destroyed something.

Mattie   We don't rise to violence, Joe.

Joe   Their violence is twenty billion times greater than mine. You just can't see it, that's all. It's a flood, a drought, a fire. A fucking asthma attack.

Clark   We're here for Mags, / Joe –

Joe   There's a representative down there – paying his respects to her family – and that's OK, but not me? He's allowed to but not us? Him not us? They haven't arrested *him*. Kept *him* in a cell. Charged *him* with criminal damage. One window.

An elderly person stands up from their chair.

A stand-off.

Joe   For fuck's sake.

Tam   Mags died.

Joe   Tens of thousands of people die every year from what those companies do.

Hadley   Our friend died.

Joe   But not because of me.

Tam   Yes.

Joe   I didn't kill Mags.

Clark   You threw a stone.

Joe   Not at Mags.

Reece   But you caused her death.

Joe   The police caused her death.

Mattie   No.

Joe   They were disproportionate in their action.

Mattie   You could have hit someone.

Joe   It was a window. I hit a window in a building. A building full of planet-murdering oil executives who say it's nothing to do with them. Windows have no feelings. They don't get scared. Their hearts don't stop when a ton of police horse bears down on them. The police were protecting the interests of the murderers and their property, not us.

Hadley   They were doing their job.

Tam   When did violent protest ever achieve anything?

Joe   Are we really going to go here again?

An elderly person stands up from their chair.

Joe   We get nowhere. We sit down in the street. We stop the traffic. We piss some drivers off. But then we have to get up again and everything continues the same. The cars keep coming.

Mattie   It takes time.

Joe   We don't have any time.

Hadley   The younger generation.

Joe   We can't leave it all to them, can we? Oh, we're past it now, dead soon, nothing we can do, leave it to the young people. What kind of message does that give? We were the ones who messed it all up for them. We have to think beyond our time.

An elderly person stands up from their chair.

Tam   That's all they'll remember now.

Joe   What?

Tam   Your violent action.

Mattie   Mags' death.

Hadley   You changed the story. It was meant to be about climate emergency and you changed it to violence.

Joe   Climate change *is* violence. It's always been about violence.

Morgan   You have to let us grieve.

Joe   Our house is on fire.

Tam   Joe.

Joe   Our house is on fire.

Hadley   I wish Mags was here.

The elderly person who came on with **Joe** *gets up from their chair and takes the banner from* **Joe***. They start to place the banner – together. The young actor playing* **Joe** *helps them.*

Banner:

'OUR PROBLEM IS CIVIL OBEDIENCE'.

The banner is placed. **Joe** *and* **Older Joe** *stand by it.*

Only one elderly person is still sitting – **Older Lily** *– the woman sitting from the start.*

Morgan   Four o'clock.

Tam   The old gang.

Mattie   The falling-apart-gang.

Hadley   Still strong.

Tam   You think?

Mattie   Mass extinction.

Hadley   And Mags gone.

Tam   Mags is gone.

Morgan   What a mess.

Reece   I said I wouldn't cry.

Tam   Here.

Tam *offers* **Reece** *a tissue.*

Reece   I'm alright.

Tam   Take it for later.

*An older person (***Older Reece***) steps forward and takes the tissue.* **Reece** *and this* **Older Reece** *stand together at the graveside.*

Daylight is fading.

Hadley   It's when I see the coffin.

Mattie   That's when you know it's real.

Tam   Yeah.

Morgan   Think about yourself in it, don't you?

Tam   Not long now, eh.

Morgan   Not long for any of us.

Tam   They wanted brass handles.

Clark   The family?

Tam   The whole thing, marble angels.

Morgan   She'd have had a fit.

Clark   The fight goes on.

Morgan   Just wrap me in a cloth and turn the earth over. Promise me.

Hadley   Wind getting up.

Mattie   Here.

Mattie *offers a shawl to* **Hadley**. *An older person steps forward and takes it – wraps it round their shoulders.* **Hadley** *and that older person stand together.*

Tam   They're coming up.

Morgan   Behave yourself, people

Mattie   Dignity, everyone.

Tam   Alright, Lil?

Lily   Maggie moo.

Tam   That's right, Lil.

Morgan   Maggie Moo's coming home.

Mattie   I can't bear this.

Tam   Want a hug?

Mattie   Yes. Yes, please.

The older person who came in with **Mattie** *(***Older Mattie***) steps in and* **Tam** *hugs them. A held moment.*

Mattie *and* **Older Mattie** *stand side by side near the grave.*

Lily *takes the folded paper out of her pocket.*

Lily   Time now?

Tam   Wait till they're here, Lil.

Lily   When they've tucked her in.

Clark   That's right.

Tam   And then we'll sing for her.

Morgan   Sing her on her way.

Lily *puts the paper away.*

Clark   See the cameras?

Morgan   Put on a good show.

Clark   Legs like jelly.

Tam   Be strong.

Older Clark *steps up to young* **Clark** *and takes their hand. They stand together.*

Morgan   What would Mags have done?

Tam   She'd have gone to the chapel.

Morgan   She'd have dug this hole herself.

Tam   Her bare hands.

Morgan   She'd have thrown the stone.

Tam   You think?

Morgan   I know.

Tam   Sometimes everything is just too complicated.

Morgan   Revolution is hard.

Tam   Painful.

Morgan   Necessary.

Tam   I wish my mum was still alive.

Morgan   She'd be 110!

Tam   She had a way of looking at you and then everything felt –

Morgan   She *is* still alive, just not in the form you remember her. So is Mags.

Tam   Here they come.

Morgan   I'm feeling the rage. Going to step back. Up by the trees.

Morgan *joins* **Older Morgan** *by the chair they're standing next to.*

Tam   Oh, God, oh God, here she comes.

Lily   Maggie Moo, we love you.

****

An understanding that Mags' burial takes place.

Each older person with their younger avatar.

*All except **Lily** who stays young until the last moment.*

The burial is completed.

****

9. OLDER LILY

The elderly woman – the one seated from the start – stands up from her chair.

*This is **Older Lily**.*

*She takes the packet of seeds from young **Lily**.*

***Older Lily** steps forward.*

Silence and stillness.

***Older Lily** speaks:*

Older Lily   Been waiting here since the beginning of this all this, all early bird, me, clack clack, premature baby, my mum said, can't kick the habit.

Alright. Alright, here goes, here I go, I go.

She scatters the seeds into the space between the stage and the audience.

She takes a folded paper from her pocket.

She reads:

My name is Lily. I am ___ years old (*age of the woman reading*). I'm told I have dementia. What do they know? I am still here.

This is my friend, Mags. Maggie Moo. One day she'll be a tree. One day we all will, I hope. If there are still trees.

The young people start to sing. Quietly at first, underscoring Older Lily's speech.

The song is your choice. A protest song. I thought of David Ramsden's anthem for Extinction Rebellion – 'We're Standing Here'.

Mags was brave. Very brave. She died fighting for something that she knew she wouldn't win in her lifetime. She was fighting for our grandchildren and their children and their children to grow up on an earth fit for living in.

Like Mags, I will fight. I will fight until I don't recognise my own hand in front of my face. Because this is not about me. I am nothing. This planet is extraordinary. What arrogance. What arrogance of us to treat it so badly. Just to go where we like and have what we want.

Our lives aren't special. Life is special – and we are killing it. Killing the chance of it. I wish that the oil would go. Had never been here. That we return to living small lives.

Do what we can. Act with love and kindness. But fight when you feel threatened. And we are threatened now.

This is not the end of Mags.

This is the beginning of us.

The song begins in earnest.

The older people join in.

The song ends.

Superglue

BY TIM CROUCH

*Notes on rehearsal and staging, drawn from a workshop with the writer,
held at the National Theatre, October 2021*

How the writer came to write the play

Superglue doesn't sit in isolation from Tim Crouch's other plays. In particular, it's connected to an earlier play he wrote called *Beginners* which was produced by the Unicorn Theatre in 2018. Like *Superglue*, *Beginners* takes its audience on a journey of discovery in its form. In *Beginners*, the audience is invited to believe that they're watching a play about adult characters performed by adult actors in a very adult way. Gradually, however, the audience begin to realise that the adult actors are not playing adult characters but children. They're just not pretending to be children in their performance style. (Crouch has issues with adults mimicking children!) In *Beginners*, the stage is haunted by real children who gradually take over the roles that the adult actors have been playing. The adults then go on to play the parents of those children. A dual game exists between what the audience see with their eyes (adult actors) and what they understand those adults actors to represent (children).

    Superglue continues this formal idea – two things in one. *Superglue* seems at first to be a play about young people – young actors playing climate activists their own age. As the play progresses, however, we realise it's a play about elderly characters performed by younger actors. (Crouch has issues with young people mimicking the elderly!) Tim Crouch is excited by the connections and parallels between young and old. In all of his work, Crouch is as excited by formal ideas as he is by narrative ideas. Form is also a story.

    Ideas around climate change are at the heart of *Superglue*. Tim Crouch was interested in how the most vocal groups around those themes are often the young and the elderly. He was inspired by Greta Thunberg, by the children's marches and by the bravery of older activists engaging in demonstrations, gluing their hands to things, chaining themselves to railings. The play is also about time. It touches on the idea of a cathedral-building mentality: working to build something which will not be completed in our lifetime. In the interests of the planet, please keep your production of *Superglue* carbon neutral. Theatre doesn't need large sets and props. It just needs people and ideas and emotions.

    Superglue operates inside the audience's head as much as it does on the stage. Let the audience do their work – it's what they're there for. There's a request to the audience to see things differently to how they're shown. The play is allusive – it operates through suggestion as much as through statement. It's ambiguous – a place where nothing is just one thing. Where chairs are both trees and the buried dead – but they're also just chairs! Actors are old and young at the same time. It's important to keep the action open to allow both states of being to co-exist. Trust that the audience will understand. They will make the transformation in their heads. The play is sending messages forward and back. Trust that the young Lily at the beginning will clearly be identified as the old Lily at the end – by the time we get there. Take your time. Trust the form.

Tim Crouch wrote the play with a particular woodland burial site in mind – in Brighton where he lives. It's on a hill, looking down to the sea. Halfway up the hill is a chapel surrounded by a traditional cemetery. Crouch used the specificity of this place to help his writing but it doesn't mean that *Superglue* is set in Brighton. The location of a woodland burial site also brings up environmental questions around people wanting to leave memorials for themselves after they die.

Superglue was written in gentle opposition to the idea that youth theatre should always be physical and energetic and loud. This play is about a held energy, a stillness, a quietness – and an understanding of age. Crouch believes these are important qualities for any actor to explore, and are particularly (and usefully) challenging for young actors. Crouch has a background in writing for and working with young people.

A writer who has inspired Tim Crouch greatly over his career is Caryl Churchill. Crouch mentioned her play *This Is a Chair* in reference to *Superglue*. In that play, headings are given to each scene that can feel to be in an interesting opposition to the action. The ideas expressed in the banners that unfurl in *Superglue* give a framework to the action of the play.

Approaching the play

Slogan exercise

Think of a question you have about the play. Then change it into a banner statement or protest slogan.

Slogans the group came up with:

LESS IS MORE

RESPECT THE SILENCE

MAKE SENSE OF EVERY SPACE

LOOK AT IT

IT'S NOT ABOUT YOU

UNDERSTAND YOUR VALUE

WHO ARE YOU?

YOU WERE YOUNG ONCE AND YOU WILL BE OLD

TRUST THE FORM

SERVE THE FORM

PLAY SITUATION NOT CHARACTER

PLAY WITH YOUR FRIENDS

KEEP IT SIMPLE

Understanding the similarities between thirteen–eighteen-year-olds and eighty-year-olds

The group was split into smaller groups of three people, and asked to collect ideas about what people their age and people aged eighty might have in common, how they are treated by society.

Thoughts from the workshop included:

'The sense of freedom in youth and age. Young people don't know the rules, the elderly feel "you can't touch me".'

'The middle generations make decisions about eighty-year-olds and teens. They can be equally marginalised in our community. There is lip service to these groups, but the middle years have the power.'

'Neither group feels the pressures of work.'

'Both groups can feel like time is running out. Young people because they will be an adult soon, and the elderly in that their life is almost done.'

'Both are waiting in anticipation for adulthood or death.'

'Character is strong as you get older and strong when you're a teenager.'

'Both groups are socially improper. They are far too passionate or tired to censor themselves.'

'They both really care about the future.'

'For older people what they've created is tangible and they fight for that, while young people are fighting to begin making their work.'

'They are both seen to be taking economically and not giving, so might be considered a burden.'

'Both can feel disillusioned.'

Themes

Some of the themes discussed throughout the workshop:

- Climate change
- The environment
- Death
- Ageing
- Time
- Protest and activism
- Morality and justice
- Nature
- Ritual
- Togetherness
- Mortality and health
- Love
- Anger
- Friendship

Structure, style and transitions

Tim Crouch feels that a key word to his plays – and *Superglue* in particular – is *simplicity*. Simplicity can sometimes be the hardest thing to achieve because people feel they need to be constantly doing things to demonstrate their excellence and ability. Simplicity means removing anything that is not essential. Simplicity invites an audience in. Over-complexity can push an audience away. Tim Crouch is wary of any reverence of virtuosity. You can spend for ever in rehearsal working on pace, space, rhythm, tone, etc. Simplicity is hard work.

Encourage your performers not to indulge. It's not about them or their performance; it's about what the audience is experiencing and the actors are servants to the audience's experience. This must be the first point of consideration. We're making work for an audience first, and ourselves second. It's a generous act of giving. This doesn't mean that Tim Crouch is encouraging the actors not to act. This is an exercise in presence. The actors become a conduit for the ideas in the play. Remind your performers that they matter in that relationship and that they are interesting in themselves – without having to project 'otherness'; without having to demonstrate everything.

Stillness and openness stalk *Superglue*. The play is an opportunity to strip back energy, as you will need to encourage your young actors to explore stillness. Held energy is a beautiful thing. Perhaps it is an old energy. Perhaps it is a reflective energy. The energy of funerals. You may want to explore this older energy with your young people, and explore how older people might feel about or behave at funerals.

Superglue should not be performed with the young people 'performing' the age of the actual characters they're playing. This is clear in the stage directions. The play is not asking them to become these characters physically – to act them out – but to hold space for those characters to exist in the audience's head. The things that make the connection between the old and the young are the writing, the staging and the audience. Theatre doesn't need you to capture absolutely the otherness of what you are presenting, as the audience will fill lots of it in. Young children don't need a cardboard box to look like a spaceship for them to understand it as a spaceship and play in it as such! Play the situation rather than the character. Crouch believes in the tensile strength of theatre, that it can be bent or stretched to take in a lot. Audiences know that it can be a long game. There is a clear release later. The audience is on your side.

There's humour in *Superglue*. It will suffer if it's too sad. There should be a sense of great detail to the performances. There is a journey in the silences, the pauses, the movements of characters entering the action. There is a big emotionality to the play, but trust that it exists without having to demonstrate it. These are old friends who are gathering to say goodbye to someone. They're sad, but deep humour is often found at funerals. They are there to celebrate a life as well as to mourn it.

The older people in the play. Crouch is cautious about calling them 'actors'. They are not there to put on a performance. They are there for their presence and their energy. Only Older Lily actually speaks – but she does a reading, not learnt lines. The older people are a great resource for your rehearsal process. They are what the actors' characters look like. You may use your older actors very minimally by giving them very basic blocking in the play – when to enter, where to sit, when to stand, etc. Or this play is an amazing opportunity to bring two generations together to make something special.

This is down to your resources of time and energy. The old people don't look at the young actors – and the young actors can't 'see' them on stage. This might change when they 'merge' towards the end with the possibility of old and young looking at each other.

Especially at the beginning, break down the fourth wall. Let Lily make direct eye contact with the audience. Let the multitude of meanings exist: old Lily, young Lily, being alone, being with the audience together, being with the older actor. Lily's first section works as a prologue.

For the final moment Tim Crouch suggested the Extinction Rebellion song 'We're Standing Here'. It could be hummed at first, then sung. You might just have eight young people sing, you might get all sixteen, you might have more people, a whole choir. You might choose another song. It should connect with the themes of the play.

Language

There are no prescribed accents for any character – use your own voices – and the language in general in the play is simple. No 'old' voices! The intention from Tim Crouch was a style which allows the themes of the play to speak clearly without over-indulgence. Each actor should explore simplicity and presence in their performance.

The biggest challenge to this is Lily. Her complex relationship with the different layers of the play is all part of her dementia and proximity to death. Her language explores this. In general she is trying to make sense of everything, despite the dementia and the medication. When Lily asks if Tam arrived in a 'helibopter' this is not a typo. It is a slippage; she believes it, it is not for effect. She's trying to be as together as she can. Alongside this, Lily also has a playful and mischievous personality which shines through what she says at other times.

There are other moments in the play where a different character forgets a word, but this is simply a normal forgetting of a word and not to do with dementia.

The forward slash in lines is known as an 'oblique'; the oblique in the line is not for the actor speaking, but cues the next line to start from where the oblique is. A dash at the end of a line is when the character is interrupted or when they run out of things to say.

Characters and characterisation

Find out who these people are and who they were. What is in the text? Collect it on pieces of paper and stick it to the walls and floors. Then use your imagination. Who were they when they were young? What lives have they lived? You may not want to spend a lot of time with them thinking about them being old. The play does this for you.

The characters are friends. That is something we all understand, and is a good access point for everyone of any age to understand this play. We all understand the moment where Tam's heart breaks for Lily. Explore their friendships.

Here are some notes on the characters:

Lily is a complex part. She see things that other characters can't see. She talks to the 'trees'. She exists between life and death, between youth and age.

Tim Crouch writes this about Lily:

> The character of Lily in the play is in her mid-seventies, maybe older. She's played by a young female actor aged between fifteen and twenty. That actor doesn't physically pretend to be old – she doesn't 'perform' old. That actor plays the truth of her character's situation. Lily is in the early stages of senile dementia. Her behaviour is erratic. Her language veers between coherence and incoherence. She finds it easier to write than to speak. Her brain mixes up her spoken words. She lives with her family – not her parents (as we might think initially) but with one of her adult children who cares for her. She mentions taking pills. The pills Lily takes are chemical inhibitors to help her memory and her judgement. For an audience, however, what their eyes will see on stage is a young woman talking about taking pills and appearing to be out of control. Their initial understanding is that this is a young person disinhibited by drugs. Someone who has run away from home. Someone whose mental state creates anxiety among her friends. Gradually the audience will understand the reality of Lily's character – which is in playful contradiction to the sight of the young actor performing it.

Tam is gentle and understanding. They are the bedrock of this group of friends, practical, understanding, helpful.

Morgan is no bullshit. They are a battle-axe, they are angry. They are not only this.

Joe is a powerful dividing figure. Discuss him with your group. What history does he have with each of them? What boundaries has he pushed before? Talk about his act of violence at the protest where Mags died.

Casting

When Tim Crouch was writing the play he intended that most characters can be played by any gender, with the exception of Lily and Joe – although these two roles are still negotiable. Crouch is interested in the difference between the nurturing, intuitive aspect of Lily and the more fiery, impulsive aspect of Joe.

There are as many older people as there are younger actors in the play. Each younger actor has their older version. The gender and ethnicity of the older actors should be the same as the younger actors they are connected with. Ideally an older relative, but connections could also be made to elder climate groups, U3A, XR, yoga, meditation, etc. Increasingly, arts organisations are offering creative opportunities for older people. (Many theatres, for example, have creative programmes for over-fifty-fives.) The older people in this show are not asked to act. The key request made of them is that they are able to sit in stillness and silence. Ideally the older people should be aged seventy plus. Certainly bus-pass age.

If you have a larger cast than eight then you could divide the lines up further for most of the characters, apart from Lily and Joe. You would, of course, need more older actors for this.

Production, staging and design

The performances in *Superglue* are naturalistic; the form of this play is abstract (even though the audience don't know this at first). There is no need to recreate the kestrel, the grave, the crows, the sea, the sun sinking, etc. Think of these as points of focus for the actors. You might use sound to support the communication of the presence of these things.

Tim Crouch imagined this play in an end-on configuration, with Mags' grave being the space between the audience and the stage. But be creative. You could do this play in a non-theatre space. It could be in thrust, perhaps even in the round. But there should be one fixed point for the grave.

Crouch has imagined a large stage space. There should be space for Lily to move between chairs/trees. The chairs for the older performers are scattered throughout the performance space, with a clearing at the forestage. This clearing should have enough space by the grave for people to congregate. There is no need to have a hole for the grave. There is an opportunity for a burial. The play allows you to decide what that burial will look like.

The banners can be wherever you want to put them, but they should be readable and shouldn't block the people on the stage. Banners can be on a stick, two sticks, on clothing, tent material, cardboard, fabric, etc. They might take effort to hang, or they might unfurl with a tug on a string. These banners are simultaneously part of the reality within the play and they connect with the ideas of the play. Within the reality of the play the characters are putting them up because they know the press are coming and they want to make their point. Within the form of the play they are communicating the themes of the production.

The costumes should be the clothes these people might wear to a funeral. With regards to the rhythm and pace of the piece, respect the silence. Embrace the silence. Be in the silence all together. Don't speed through the text, explore all its spaces. Sometimes the language is quickfire, but sometimes the conversations are thought out idea by idea. This is the task of rehearsal.

Specific moments that were looked at in the workshop

In the beginning of the play Lily may find herself facing out and looking into the audience's eyes, breaking the fourth wall. This should allow the play to bleed into being. With regards to her performance, there is a rich chain of thought happening with her throughout the play, even before she has spoken. Encourage the actor playing Lily to hear the thoughts or the other words in between.

In the moment where Lily sees the older people, Lily is looking at them but they probably don't look back at her. This could change towards the end.

In the moment where Mattie hands the tissue to Rhys, as the older Rhys approaches, Mattie might flick their attention to the older Rhys, and young Rhys might have a moment of connection with older Rhys. It is a moment of transference or slippage.

In the moment where older Hadley takes the shawl and puts the shawl round younger Hadley it might be the same. These are complicated moments where little things happen where we see two worlds colliding. There are a few moments like these, and they should feel like a chemical reaction which builds until the end.

In these complex moments of transference, slippage or collision, you may not want to overlay too much music or sound. Allow the connection of the older and younger characters to speak for itself. When you do use music and sound, remember not to push the audience to feel too much. The ending likely breaks this rule.

Exercises for use in rehearsals

Lots of these exercises centre around ensemble, listening, presence and openness. Stillness and openness are key qualities in this play. One way to be open is to listen. Active listening is a great way to be open. If you are actively listening you cannot be in the past or in the future, but in the present.

Monsters/Penguins – chair game

Everyone is spaced on chairs around the room, all facing in different directions. There is one empty chair. One person is the penguin and starts at the other side of the room from the empty chair. This person's aim is to sit in a chair, but the group must work collectively to stop them by keeping the chair occupied. The person seeking the chair moves with their knees together, like a penguin. Once anyone leaves their chair to block the seeking penguin, with their bum leaving the seat, they must finish their move. The person who bears the most of the fault of the seeking penguin managing to sit becomes the new seeking penguin. Encourage the group not to be vocal, and use eye contact only. This game is useful for collective responsibility; it is useful to see how people start to take control of the game. After a while change the rules, make the game less about winning and more about playing. Flirt with the game, playfully punish people by sitting if they make silly mistakes. A good game for being sensitive and being open to the periphery.

Walking and stopping ensemble exercise

Spread the group around the room, standing. At some point, without anyone leading this exercise, one person will move and walk and then stop. And then at the same time, two people will start to walk, in any direction, but at the same time, and then they will stop at the same time. Then three. Try the sequence one, two, three, two, one. Ask your group not to start this exercise for at least ten seconds after the game starts, it can be longer. Many will have to sacrifice their intention for the group. Everyone can move how they like if they are the mover. Pause the exercise and start again from an appropriate point if the wrong number goes. Watch out for a performative presence. As the group becomes connected and relaxed they can be more playful, and enjoy how exciting the waiting can be (a pre-expressive energy, as we connect before movement). The more you find this, the more present your group will be. Caution is the death of theatre, so avoid a cautious energy. It's playful, and doesn't have to be serious.

Filters to add to this: Encourage people to have their focus about three metres from the ground. This prevents people from going into themselves and gives an emotional quality to this exercise. It can add a sense of being outdoors in a great space. It creates an understanding that you are engaged in something.

Counting to twenty

Count to twenty as a group – with no one determining who speaks next. If two people speak at the same time then you must go back to the beginning.

Three people standing

A circle of chairs – the whole group seated. At any one time, three people must always be standing up from their chairs. No more than three, no fewer than three. They can stand for a maximum of ten seconds before they have to sit down. It is the group's job to keep the balance of three standing throughout the game.

Exercises for understanding the play

A writing exercise to understand the writing style

This is an writing exercise that explores the kind of 'double exposure' that is present in *Superglue* (and *Beginners*).

Write a scene between two characters – A and B. The scene you write must sustain the possibility of two scenarios at the same time. (In *Superglue*, the writing sustains the thought that the characters are both young and old.) An example of this: write a scene that should be able to be read both as:

1   two people putting up a tent
2   one person counselling the other away from suicide

Think about phrases and qualities that can exist in both scenes. You might write as little as three lines; just think about creating a scene where both these things can co-exist without one shutting the other down. The intention is to make an open piece of writing.

Come up with your own scenarios.

Walking together

Put five to ten people in a line at one end of the room. Make sure they have lots of space in front of them and that you have an audience. At an unspecified moment the people will all begin to walk together and then stop together – with no one leading the movement. This is about pre-expressive energy; it is about peripheral vision. Ask the audience what they notice. There should be huge tension. Next give them a focus, maybe above the horizon and ahead. See if that brings the group more together. Find the beauty in this moment. The purity in the presence of performance of this task. See what happens if you put music under it.

Question and answer with Tim Crouch

Q: How do you define the space of the hill?
TC: Allow the young people to define the space.

Q: Is there an empty grave? Where is it?
TC: It's at the forestage, the space between the stage and the audience. There is no need to have a hole for the grave.

Q: How do I prevent indulgence?
TC: Make sense of every space, of every moment. Define indulgence with your company. A reminder that simplicity is hard work. And hard work is never indulgent.

Q: How do you support neurodiverse performers in these stillnesses and silences?
TC: Find their own stillness and silence. It can be different to different people. Interpret your silence as appropriate for your company. Find your inner stillness. This may include outer movement to find the inner stillness.

Q: What can I do if I can't achieve a blackout?
TC: There doesn't have to be a blackout. There's no mention of a blackout in the play. A blackout is a sense of displacement. Don't pretend you are not where you are. You're in a theatre and this is a play! The energy changes and then resumes. The audience release and then re-engage. It's simple.

Q: How much do the entrances of the older actors demand focus from the audience?
TC: They should have their moment, it is important the audience notice these moments and have space to contemplate their meaning. Let things take their own time. Don't try to rush things.

Q: Can we involve those who aren't assigned characters?
TC: There are opportunities to integrate other performers outside of the eight characters and their older mirrors. The unfurling of the banners, the transitional moment, a chorus as the numbers of people grow on stage for the funeral, though perhaps not to accompany the older actors on stage. At a push you might be able to split characters' lines. But not Lily or Joe.

Q: Can we represent anyone digitally?
TC: This play depends on the presence of the older actors for the interaction and transference of meaning. If this were a film we would direct it with old actors in the main parts, but film generally carries less symbolism. Theatre does a lot of heavy lifting, and can carry that symbolism. What can theatre do without loads of tech? Instead of finding inventive ways to perform *Superglue*, think about how you can meet the writer's ideas in the play.

Q: What year do we set the play in?
TC: It is a play for right now, so the 'now' of the older actors would be the same as our now.

Q: How do you find your older actors?
TC: If the grandparents or great aunts and uncles of the actors are not available then you could approach older acting groups in your local area, or older dance groups. You

could also approach your local Extinction Rebellion group, the governors of the organisation you work for or the University of the Third Age.

Suggested references

Beginners by Tim Crouch (Bloomsbury)
Max Richter's album *Sleep* was the soundtrack to much of Tim's writing of *Superglue*
Survey which shows that older people are the happier demographic:
https://www.bbc.co.uk/news/uk-35471624
'Warning', a poem by Jenny Joseph.
'Is That All There Is?' Peggy Lee song
Greta Thunberg's book *Our House Is on Fire*
Extinction Rebellion Handbook – *This is Not a Drill* (Penguin)
This Is a Chair by Caryl Churchill
'Joe Hill', a protest song by Alfred Hayes:
https://www.youtube.com/watch?v=n8Kxq9uFDes&t=37s
Our Town by Thornton Wilder: Act Three, where the dead of the town's cemetery talk
What Dementia Teaches About Love by Nicci Gerrard (The Alzheimer's Society)
Films of people with dementia listening to music:
https://www.youtube.com/watch?v=OT8AdwV0Vkw

From a workshop led by Tim Crouch
Consultant Director Kirsty Housley
With notes by Stephanie Kempson

Variations

by Katie Hims

Katie Hims is a writer for stage, screen and radio. Her stage work includes *Three Minutes After Midnight* for The Globe Theatre, *The Stranger On the Bridge* at The Tobacco Factory, *Bristol and Billy the Girl* for Clean Break at Soho Theatre. She has also spent time on attachment to the National Theatre Studio. Katie was lead writer on BBC Radio 4's First World War series *Home Front* for five seasons and she wrote the feature length final episode (shortlisted for the Peter Tinniswood prize.) Other radio includes *Black Eyed Girls* (winner of the BBC Audio Drama Award for Best Original Drama) and *Lost Property* (winner of the BBC Audio Drama Award for Best Original Drama). Radio adaptations include *Tess of the D'Urbervilles*, *Middlemarch* and *The Martin Beck Killings*. She is currently under commission to The Unicorn Theatre.

Characters

Alice, *thirteen*
Dan, *sixteen* (**Alice**'s *brother*)
Lucas, *fourteen* (**Alice**'s *brother*)
Cinnamon, *thirteen* (**Alice**'s *friend*)
Chloe, *thirteen* (**Alice**'s *friend*)
Postman, *sixteen*

Jasmine, *seventeen* (**Alice**'s *sister*)
Pearl, *fifteen* (**Alice**'s *sister*)
Pablo, *thirteen* (**Alice/Joe**'s *friend*)

Shelly, *thirteen* (**Alice** *as her mother*)
Dean, *fifteen* (**Shelly**'s *brother*)
Bex, *seventeen* (**Shelly**'s *sister*)

Joe, *thirteen* (**Alice** *as a boy*)

Scene One

2018. The kitchen is stacked high with dirty cups, plates and saucepans. **Dan** *is eating cereal.* **Lucas** *is holding a laminated piece of A4 card.* **Alice** *comes into the kitchen, doesn't speak to her brothers and starts looking for some breakfast. All three of them are in school uniform.*

Lucas Do you know what colour you are?

Dan No.

Lucas You're the colour blue.

Dan *doesn't respond.*

Lucas You're the colour blue.

Dan OK.

Lucas And look what colour it is.

Dan I can't believe you've actually laminated that thing.

Lucas It's blue.

Dan Stop waving it in my face.

Lucas That's you.

Dan Alright!

Alice *switches on the radio. It's an eighties song. Take your pick from 1980/81/82/83.*

Dan Alice.

Alice What?

Dan Can you turn that shit off.

Alice I like this shit.

Dan Well, I don't.

Alice Well, I do.

Dan *gets up and switches it off.*

Dan It makes me feel like killing myself.

Alice All the more reason to keep it on.

She switches it back on. **Dan** *switches it off again.*

Alice Dan!

She switches it on.

Dan *switches it off.*

Alice Mum! Mum! (*Calling for their mum to adjudicate.*)

Lucas   She's not here.

Alice   Where's she gone?

Lucas   Work.

Alice   Already?

Lucas   Yes.

Alice   Well, where's my phone?

Dan   How should I know?

Alice   Did she take it with her?

Lucas   How should we know?

Alice   She wouldn't. She wouldn't take it with her. Would she?

Lucas *shrugs.*

Alice   Did she say anything before she left?

Lucas   She wrote us a note.

He reads the note.

'If you don't sort the kitchen out before I come home I will kick you all out and you can go and live with your feckless –' (*Hesitates.*)

Dan   – bastard –

Alice   Does it actually say 'bastard'?

Lucas   – yeh – 'feckless –'

Dan   – bastard –

Lucas   '– of a father' – I think she's given up trying not to criticise him –

Dan   Do you reckon?

Lucas   '– and his twenty-seven-year-old Aussie witch of a girlfriend – and their new baby. I mean it.' (*More emphasis.*) 'I MEAN IT.'

Alice   Wow.

Lucas   Yeh.

Dan   She doesn't. She doesn't mean it.

Lucas   Second time is in capitals.

Alice   They've got their scan today.

Lucas   What?

Alice   Dad and Lilia.

Lucas   Oh.

Alice   So they'll find out. What they're having.

Dan   Great.

Alice   I dreamed last night that they had a girl.

Dan   Was it ugly?

Alice   No she was lovely. She'd just been born and I held her in my arms.

Lucas   Was she covered in blood?

Alice   No.

Lucas   That's not very realistic.

Dan   That's cos it was a dream.

Alice   I held her in my arms and she smiled at me.

Lucas   Babies don't smile till they're six weeks.

Dan   It was a dream, you doughnut.

Alice   Do you think they're having a boy or a girl?

Dan   I literally couldn't give a shit.

Alice *looks in the breadbin/cupboard.*

Alice   Have you two eaten all the chocolate croissants?

Lucas   Otherwise known as pains au chocolat.

Alice   Have you?

Dan   Probably.

Lucas   I only had one.

Alice (*to* **Dan**)   How many did you have?

Dan   Dunno. Three?

Alice   Three? Three chocolate croissants?

Lucas   I prefer pains au chocolat.

Alice   You're so selfish –

Lucas   – although they look at you a bit weird when you say it with a French accent.

Dan   That's because you say the whole sentence in French.

Lucas   *Je voudrais un pain au chocolat.*

Alice *looks in the fridge, takes out an empty bottle.*

Alice   There's no milk. (*To* **Dan**.) Did you use all the milk too?

Dan   Yep.

Alice   You don't care about anyone do you.

Lucas   Your friend is quite a mercenary. I wonder if he cares about anything or anyone.

Dan   What are you babbling about?

Alice   It's from *Star Wars*.

Dan   I know it's from *Star Wars*.

Alice   There is nothing to eat. There is literally nothing to eat.

Lucas   Actually that's not true.

Lucas *goes to the cupboards.*

Lucas   There's pasta and flour and golden syrup and and glacé cherries and lentils and –

Alice   But I don't want to eat pasta and golden syrup for breakfast do I.

Lucas   No – course not – that's not the point – the point is that you should have said 'figuratively' not 'literally'. People get it wrong all the time. And it's not a modern phenomenon. I expect you think it is – most people do – but it isn't. It's actually been going on for about five hundred years.

Dan   Lucas, can you shut up.

Lucas   But people need to know.

Dan   I don't need to know. I mean I – literally – couldn't give a shit.

Lucas   Why do you have to swear?

Dan   The whole world swears – except you –

Lucas   Nuns don't.

Dan   I'm sure some of them do.

Lucas   Priests don't.

Dan   I'm sure they do. I would. If I was a priest.

Lucas   Then you wouldn't be a very good priest.

Dan   No. I wouldn't.

Alice   Auntie Bex swears. Auntie Bex swears like a trooper.

Dan   What's that got to do with anything?

Alice   Well she was a nun wasn't she.

Dan   No she wasn't.

Alice   She was. She was.

Dan   How long for?

Alice   I dunno. But like years.

Dan (*to* **Lucas**)   Well, there you go.

Lucas   What?

Dan   Nuns do swear.

Alice   That was my point.

Lucas   But she's an ex-nun. Ex-nuns don't count.

He picks up the note and looks at it again.

Is no one else worried she's going to kick us out?

Dan   No. Because she's not.

Alice   What's that?

Lucas   What's what?

Alice   On the other side!

Lucas   Oh oh . . . (*Lucas turns the note over, nods slowly, frustratingly.*)

Alice   What does it say?

Lucas   'PS Alice, I have taken your phone.'

Alice   Shit!

Lucas   'You can have it back when you apologise.'

Dan   Apologise for what?

Lucas   What did you do?

Alice   Nothing.

Dan   Ha.

Alice   I didn't. I didn't do anything.

Lucas   You must have done something.

Alice   I can't believe she's taken my phone.

Dan   You must have pissed her right off.

Alice   It's like. It's like taking someone's life. It's like she's taken my life.

Dan   Drama queen.

Lucas   People used to live without phones you know.

Alice *rolls her eyes at* **Lucas**.

Lucas   People used to use phone boxes.

Dan   Phone boxes smell of piss.

The landline phone rings.

Dan   That's weird.

Alice   Yeh.

Lucas   I sort of forget it exists.

Dan   Me too.

Lucas *goes to answer it.*

Alice   Don't answer it!

Lucas   Why?

Alice   It might be Cinnamon.

The answer machine kicks in.

Mum   You're through to Shelly, Dan, Lucas and Alice. We can't take your call right now but please leave us a message and we'll get back to you.

Cinnamon *on the answering machine.*

Cinnamon   Alice, it's Cinnamon.

Alice   See.

Cinnamon   Are you there? Alice are you there?

Lucas   Aren't you going to pick up the phone?

Cinnamon   I tried ringing your mobile but you didn't answer. I tried you a couple of times. Cos you said we might walk to school together but I don't know if . . . I'll just try you again. I'll try you one more time. OK. OK. Hope you're OK. Bye.

She hangs up.

Lucas   Why don't you want to speak to her?

Alice *shrugs.*

Alice   Cos we're not really friends any more.

Lucas   So why's she ringing you?

Alice *shrugs.*

Alice   I mean we are friends sort of. Her and Chloe don't really – get on.

Dan   That's cos Chloe is a bitch.

Alice   She's not a bitch.

Dan   She looks like a bitch.

Alice   That's a very misogynistic thing to say.

Lucas   How do you spell misogynistic?

Alice   I don't know.

Lucas   You should know that. As a feminist.

The doorbell rings.

Alice   That'll be her.

Lucas   Who?

Alice   Chloe.

She answers the door.

Chloe   What have you done to your eyebrows?

Alice   Nothing.

Chloe   They look funny.

Alice   Do they?

Chloe   Like you've over-plucked them.

Alice   I haven't touched them.

Chloe   Well, maybe you've under-plucked them then. You ready?

Alice   Erm. No, sorry. Erm.

Chloe   Can I come in then?

Alice   Er yeh sorry yeh come in.

Chloe *follows* **Alice** *into the kitchen.*

Chloe   Hi, Dan.

Dan *does not look up.*

Dan   Hi, Chloe.

Chloe *looks round.*

Chloe   This kitchen is disgusting. Did you ask her?

Alice   Ask who what?

Chloe   Did you ask your mum?

Alice   Er no cos erm she had to leave really early this morning so.

Chloe   Ring her. Ring her now.

Alice   I really don't think she's going to say yes.

Chloe   Don't tell her that you're going to a party! Just say you're staying at mine.

Alice   But she can't answer her phone while she's on a shift.

Chloe   Leave her a message. She can text you in her break.

Alice   Erm. She can't text me cos she's taken my phone.

Chloe   She took your phone?

Alice   Yeh.

Chloe   She took your phone?

Alice   Yeh.

She starts packing her school bag, looking for something.

Chloe   I would never ever let my mum take my phone.

Alice   Well, I didn't *let* her.

Chloe   I mean that's like, that's like taking someone's *life*.

Alice   I *know*.

She picks up her pencil case to pack it. The pencil case is open and all the pencils fall out. At the same time she knocks a mug of cold tea over and it splashes on **Chloe***'s shoes.*

Chloe   Alice!

Alice   Oh my God. I'm so sorry.

Chloe   You're so clumsy.

Alice   I'm sorry.

Chloe   You're always spilling things or knocking things over or dropping things or whatever. You're like a – you're like a – boy.

Alice   I'm sorry.

Chloe   It's all over my bag.

Alice   Do you want me to. I could clean it.

Chloe   I'll do it.

She goes to the sink.

The sink is full of crap.

Alice   You could clean it in the bathroom.

Chloe *goes offstage to the bathroom.*

Alice (*calling after her*)   I'm sorry. I'm really sorry.

Lucas   Why are you friends with her?

Alice   Shush.

Lucas   But why are you?

Dan   Whose party is it?

Alice   What?

Dan   This party that Chloe's trying to get you to go to?

Alice   It's this boy – called Pablo. His mum and dad are away. So.

Dan   Sounds dodgy.

Alice   What do you care?

Dan *picks up his bag.*

Lucas   Where you going?

Dan   School.

Lucas   You can't leave it like this. (*Gestures to kitchen.*)

Dan   I can. I will. I am.

Lucas   I'm not letting you leave.

Dan   Don't be ridiculous.

Two text messages arrive on two separate phones. Both **Lucas** *and* **Dan** *look at their phones.*

Lucas   It's a boy.

Alice   What?

Lucas   Lilia and Dad.

Dan   They're having a boy.

Alice   I really wanted them to have a girl.

Dan   Get out of my way.

Lucas   No.

Dan   I will hit you. You know I will.

Alice   I really wanted a sister.

Dan *goes to hit* **Lucas** *and* **Lucas** *grabs* **Dan***'s arm.* **Dan** *starts trying to hit* **Lucas** *with his other arm.* **Lucas** *dodges him but doesn't let* **Dan** *go. It descends into a pathetic fight/wrestle as the conversation goes on.*

Dan   Let go of my arm!

Lucas   I'm not getting kicked out of the house – because of you –

Dan   She's not going to kick us out!

Alice   I wish Jasmine hadn't died.

Lucas   Who's Jasmine?

Alice   Who's Jasmine?

Lucas   Yeh.

Alice   Mum and Dad's stillborn baby.

Lucas (*not very interested*)   Oh yeh yeh yeh.

Alice   Lucas.

Lucas   What? She died before any of us were born. So I forget she existed. She's a bit like the landline.

Alice   She is not like the landline.

Lucas   I mean I never think about her.

Alice   I think about her all the time.

Dan   Let go of my arm!

Lucas   Say you'll do the washing-up!

Dan   No!

They keep fighting.

Alice   Dan.

Dan   What?

Alice   If Jasmine hadn't died then you would never have been born. Do you ever think about that?

Dan   No.

Alice   And I'd have a sister.

Lucas   But you wouldn't have been born either.

Alice   I might. I might have.

Lucas   No none of us would.

Alice   It could have gone like Jasmine and then another girl and then me.

Lucas   No because you change one thing and all of it changes.

Alice   Unless you subscribe to string theory.

Lucas   String theory isn't science.

Alice   Some people think it is.

Lucas   It's science fiction.

Alice   Some people think it's possible. Cosmic microwaves. Left over from the Big Bang. Unless there was no Big Bang and it's just bubbles. Just bubbles. One bubble leading to another.

Lucas   The universe is not an Aero.

Dan (*to* **Lucas**)   Let. Go. Of. My. Arm.

Lucas *lets go of* **Dan** *and they collapse onto the floor.*

Dan   Twat.

Lucas   Dickhead.

Dan   Wanker.

The doorbell rings.

Alice   I'll go.

Alice *goes to the door. It's the* **Postman** *with a massive box wrapped in brown paper.*

Alice   I hate my brothers.

Postman   Are you Alice?

Alice *nods.*

Alice   I hate my mum. I hate my dad. I hate my best friend. I hate my whole life.

Postman   This is for you.

Alice   What is it?

Postman   How would I know?

Alice   Good point.

Postman   Can you sign here please?

Alice   Aren't you a bit young for a postman?

Postman   I'm sixteen.

Alice   That's young though isn't it?

Postman   Are you going to sign it or not?

Alice   Yes. Sorry. Yes.

She signs.

Scene Two

2018. The kitchen is stacked high with dirty cups, plates and saucepans. **Jasmine** *is eating cereal.* **Pearl** *is holding a piece of paper. They are both in school uniform.*

Pearl   Do you know what colour you are?

Jasmine   No.

Pearl   You're the colour blue.

Jasmine *doesn't respond.*

Pearl   You're the colour blue.

Jasmine   OK.

Pearl   And look what colour it is.

Jasmine   Don't shove it in my face.

Alice *walks into the kitchen and stares at them both. She is entirely freaked out but sort of frozen too.*

Pearl   It's blue.

Jasmine   Alright!

Alice   Who are you?

Pearl   What?

Alice   Who are you and what are you doing in my kitchen?

Jasmine   You're not funny, Alice.

Pearl   Mum's gone to work and she's left us –

Jasmine   – a really shitty note.

Pearl   It says.

She reads the note.

Pearl   'If you don't sort the kitchen out before I come home I will kick you all out and you can go and live with your feckless –'

Jasmine   – shithead –

Pearl   – yeh – 'father and his twenty-seven-year-old neurotic of a girlfriend and their new baby. I am not joking.' (*With emphasis.*) 'I AM NOT JOKING.' Second time in capitals.

Alice   Oh my God.

Pearl   Are you OK?

Alice *shakes her head.*

Jasmine   You don't need to freak out and get all dramatic and emotional. She won't do it. She won't actually kick us out.

Alice   Oh my God. Oh my God.

Pearl   Have a pain au chocolat.

Alice   There's none left.

Pearl   Yeh there is.

She give **Alice** *a pain au chocolat on a plate.*

Alice   Thanks.

Pearl   Do you want a cup of tea?

Alice *nods.* **Pearl** *gets a bottle of milk out of the fridge and pours* **Alice** *a cup of tea.*

Alice   Can I see it? Can I see the note?

Jasmine *passes her the note then switches the radio on. It's the same eighties song from Scene One.*

Jasmine   Oh, I bloody love this song.

Pearl   So do I.

Jasmine *starts dancing.* **Pearl** *sees* **Alice** *reading the back of the note.*

Pearl   What's that?

Alice   'Alice, I have taken your phone.'

Pearl   She's taken your phone?

Alice *nods.*

Jasmine   Why's she taken your phone?

Pearl (*taking the note and reading*)   'You can have it back when you apologise.'

Jasmine   Wow.

Pearl   What did you do?

Alice   I didn't do anything.

Pearl   Mmm, not likely.

The chorus of the song begins. **Jasmine** *turns it up louder and* **Jasmine** *and* **Pearl** *begin to sing along. Then* **Pearl** *joins* **Jasmine** *dancing.* **Pearl** *and* **Jasmine** *dance together while* **Alice** *watches. The dance goes slightly wrong and they both laugh.* **Alice** *joins in with them despite being freaked out. This may be the only chance she ever gets to dance with her two sisters. The dancing can be as impromptu or coordinated as you wish.*

Alice   This is so nice.

She dances a few moments longer.

This is amazing.

The song ends. The dancing ends. She looks incredibly happy. She switches the radio off.

Is this real?

Pearl   Is what real?

Alice   I mean it feels real. But it can't be. How can it be?

Jasmine   What are you talking about?

Alice   This.

Jasmine *picks up her bag.*

Pearl   Where you going?

Jasmine   School.

She is about to leave.

Pearl   You're not allowed.

Jasmine   Ha.

Pearl   I mean it. Jasmine!

Alice   You're Jasmine. Are you Jasmine?

Jasmine   Are you trying to be funny again?

Alice   No no no I'm not. See my whole life I've wondered what you'd look like.

She goes up close to **Jasmine** *and touches her face.*

Jasmine   What are you doing?

Pearl   Are you crying?

Jasmine   Can you stop touching my face?

Alice   But you're so lovely.

Jasmine *backs away.*

Jasmine   Stop it!

Pearl   Why are you crying?

Alice   Because she's the baby who died.

Peal   What? (*Together with* **Jasmine**.)

Jasmine   What?

Alice   You died when you were a baby. You were stillborn. Because Mum had pre-eclampsia but no symptoms. And so they didn't know. And Dad felt bad. Because he was medical. Like he should have done something that he didn't do.

Jasmine   Is this a drama project?

Alice   In real life I don't have sisters, I have two brothers.

Jasmine   Is this like some kind of weird school project?

Alice   No. It's real.

Jasmine   It's twisted.

Alice   I'm sorry.

Jasmine   You are completely freaking me out.

Pearl   I don't think she's doing it on purpose.

Alice   I'm not.

Jasmine   Why are you always on her side?

Alice   Are you?

Pearl   No. Yes. Sometimes.

Alice (*to* **Jasmine**)   When's your birthday?

Jasmine   Stop it, just stop it.

Pearl   It's 19 September.

Alice (*to* **Jasmine**)   That's the day you died.

Jasmine   That's the day I was born.

Alice   I used to imagine you all the time. I imagined that we'd really get on.

Jasmine   Ha. (*Together with* **Pearl**.)

Pearl   Ha.

Alice   Do we not, do we not get on?

Pearl   No.

Jasmine   She knows we don't! You know we don't!

Alice   But I don't!

Pearl   She could be having a psychic fugue. You could be having a psychic fugue.

Alice   Could I?

Pearl   I watched a documentary on it. And you just kind of forget everything. And you disappear.

Jasmine   Well, Alice hasn't disappeared. She's right here.

Pearl   But she might disappear. She might disappear later. Especially if we don't handle the situation carefully.

Jasmine   For God's sake.

Pearl   You're very cold, Jasmine.

Alice   Dan's very cold.

Pearl   Who's Dan?

Alice   My eldest brother.

Jasmine   Jesus Christ.

Alice   And I always thought that Dan was cold because he came after you. And that Mum was in such a state when he was born that she wasn't quite there or something.

Not that it was her fault. Although I think she did blame Dad – for your death. Or he thought she blamed him. But if you didn't die . . .

Jasmine Can you STOP talking about me dying?

Alice Sorry. I'm sorry but you did die. But you're not dead now.

Jasmine No I'm not!

Pearl (*to* **Jasmine**) Why are you so angry?

Jasmine Why are you not angry?

Pearl (*to* **Alice**) She gets angry a lot.

Alice So does Dan.

Jasmine Will you shut up about Dan? Dan doesn't exist. He doesn't exist. I exist, alright?

Pearl The other thing it could be is a brain tumour.

Jasmine It's not a brain tumour.

Pearl How do you know?

Jasmine Because they're extremely rare!

Pearl But a rare occurrence still happens doesn't it. A rare occurrence does still occur.

Alice I don't want to have a brain tumour.

Pearl No one *wants* to have a brain tumour.

Jasmine (*to* **Alice**) You haven't got a brain tumour.

Pearl You don't know that.

Jasmine I do because she's obviously making the whole thing up!

Alice But why would I make this up?

Pearl Why would she make this up?

Jasmine Why are you always on her side?

Pearl I'm not!

The doorbell rings.

Alice I'll get it.

She answers the door. It's **Pablo**.

Alice Pablo.

Pablo What have you done to your eyebrows?

Alice Nothing.

Pablo   They look funny.

Alice   Do they?

Pablo   Like you've over-plucked them.

Alice   I haven't touched them.

Pablo   Well, maybe you've under-plucked them. Are we walking to school or not?

Alice   Me and you. Walking to school?

Pablo   Unless you're walking with Chloe.

Alice   Erm, I'm not walking with Chloe, no.

Pablo   I can't cope with Chloe today. Things are bad enough.

Alice   What things?

Pablo   Oh, I'm just really stressed about the party.

Alice   Oh right.

Pablo   You ready?

Alice   Er sorry no um can you come in for a minute?

Pablo   Certainly.

He follows **Alice** *in to the kitchen.*

Jasmine   Hi, Pablo.

Pearl   Hi, Pablo.

Pablo *ignores them and looks round.*

Pablo   This kitchen is disgusting. Did you ask your mum?

Alice   Ask her what?

Pablo   About the party?

Jasmine   What party?

Pablo   I'm having a party at my house.

Jasmine   Really?

Pablo   It's very nerve-wracking. Did you ask her?

Alice   Erm no cos she didn't come home till late last night. And then she had to leave really early this morning so.

Pablo   Ring her. Ring her now.

Alice   She's got my phone.

Pablo   Why's she got your phone?

Alice   It's a – punishment.

Pablo   Wow. What did you do?

During the following dialogue **Alice** *starts packing her school bag, looking for something, a pencil case. The pencil case is open and all the pencils fall out.* **Pablo** *helps her pick them up.*

Alice   Nothing. Honestly she's been a bit crazy since my dad left.

Pablo   But taking your phone, I mean that's like taking your life.

Alice   Yeh. I know.

Pablo   So you must have done *something*.

Then **Pablo** *knocks a mug of cold tea over.*

Pablo   Oh my God. I'm so sorry.

Alice   It's alright.

Pablo   It's just nerves.

Alice   What are you so nervous about?

Pablo   The party.

Alice   Oh yeh. Sorry.

Pablo   No I'm sorry. About the tea.

Alice   It's fine.

Pablo   Shit.

Alice   What?

Pablo   It's all over my bag.

Alice   Do you want me to. I could clean it.

Pablo   I'll do it.

He goes to the sink.

The sink is full of crap.

Alice   You could clean it in the bathroom.

Pablo *heads offstage to the bathroom.*

Alice   You didn't tell me I was friends with Pablo.

Jasmine   Why would we tell you something that you already know?

Alice   In my other life. In my real life I'm not friends with Pablo. He's just a boy. Who's in my geography class.

Jasmine   This *is* your real life, you freak.

She picks up her bag.

Pearl   You can't leave now.

Jasmine   Yes I can.

Pearl   What about Alice?

Jasmine   She's fine. She's faking it.

Alice   I'm not faking it.

Jasmine   You are. You are faking it. And you're being a complete bitch.

Alice   That's internalised misogyny.

Jasmine   What?

Alice   Calling another woman a bitch.

Jasmine   I don't care about things like that.

Alice   But you should. You should care.

Pearl   I care.

Alice   That's a line from *Star Wars*.

Pearl   Your friend is quite a mercenary.

Alice   I wonder if he cares about anything or anyone. And then Luke says.

Pearl   I care.

Alice and **Pearl** *smile at each other, inexplicably pleased.*

Jasmine   I've got to go. Alice, you're not a woman. You're only thirteen. And you are being a bitch. If you're not faking it go to the doctor's.

Pearl *stands in* **Jasmine**'*s way.*

Jasmine   What are you doing?

Pearl   I'm not letting you leave.

Jasmine   Don't be ridiculous.

Pearl   I'm not.

She grabs **Jasmine**'*s arm.*

Jasmine   Get off my arm!

Pearl   You have to do the washing-up!

Jasmine   You're mad, you're madder than her. (*Indicates* **Alice**.)

Jasmine and **Pearl** *get messages on their phones at the same time . . .*

Pearl   Dad and Lilia are having a girl.

Jasmine   Great. Another girl.

Pearl   I really wanted a brother.

The doorbell rings.

Alice   I'll get it.

She opens the door. It's the **Postman** *with the same parcel.*

Alice   It's you.

Postman   Yes it's me.

Alice   You're the same postman.

Postman   Yeh.

Alice   I thought you might be different.

Postman   Different from what?

Alice   From the other one.

Postman   What other one?

Alice   Erm. It doesn't matter. Sorry.

Postman   Can you sign this?

Alice   Er – yeh.

She signs.

Scene Three

2018. The kitchen is stacked high with dirty cups, plates and saucepans. **Dan** *is eating cereal.* **Lucas** *is holding a laminated piece of A4 card.*

Lucas   Do you know what colour you are?

Dan   No.

Lucas   You're the colour blue.

Dan *doesn't respond.*

Lucas   You're the colour blue.

Dan   OK.

Lucas   And look what colour it is.

Dan   I can't believe you've actually laminated that thing.

Lucas   It's blue.

Joe *comes into the kitchen.* **Joe** *is actually* **Alice** *in the body of a boy. All three of them are in school uniform.*

Dan   Don't shove it in my face.

Lucas   That's you.

Dan   Alright!

Joe   I'm back. I'm back. Ha! I'm back.

Lucas   We didn't know you'd gone anywhere.

Joe   Didn't you?

Dan   Where did you go?

Joe   Er, nowhere.

He picks up the note.

'If you don't sort the kitchen out before I come home I will kick you all out and you can go and live with your feckless dickhead of a father and his twenty-seven-year-old skank of a girlfriend.' Blimey. Bit harsh.

Lucas (*to* **Dan**)   This is why you've got to wash up.

Dan   She's not going to kick us out.

Joe   I meant calling Lilia a skank.

He turns the note over and reads the postscript. Stops dead.

'PS Joe I have taken your phone' . . . Is my name Joe?

Dan   She's taken your phone?

Joe *slowly realises that he's a boy. Looks at himself.*

Joe   I'm a boy.

Dan   Well, sort of.

Joe   What?

Lucas   Why's she taken your phone?

Joe   Erm, I dunno.

Lucas *looks at the note.*

Lucas   She said she's not going to give it back till you apologise.

Dan   What did you do?

Joe   Er – nothing.

Dan   Yeh right.

Joe   Do I look different to you?

Lucas   No.

Dan   You look as shit as usual.

Lucas   Why have you got to swear?

Dan   The whole world swears, Lucas – except you.

Joe   So I don't? I don't look at all different?

Lucas   No you don't.

Lucas *and* **Dan** *get a text message. They look at their phones.*

Lucas   It's a boy.

Joe   Dad and Lilia are having a boy?

Lucas   Yes.

Joe   So it's gone back to a boy but now I'm a boy.

Dan   What?

Joe   Nothing. Nothing at all. Ignore me.

Dan   I do.

Joe   I thought some things might have changed. Some things have changed – significantly – but not the things I was expecting. Or hoping for.

The doorbell rings.

Joe   I'll get that.

He goes to the door.

Pablo.

Pablo   Yeh.

Joe   What are you doing here?

Pablo   I thought we were walking to school.

Joe   Right. Right. Yes.

Pablo   Are you ready?

Joe   No. No, erm.

Pablo   What's wrong?

Joe   I'm having a really weird day.

Pablo   It's only just started.

Joe   No no no, that's the thing.

Pablo   What? What's the thing?

Joe   You won't believe me if I tell you. Or you'll think I've got a brain tumour. Or I'm having a psychic fugue.

Pablo   What's a psychic fugue?

Joe   I don't really know.

Pablo   OK . . .

Joe   I'm not. I'm not a boy. I'm a girl. My name's Alice.

Pablo   Are you saying you want sex reassignment surgery?

Joe   No.

Pablo   It's OK. It's OK. You can talk to me. Because I've been wondering lately if I might be non-binary.

Joe   Oh.

Pablo   So this is brilliant. This is amazing. Because I had no idea about you. And you clearly had no idea about me.

Joe   Erm. OK, well, anyway –

Pablo   Can I just tell you one other thing.

Joe   What's that?

Pablo   I've got a paralysing crush on your brother Dan.

Joe   But he's a dick.

Pablo   But he's a gorgeous dick. That sounded weird – I didn't mean it like *that*.

Joe   I know, it's fine. Don't worry.

Pablo   Sorry, sorry, we were talking about you. Erm. Where were we?

Joe   I'm not thinking about what did you call it. Sex reassignment –

Pablo   Surgery.

Joe   Yeh yeh, I mean I am a girl. I am actually a girl. I was born a girl.

Pablo   I know, I know, and that's how a lot of people feel. But you mustn't rush into anything.

Joe   I'm not going to rush into anything.

Pablo   Good. I think that's good. You could just start wearing women's clothes couldn't you. And see how that went. Because that's like reversible. Because clothes are just clothes aren't they. But cutting your (*gestures to his crotch*) off. Well, that's like getting a tattoo. But worse. Because actually now with laser treatment and everything you can get a tattoo lasered off and it's not that bad. I mean there's scarring but you know. You can live with that can't you. Whereas no – you know. The regret if you feel regret. I mean you might not of course. I don't want to discourage you. I want to be supportive. You're my best friend. And I'll stand by you. Only don't tell anyone at school because of how we'll both get the shit beaten out of us.

The **Postman** *arrives with the parcel.*

Postman   Can you sign this?

Joe   It's you.

Postman   It's me.

Joe   Is it you?

Postman   What?

Joe   Is it you that's making this happen?

Pablo   Making what happen?

Joe   This.

Postman   I don't know what you're talking about.

Joe   Why am I a boy?

Postman   How should I know?

Pablo   He's just a postman.

Joe   No I don't think he is.

Postman   Actually I really am.

Joe   If I sign it will we go back to the beginning?

Pablo   The beginning of what?

Postman   I haven't got time for this.

Pablo   I can sign it. If you want.

Joe   No erm no I think it has to be me.

Postman   Well, are you going to sign it or not?

Joe   Yes.

He signs.

Scene Four

2018. The kitchen is stacked high with washing-up. **Dan** *is eating cereal.* **Jasmine** *is holding up a piece of paper. Both of them are in school uniform.* **Alice**, **Pearl**, **Lucas** *and* **Joe** *do not exist.*

Jasmine   Do you know what colour you are?

Dan   No.

Jasmine   You're yellow.

Dan *doesn't respond.*

Jasmine   You're yellow.

Dan   OK.

Jasmine   And look what colour it is.

She doesn't stop.

It's yellow.

Dan *grabs it and tears it up. And scatters the bits.*

Jasmine   Great. That's great.

Dan   It is actually.

Jasmine   I should have got it laminated.

Dan   Yeh. You should.

Jasmine *switches the radio on. It's the same song again.*

Dan   Can you turn that shit off?

Jasmine   I like this shit.

She dances on her own.

Dan   Well, I don't.

Jasmine   Well, I do.

Dan *switches it off.*

Dan   It makes me feel like killing myself.

Jasmine   All the more reason to keep it on.

She switches the radio back on. **Dan** *switches it off.*

Jasmine   Dan!

Then they both get a text on their phones. They both look at the phones.

Jasmine   Jesus.

Dan   Christ.

Jasmine   Twins.

Dan   Ha.

Jasmine   Poor cow.

Dan   She brought it on herself.

Jasmine   Yeh Dad had nothing to do with it.

Dan *picks up his bag.* **Jasmine** *stands in* **Dan**'s *way.*

Dan   What are you doing?

Jasmine   I'm not letting you leave.

Dan Don't be ridiculous.

Jasmine *grabs* **Dan***'s arm.*

Dan Are you insane?

Jasmine I'm not letting go.

They start to actually fight or wrestle. **Dan** *trying to get away and* **Jasmine** *not letting him.*

Dan Bitch.

Jasmine Wanker.

Dan Dickhead.

Jasmine You can't call a girl a dickhead, you prick.

Dan Yeh you can. I just did.

The fight ends with both of them slumped on the floor and **Jasmine** *holding onto* **Dan***'s leg. They stop for a moment.*

Jasmine Does it feel like?

Dan What?

Jasmine Like someone's missing?

Scene Five

2018. The kitchen is stacked high with dirty cups, plates and saucepans. There is no one there. **Dan**, **Lucas**, **Jasmine**, **Pearl** *and* **Joe** *do not exist.* **Alice** *comes into the room. Looks around. Goes to the note on the kitchen table, reads it. Then turns it over and reads the message on the back. Looks in the cupboard. Takes out a packet of four pains au chocolat. Looks in the fridge. There's plenty of milk.*

The phone rings.

Alice *waits.*

The answer machine kicks in.

Mum You're through to Shelly and Alice. We can't take your call right now but please leave us a message and we'll get back to you.

Chloe *is on the answering machine.*

Chloe Alice it's Chloe. Are you there? Alice, are you there? Why aren't you answering your phone? Are we walking to school or not? Call me or I'm just going to go without you.

She hangs up.

Alice *switches the radio on. It's the same eighties song.*

The doorbell rings.

Alice *switches the radio off. Goes to the door. It's* **Cinnamon***.*

Alice   Cinnamon.

Cinnamon   You said we might walk to school together but then you didn't answer your phone so then I thought she's probably walking to school with Chloe. But then I thought what if she's not alright. So then I thought I better come round and see. But you're alright. You're fine. So I can just go.

Alice   My mum took my phone. That's why I couldn't answer.

Cinnamon   Why did she take your phone?

Alice   Because she's crazy at the moment.

Cinnamon   So it was nothing to do with you?

Alice   Well, we had a sort of argument. Quite a big argument.

Cinnamon   What about?

Alice   She won't let me do anything. She's like over-the-top protective. Do you want to come in?

Cinnamon   Is Chloe there?

Alice   No.

Cinnamon   But is she coming round?

Alice   I don't think so. And I've got four uneaten, unopened pains au chocolat. So we can have two each.

Cinnamon   OK.

She follows **Alice** *into the house.* **Alice** *opens the pains au chocolat and finds them both a plate. Maybe makes them both a cup of tea too.*

Alice   I'm having a really weird day.

Cinnamon   It's only just started.

Alice   No no, that's the thing. The day keeps starting again. But each time it's different so this morning I've woken up with two sisters instead of two brothers. And then I woke up as a boy. Like with a boy's body. Which was insane. Then a minute ago. It all went blank.

Cinnamon   What did?

Alice   The world. It was white. And I was nothing.

Cinnamon *nods.*

Alice   Do you believe me?

Cinnamon   Yeh.

Alice   Do you?

Cinnamon   Yeh.

Alice   Why?

Cinnamon   Well, why would you make something like this up?

Alice   That's what Pearl said.

Cinnamon   Who's Pearl?

Alice   My sister.

Cinnamon   But you haven't got a sister.

Alice   Have I got any brothers?

Cinnamon   You're an only child.

Alice   Right.

Cinnamon   Sometimes I'm a bit jealous.

Alice   Of what?

Cinnamon   Of the fact that you're an only child. I know I shouldn't say that cos you did have a sister who died.

Alice   But she died before I was born. I mean I don't know if that counts. As having a sister. If I wasn't alive at the time.

Cinnamon   Oh my God.

Alice   What what?

Cinnamon   Is this a trick?

Alice   No!

Cinnamon   Is Chloe here? Is Chloe here all along? Is she, like? Is she, like, hiding? Listening to this?

Alice   No no, course not.

Cinnamon *starts looking for her.*

Alice   Cinnamon she's honestly not here. I wouldn't do that. I wouldn't do that.

Cinnamon *stops looking.*

Cinnamon   Do you think I should change my name?

Alice   No. No I don't.

Cinnamon   Chloe thinks I should change my name.

Alice   Well – she's wrong.

Cinnamon   It's really lonely since you started hanging out with her.

Alice   I'm sorry.

Cinnamon   She's not even nice.

Alice   She's not. She's not really. She's just sort of – powerful.

Cinnamon   Sometimes I wish we were still at primary school.

Alice   So do I.

Cinnamon   It was easier.

Alice   What do you think of my eyebrows?

Cinnamon   What?

Alice   Do they look alright to you?

Cinnamon   They look fine.

Alice   Not over-plucked or under-plucked or wrong somehow?

Cinnamon   No.

Alice   How am I going to get back to normality?

Cinnamon   Do you want to get back to normality?

Alice   Yes.

Cinnamon   Why?

The doorbell rings.

Alice   That'll be the postman.

She goes to the door.

Postman   Can you sign this?

Alice   Have I got a brain tumour?

Postman   Sorry?

Alice   Would you know anything about that?

Postman   About what?

Alice   If I had a brain tumour or not.

Postman   I'm a postman, love.

Alice *signs.*

Scene Six

1983. Kitchen. The kitchen is stacked high with dirty cups, plates and saucepans. **Bex** *is looking in cupboards.* **Dean** *is doing a Rubik's cube.* **Shelly/Alice** *comes into the kitchen.* **Shelly** *is actually* **Alice** *in her mother's body. They are all in school uniform.*

They all have eighties hair and **Shelly** *and* **Bex** *wear leg-warmers.* **Shelly** *wears a headband just for added eighties value.*

Bex   There's nothing to eat. I can find literally nothing to eat.

Dean (*to* **Shelly**)   What are you staring at?

Shelly   This is a very eighties kitchen.

Dean   That's because this is the eighties.

Shelly   The eighties. I wasn't expecting that.

Dean   What?

Shelly   Nothing.

Bex   I could make custard I suppose.

Dean   Custard?

Bex   There's custard powder.

Dean   But we haven't got any milk.

Bex   We've got powdered milk.

Dean   Can you make custard with powdered custard and powdered milk?

Bex   Shall I try it?

Dean   Why not?

Bex *switches the radio on. It's the same eighties song we heard in the first two scenes.*

Bex   I *love* this song.

Shelly   Me too.

Bex *sets about making the custard. Dancing now and again.* **Shelly** *watches her. Watches* **Dean**. *He has nearly finished the Rubik's cube.*

Bex   Shelly.

Shelly *doesn't respond.*

Bex   Shelly.

Shelly   Er – yeh?

Bex   Are you alright?

Shelly   Have we got a mirror?

Bex (*confused*)   Er – there's one on the wall.

Shelly   Oh yeh.

She goes to the mirror and sees herself. Looks at her face and sees her mother at thirteen.

Shelly   Oh my God.

Bex   What?

Shelly   I'm her.

Bex   You're who?

Shelly   I'm my mother.

Bex   What do you mean?

Shelly *is saved from having to explain further by the phone ringing.* **Bex** *and* **Dean** *look at each other in a slight panic about the phone.* **Bex** *switches off the radio.*

Bex   What shall we do?

Dean   Can we just ignore it?

Bex   Yeh.

Dean   OK.

Shelly   Do you want me to answer it?

Bex   It's alright.

Dean   It'll stop ringing in a minute.

The phone is still ringing.

The three of them wait.

Wait another three rings.

Shelly   I don't mind. I don't mind answering it.

Bex   OK. OK. Answer it but if it's any of the utilities –

Shelly   Utilities?

Dean   British Gas. British Telecom. Or the Electric.

Bex   If it's any of them.

Dean   Just hang up.

Shelly   OK.

She picks up the phone.

Hello? . . . Erm hello – Mick.

Bex *rolls her eyes at* **Dean**. **Dean** *puts his head in his hands.*

Bex   Great.

Shelly (*whispers to them*)   It's Mick.

Dean   Mick the dick.

Shelly (*to* **Mick**)   No no, I was just saying to (*looks at them, hesitates because she's not 100 per cent sure*) Bex and and Dean (*this is clearly correct*)– that it was you – on the phone . . . (*to* **Bex** *and* **Dean**) Erm he wants to know where Mum is. Where where is she?

Bex   We thought she was with him.

Shelly   Oh. (*To* **Mick**.) Erm, erm . . . she's not here. We thought she was with you. No no we really did . . . But she isn't here . . . (*Whispers to* **Bex** *and* **Dean**.) He says he's coming round.

Bex   Great. That's great.

Shelly   But she isn't here, Mick. She really isn't . . . Honestly I swear. (*Whispers to* **Bex** *and* **Dean**.) He doesn't believe me.

Bex *rolls her eyes.* **Shelly** *holds the phone away from her ear.*

Shelly (*whispers*)   Now he's just yelling.

Bex (*whispers*)   Hang up.

Shelly *hesitates.*

Dean (*whispers*)   Just hang up.

Shelly (*whispers*)   Won't that piss him off even more?

Bex   Yeh but. (*She shrugs.*)

Shelly (*holds the phone back to her ear*)   Erm, Mick, Mick. Listen. Erm, I'll tell her you called alright? I'll tell her you called. I promise. I'll tell her to call you right back. Yeh. Cross my heart hope to die . . . OK OK OK, Mick. Yeh OK. Bye, Mick.

She hangs up.

He's insane.

Dean   Yeh.

The doorbell rings.

Shelly   Is that him?

Dean   It can't be.

Bex   It can't be.

Shelly   Why can't it be?

Bex   Well, how's he going to get from his house – all the way here – that quick?

Dean   He can't. He couldn't.

Bex   Unless he was calling from a phone box. Did it sound like a phone box?

Shelly   What does a phone box sound like?

Dean   Echoey.

Bex With beeps.

Shelly Erm, there weren't any beeps. I don't think.

The doorbell rings.

Bex If it's him. I just won't open the door.

Dean OK.

Bex OK.

She goes to the door.

Shelly You must be really clever.

Dean Why?

Shelly I can never do them. Rubik's cubes. I mean I can do one side but that's pathetic isn't it. Anyone can do one side. Most people can do one side. But I think even if I had forever I wouldn't be able to do all of them. All of the sides. I think it's got something to do with being bad at physics.

Bex *returns to the kitchen.*

Bex It's a man. Wants to see our TV licence.

Shelly Have we got one?

Dean No.

Shelly Oh.

Dean What shall we do?

Bex Hide the telly.

Dean OK.

Bex It's only little. Carry it upstairs and put it in the airing cupboard.

Dean OK. OK yeh.

He leaves the kitchen.

Shelly Bex.

Bex Yeh?

Shelly I'm not Shelly.

Bex You're not Shelly?

Shelly I look like her but I'm not her.

Bex Who are you then?

Shelly I'm Alice. I'm Shelly's daughter. I'm from the year 2018 and you're my Auntie Bex.

Bex   If this is a joke I don't get it.

Shelly   It's not a joke. Erm, it's not a joke – but I don't know how I can convince you and I don't know how much time I've got before it ends.

Bex   Before what ends?

Shelly   This.

Bex   Do you mean like a nuclear holocaust?

Shelly   Er, no I mean this. This. It's like, it's like I'm in, um, *Back to the Future*.

Bex   What's *Back to the Future*?

Shelly   The film. You must know that film.

Bex   I've never heard of it.

Shelly   Maybe it's not out yet. What year is this?

Bex   1983.

Shelly   *Back to the Future*. Oh I think it was later than that. I could Google it if the internet exists?

Bex   What's the internet?

Shelly   OK, so it doesn't. Forget it. The internet I mean. But you should go and see *Back to the Future*. When it comes out.

Bex   OK.

Shelly   Michael J. Fox goes back in time to when his mum and dad are kids – teenagers – although he doesn't actually end up in his dad's body. That's more like *Freaky Friday*.

Bex   Oh I've seen that. I've seen that. With Jodie Foster.

Shelly   I haven't seen that one. But they did a remake with Lindsay Lohan.

Bex   Right.

Shelly   So I'm in a kind of mash-up of *Back to the Future* and *Freaky Friday* and something else. *Groundhog Day*! *Groundhog Day* is brilliant. You should see that too. But oh God oh God. I shouldn't be telling you stuff about the future. In case it changes the past.

Bex   Well, you've only told me to go and see two films.

Shelly   Three. If you include the *Freaky Friday* remake. Which I would definitely recommend.

Bex   Three films. So I mean. That could completely change my future but it's not like –

Dean *returns to the kitchen.*

Dean   I put the TV in the attic. In case he goes in the bathroom.

Bex   Perfect.

Dean *grins, pleased.* **Bex** *smiles.* **Bex** *goes back to the front door.*

Shelly   I wish I had a brother like you.

Dean   You have. You have got a brother like me.

Shelly (*realising her mistake*)   Yes yes I do and I'm really glad.

Dean   By the way.

Shelly   What?

Dean   You don't look anything like Mum.

Shelly   Why did you say that?

Dean   When you looked in the mirror you said oh my God I'm my mother or something. But you look nothing like her.

Shelly   I think I do – I think I do a bit.

Bex *returns.*

Bex   TV man's gone.

Dean   What happened?

Bex   He wasn't authorised to come in the house.

Dean   Oh. Shall I bring it back down?

The doorbell rings.

Do you think it's him again? Trying to trick us?

Shelly   Or Mick. What if it's Mick?

Dean   I'll go and look. Out the bedroom window.

Bex   OK. OK yeh.

Dean *leaves the stage.*

Shelly   I shouldn't say this cos it's about the future but don't become a nun alright?

Bex   A nun?

Shelly   You become a nun and you're in a convent for five years. One of those ones that doesn't talk or go out or anything.

Bex   Blimey.

Shelly   But then you give it up and become a lesbian.

Bex   Oh.

Shelly   And you always said that you should have become a lesbian sooner and not bothered with the nun bit.

Bex   OK. OK thanks.

The doorbell rings again.

Shelly   I had no idea. No idea at all that my mum's life was like this. She never said anything.

Dean *returns.*

Dean   It's alright. It's alright. It's just the postman.

Bex   I'll get it.

Shelly   Can I get it?

Bex   If you want.

Shelly *goes to the front door. Opens it.*

Shelly   It's you.

Postman   What's me?

Shelly   Is it you?

Postman   What?

Shelly   You look really similar to our postman.

Postman   That's because I am your postman.

Shelly   No I mean our postman from 2018.

Postman   Are you having a laugh?

Shelly   Not really. This is quite stressful.

Postman   Sign here.

Shelly   If I don't sign it will I be like stuck in 1983 forever?

Postman   I honestly don't know what you're talking about.

Shelly   Me neither.

Postman   Are you going to sign it or not?

Shelly   I think I should. I think I better. OK.

She signs.

Scene Seven

2018. The kitchen is stacked high with dirty cups, plates and saucepans. **Dan**, **Jasmine** *and* **Pearl** *are all eating breakfast.* **Lucas** *has the same laminated rota as usual.*

A note for this scene: the asterisks in the dialogue during the dancing are intended to denote gaps in which the characters are just dancing. These gaps can be as long or as short as you like.

Lucas   Do you know what colour you are?

Dan   I'm blue.

Lucas   No you're pink.

Dan   Pink.

Lucas   Yes.

Dan   Why did you make me pink?

Pearl   Why shouldn't he make you pink?

Dan   Because it's a girl's colour.

Pearl   For God's sake.

Jasmine   He's got a point.

Pearl   No he hasn't.

Lucas   You are pink.

Dan   Don't shove it in my face.

Lucas   Pink

Dan   Lucas, stop shoving it in my face or I'm going to hit you. I swear.

Lucas   He's got to do the washing-up.

Jasmine   He does. You do.

Dan   I do not.

Lucas   But you're pink.

Dan   Can you stop saying that?

Alice *comes into the kitchen.*

Alice   This isn't normal.

Jasmine   Yeh it is.

Alice   I mean it's not normality.

Jasmine   Who ate all the chocolate croissants?

Dan   Me.

Lucas   I prefer to say pains au chocolat.

Alice   I was hoping for normality.

Lucas   Why?

Alice   I don't know.

Jasmine   You're so bloody selfish.

Alice   Me?

Jasmine   I was talking to Dan.

Alice   Oh.

Jasmine   But you're not much better.

Pearl *picks up the note on the kitchen table.*

Pearl   Mum's going to kick us out if we don't do the washing-up.

Alice   I know.

Pearl   And she's got your phone.

Alice   I know.

Lucas   Why did she take your phone?

Dan   What did you do?

Jasmine   Yeh what did you do?

Lucas   What did you do?

Alice   I said things. That I shouldn't have said.

Pearl   What things?

Alice   I don't want to talk about it.

A text message arrives on everyone's phones and they all read the message. Except of course **Alice**.

Alice   Is it a boy or a girl?

Pearl   One girl. One boy. And the other one they couldn't tell.

Alice   They're having triplets?

Pearl   Poor Lilia

Dan   She brought it all on herself.

Pearl   Yeh women just get themselves pregnant all the time. They're very irresponsible like that.

Dan   They are! That's how they trap men.

Pearl   Jesus, Dan.

The doorbell rings.

Alice   I'll get it.

It's **Cinnamon**, **Pablo** *and* **Chloe**.

Chloe   Who are you walking to school with?

Alice   I don't know.

Pablo   We could all walk together.

Chloe *pulls a face.*

Cinnamon   Or not.

Alice   Will you come in? Just for a minute?

Cinnamon, **Pablo** and **Chloe** *go into the house.*

Chloe   Hi, Dan.

Dan *doesn't look up.*

Dan   Hi, Chloe.

Alice *switches the radio on. It's the same song we've heard all along.*

Dan   I hate this shit.

Jasmine   Oh shut up, Dan.

Alice *starts dancing.*

Chloe   Why are you dancing?

Alice   Because this may be the only chance we get.

Pablo *starts dancing.*

Cinnamon *starts dancing.*

Chloe *rolls her eyes and starts dancing.*

The following conversations take place amid the ramshackle dancing. At some point in time **Pearl** *and* **Jasmine** *and possibly even* **Lucas** *join in. And everyone except* **Dan** *sings along to the chorus.*

Chloe   Your brother is gorgeous.

Alice   My brother is a meathead.

Chloe   I don't really mind that.

Alice   What is wrong with you?

Chloe   What do you mean?

*

Alice   You can do better than my brother Dan.

Pablo   What?

Alice   You've got a paralysing crush on him but you can do better.

Pablo   How do you know about that?

Alice   I. Guessed.

Pablo   Is it that obvious? Is it like written on me?

Alice   No. No. Not at all. Honestly

*

Cinnamon   Your brother is gorgeous.

Alice   My brother is a dick.

Cinnamon   I didn't mean Dan I meant Lucas.

Alice   Lucas?

Cinnamon   Yeh.

Alice   Really?

Cinnamon   Don't tell him I said that.

Alice   I won't.

*

Alice   Pablo's having a party.

Cinnamon   I know.

Alice   Do you want to come?

Cinnamon   I'm not invited.

Alice   Well, I'm inviting you. I mean if I'm going. If I'm allowed to go. Which I'm not sure I am or will be. But if I am.

*

Alice   I'm going to walk to school with Cinnamon from now on. And maybe Pablo too. Sometimes we'll walk with Pablo.

Chloe   And what am I supposed to do?

Alice   I don't know. Be nicer to people.

*

Alice *takes the landline phone and moves away from the dancing. The song ends and everyone else leaves the stage.*

Alice   Mum? It's Alice. I'm sorry for what I said. About how I wished I'd never been born. And that you were ruining my life. And also calling you a bitch. You're not. A bitch. I mean.

She is crying.

Erm but this party is not what you think. I mean it's at Pablo's house and Pablo's my friend. And Cinnamon's going to come with me. To the party. If I'm allowed to go. And we'll all look after each other. So nothing bad is going to happen. I mean I can't promise that nothing bad is going to happen ever ever. Cos it's like Yoda says – the future is always in motion. But erm erm erm just because you had one daughter who died. It doesn't mean that I'm going to die too. OK? OK. OK. I love you. Bye.

The doorbell rings. **Alice** *goes to the door.*

Alice   Hi.

Postman   Can you sign this please?

Alice *signs.*

Scene Eight

2018. The kitchen is stacked high with dirty cups and plates and saucepans. **Dan** *is eating cereal.* **Lucas** *is holding a laminated piece of A4 card.* **Alice** *comes into the kitchen. All three of them are in school uniform.*

Lucas   Do you know what colour you are?

Dan   No.

Lucas   You're the colour blue.

Dan *doesn't respond.*

Dan   Stop waving it in my face.

Lucas   It's blue.

Alice *goes to the note.*

Alice   It says twenty-seven-year-old witch of a girlfriend . . .

Dan   We know.

Lucas   We've read it.

Alice   Ha! It says twenty-seven-year-old witch of a girlfriend! (*To* **Dan**.) And you're the colour blue. You're the colour blue aren't you?

Lucas   Yeh he is.

Alice   Ha! That means I'm back.

Dan   What?

Alice   Nothing.

Lucas   You have got to do the washing-up.

Dan *takes the rota from* **Lucas**. *Looks at it.*

Dan   Why have I got to do the washing-up – when – whoever's yellow didn't do their washing-up from the morning –

Lucas   I did do my washing-up from the morning but Alice who by the way is pink – she left all that stuff on the side from the night before.

Alice   Because half of it was Dan's from the morning!

Dan   Why can't Mum just get the dishwasher fixed?

Alice   Because she's broke.

Dan *gets his bag.*

Alice   Dan.

Dan   What?

Alice   We have to clean this kitchen up right now. All of us. Because erm because erm Mum had a really shit childhood.

Dan   What?

Lucas   I don't think she did.

Alice   No she did. She definitely did. I know she did.

Lucas   She's never said that.

Alice   Because she was protecting us.

The doorbell rings.

Alice   I'll get it.

She goes to the door. It's the **Postman**.

Postman   Can you sign here?

Alice   No.

Postman   Sorry?

Alice   I'm not signing it. I refuse.

Postman   Why?

Alice   Whatever it is. I don't want it.

Postman   OK.

Alice   I want what I've got.

Postman   OK.

Alice   OK.

Postman   OK.

Alice   So, so that's it?

Postman   Yeh, that's it.

Alice   Great.

Postman   OK. OK.

Alice   It's about playing the cards you're dealt with, isn't it? That's what it's about. Isn't it?

Postman   I have no idea what you're talking about.

Alice   I mean instead of wishing that your life was different from what it is you have to play the cards you're dealt with. That's it, isn't it?

Postman   I still no have no idea what you're talking about.

Alice   OK.

Postman   OK.

Alice   Be like that.

Postman   I will.

Alice   Bye then.

Postman   Bye.

Alice *goes back to the kitchen.*

Lucas   Who was that?

Alice   The postman.

Dan   So where is it?

Alice   What?

Dan   The post.

Alice   Oh. He had the wrong house.

She switches the radio on. It's the same 1980s song. She starts washing up. **Dan** *and* **Lucas** *don't move for a while. Eventually they join her.* **Lucas** *first and then* **Dan**.

Variations

BY KATIE HIMS

*Notes on rehearsal and staging, drawn from a workshop with the writer,
held at the National Theatre, October 2021*

How the writer came to write the play

Katie Hims was originally commissioned to write the play by the National Theatre
nearly three years ago. She knew she wanted to write something that incorporated her
love of plays that are on some sort of time loop, like *Constellations* by Nick Payne and
Blue Heart by Caryl Churchill. She has had an obsession with time loops since she was
seven from watching a *Doctor Who* episode with Tom Baker which loops and this has
stayed with her.

In addition, she is also a massive fan of the concept of a multiverse, so she knew she
wanted to bring these things together. She can't remember at what point the story
became about a girl who wanted sisters instead of brothers, but she knew she wanted to
write something very ordinary and domestic in order to give young actors something
close to their own experience.

Everybody is born into some sort of family set-up. Everyone has an opinion on that
family set-up. Hims wanted to give as many variations of Alice's life as possible in
order for as many similarities to be found as possible. And of course in the play, today
is the day that Alice finds out she might be getting a sister that she has wanted for
thirteen years, which is the inciting trigger for the events that follow.

Introductions and icebreakers

Game: Things in common

This game involves quickly getting into groups of a certain number when that number
is called. Then in those groups, finding three things you have in common within
thirty seconds. The game leader keeps the time. Each round can have different 'bans'
on what can be discussed as things in common. At the end of thirty seconds, you will
have five seconds to nominate a spokesperson who will say the things that you all as a
group have in common. Give a round of applause after each spokesperson. Between
each round, walk very quickly around the room and make eye contact with each other.
No eyes on the floor.

Round 1: Group of four. Ban on using National Theatre Connections or the play as
something in common.

Round 2: Group of five. Ban on anything to do with drama, pets, holidays or children.

Round 3: Group of seven. Really try to delve. In this final round the spokesperson
should also introduce everyone in the group by name.

Game: Prison guard

Create a wide circle of chairs with room to stand behind.

There were nineteen in the group, so nine people sat down and ten people stood behind. *(There must be one empty chair with one missing prisoner in the circle.)*

The game does involve physical contact; tapping people on the shoulder. It doesn't have to be a hand so you could get something else which is soft.

If standing, you are a guard. If sitting, you are a prisoner.

The aim of the game is for a guard to have a prisoner. If you are a guard without a prisoner (i.e. the empty chair in front of you) then you need to call a prisoner to you. As a prisoner, if your name is called, then you must leave your seat and move quickly to the empty chair and prison guard who has called you. However, guards are allowed to stop their own prisoners from moving with a gentle tap. It is important at the start to check people's comfort levels with being touched, and to remind everyone the tap should be very gentle and either done with soft hands, fingers or perhaps something like a cloth. Let the game run for a little while, then give a thirty-second countdown. When the round is finished ask two guards to name all the prisoners. Then switch guards and prisoners and play again.

Approaching the play

Questions

Lead director Ria Parry invited the group to answer four questions in order to approach the play. She asked them to be strict with these questions and only give one response to each. She then split the room into groups of four to discuss their answers. The four questions are:

1   What question do you have about the play?
2   What question do you have about staging the play?
3   What excites you about the play?
4   What will challenge you about the play?

This exercise is to see what is instinctively in your mind when thinking about the play.

Parry pointed out that she finds it really important to have a good list for what excites her about the play. Put it in the front of your notebook and when the play or rehearsals gets tough you can come back to it to remind you.

Rhythm, pace and language

Ria Parry proffered that it is the responsibility of the director to ensure that the structure is clear to the audience.

Exercise: Scene work

Ria Parry invited the group to read aloud the beginning pages of every scene in order to explore the rhythm and language of the piece and the structure of the time loop.

It is easy to mark the repetition and the pace of the play from the first few scenes. Ria Parry and Katie Hims discussed with the group how important it was to be tight on the repetition of language and action. Many of the practical elements, such as the cup of tea being knocked over, are visual markers for the audience. However, it is the tightness of the text, where lines are clearly repeated by either the same characters or the alternative multiverse version that clearly demonstrates the time loops to the audience.

It is important for a line to have the same rhythm, intonation or gesture each time. Cue lines in particular need to be picked up quickly and with energy, or what Ria Parry describes as a tight pick-up. For example, the first half of the page of nearly every scene should feel similar so the audience can feel, hear and see that they are in a time loop.

When you are working with actors of varying experiences, using phrases such as 'tighter' or 'quicker' are not always useful and so the verbal reasoning in the room needs to be linked to character and situation, making sure it isn't just because they have been told to be pacier. A good note; if the play is two hours in length then you haven't found the production yet.

For Katie Hims, rhythm of the language is the most important thing when listening to the actors. The meaning of everything is in the rhythm. If you say something in a certain way in a certain rhythm, you can feel the meaning/sadness. Whilst your actors aren't professionals they may have great instincts and Katie Hims reminded the group that when you listen to young people talking to each other they talk very fast, they often don't think too hard on what they are saying. There is a joyful lightness in just chucking thoughts and words about that exist on the page.

Ria Parry suggested that it is important to think about what your actor might need in order to find the rhythm and tight pick-ups. Some actors may need the work to centre on character conversations to get them to understand the pace and rhythm. If they have siblings themselves you can ask them questions such as: do you listen to your siblings or put any thought behind what you say to them? What is it like at home at breakfast time before school? Is everyone rushed? Setting up the location, the external circumstances and the characters can greatly help an actor understand the need for tight pick-ups. Character conversations can impact on the delivery. You know your actors and what they are most likely to respond to. There are also warm-up games to help work on this.

One exercise offered from the group would be to use a scene from a David Mamet play, where character is found in the rhythm and the text. Have your actors work on the scene to get an understanding from the words only. Character work can then come later as well.

Casting

Casting can be difficult with *Variations* depending on the needs of the company.

A big topic that came up was that of gender and whether the gender of characters could be altered to suit the needs of the company rather than having girls play boys or vice versa.

When Ria Parry is working with a piece of new writing, clarity is everything. The audience has no reference to anything before they come in. Your responsibility as a director is to be as clear as possible with information given to the audience in terms of the story.

The ideal, and what you should strive for, is to cast according to what Katie Hims has written in terms of descriptions and gender. But there is also the reality that this isn't always possible, so if you need flexibility, think about what you can do that doesn't take away from the clarity of what you are trying to communicate.

As soon as the audience is having difficulty trying to understand who is who, then the play is scuppered. The story is clearly one character, one girl, trying to work out if her current life is good enough. She is going through a huge learning curve, going through the body of a boy, the body of her mum, not having siblings, to not existing at all. Doubling the role of Alice could potentially cause confusion.

A question from the group was: with regards to gender, is it better to change a character to a boy or girl to match the make-up of your cast than to have a girl playing a boy or vice versa?

With new writing, the focus must be on keeping the relationships as clear as possible. For this play, in order to keep the clarity, if you have an all-female cast, keep the gender of the character as written; for example, Dan should remain male, even if played by a female. This will open up conversations with your company about what it means to play a boy/be a boy, etc. These are great conversations to be having with your cast. Gender-blind casting is different in some other plays, but in this play gender is a key theme. It has to be clear all the way through. If you change the casting it will skew the communication to the audience.

Ria Parry and Katie Hims both urge you to serve the play, but as a director you will also need to serve your company. Parry would change the postman before changing Lucas. There is something about returning to the same Dan and Lucas in scenes to help the audience understand that this is a play about time loops and multiple universes.

However, Ria Parry suggested that if you do have more than twelve actors in your company, and you must double up characters, keep asking yourself as director: how do I help the audience understand what they are about to see? So if you have to have three actors play Lucas, do you have an image flash of all them dressed identically at the beginning? You know what your parameters are and you have to do what you can to make it as clear as possible.

With a large company, using actors for transitions and other magical set change moments could be possible and if so creating an 'ensemble mentality' early on in rehearsal will be very important. Try to make the company see the whole production as 'their' moment as opposed to individual actors wanting 'their own' moment. There is a necessity for each actor to spend time with their own character in this play, but if you spend too much time on that in the beginning rather than on building your ensemble, then the individual will drive the play not the whole.

Characters and characterisation

Alice

The casting of Alice is open and Katie Hims has seen versions where she is bold and boisterous and also shy and little. She is a bit of an 'every-girl'. What is striking in every story is that we can identify with the hero. Alice can be any of the young people who will end up playing her.

Dan

He's a bit of a git! Katie Hims sometimes worries he is too much of a git, but it's nice to see him finally break out of his shell by the end. He does care for Alice and his siblings. He can be mean to them but doesn't want them to be unsafe. He is sexist and unreconstructed.

Lucas

He is moderate, he can't read social cues. He can't read the room but he has a good heart. You can see he is a nice person, whereas Dan's nice person is hidden!

Jasmine and Pearl

Alice's fantasy sister is not Jasmine; she is too similar to Dan and non-feminist. Pearl is similar to Lucas and close to the fantasy idea that Alice has of her sister. With siblings, you get what you're given.

Cinnamon and Chloe

They are another reflection of Pearl and Jasmine, so Alice longs for sisters and she had that relationship with Cinnamon, which she had been undervaluing. Chloe is a classic mean girl, but the point is that she doesn't think she is a mean girl. It's not all who she is and she has the capacity for change. Katie Hims doesn't want her played super-mean as it's all in the writing and she doesn't need to be evil. Cinnamon is not cool but sincere and a good friend.

Shelly

She is a strong human being who has had a crappy life, but has established a solid life as an adult and kept her childhood out of sight for her kids. She doesn't want that burden to be on the kids.

Dean and Bex

The three of them have pulled together with the odds against them. This version is a slightly romanticised set-up.

Pablo

A good person for Alice to have connected with in this process, which expands her universe. At the end she has two excellent best friends in Pablo and Cinnamon.

The Postman

The Postman is a real postman but also a mythical character. He is magic. But they should be played as a postman who doesn't know they are a mythical character, or part of sci-fi. They are inside it as opposed to being aware of it. There is a version of the Postman where they get a bit more knowing as the play goes on, but it is not in the writing. The danger of making the Postman more knowing as the play moves on is that it will shift the tone and structure of the play.

A note on tone

You can encourage your actors to bring themselves to the characters, but remember to trust the text. There are serious themes and subjects and there is comedy and fun and joy in here. It is all present in the text and so you can encourage your actors to trust in the tone. A helpful suggestion is to use the phrase 'play it truthfully'.

Design

The room split into groups to discuss design in terms of what the play *needs* and what you may *want*.

They were asked to consider – what is the absolute basic set that you need to tell this story? From there you can scale up according to budget.

What you *want* can be more of a design choice whereas what you *need* is about serving the story.

You could make a list for what you need practically for the set and another list for what can be representational. For example, a door is needed for all the entrances and exits and seeing the Postman deliver the parcel, but does it have to be a real door or could lighting be used instead?

Decisions will come down to budget and your own resources within your company. To begin with, each company will have the same list of actual items but then the visual representation of those things will come down to visual choice according to constraints of your company.

You could use lights to make the space feel different; e.g. a spotlight could close a space down to be a different place.

What resources do you have and what creative choices can you make according to your constraints/parameters?

It is important to look at the moments involving props and spillages, breakages, etc. What can you do on stage to show the moment that perhaps doesn't involve spilling actual tea?

How can you play with creating the kitchen for each scene that then becomes slightly different according to which multiverse you are in? There also needs to be consistency so that the story and link for the audience is clear.

Ask yourself how you would do it if you had to do it tomorrow? What are the bare basics that you can communicate this play to an audience with?

Then ask yourself: what do I want? What is the visual dream in your head? If a revolving stage keeps popping into your head, what is the revolving stage giving to the production for you? How could you explore the journey of transitions using your company and ensemble that gives the smooth movement that a rotating stage would?

Asking yourself these questions also helps figure out what the problems are ahead of rehearsal. It's worth thinking through why you want those big things; for example, if you want a fully formed room in the middle of the stage, is it that you want to be able to create clear lines and angled lighting?

A general note on design is to lean into the resources that you have around you. Be honest about what you don't know or don't have.

Music

You can bring in other music for the transitions and scenes, but make sure there is only the one 1980s song. Ria Parry also suggested not dating the music very clearly elsewhere, then it won't affect the impact of the number from the 1980s.

The song

For Katie Hims, the song is a gift for the company to choose themselves. Previous groups have used 'Come on Eileen' – recognisably of the era – and disco tracks. 'Girls Just Wanna Have Fun' was another suggestion. Katie Hims recognises the dance is one of the trickiest moments of the play so it could help if the song is a group choice.

Scene seven and the dancing

A lot of the group commented that this scene and the dancing felt like a particularly daunting challenge to tackle with young people. Ria Parry suggested that it was important to know *when* to work on this scene according to your company. It is important that some bonding has happened for their comfort levels and to create a moment of *carpe diem* for Alice.

Ria Parry asked the following question: 'What does the dancing do in this scene?' The group's thoughts included the following:

- It allows us to zoom in to the little conversations, framing them conversations.
- It allows the audience to see the largeness of all the siblings and friendships. It allows it to be seen visually as well as heard through the text.
- It allows Alice to come into her own and celebrate the changes she is making in her life and allows her to connect to the people who have helped her (unknowingly) on her journey.
- It enables them all to be honest under the cover of the music and dancing. They have dropped the pretence now they are dancing.

- The dancing is a brilliant device at the end of the play to bring all the strands together.

The word 'honest' is a great one to use for this scene as sometimes dancing can cause an issue for people and create worry over choreography, etc.

How do you get your company to a point where there is a sense of comfort, trust and ease in the scene?

In the text it says 'ramshackle dancing'. It is important that it shouldn't feel rehearsed, but there could be spontaneous moments of rhythm and movements that have been known over the years amongst siblings.

You could start rehearsals with the dance and the movement, so it isn't a big thing you are building up to.

Ria Parry reminded everyone that scene seven is filled with many directorial choices, where you will need to marry your vision with serving the play.

The decision of what song is played is an important one. If you are looking for something celebratory, it could be a lovely project for the company to work together on, or it could be the director's decision to bring a particular feeling onto the stage.

Think about whether you will play the complete song or if you will fade it out.

This is a big celebratory scene where it can be joyful to see all the personalities come out in their dancing. Try and embrace the moment and encourage your company to seize the energy and really let go and enjoy it. It should be fun!

Question and answer with Katie Hims and Ria Parry

Q: Is there room to add people into the transitions to express the multiverse?
A: Yes there is; however, Katie Hims doesn't want any young person to feel as though they are less for not being a 'named' role and so it is essential that any ensemble work has time and energy spent on it so everyone feels important. One production Hims saw had every version of Alice's life pass through Alice in the transition right at the end, which made Hims realise that there is a lot of scope in the gaps between the scenes.

Q: Is there scope to use the ensemble to make the changes – for example, a magical stage crew?
A: This is a very creative way for the ensemble to have a huge part to play. It could become integral. Ria Parry would suggest creating a significant role for an ensemble before doubling up named characters, which could cause confusion for an audience with regards to understanding the structure of the play.

Q: For some young people this might be the first time they have had conversations around gender roles. Are there any supporting documents or resources that can help us navigate this journey?
A: Katie Hims pointed out that the gender conversation has moved on greatly since she wrote the play and that conversations between young people are moving far quicker now than when it was commissioned and set (2018). Some suggestions for resources were made by members of the group and they are listed at the end of these notes.

Q: Pablo and Joe's conversation and referencing 'sex reassignment surgery' (Scene Three, page 506) is now considered to be wrong terminology and adds to the gender-dysphoria trans people face. It is now referred to as gender confirmation surgery. Could this be changed?
A: This is a good discussion point. The language reflects Pablo's own ignorance of the subject, and whilst his intention is to be a good friend to Joe/Alice, he doesn't have the language to do that sensitively. Changing his terminology would require a larger rewrite.

Try having an open discussion with the group about Pablo's language, why his terminology is inappropriate, and what that tells you about the character, and the gap between his intentions and his understanding.

Q: How far can we push the multiverse idea within the design or does it need to stay domestic/ordinary?
A: You can push it as far as you like!

Q: Is it an actual 1980s kitchen? Is this all really happening or is she dreaming? So would it be cliché 1980s?
A: This is absolutely a personal choice for the company, and a fun conversation to have.

Q: Does the Postman need to be dressed in the appropriate costume for the 1980s?
A: You could do some research into the era. This is a design decision based on your production. However, remember the script says it is the same person but there is no reference to the visual, so the look is based on design and directorial decision.

Q: Do we update it from 2018 to 2022?
A: No. It was written in 2018 and is of its time; in particular due to the gender conversation happening at the moment, it wasn't as far along as we are now. This is also pre-Covid. This play is set in 2018 and needs to stay that way. It cannot be updated to now, as it will shift characters' ages and dates.

Q: What is in the box?
A: Katie Hims believes it is Alice's life in the box. Every time the Postman gives the box he is giving her a new version of her life to see. She doesn't know this but at the end she doesn't sign as she is happy with her life. Potentially you could have different boxes each time as a design choice.

Q: Why is there no Postman in scene four?
A: Katie Hims originally said it has to be Alice to sign, so this is an aberration and there's no Postman. If there is no Alice, there's no Postman; this could highlight his importance. Ria Parry suggested that when you don't have the writer around, it becomes a set text, so how do you interpret this scene so that it's solid and purposeful? Can it prompt your design and production choices? For example, is there something different visually or in the sound in scene four as there is no Postman or Alice? Alice is aware that at some point she didn't exist and Katie Hims is sure that there isn't a Postman.

Q: Can we change certain terms according to where we are in the world?
A: It should be free from any regional terminology or phraseology as it would change the rhythm and change the text. It can be performed in their own accents and placed

anywhere, but phrases need to stay the same. The text is neutral enough to stay. A particular reference to British Gas can be altered to local utilities and 'Mum' and 'Mam' can be shifted. Katie Hims referenced a past Connections performance where the company used props to help identify or give a local setting to their version; for example, a can of Irn-Bru in the kitchen as a link to their Glaswegian location.

The precision of dialogue is incredibly important. It is a commissioned play that has been written by a live writer. Every word and comma has been chosen purposefully and must be adhered to. Bring yourself to the text but accuracy of dialogue is something that young actors need to learn.

Rhythm is very important to Hims. Everything on the page is very deliberate.

Q: With props and costumes, do we try and do the best with what we have been given?
A: Yes, absolutely. These are all directorial choices, though it's nice for the actors to have a contribution as well. Do let the actors follow their instincts for what their characters would wear. Anything your young people want to bring to the table is potentially very useful, but of course you need to be the guidance on that.

Q: How important is the swearing in the play?
A: If the swearing is problematic in your setting, you could look at changing the swear words, but please be aware this will alter the rhythm of the language, so as far as possible you should do the play as it is written.

Suggested references

http://genderedintelligence.co.uk/professionals/resources
https://thebeyouproject.co.uk/resources/
https://www.nspcc.org.uk/keeping-children-safe/sex-relationships/gender-identity/

From a workshop led by Ria Parry
With notes by Jemma Gross

You don't need to make a Big Song and Dance out of it

by Abbey Wright, Shireen Mula and Matt Regan,
in association with Tackroom Theatre

Abbey Wright is a theatre director and maker.

Abbey is Artistic Director of Tackroom Theatre with whom she created, directed and produced *Why is the Sky Blue?* (Southwark Playhouse), *Go On* (a podcast series featuring Simon Stephens, Ben Okri, Maxine Peake, Toby Jones) and *Resolution* (a global climate action music project with Decca Records and Music Declares Emergency and with musicians in every country in the world). Other direction for Tackroom includes: *Mrs Lowry and Son* (Trafalgar Studios); *The Eisteddfod* and *Holiday* (Bussey Building); *The Glass Supper* (Hampstead Downstairs).

Other recent directing includes: *The Outsider* (Winner of Offie Award for Best Production); *The Cocktail Party* (The Coronet); *The Father*, *Dublin Carol* (Donmar at Trafalgar Studios); *The Mentalists* (Wyndham's, West End); *Diana of Dobson's*, *Ghosts*, *Talent*, *The Mountaintop* (New Vic) and *The Grapes of Wrath* (Leeds Playhouse, Nottingham Playhouse, Royal and Derngate, NST).

Abbey was Resident Assistant Director at the Donmar, Staff Director at the National Theatre, Associate Director at the New Vic and Nuffield Southampton Theatres.

Shireen Mula is a playwright and theatre-maker.

Shireen has been playwright on attachment at the Royal Court Theatre and Associate Artist at both Ovalhouse and Nottle Theatre Company, Korea. She is an Associate Artist with FastFamiliar (previously fanSHEN) with whom she's created numerous works, most notably *Lists for the End of the World* (Summerhall) and *The Justice Syndicate* (UK and Ireland tour). She co-authored *Why is The Sky Blue?* (Southwark Playhouse) which was nominated for two Offies. Her other plays include: *39 and Counting* (Park Theatre); *The Rise & Fall* (Somerset House); *Soon Until Forever* (Theatre503); *Same Same* (Ovalhouse) and *Nameless* (Arnolfini Theatre). *Same Same* was presented by the British Council in Italy as well as being shortlisted for the Royal National Theatre Foundation Playwriting Award, formerly the Meyer Whitworth Award. Shireen is currently working with Secret Cinema and Tangled Feet Theatre Company. She lectures on the Drama and Performance MA and BA at London South Bank University.

Matt Regan is a Belfast-born award-winning composer, songwriter and theatre-maker. His work aims to be accessible, socially conscious and formally adventurous. His critically acclaimed first album and stage show, *Greater Belfast*, 'made a mockery of all the old boundary-defining labels such as "gig", "theatre" and "spoken word", or indeed "pop" and "classical music"' (*Guardian*).

As a collaborator and associate artist, he has worked with the National Theatre, the National of Scotland, filmmaker Mark Cousins, Tackroom Theatre in their issue-based contemporary musicals, Vanishing Point and more artists and organisations across the UK and Ireland over the last ten years.

Note on the content

All of the words spoken or sung in the show are verbatim. This means all of the words in the show were originally spoken by children or young people aged between thirteen and twenty-two – and, in one case, a teacher. Abbey Wright and Tackroom Theatre carried out interviews with over ten thousand children and young people right across the UK. And the content of these interviews was used to make this show.

Each scene represents young people from a different school or youth theatre in a different part of the UK.

Note on the setting

All of the words spoken in this show were spoken by young people in schools, or youth theatres. Often they were sitting in a circle of school chairs and wearing uniform or their own clothes. If you would like to replicate that on stage, then this can be a very easy show to produce. But, of course, you may have other ideas regarding set and costumes, etc.

Note on the casting

The songs and scenes can be divided between your performers however you see fit. Text that appears as monologue can be shared between as many speakers as you like.

Occasionally in the text, it is clear that the original speaker is a particular age, gender, sexuality or ethnicity but it is not necessary that the performer is the same age, gender, sexuality or ethnicity. It can be presented in a more Brechtian way than that. We would welcome any interpretation: girls reading boys' lines and vice versa, etc. It is all up for grabs.

In the same way, it is your choice whether you try to use accents in the piece for characters from diverse locations or whether the performers use their own accents. Either choice is entirely valid.

It is perhaps nice to have some musical numbers as solos or duets and some as full company numbers.

Note on performance

Ideally all songs should be performed as in the demos.

Despite being a 'musical', we suggest using the authenticity of the young people's voices. We wouldn't suggest big, American-style musical theatre singing, but more colloquial, pedestrian, authentic singing.

List of musical numbers

'The Beauty of Porn'
'Squirt'
'Little Spoon'
'Never Have to Leave the House'
'Fleshcoats'
'Good to Chat'

As the audience enters, audio plays: The content of this audio will be banal chat and use the word 'chat' a lot. For example: Shall we get more chairs? We are just going to have a little chat. How are you going to keep the memory on your phone? Each of the extracts features diverse groups doing bits of last-minute 'admin' before the session begins.

The actors can already be onstage as the audience comes in or they can make an entrance at the top of the show now.

Scene One

Teacher   Hello, class. Hello – Hello, everybody.

Um, is this everybody?

Come on in, everyone.

Are you all coming to the chat?

OK. Great.

Have we got Claudie?

Claudie   Yeah.

Teacher   Lee Anne?

Lee Anne   Yeah.

Teacher   David?

David   Yeah.

Teacher   Have you got enough room there, David?

David   Yeah.

Teacher   Are you a wee bit squashed? Are you OK?

David   Yeah.

Teacher   Are you sure?

I think you should move. You look a wee bit squashed, OK.

Where are you ladies off to?

Chorus of Three   Toilet.

Lee Anne   Where should we put the chairs, miss?

Teacher   Just – er – leave them where they are. Hang on. I'm just gonna press the red button – yep – we're recording.

Thank you all for coming out rather than staying home and watching *Made in Chelsea* and having your tea.

Now. We are taking part in a big research project with ten thousand other young people.

All   Whooooo.

Teacher   And they are going to make a play with your words. The play is going to be a musical and all of the words in it – even the words to the songs – will have been spoken by young people like you lot all across the UK.

David   What's it about?

Teacher   Well, at the moment they're looking into – ummmm – (*The teacher is shy to say the word 'pornography'.*) just doing some research. And they would like to talk to you – ummmmmm – to help them do their research. Is that OK? What's wrong with your face, Patrick?

Pardon?

That's your normal face, did you say?

Claudie   Is it like reality TV the play they're doing? Kind of like – the real living insights of young people. Will it have a story?

David   Will this get to San Francisco?

Lee Anne   What? Don't you mean New York?

Claudie   Are we going to be famous like?

Patrick   Hello, Mum!

He waves and the others all join in waving and calling out: 'Hello, Nan', 'Hello, Mum', 'Hi, Dad', etc.

Teacher   OK, guys. Let's get cracking, shall we? – If you – if you're not comfy about anything that's being said or discussed, you can just – you don't need to make a Big Song and Dance out of it – you can just take yourselves out.

Basically, it's going to be a big old chat.

Claudie   You know we're good at that! Ha! Yeah we like to chat!

Scene Two

Claire (*aged fourteen*)   It's not usually the kind of thing you talk about with someone you just met. It's quite a close personal thing. I'm fourteen and I'm from Glasgow.

I find adults are really frightened of talking to children about porn.

They are afraid of safeguarding where you don't actually need to be afraid of it. They're just really afraid of getting into trouble. But obviously we know much more than they do, so that's pretty strange.

Whenever teachers, parents, whatever, talk to you about sex, they use a whole load of metaphors, books, videos, those cartoons. Stuff like:

'The birds and the bees' – the whole special cuddle. Not that useful. I mean what does the birds and the bees have to do with sex? I had a book when I was little called *Hair in Strange Places*.

And my brother had one called *Living with a Willy*. About a boy and when he opened his trousers, fireworks went off and as a kid he was *terrified* of his trousers.

There was this man who was chasing – in like a cartoon – chasing a girl with a feather duster. And that was in Year 7 and they just showed that and – it was like – they were kind of like running around and like dusting each other and then they like took their clothes off – but they didn't have any like – they didn't have any like genitals. And then they just jumped into the bed and then feathers came up and they were like – that is sex.

I can't look at a pigeon in the same way now.

It is quite a religious high school where I go and so there is a kind of: 'Even the Virgin Mary didn't even have to do it so you don't have to do it either. A testicle is the same size as a walnut, celibacy is fun. Here's a Bible.'

I feel sorry for parents because they didn't make the internet. They don't know how young their children are viewing these things.

Because they've raised you from like a baby and you have grown from this innocent child – I think – I think they just want to hold onto that.

The trouble is that I want to say to anyone who is a parent, your kid has seen porn. They have. And you probably have parents who are like – 'Oh I know that kids see porn around this age, but not my Jimmy'. But I want to say to you – 'Jimmy has seen it. He's seen it. And so's Jenny and so's Sue and so's Graham. They've all seen it.'

And it *is* like a rite of passage. We have to discover some stuff for ourselves. There are things that no one else can teach you. Like, there's a limit – you can't talk to your Mum and Dad about everything.

But yeah, porn is everywhere. And it's pretty mindboggling what is out there. What do they say? What is that rule? Is it rule 42? If you have thought of it, or if the human mind can think of it, then there is porn like that out there on the internet? Oh yeah, no, not rule 42 – that's something else.

Song: 'The Beauty of Porn'

Rule 34.
If you can imagine it, there's porn of it.
There are dwarves, goblins, leprechauns – all the woodland creatures.

There's *Game of Thrones*, Ebony, Asian;
– all the racey racist ones.
There's categories like BBC.
When I first heard BBC, I was like – why does the British Broadcasting
Corporation have a porn channel?

The Greatest Hits
Stuff you just can't say out loud.
So you'll have to imagine.
It's literally like the Wild West.
That's the Beauty of
That's the Beauty of
That's the Beauty of
Porn.

Like
women with beards in the circus.
You're like a kid at the fair.
You've broken into a haunted house and
you really shouldn't be there.
Am I gay, straight, pansexual, bisexual?
Do I like making love to a man dressed like a teddy bear?

There are costumes, and carriages, breeches.
Smoking a cigarette, eating spaghetti.

Sometimes, that's all – no rumpy pumpy or anything – they just eat the spaghetti.
And then they're like, 'Oh I'm full now. Thank you. That was a lovely meal.'
And I'm a bit like – 'Oh. That really was a film about someone eating spaghetti.'

Somewhere out there that's ticking someone's box.

Titanic, Love Actually – there's lots of Richard Curtis films
The Simpsons, SpongeBob, Scooby and Scrappy Doo.
That's when you've made it –
They're ripping you off for porn.
There's this thing called Sexy Disney – 'Whistle while you twerk';
'The Lion Fling';
and 'The Hunchback of Notre Dyaaaaammmm'.

You know someone, somewhere has searched the same thing as you.
So if you're a freak, somebody else is too.
That's the Beauty of

That's the Beauty of
That's the Beauty of
porn.

Masturbate. Masturbation. There's not much wrong with masturbation.

Repeat.

My friend Billy had a ten-foot willy and he showed it to the girl next door. She thought it was a snake so she hit it with a rake and now it's only five foot four.

Repeat.

Scene Three

Hugh (*aged eighteen*)   Sometimes my little brother will stay with me in Aberystwyth – you know – if it's a bit rough at home – or if he just can get away with it. One of his friends – Joe – I don't know why I need to say his name but – he was like I love coming here. We're able to talk about things that we wouldn't at home. I was like 'AAAHH!' And then he started talking about porn. But he was talking about it so – *vividly*. It's weird seeing my little brother involved in a conversation about porn because I can't look at him the same sometimes – you know.

He laughs.

He's eleven and I've just turned eighteen.

It's interesting how people overcompensate. And how they feel the need when they discuss it be like '*Yeeeeaaah* I really love boobs and this and that' and I feel like he's almost trying to make himself believe that.

With porn, there are set labels, you're either this or that in porn, it's a category. You're the dominant aggressive this or you're nothing – like that's what it is and it forces people to say, 'OK, am I going to choose to be this, or be that, or be this, or be that.'

As a guy, I can say, yeah I know it's not real, I get that. But to be honest, am I really that evolved that I can say I am that in control? If you spoon this stuff in it has an effect. It messes up I think because you – you – you sort of view people as part of like a sexual – a porn category. As opposed to seeing people as individuals and their struggles and their life or who they are as people. You look at them and you're like, you're Ebony, OK. I watched a video of Ebony. I watched a video of lesbians and you guys do it like this – it messes up your perception of people. And it's quite – dangerous, I think. For young guys looking at women and what you think the women are meant to do. Like you had the whole fake news. Like not all women bend like that!

Song: 'Squirt'

You're either
slim thick. Or

thick. Or slim.
Slim thick is the Kim Kardashian hourglass. She's got the flattest
stomach . . .
The
tiniest waistline but you've got the
boobs and the bust size.
There's
Slim, you're you're a bit rectangular.
And then you have the
thick
where obviously like you're very curvy and

you can shake it
you can like
break your back
like, you're
moving like the space when
you're dancing you're taking up the floor

like honey yes!

Go for the mainstream
Get yourself peng
Do squats and lunges
Get the big booty
Why can't you do this?
Why won't you do that?

Join the skinny, hairless women.
Tits like a porn star. Hips like a porn star.

Why can't you do this?
Why won't you do that?

Being skinny's not in any more.
Follow the changes.
You're supposed to have curves.

'You're supposed to squirt now.'

Squirt. Squirt. Squirt.

'You're supposed to squirt now.'

Squirt. Squirt. Squirt.

'You're supposed to squirt now.'

You're peng you're peng you're peng
You're slim you're slim you're slim
You're dank you're dank you're dank
You're thick you're thick you're thick

(Spoken) OK. I have like really massive boobs but seriously if you knew how it was to have really massive boobs then – you're just walking around. You can't run anywhere – you can't. But it looks good on screen so –

Let's all look like a Kardashian
Any Kardashian
Be sexy but don't be a slut.

Why can't you do this?
Why won't you do that?
Why do you not like your body?
Why do you not love yourself?
You're supposed to have curves.

'You're supposed to squirt now.'

Squirt. Squirt. Squirt.

'You're supposed to squirt now.'

Squirt. Squirt. Squirt.

'You're supposed to squirt now.'

You're peng you're peng you're peng
You're slim you're slim you're slim
You're dank you're dank you're dank
You're thick you're thick you're thick

Don't be a slag ra ra
Don't be stoosh. Don't be a ho
Be sexy – don't be a slut.
Be sexy – don't be a prude.
Girls, close your legs. Guys, go ahead.
Scissor, scissor
Be a lipstick les
Be femme,
Be well up for a random bloke joining in.
Be obsessed with strap-ons
Make out with your sister

Keep your bits under –
Don't get a reputation.
Don't be dirty, slutty frigid. Or –
Enioy it.
But not too much.

Why do you not like your body?
Why do you not love yourself?
You're supposed to have curves.

'You're supposed to squirt now.'

Squirt. Squirt. Squirt.

'You're supposed to squirt now.'

Squirt. Squirt. Squirt.

'You're supposed to squirt now.'

Watch porn to
learn what to do to please the man
You know your vagina is meant to look like that.
Get down on your knees and do it.
Be as bendy as you can.
Fake it till you make it.
Always be ready for sex –
no matter what time of the month it is
Shave, shave, every little thing.
You don't want to be a gorilla.
Don't be gross.
Impress them and please them.
Don't be clingy and don't fanny fart.
Toss your hair around.
Let them in the back door.
Be freaky
Get straight to it.
I seen a video where the girl wanted me to
Do this to her
So why can't you?
They do that here so I don't get why you're upset.
Orgasm and reach climax and often yeah and very loud.
Do all this stuff and pretend you know what half of these things are.

Try and act normal. Try and act normal.

Why can't you do this?
Why won't you do that?

Being skinny's not in any more.
Follow the changes.

You're supposed to have curves.

'You're supposed to squirt now.'

Squirt. Squirt. Squirt.

'You're supposed to squirt now.'

Squirt. Squirt. Squirt.

'You're supposed to squirt now.'

You're peng you're peng you're peng
You're slim you're slim you're slim
You're dank you're dank you're dank
You're thick you're thick you're thick

Scene Four

Beth (*aged thirteen*) and **Joseph** (*aged thirteen.*)

Beth   I'm Beth. I'm thirteen. You know what's weird in pornography, then in the videos, the camera always seems to zoom in and focus on the actual intercourse but then in reality you don't see it up close. That's not what you're watching. That's not your viewpoint. Like if you were having sex with someone you wouldn't just be staring at their (*whistles*). You would both be up the head end, face to face.

Joseph   Or you would hope! Imagine you're getting into it and the person keeps going down to the (*whistles*) and looking at it – like Inspector Gadget.

They are both laughing a lot.

Joseph   I'm Joseph. I'm also thirteen. My experiences with all my pals – it is – it's like a big competition. You see it with all the boys at school. At my school the girls are kind of like – it's proper honestly again at my school – in my school – it's like – Oh if it's below nine inches non-erect you're not cool.

They are both laughing a lot. Hysterically. From now on.

Beth   Excuse me! Do you know how big nine inches is, Joseph? What girls go to your school?

Joseph   But that's literally what it is.

Beth   JESUS!

Joseph   That's just an example. But that's –

Beth   Like the whole thing in porn of the camera getting as close as flipping humanly possible to the action. I saw this one thing where I was like – eugh – are they actually going to put that camera in her bottom now?

They are laughing.

Joseph   Like a colonoscopy. Like a flipping colonoscopy.

Beth   It's weird – cos with porn – it gets in your brain – and so – and it sows a seed – and it's weird to think all of our private fantasies are being shaped by creepy old white dudes.

Joseph   Yeah. And, our generation is different on gender anyway. We all know that everything flows.

Song: 'Little Spoon'

Have you heard of the saying 'Boys will be boys?'
Yeah.
Yeah.
kind of like
Boys are rough and tumble, playfightyish, not very sensitive.
Well, that's boys for you.

You know how porn –
Yeah –
Is like 'Guys take what you want.'
Like 'We know you want to.'
WINK WINK WINK WINK
But I'm actually like – I don't want to.

People always say –
'Oh I know what teenage boys are like.'
And I'm always like – 'Oh really. Do you?'
'We ain't all the same, because
Sometimes I want to be
Sometimes I
Sometimes I want to be
Sometimes I want to
Be the little spoon,
Oh it's nice being hugged
Nice to be hugged
Everybody needs a bit of love love love love love love love

I got bullied cos I'm-not manly
By one of these
fellas who walks with a wide stride.
I know those fellas.
It's
hard to know what to do
really as a boy.
Yes, it's confusing
all these rules.

Sometimes I want to be
Sometimes I
Sometimes I want to
Sometimes I want to
Be the little spoon,

Oh it's nice being hugged
It's nice to be hugged
Everybody needs a bit of, a bit of love.

At the moment though it's gone too far.
All we hear is masculinity equals toxic.
Just the fact that I'm a young man –
there's something wrong in that –
in just being a young man. You know?
Sure. I know.
Porn really don't help.
There are so many ads for gigantic penises –
like penises the size of a small country.
You see it in a lot of them
the way these really like sexually aggressive men
it's kind of rewarded –
it feels like
it's kind of –
It's saying if you act in this way you get rewarded with sex
If you're the bear you get the honey.
Try being Black and a man.
It's all 'White woman gets demolished by Black man'.
Why do I have to demolish her?
Why can't make sweet love to her?
Cos the whole Harvey Weinstein thing
Uh-oh
and Donald Trump –
Oh you've gone there.
These white guys
Who are obviously doing something wrong
And taking advantage
I don't wanna be seen like that.
I don't wanna be seen as this villain.
You don't want people to presume.

But I want to
Be the little spoon.
Oh, it's nice being hugged.
It's nice being hugged.
Everybody needs a bit of love, love, love, love, love, love, love.

Have you heard of the saying 'incels'?
Er – I don't believe I have.
Involuntary celibates.
There are websites full of these people
The geeky introverted sort of people.
Uh-huh.

There's porn videos where people are
Actually violently hurting somebody,
These are the kind of videos that get shared a lot
On incel sites; it's like revenge against the world.

Like people chained up and I
It kind of makes me feel internally sick
Like females, I don't know,
Gags and stuff where you can see somebody
Sometimes they'll have like hooks!
Hooks!
Like metal, metal hooks.
What?
. . . so like you know . . .
so . . .
That's a thing?
Yeah.
That's an actual thing?
Yeah.
That's . . .
She literally has to . . .
She can't like . . .?
If . . .
Yeah that's a thing.
Ugh. Oh my God.
That's a thing?
Yeah.
That's an actual thing.

Note on that section above: The omission of detail on the event depicted in the pornographic scene is deliberate so that we safeguard the young people from too detailed a description. In performance, therefore, the intention is that the omission of detail provides an indication that something violent is being discussed by the speakers.

I'm obviously a trans man so I maybe don't face the same issues as like a cis man, but like, um, my first girlfriend was like quite like physically dominant like she would always initiate kisses. And I really enjoyed that. She was also taller than me. I actually really liked that, I was like 'Oh I feel protected'.
And I know other guys *who are like*:

Sometimes I want to be
Sometimes I
Sometimes I want to
Sometimes I want to
Be the little spoon
Oh it's nice being hugged
It's nice to be hugged.
Everybody needs a bit of love love love love love love love.

Scene Five

There could be a few chords underscoring this speech.

LaShane (*aged fourteen*)   I think a lot of things can happen that you kind of let happen.

You sit down and you's end up with a train of videos. You're not really sure how one led onto another.

You go further down the rabbit hole.

You can't really get out of it.

And it's honestly quite scary – you find it quite scary.

You just keep going down into that abyss.

There's no bottom to it. If you do get lost in it.

When you're in that space – you kind of blur into – you are in that zone – you are in the computer.

My name is LaShane. I am fourteen. I'm from Coventry, which is in the Midlands.

Then you go up in the rankings – you watch something a bit worse – you look for something a bit more shocking.

One, then another and another, and just again threesomes or foursomes – to make it more crazier and wilder – like ooh you haven't seen this before. You know? Like.

You have eight to ten different tabs, different videos each of different like things. Playing at the same time so you can go between them.

And it's like that buzz – you get one – OK yup, bored of that – that one – OK bored of that – bored of that.

You can have that instant you know all the variety in the world.

That intimate thing that's with only one person feels boring.

The internet is so big now, you can almost find anything.

It's like another room in your imagination.

It's like a drip feed into your brain.

You go through and nup, nup, nup, nup and you're on the twentieth page. Imagine having loads of girls in front of you in real life standing there and you being like, 'No, no, no, no.' The power of that is crazy.

You can completely shut off from your thoughts.

It's easier to watch than to think maybe.

You stop thinking. You are shoving it in like –

Imma have a chocolate and Imma have a Curly Wurly, Imma have a Dairy Milk and Imma have Mars –

You're always with these porn women. The most often comment on any of the videos is 'What's her name?' They've taken an attraction and 'What's her name? What's her name?'

Song: 'Never Have to Leave the House'

My bedroom is my style. It's how I like it.
You put yourself in a bubble and you live this other world.
It's the perfect love.
It's a private embrace.

You never have to, never have to leave
You never have to, never have to leave
You never have to, never have to leave
the house . . .

It's something you do on yourself by yourself
I'm normally in my room and my
mum says come downstairs
part of me wants to go
part of me wants to stay

everybody lies
about the chaos inside
you can hide
I'm on my own so I'm gonna to do what I want

You never have to, never have to leave
You never have to, never have to leave
You never have to, never have to leave
the house . . .

I have tried
but girlfriends are hard.
People muddy the waters.
It's free and not saying that girlfriends aren't free but sometimes you're going to have to get them
something or – like this guy in my year – gave this girl a fifty pound ring to stay with him – we kind of
make gold digger jokes now. That's a little bit off topic.

It's stress-free –
because really
with boyfriends there's complications.

It's two clicks away
Your phone won't let you down
And you won't let it down.
You can only do so much
I'm on my own
So I'm gonna do what I want

You never have to, never have to leave
You never have to, never have to leave
You never have to, never have to leave
the house . . .

Scene Six

Carrie (*aged sixteen*)   My name is Carrie and I am sixteen years old. I grew up in Hackney. It's quite a widespread thing. People clocking out of life a bit. And I think porn is a part of that. I've never been addicted to porn but I have been obsessed by it. By it not of watching it – but of thinking like if I was with a guy just whether – what their porn habits were. How they watched it, what they thought of me because of it, what they were expecting because of it – all of that kind of thing. I think I get very unlucky in the rain. I'm sitting here talking to you dripping all over the floor. And I don't know why I get more unlucky than everybody else. I tried to get into the British Library once and they wouldn't let me go in because I was soaking. Porn is so pervasive and it shapes so many things without us even realising it. There's a darkness. And I don't know how to describe it in any other way than there's this darkness. I think it's stopping people from being able to connect with each other. And honestly see each other. So often you put yourself in a bubble and you live in this other world.

I'd say you feel connection instantly with someone. You just know. This will be a person I'll have a connection with.

You have an automatic connection with your mum. You made that bond so early on without even knowing it when she's got you in her tummy.

Something slotting into place. A safety. There's something there. You feel in tune. It feels right.

Like 'this feels right to me'.

I feel the bubble around me. If you connect with someone they burst through the bubble.

But it's not that easy. It's much easier to stay in the bubble. And I worry – I do worry – that porn encourages that. Because it can be done on your own – without anyone else – just you know – you never have to leave the house.

When someone touches you, it's just a very clear way of saying 'I'm here and you're here'. It's like we are all fleshcoats and we all want to be touched but we don't want to be touched. We are all looking for connection but we are all scared. Maybe that's just being a teenager but I asked my dad and he said, no that's true for everyone. If I'm not sure if what I think is right or not, I ask my dad and he says, yup, that's another thing about the human condition you are going to have to live with.

It's like – 'Thanks, Dad.'

She does a thumbs-up.

Song: 'Fleshcoats'

> When monkeys climb
> One hand forward
> And the other holds back.
> The one that holds back
> Stops it from falling
> down from the trees
>
> So people don't rush to touch new things or something like that
>
> They want to touch. They don't want to touch.
> They want to love and they don't want to love.
>
> They are fleshcoats
> Rubbing together.
> Fleshcoats
> Rubbing together.
>
> There is nothing a human fears more
> than the touch of the unknown
> You sit on a train
> with an empty seat
> Between you.
>
> They want to touch. They don't want to touch.
> They want to love and they don't want to love.
>
> They are fleshcoats
> Rubbing together.
> Fleshcoats
> Rubbing together.
>
> I've always been afraid of pornography.
> There's something about it that makes me feel hollow.
>
> They want to touch. They don't want to touch.
> They want to love and they don't want to love.

They are fleshcoats
Rubbing together.
Fleshcoats
Rubbing together.

Scene Seven

Michael (*aged nineteen*)   Yes, I remember seeing pornography when I was very little. Sorry, I'm Michael, I'm nineteen. I like beatboxing and my special subject is geography – Hello, everyone.

Yeah, it was when we were living on the estate – this was in Bradford – I'm from Bradford – so I must have been five or six max. Well, my brother showed it to me – just being a clown and thinking it would be funny to show a little boy or something. And anyway, my heart pounding, and yeah, just my eyes out on stalks. I don't know. It felt very gruesome and very adulty and yeah like, OK, so this is another new thing I need to get into. Seeing pornography from such a young time – when I didn't even really know what having a girlfriend – or having a boyfriend – meant – I'd never had any feelings in that direction – well, it's like being in a catapult and being catapaulted into the future. I don't know. When I was twelve or thirteen, I spoke to my dad and he was really taking me through it then. That I should stop watching pornography because it was closing me off. I wasn't having many hobbies or friends. Yeah, I was addicted to it and I was watching it every day and I couldn't stop. But my dad took me through it to make sure I got it right in the end. And yeah, it was a thing but it's not a thing now. But yeah, I don't like the idea of it – with my little cousins.

It's the shame – the returning shame when you are watching it every day and the drainingness. But also like mixed – because you're watching something and you are sort of having like – it's fun . . . it's a treat – so it's very mixed like – it's like – toxic – I think that's a really difficult combination is mixing feelings of pleasure and arousal with shame and guilt and loneliness as well. Like I don't think the two things should be – like go together. And I think in porn they almost constantly go together.

But yeah, when people talk about porn, the conversation is immediately negative but there are some positive things about porn as well. Because if porn just made you feel lonely and ashamed you wouldn't watch it.

He laughs.

I'm going to be honest here. For *me* like I was coming to terms with being gay, the liberation of letting myself watch it and being like 'ahhhhhh' (*sigh of relief*) . . . when I actually like, gave in, I guess, and let myself watch the ones I really wanted to watch it was so, it was like one of the best feelings ever – and it sounds funny – but it really was for me. It was like, 'Oh I can actually enjoy this'. So for that, it then made me feel way better about my own personal experience because you sort of like become more comfortable in yourself. So for me like, definitely there are so many negative parts to porn, but for me, like there were positive aspects of it. And that's what's so confusing.

But not when you're too young. And not when you watching it too much. And not when it's a secret. Do you see I'm confused here?

He laughs.

It's bad . . . it's good . . . it's good , . . It's bad . . .

I have a lovely boyfriend, thank you. He's a big strong hunk. Ha! Chalk and cheese.

Scene Eight

Fragments (*to be divided among the company with no intro to different speakers*)   Modern life is pretty much all that I know but at the same time I think there's a big part of me that's trying to be living at another time. I go days without being on my phone and I read books. It seems like it's impossible not to be connected to the internet. I want to reduce modern life – but I'm still trying to figure out how to. I want to get the most out of simple life – traditional, standard, simple life.

If I could live in a different era – maybe when there was no one on Earth.

I'd love to be in a time where – I love the idea of not being settled in one place and just moving around and having to survive. I think that idea excites me.

And I know that the people that lived in that time they were a lot different to us.

These people like – were on a *higher* level. A ridiculous level.

The standard was probably being an athlete because you couldn't not survive.

So I'd love to be in that time just to see – because I think in that time I would be able to see – just people being on an entirely different level.

I don't have any solutions other than this is the only thing I would say. There have always been dangers in the world. And you always want to protect children from dangers.

But – if you want a child to know that fire is hot then you teach them about it. You don't pretend it doesn't exist and then lock them in a room with a fire to work it out for themselves.

If you put a phone in a child's hand you are putting porn in a child's hand. Don't put a phone in a child's hand unless you are ready to talk to them about porn. I mean the internet is so big now and it's in your pocket. So you can't ban anything. If you want to know how to get around parental locks google 'how to get around parental locks'. And with the age verification stuff the government is doing – it's like, um, hello – the truth is that kids understand the internet in a way that adults really don't. So the adult is trying to protect the child but actually they rely on the child to show them how to use Word. Five-year-olds are learning to code now. Do you know what coding is? OK, but can you do it?

Talking about this stuff might not make it better . . . but it might.

So, thank you for listening to us.

It's actually been really good to chat.

Song: 'It's Been Good to Chat'

Where shall we put the chairs?
Just – er – leave them where they are.
Thank you all for coming out.
Rather than just stay at home watching *Made in Chelsea*
And have your tea.
We've got three
minutes then
they chuck us –

I wasn't aware that you could share your feelings without making a joke out of it.
It's been
really nice to chat
It's been good so good to chat
Good to let your feelings out on the town
It's been good to chat.

Where shall we put the chairs?
Just – er – leave them where they are.
Maybe you can come back.
We can do Chapter Two,
Chapter Three and Four.
Tonight is Chapter One.
There's a lot
More to say
On this one.

I wasn't aware that you could share your feelings without making a joke out of it.
It's been
really nice to chat
It's been good so, good to chat
Good to let your feelings out on the town
It's been good to – chat.

We're finishing in thirty seconds.
Can you guys line up by the door.
I need a pen.

I need the toilet.
Do I press the red button again?

It's been
really nice to chat
It's been good so good to chat
Good to let your feelings out on the town
It's been good to – good to – good to – chat.

'The Beauty of Porn'

That's the beau-ty of   porn   Like wo-men with beards   at the

cir-cus   You're like a kid   at the   fair   You've bro-ken in   to a

haun- ted house and   you rea-lly should-n't be   there   Am I   gay straight

3

they just eat the spaghetti   and then they're like   Oh! I'm full now   thank you, that was a lovely meal

and I'm a bit like   Oh. That really was a film   about someone eating spaghetti   Some-where out

there it's   ti-cking some-one's   box   Titanic, love actually   there's a lot of

5

'Squirt'

Music & lyrics by Matt Regan
Orch. Jen Green

02. Squirt - Voice

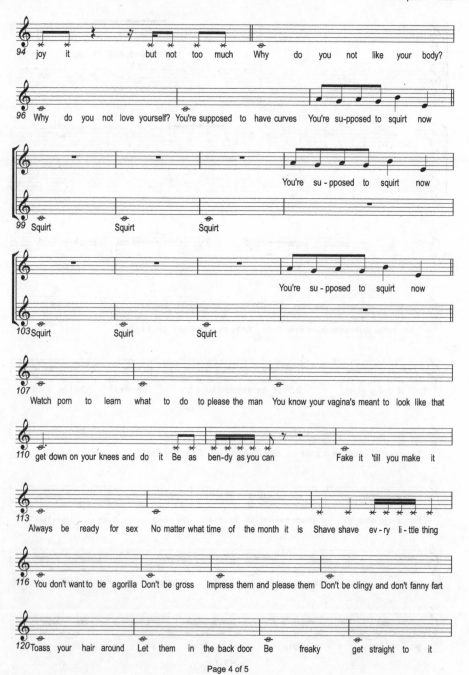

94 joy it but not too much Why do you not like your body?

96 Why do you not love yourself? You're supposed to have curves You're su-pposed to squirt now

You're su - pposed to squirt now

99 Squirt Squirt Squirt

You're su - pposed to squirt now

103 Squirt Squirt Squirt

107 Watch porn to learn what to do to please the man You know your vagina's meant to look like that

110 get down on your knees and do it Be as ben-dy as you can Fake it 'till you make it

113 Always be ready for sex No matter what time of the month it is Shave shave ev - ry li - ttle thing

116 You don't want to be agorilla Don't be gross Impress them and please them Don't be clingy and don't fanny fart

120 Toass your hair around Let them in the back door Be freaky get straight to it

02. Squirt - Voice

'Little Spoon'

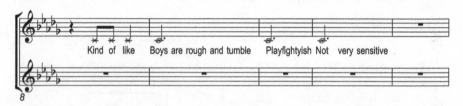

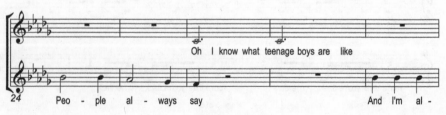

4

03. Little Spoon - Vox

with a wide stride   It's hard to know what to

101   I know those fellas

do   Yeah it's con - fu - sing

106   really as a boy   All these rules

Some-times I want to be   Some-times I want to

112   Some-times I   Some-times I want to

Be the li - ttle spoon   O - h it's nice be-ing hugged   Nice to be hu - gged

120   Be the li - ttle spoon   O - h it's nice be-ing hugged   Nice to be hu - gged

ev - er - y   b - o - dy   ne-eds a   bi - t   of   a - a   a   bi - t   of   love

129   ev - er - y   b - o - dy   ne-eds a   bi - t   of   a - a   a   bi - t   of   love

At the moment though it's gone too far   All we hear ismasculinity equals toxic   Just the fact that

136

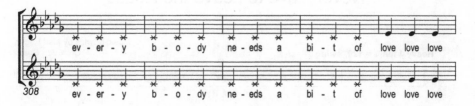

ev - er - y   b - o - dy   ne - eds   a   bi - t   of   love love love

308   ev - er - y   b - o - dy   ne - eds   a   bi - t   of   love love love

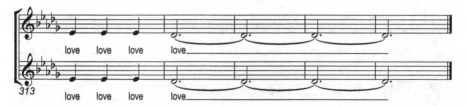

love   love   love   love____

313   love   love   love   love____

Vox

'Never Have to Leave the House'

Music & lyrics by Matt Regan
Orch. Jen Green

04. House Vocal - Vox

04. House Vocal - Vox

05. Fleshcoats - Voice

06. Good to Chat - Vox

06. Good to Chat - Vox

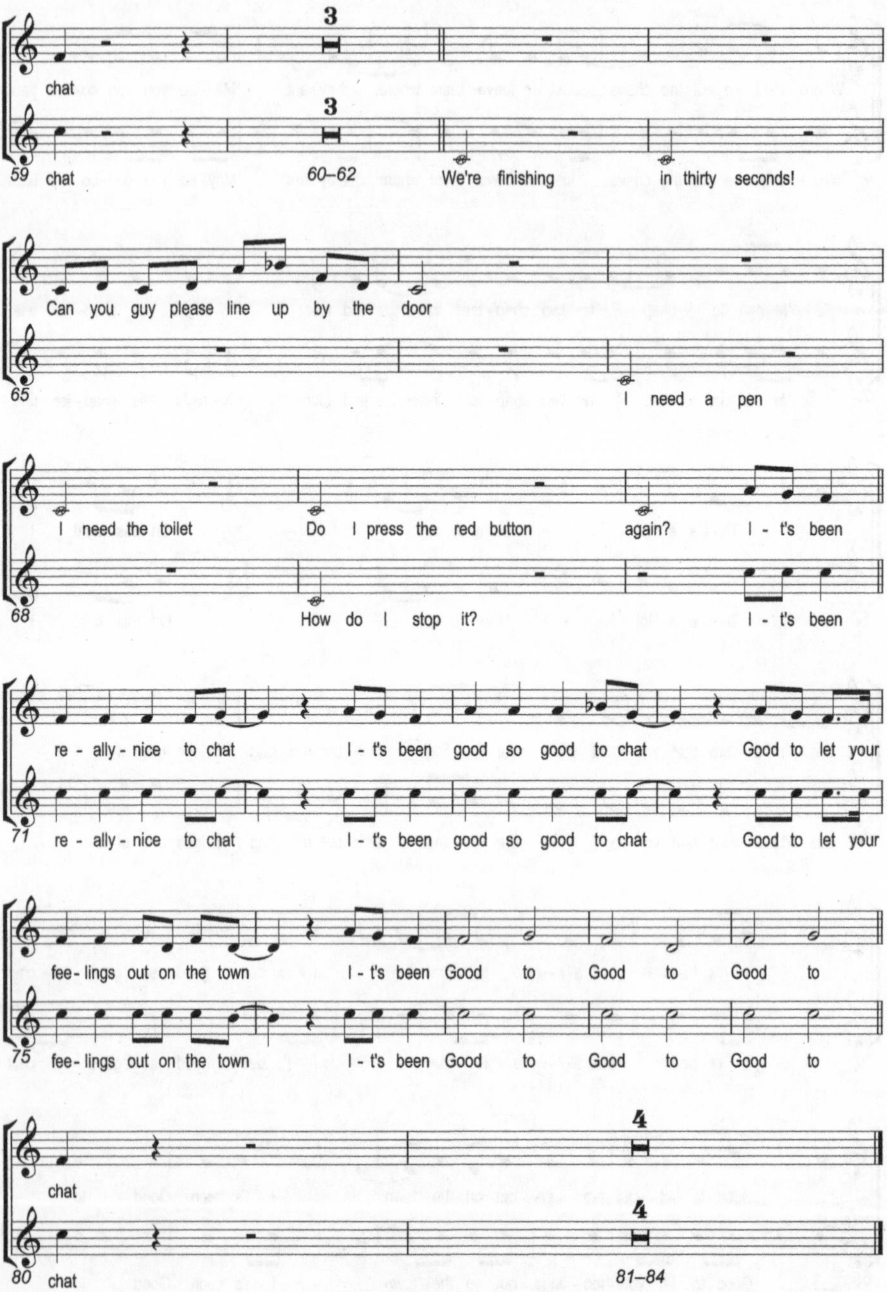

You don't need to make a Big Song and Dance out of it

BY ABBEY WRIGHT, SHIREEN MULA AND MATT REGAN

*Notes on rehearsal and staging, drawn from a workshop with the writer,
held at the National Theatre, October 2021*

How the writer came to write the play

Writer Abbey Wright spoke about her experience of creating the show (originally called
Why Is the Sky Blue?) with Shireen Mula and Matt Regan:

> I wanted to create a piece of theatre about children and young people's
> experiences of pornography. I spoke to 10,000 children and young people aged
> six to twenty-two and of diverse backgrounds, genders, sexualities and from
> right across the UK from Dundee to Cornwall. This was a huge privilege. I
> found young people were very keen to talk about this complex subject and to
> share their own insights and experiences. I wanted to platform the voices of
> these young people and to make the audience feel as though they were in the
> room listening to these extraordinary conversations – and so we decided that
> verbatim would be the most effective way to do that.
>
> I initially envisioned a cabaret-style musical as the form of the piece. There
> are certain similarities with cabaret and pornography: hyper-sexualisation; big
> caricatures; a merge of sex and violence that is reflected onstage; but then also
> there is a humour you can get from the musical form that really reflects the
> nature of many of the conversations we had with young people across the
> country too. The songs allow us to create a poetic feeling of a chorus of young
> people's voices.
>
> Young people's exposure to pornography happens way earlier than any of us
> are comfortable admitting. It has a very invasive impact on their development
> and sense of self, relationships and intimacy. It is a topic that adults can shy
> away from and I am very glad to be able to share these young people's words
> and to encourage a national conversation on this vital subject.

Approaching the play

As a starting point, lead director John Haidar suggested an exercise that could be done
either as director preparation or with your company of young people.

Exercise: Ten words

Without thinking too much, write down ten words that you associate with this piece –
it's not a test, and the words can be as abstract as you like. Some words shared from the
group included:

Funny / Honest / Youth / Risky / Embarrassing / Connection / Care / Ensemble / Wow / Openness / New / Shame / Inclusive / Exploration / Puberty / Terrifying / True / Relatable / Anxiety / Pride / Squirt / Fun / Listen / Change / Dynamic / Sweet / Isolation / Failure

Then cross out all but the five words that mean the most to you and what you think best represents the work you're going to make.

Then cut out two more and leave the three that mean the most and resonate the most.

Finally, delete two more so that you are left with a single word.

Ask each member of the group to talk about the word they've chosen to stick with – why that word is important to them in relation to the play and what it means.

This can be a useful exercise to do with your young people – it will tell you a lot about what they think. It's a useful exercise to do again at the end of the rehearsal process to see if it's shifted. It will also help them to be able to focus on that one word.

Discussion

The group discussed the influence of the internet and the challenge of talking to young people about this topic. Everything happens at a much younger age now because of, and with, smart phones.

Society has changed incredibly quickly, and young people have less of a sense of the difference between real life and what happens on the internet – so many of their experiences are already mediated.

Not everyone's parents have sat them down to talk about pornography or sex, so every single student will have a different relationship with this text – and be coming to it with a different set of conversations and experience.

John Haidar reflected that this play needs directors who will bring it to people who may not be receptive and to make space for it.

Exercise: Image gallery

Invite your group to bring in images and create a gallery in response to the play.

Discuss each image in turn, then the person who brought that image tells the group why they brought it in, and what element of the play they feel it speaks to.

This exercise is a great one to do with young people. You can keep it abstract, and choosing images might be an easier way in for them. By osmosis from these conversations, you might learn more about what you want your production to be.

Exercise: I'm going to make a show about . . .

An exercise for you to do as a director.

Ask yourself the question: What do you want your production to achieve?

1 I'm going to make a show about . . .

Take this sentence and keep checking in on why you're making it. You can measure the success of the project on the terms you set for yourself. It's hard to know how well you're doing at directing while you're directing it. But if you keep checking in with your intentions, if you're achieving those things then you can measure your success. It's useful to come back at the end of the process and think about how well you did and it helps you to debrief on where you got to.

Exercise: Analogy

If this musical were a song (not from the musical itself), what would it be? An existing song.

If this musical were an artist, who would the artist be? The definition of the artist can be as broad as you like.

If this musical were a smell, what would it be?

If this musical were a colour, what would it be? Be as precise as you can be.

When you make the Hollywood film of this musical, what do you want the camerawork to be like? How do you want the audience to experience it – immersive, up close, wide screen? What do you want the audience to take from it?

You can do this with your company and share and discuss everyone's answers.

It is also really useful to do for yourself as director preparation. The answers can inform your design choices, but really this exercise is more about the tone that you want to set. How can you get to the spirit of, for example, the song you chose? It's useful to do before you get into the room – even if you end up sharing some of these ideas with your company.

Exercise: Write five sentences that begin:

This is a world where . . . / This is a world in which . . .
Again, this is a useful exercise to get conversations about the production going – you can highlight the responses you and your group are particularly interested in.

Exercise: Backstory

Choose a character and write as detailed a backstory for them as possible. In the workshop, the time set for this exercise was ten minutes, but you might set it as homework overnight.

You could start with: who/what/why/where/how/other questions. For example: What is their social background? What school do they go to? What sexuality are they? What is their sexual experience? What is their relationship to the teacher or to school? What football team do they support? What do their parents do?

You could also ask your company to design a floorplan of the home of their character.

Next steps

You could give this as an overnight exercise or over the weekend and follow it up at your next rehearsal with hot-seating – where you question them in character. Keep the rest of the company watching in a circle – so they all have a shared understanding of each character. Keep the conversation going – sometimes answers are hard to think of on the spot, even if they've looked over it in advance; the important thing is to keep trying. John Haidar uses the *Observer* Q&A questions as a starting point. They can be found here: https://www.theguardian.com/lifeandstyle/series/qa

Design and space

Thinking about the spaces you're working in for your production – what are the rules of that space, who is allowed to go in there? How might characters transgress the rules of the space?

Is everything literal, or can its meaning or use change? E.g. a piece of furniture that has one function which changes throughout the play.

Who takes up what space in each environment – how much do you want to create a sense of disparity through space, such as between students and teachers?

What is the incentive for the student characters to be there in the first place – what are they hoping to get out of it?

There's always something that's being preserved, worshipped, upheld. What are the gods or totems in the space? How are those things protected and upheld?

What isn't being said in a room with connection and communication?

What's the normality of the space on any given day, what is special about today and how does it interrupt that normality?

Verbatim theatre

Writer Shireen Mula led an exercise to give the group an insight into how the work was made, which may in turn inspire the choices they make in presenting *You don't need to make a Big Song and Dance out of it.*

Recording

- Find a partner and find a space in the room together. Bring a notepad, a pen and your phone.

- Write down five questions that you would like to ask your partner. These could be about their work, or they could be more personal or fun questions. Don't tell your partner what they are. Keep the questions open. When you have five, cut two – sometimes the later questions are more interesting than the first things that come into your heads. Writing five helps you to get to a clearer three.

- You are going to record your interviewee so you need their permission and consent. Tell them your name, your role, why you are interviewing and ask them if it's OK for you to record your conversation. With your phone, include the question and record for a minute and try to keep talking until the minute is up. If the interviewee is struggling, you can keep asking follow-ups to help them, but it's best if your partner can try to keep talking for the full minute. Pick who goes first and the first person asks their first question. Some verbatim practitioners video record so they can later pick up on gestures and movement, though you will have to ask for additional permission if you wish to do that.

- At the end of the minute, swap around and the second person asks their first question. Swap back and forth and ask all your three questions each, with the person asking the question doing the recording.

Creating

Alone, spend twenty minutes working on your three minutes of audio. You can transcribe, you can work on just one question, you could try recorded delivery.

Recorded delivery is a technique from verbatim theatre, created by practitioner Anna Deavere Smith. You wear headphones and listen to the audio. The audience cannot hear what you are listening to. You try to speak along exactly with the audio and match the tone, laughs, vocal mannerisms, etc. of the person speaking in the audio.

The participants shared their work and had the following reflections:

Reflections

It can be cringey hearing yourself, and also you can absolutely see yourself in it.

Characters come across as really clear.

Rhythm – naturally we elongate and shorten in an uneven way. When we write like this, it seems fake, but it's more real.

Pace – it's hard to keep up in recorded delivery and get all the exact details in, or get the gaps between words exactly right. Speed is tricky, slowing down and speeding up, it catches you by surprise and you end up behind.

In verbatim, do you want to show the artist's hand or not? There is an honesty in this. What does it add, what is lost?

Even though you don't have the audio for your production, this exercise can hopefully be useful in thinking about what choices you might make when performing it. For example, perhaps when we're embarrassed we speed up, or speak softly or quietly.

In verbatim theatre, you can decide which performer delivers what text – is the performer similar to the original speaker or very different? How does this alter the meaning that's created?

Music

Questions and answers

Q: The songs follow a clear tune. Some are so verbatim that they go all over the place. Musicians have sheet music to keep them right – what would you suggest for learning the music?

A: Because it's verbatim, you can treat the audio tracks like a verbatim recording. You can listen to the demos like you do with recorded delivery. You have a concrete version of it that works as a demo. So layer it up – speaking, then singing, then backing track. There are three key styles of singing in the show:

1 You've got a bar's length and four words to say – speaking in your own rhythm with a bar's length. You'll know instantly if you need to stick with the tempo. It's generally easier to have one voice here.

2 In the music it has scored rhythms which are the least natural, and this is the one where the demos are really useful to show how it works. When you first do it, you'll sound like a robot, so it's about figuring out the rhythm first and then you can start to find the meaning and character in it.

3 Singing – it's not a conventional musical, it's a pedestrian style and very natural.

The show constantly flips between the three styles, which makes it really unique and interesting. Musical theatre doesn't usually have people speaking in a rhythm. It might be a challenge that takes a few weeks.

Q: Can we add more singing, harmonies, etc. that are spoken on the demos?
A: The team would prefer it if you didn't do this. They have made specific choices about which sections are sung and which are spoken and feel the concept would become diluted/ muddied if more sections were sung.

Q: Could actors accompany themselves if they play an instrument?
A: If you think it works, then go for it!

Q: For one of the monologues it says 'this could be underscored'. Could other monologues be underscored too?
A: This could be an option if it sounds good when you try it out. However, the team did try this in *Why Is the Sky Blue?* and they didn't feel it worked.

Q: I was interested in the connection with cabaret mentioned in the recorded conversation – how much has that fed into this version?
A: A cabaret format was used in the original show (*Why Is the Sky Blue?*), so that's how it existed in a prior life – cabaret feels less of an element of it now.

Song exploration

There are fairly manageable band parts for a musical department of students if you have them. Matt Heslop, who was musical director for the workshop, reassured participants that while it can feel complex to start with, once you've got it it's hard to get wrong, and it really does click in.

Matt Heslop played the songs for the participants and, as he did so, he invited them to write down words, phrases and responses as they listened, which they then shared as a group.

Some of the responses are outlined below.

'The Beauty of Porn'

Joyous song, anticipation and trepidation about the subject so this as the opener might be unexpected.

A bit *Avenue Q*, a bit Victoria Wood.

Breaking the ice.

The staging will really change across each production and there's lots of room to do it in different ways. The different genres of song mean there's a lot of scope for staging, and you can make it accessible for lots of people.

A nice wide overview and fun, allows them to be kids, not necessarily judgemental.

This song covers the three forms – free to do your own rhythm, singing and rhythmic speaking, so it's a good introduction to those styles too.

'Squirt'

How do you make 'squirt' and whispering that word not embarrassing? Perhaps you could lean into the genre, make it 'look' like musical theatre, the *Little Shop of Horrors* kind of way, something quite jazzy and glamorous.

There is repetition in the structure of this song, so it could be good to do something episodic so it's moving along or changing each time you revisit the same section of repetition.

Strong female voice.

Plenty of parody can be found within it.

The lyrics become quite dark but the music can stay uplifting and disco.

Could bring a lot of visual references and pop culture references into the blocking.

'Little Spoon'

Flips between set rhythms and loose rhythms which can make it sound more complicated than it is, and constant listening will help.

Potential for acting out these moments for larger groups.

It is a sweet song and there is potential for a nice staging moment.

'Never Have to Leave the House'

Much more of a sung song, more of a traditional musical theatre song. Should be fine to rehearse with a piano or backing track.

Explores how watching porn is a low-risk thing for people to do – they don't have to risk themselves by going out and connecting.

'Proper' song – the meaning is something you have to dig for; it sounds reassuring but the meaning dawns on you. Its normal, familiar sound is part of the point – making it a normal thing to stay at home and not go out and connect.

'Fleshcoats'

Another chance to showcase a great singer.

It is very visual in terms of the movement, very gestural.

Themes of intimacy and isolation.

This is the heart of connection, intimacy; pornography as a barrier to those things.

Nice opportunity to listen to quite a calm song; there's an opportunity to counteract that in the staging visually (also true of 'Never Have to Leave the House').

'Good to Chat'

A good way to finish the show.
   The least we can do is talk about it.
   Sending the audience out; almost like an encore to cap off the show.
   A message to the parents that talking about it is good.
   Lots of potential for a lot of people to sing at the same time.

Question and answer with Shireen Mula

Q: With the opening scene, it starts with young children in school, and then the monologues feel like they're from a separate place or not in school?
SM: The first scene is one of the groups we've met, and then the play splits out into people from all over the country and different school groups, and comes full circle at the end.

Q: In terms of breaking up the monologues, can we make them conversations and assign how we like?
SM: Yes – simultaneous speaking, conversation, switching genders, etc. is totally fine.

Q: Some songs have uneven rhythms – how do we teach this?
SM: From experience of teaching these songs to people, if there's complicated speaking rhythms, split those up early so that they have time to get on it. It is counter-productive to use loads of time splitting them up, so make clear decisions about who is singing or doing what.

Q: The ending – it talks about breaking it down into loads of different lines specifically. Why does that particularly happen at the end?
SM: We just structurally felt like it was nice to have everyone involved, so everyone gets a final say and gets brought back on – it's a moment of culmination before the final song – and then everyone sings 'Good to Chat' as an encore together.

Q: And is it the group that starts the show off coming full circle?
SM: The 'Fragments' section can include anyone and everyone. The song 'Good to Chat' should feature the first group but can also involve your whole cast.

Q: Can we do that opening section as live speech rather than recording it, as they set up the room and bring everything on?
SM: Yes, that's fine.

Q: The relationship between performers and audience. Are they speaking to the audience directly, or are they inside characters and in their own world?
SM: Direct address can be helpful in making the audience understand that they are complicit in it. John Haidar gave a provocation to require the audience to feel involved because they are. If there's a moment where you have one person on stage doing a monologue on their own, it would be a missed opportunity not to give that in soliloquy, and put the audience inside the head of that character – that isn't as easy when you have fourteen people doing a monologue. It's a big level of responsibility and of comfort for that young actor.

The feeling is that the more the production style can simulate the feeling, atmosphere of conversation/conversational intimacy in the monologues and duologues, the better. As a general rule, soliloquies are best spoken directly to the audience rather than with a gaze off to the side or other imaginary speaking partner. Explore the direct address and cast the audience in the role of the person the character is speaking to.

From a workshop led by John Haidar
With notes by Katherine Nesbitt

Participating Companies

10 TO 13 Collective
20Twenty Connections Youth Theatre
1812 Youth Theatre
Aberystwyth Arts Centre Youth
  Theatre
Acorn Young People's Theatre
Act 2 Academy
ACT Youth Theatre
Actors Workshop
Alderbrook School
Ardclough Youth Theatre
The Archer Players
artsdepot Youth Theatre
ArtsEd EXTRA Youth Theatre
Astor Youth Theatre Company
Atlantic Coast Theatre Co.
Barton Peveril Sixth Form College
Bathgate Academy Drama Club
The Baylis Blue Ties
Bedlington Academy
Beechwood School Youth Theatre
Best Theatre Arts
BHASVIC Theatre Company
Bilborough Sixth Form
Birkenhead High School Academy
Bishops High School
The Boaty Theatre Company
boomsatsuma
Brewery Youth Theatre
Bury Grammar School
CAPA College
The Carlton Academy
Carmel College Performing Arts
The Canterbury Academy
Cast Youth Theatre
Castleford Academy
Cavendish School
Cheltenham Youth Theatre
Chestnut Grove
Cockburn School
The Colfox Drama Project
The Company
Corn Exchange Newbury Youth Theatre
County Limerick Youth Theatre
Craven College
Crescent Arts Youth Theatre
Croydon Youth Theatre

Csaw Theatre Company
Curious Connections
The Customs House Youth Theatre
CWC Company
Cramlington Youth Dramatic Society
CYT Harris Church of England Academy
Dalton Theatre Company
Delanté Détras Theatre Company
Demesne Community Centre Youth Theatre
  Group
Derby Theatre
Devizes School
Diocesan School for Girls
Dorchester Youth Theatre
Dorset Drama Academy
The Drama Studio
Dreams Theatre School
Duckegg Theatre Lincolnshire and North
  Nottinghamshire
Dudley College Performing Arts
Dumfries Youth Theatre
The East Manchester Academy
Easy Street Theatre Company
Emerson Park Academy
Everyman Youth Theatre
Farlingaye High School
Felpham Community College
Fisher More RC High School
Fleet Street Studios
Flying High Young Company
Footlight Theatre Company
Forest Hill School
Framingham Earl High School
Fred Longworth High School
The Garage, Norwich
Gateshead College
GHS Senior Drama
Goresbrook School
Grantham College Theatre Group
Griese Youth Theatre
Guildford College
Gulbenkian Young Company
Hackney Shed Collective
Hayworth Players Ipswich High School
Headington School Oxford
Heathcote School and Science College
The Heathland Players

Heles School
HGS Herschel Grammar School
Highdown School & Sixth Form Centre
Huntingdon Youth Theatre
IC Drama
Ignite Youth Theatre
InterACT Youth Theatre (Neston)
Inverclyde Youth Theatre (Kayos)
JCoSS School
Kesteven and Grantham Girls' School
KEVICC King Edward VI Community
   College
Kildare Youth Theatre
Kindred Youth Theatre
Kingsthorpe College
Kirky High Playhouse
Knightswood Secondary School
Kola Nuts
KPYT
Launceston College
Launch Theatre and Performance Training at
   Cornwall College
Let's Act Drama School, Doncaster
Let's Act Drama School, London
Light UP
Lincoln Young Company
Lipson Co-operative Academy
Lister Drama
Liverpool Empire Youth Theatre
Lochend Community High School
LORIC Players
Lumos Theatre
M6 Youth Theatre
Malton School
Mark Rutherford School
Marlowe Theatre Youth Company
MAST Mayflower Studios
Mayflower Youth Theatre
Mid Powys Youth Theatre
Milton Keynes Theatre Academy: Young
   Company
Mishmak Youth Theatre
Mulberry Academy Shoreditch
Mull Youth Theatre Comar Arts
Multiplicity Theatre Company
N10 Productions
Nine Lives Theatre Company
Norlington School
Northampton High School
Northampton School for Boys

The Nottingham Emmanuel School
Nottingham Playhouse
Oasis Academy Coulsdon
Oldham College
On Point Theatre Company
Open Door Drama
Orchard Park Theatre Company
Ormiston Rivers Academy
Outwood Academy Hemsworth
OX2 Collective
PACT Theatre Company Soham Village
   College
Page2stage Youth Theatre
Passmores Academy
Perfect Circle Youth Theatre
Pike and Musket
PlayActing Youth Theatre
Playmakers
PQA Swindon
Prendergast Players
Proteus Young Company
Queen Elizabeth's School
Queen Mary's College
Rainham Mark Grammar School
Ravens Wood School
Raynes Park High School
Reading College
Reepham High School and College Drama
   Club
Regent Theatre Academy
The Repertory Theatre Project
ResLife Youth Theatre Newcastle
The Ridgeway School & Sixth Form
   College
Ringwood School
Robert Barclay Academy
Roding Valley High School
Roundwood Park School
Royal & Derngate Young Company: Connect
Rugby School
Sackville School
Saracens High School
SGS Theatre Academy
Shenfield High School
Sherman Youth Theatre
Shetland Youth Theatre Company
Shirley High Theatre Company
SHSG Young Actors Company
Silhouette Youth Theatre
Smithills School

Southwark Playhouse Young Company
Spotlight Drama Youth Theatre
Springwest Academy
SRWA Theatre Company
St Brendan's Sixth Form College
St Gregory's Bath
St Mary's Catholic School
St Richard's Drama Stars
St Saviour's and St Olave's School
St Thomas More Catholic High School
St Ronan's College Youth Theatre
Stag Youth Theatre
Stagecoach Buckingham Further Stages
Stagedoor Learning
Steel Valley Beacon Arts
Stockton Riverside College
Straffan Drama Club
Strathaven Academy Drama
Strive Drama
Strode College
Suffolk New College Performing Arts
Sundial Theatre Company
Swan Theatre Young Rep Company
The Swanage School
Telford Priory School
Thame Youth Theatre
Theatre Peckham JAC
Theatre Royal Youth
Theatre Unboxed
Theatre Works
Theatreworks Deal
Through the Wardrobe

Titchfield Youth Theatre
Towers School and Sixth Form
TQ1 The Spire College
Trinity Youth Theatre
Triple Act Theatre and Arts
Turing House Drama
The Upstarts
UROCK Theatre Company
Valley Park School
The View from Here
Waterford Youth Arts
Weavers Academy
West London Free School
Westacre Theatre
Westfield Arts College
Westminster Kingsway Performing Arts
White City Youth Theatre
Winstanley College
WKGS West Kirby Grammar School
The Workshop KL
Wollaston School Theatre Company
Worlds End Productions London
Worthing College
Yew Tree Youth Theatre
York Theatre Royal Youth Theatre
Young Actors
Young Dramatic Arts
Young Octagon
Young People's Theatre
Young Theatre Royal
Youth Arts Centre, Isle of Man
Ysgol Aberconwy

Partner Theatres

Aberystwyth Arts Centre
artsdepot
Beacon Arts Centre
Bristol Old Vic
Cast Doncaster
Crewe Lyceum
Derby Theatre
The Fire Station, Sunderland
The Garage, Norwich
HOME Manchester
Lighthouse, Poole Centre for the Arts
The Lowry
Lyric Theatre Belfast
Lyric Theatre Hammersmith
Marlowe Theatre
MAST Mayflower Studios
The North Wall, Oxford
Nottingham Playhouse
Queen's Theatre Hornchurch
Reading Rep Theatre
Royal & Derngate
Sheffield Theatres
Sherman Theatre
Soho Theatre
Southwark Playhouse
Theatre Peckham
Theatre Royal Plymouth
Trinity Theatre, Tunbridge Wells
Wiltshire Creative
York Theatre Royal

National Theatre Connections Team

Performing Rights

Application for permission to perform, etc. should be made before rehearsals begin to the following representatives:

For *Cable Street, Hunt, Like There's No Tomorrow* and *You don't need to make a Big Song and Dance out of it*:
Permissions Department
Bloomsbury Publishing Plc
50 Bedford Square
London WC1B 3DP
performance.permissions@bloomsbury.com

For *Chat Back*:
Sheil Land Associates
52 Doughty Street
London WC1N 2LS
info@sheilland.co.uk

For *Find a Partner!*:
Independent Talent Group Ltd
40 Whitfield Street,
London W1T 2RH
alexrusher@independenttalent.com

For *Remote*:
TEAM Artists
2 John Kings Court
67 St John's Grove
London N19 5QR
davina@team-artists.co.uk

For *Superglue*:
United Agents
12–26 Lexington Street
London W1F 0LE
gsmart@unitedagents.co.uk

For *The Ramayana Reset*:
The Agency
24 Pottery Lane
Holland Park
London W11 4LZ
info@theagency.co.uk

For *Variations*:
Curtis Brown Group Ltd.
Haymarket House,
28–29 Haymarket
London SW1Y 4SP
jenn.lambert@curtisbrown.co.uk